Instructor's Resource Manual with Test Items

Those Who Can, Teach

TENTH EDITION

Kevin Ryan/James M. Cooper

Leslie A. Swetnam
Metropolitan State College of Denver

Houghton Mifflin Company   BOSTON   NEW YORK

Senior Sponsoring Editor: *Sue Pulvermacher-Alt*
Senior Developmental Editor: *Lisa Mafrici*
Editorial Associate/Development: *Sara Hauschildt*
Editorial Assistant/Editorial Production: *Talia Kingsbury*
Senior Manufacturing Coordinator: *Jane Spelman*

Printed in the U.S.A.

ISBN: 0-618-30705-2

23456789-MA-07 06 05 04

Contents

Preface

The first section of this Instructor's Resource Manual provides instructors with model syllabi for an introduction to education course for both a 10- and 16-week semester schedule.

The section on instructional resources includes, for each chapter of the text, learning objectives, a chapter overview, a chapter outline, supplementary lecture and discussion topics, student study guide, additional resources for instructors, media resources (Appendix I includes contact information for the most frequently cited distributors), student activities including school observations, and student assignments, including:

- Independent Readings from *Kaleidoscope*
- Reflective Paper Topics
- Journal Probes
- CD-ROM Video Clips for selected chapters

The learning objectives and chapter overview orient the instructor to the purposes of the chapter and its contribution to students' professional development. The supplementary lecture and discussion topics offer a sampling of suggestions for elaborating on the chapter's contents. The copy-ready student study guide pages focus on the recognition and comprehension of major points in each chapter and are an easy resource for instructors to provide to support student learning. There are no answer keys included for the study guide since the answers are clearly indicated in the corresponding chapters and the intent of this section is to provide a study aid for students, not an assignment for the instructor to grade. The annotated references—both print and media—show where additional information or insights can be found. The student activities are designed to engage students in reflective thinking and role-plays that simulate aspects of a teacher's work. The student assignments can be used to produce portfolio examples and as alternative means of assessment.

The next section and the test bank disks include sample quizzes that may be used by students to prepare for exams and review the material in the chapters. These questions may also serve as a resource for instructors when constructing a test using the test bank. The test bank section for each chapter contains 30 to 40 multiple-choice items. The distractors for each item have been formed with the intention of stimulating careful thought; to reject a distractor is to have reviewed its meaning and recognized its inappropriateness. Items have been developed according to accepted principles of test construction and are designed to elicit student thinking at various levels. The evaluation section also contains two or three short-answer and essay questions per chapter, along with suggested responses.

To supplement the cases presented in the text and the short cases in some of the activities in the Instructor's Resource Manual, Appendix II contains four longer case studies that present interesting dilemmas or issues that prospective teachers may encounter in their professional career. It is included at the end of the manual. Discussion questions help to guide the analysis of the cases and to bring the prospective teachers to some resolution of the issue at hand.

The sample quiz and test items contained in the Instructor's Resource Manual are also available on the HMClassPrep/HM Testing 6.0 CD-ROM for use with IBM or Macintosh computers.

Our goal in providing these materials is to help students learn about themselves and the teaching profession. We strongly believe that the student activities should include follow-up. In addition, tests should be reviewed in class, with correct answers made available and alternative responses discussed. Such follow-up and discussion allow for clarification and consolidation of new information.

Although many individuals helped develop this manual, we express special gratitude to Leslie Swetnam, who revised this edition of the *Instructor's Resource Manual with Test Items;* to Diana J. Doffing, who aided with manuscript preparation; and to Brooke Graham Doyle, who reviewed the materials for Chapter 6. We also thank Cathleen Kinsella Stutz, Susan Tauer, Mary S. Leighton, Gloria Thompson, Kathryn Rabinow, Debra Hallock Phillips, and Lee McCanne, whose work on earlier editions was most valuable. To those readers who took the trouble to comment on previous editions, we also offer thanks. The changes made for this edition are based on their helpful advice.

Information regarding your own experience with this manual will be used in preparing future editions. Comments may be recorded on the instructor evaluation sheet at the end of the manual. If you develop or discover activities that you would like to recommend to us, we would be delighted to hear of them.

Good luck in your teaching!

A TRANSITION GUIDE

Those Who Can, Teach, Tenth Edition

This book, *Those Who Can, Teach*, is a book of questions. In fact, it was written in the first place to answer the question, "What are the things people beginning their formal study of education should know?" We have organized the chapters of our book around a series of questions that are likely to be of special concern to prospective teachers, and which we believe are keys to the central issues and concerns of teaching and learning. We hope that these questions provide direction and focus to readers' study well beyond the time they spend with this book. In addition, for those who are simply considering careers in teaching, we believe that the search for answers to these questions will help them clarify their career goals.

AUDIENCE

Those Who Can, Teach is intended as a basic text for courses variously titled "Introduction to Education" or "Foundations of Education." We originally wrote this book because we couldn't find the kind of textbook our own students and the students of many of our colleagues needed and wanted—a book that involves prospective teachers in the real issues of schooling and education and gives them a clear view of the skills and knowledge they will need to be successful professionals.

CONTENT OF THE TENTH EDITION

Those Who Can, Teach, Tenth Edition, presents a frank, contemporary examination of the field and foundations of education and, especially, the teaching profession. Although the text is firmly based in educational research and scholarship, it seeks to convey the important knowledge and issues in the field of education in a way that effectively bridges educational research and classroom practice. For this purpose, we rely heavily throughout the book on a narrative style, attempting to place the book's content in very human terms.

We have organized the book around four themes, each theme representing one of the four parts. *Part 1*, "Schools and Students," includes an examination of the dynamics of school life from many different angles to give the prospective teacher a multilayered view of schools. It attempts to provide the reader with a vivid grasp of the diverse and changing nature of today's students in the United States and examines the critical social issues that affect them and schools today. *Part 2*, "Teachers," begins with the knowledge base about effective teaching and the growing role of technology in both teaching and learning. It also describes the ethical and legal issues facing teachers. *Part 3*, "Foundations and the Future," contains chapters on topics that are "foundational" or basic to the practice of teaching: the economic and political issues underlying the control and governance of schools, the philosophy of education, and the history of American education. It is in this mix of our educational past and present that we have placed an important chapter on educational reform. *Part 4*, "The Teaching Profession," presents timely information on salaries and employment opportunities, and an examination of teaching as a profession. It includes a chapter that tries to give the reader a behind-the-scenes look at what we know about the experiences of beginning teachers and concludes with an examination of the various motivations for teaching.

FEATURES OF THE REVISION

Teaching, learning, and the condition of our schools have been in the headlines almost continually in the past ten years. Education is big news from Main Street to Pennsylvania Avenue. As the link between education and the well-being of both the individual and the nation becomes more obvious, both real change and proposals for change become apparent. Therefore, we—Kevin and Jim—try to sort out the most significant developments without losing sight of the enduring issues facing students and teachers. The changes in this edition include:

Most Important Changes:

- NEW **Voices from the Classroom** feature in every chapter, with stories written by actual teachers about their real-life teaching experiences.

- NEW **Open to Debate** features in some chapters, in which the authors explore opposing viewpoints on controversial education issues, such as school choice, teacher tenure, and more.

- Increased emphasis on standards-based education, including INTASC teacher standards, throughout the text, particularly in chapters 4, 5, 6, 11, 13, and 14.

- Strengthened emphasis on reflection and reflective teaching throughout the text, especially in chapters 1, 5, 13, and 15.

- NEW **Pause and Reflect** critical thinking questions appear three to four times in each chapter to reinforce the reflection theme.

- Extensive technology content for students including companion Web site and CD-ROM, both carefully integrated with textbook content.

Significant to Many Instructors:

- Careful balancing between coverage of secondary and elementary education

- Continued emphasis on diversity, with added statistics on minority groups, including Asian/Pacific Islanders and Native Americans, in many chapters

- Continued emphasis on technology, with new EOC sections listing Web resources, and direct tie-ins to media package throughout the text marked by special marginal icons

- Improved chapter cross-referencing

- NEW biography of Marva Collins (chapter 11)

- Chart inside book covers correlating text content to INTASC standards for new teachers

ACCOMPANYING TEACHING AND LEARNING RESOURCES

The tenth edition of *Those Who Can, Teach* is accompanied by an extensive package of instructor and student resources.

Kaleidoscope: Readings in Education, **Tenth Edition,** is a companion book of readings that can be used either in conjunction with the text or as a separate volume. This collection of reading selections contains works by some of the most distinguished scholars in education, along with the writings of practicing teachers. A mixture of topical and classical studies, the readings include diary entries, letters, teacher accounts, journal articles, and reports. Many of the authors and research reports cited in *Those Who Can, Teach* are included in this book of readings. Also, an easy-to-use chart cross-references topics discussed in *Those Who Can, Teach* with the readings in *Kaleidoscope*.

Accompanying the text is an ***Instructor's Resource Manual*** (IRM) ***with Test Items,*** prepared by Leslie Swetnam of Metropolitan State College of Denver, a highly skilled teacher educator and long-time user of previous editions of this book. The IRM contains a transition guide from the ninth edition to the tenth; model syllabi; and instructor and student support resources including lecture outlines, media resources, sample chapter quizzes, activities, case studies and a full bank of test items.

The **HMClassPrep CD with HM Testing 6.0** provides instructors with a variety of teaching resources in an electronic format allowing for easy customization to meet specific instructional needs. Files encoded on the disk include a brand new PowerPoint package for classroom presentations as well as Word files from the Instructor's Resource Manual which can be easily edited and customized (including lecture outlines, class exercises, debate issues, chapter quizzes, answers to discussion and review questions, comments on the cases, and video guide information).

A new **CD-ROM for students** includes video, graphic, and primary text resources with reflection questions. Video topics include the history of education, the digital divide, gender bias in the classroom, alternative and charter schools, and classroom discipline, to name a few. Graphic resources include a variety of thought-provoking images and questions for each chapter, and the primary text resources include the full text of the Education for All Handicapped Children Act, the Bilingual Education Act, the No Child Left Behind Act, court cases, and more.

The **companion Web site** for *Those Who Can, Teach* includes ACE Self Quizzes, links to key topics in each chapter, additional "Voices from the Classroom" articles, enhancements of the "Biography," "Open to Debate," and "Policy Matters!" features with links to updated and expanded information and additional reflection questions, a sample classroom observation guide, tips for creating a teaching portfolio, and more resources for both students and instructors.

Blackboard and WebCT Course Cartridges contain text and study guide content made platform-ready for online courses.

Major Chapter-by-Chapter Changes:

Chapter 1: What Is a School and What Is It For?

- New emphasis on reflection at the beginning of the chapter

- Major new section on "Four Basic Purposes of Schooling" (intellectual, political and civic, economic, and social), featuring quotations from famous educational theorists

- New "Voices from the Classroom" box, with a teacher answering the question "What is a Good School?"

Chapter 2: Who Are Today's Students in a Diverse Society?

- New definitions of race and ethnicity

- Thoroughly updated statistics on primary languages of students, racial and cultural diversity, and students with disabilities

- New description of equity pedagogy

- New examples to help explain learning styles

- Updates on bilingual education and inclusion controversies

- New "Voices from the Classroom" box, with a special education teacher and classroom teacher describing their co-teaching experience

- New box, "Breaking Out," about one school's success with children who have autism

Chapter 3: What Social Problems and Tension Points Affect Today's Students?

- Thoroughly updated statistics on single-parent families, parental work schedules, poverty, teenage parenting, child abuse, alcohol and drug abuse, suicide, school violence, and school dropout

- Emphasis on teen parenting, rather than teenage pregnancy, to acknowledge the role of males

- New information on outcomes for children of teenage mothers

- New section on bullying and prevention efforts, including advice for teachers.

- Update on school choice, including most recent (6/2002) Supreme Court ruling on school voucher programs and research on charter schools

- New "Open to Debate" box on whether public schools have a monopoly on American education

- Update of gender and sexuality section, including research on gender differences in schools, sexual harassment, and abstinence versus comprehensive sex education programs

- "Voices from the Classroom" box on teaching children whose lives have been affected by social problems

Chapter 4: What is Taught?

- Section on history of curriculum deleted; history information has been consolidated in history chapter

- New section on standards-based education, including new table with examples of curriculum standards at several levels from several states

- Updates on issues and trends in curricula for major subject-matter areas

- Update with most recent available NAEP scores

- New section on differentiated instruction, with a new table listing several methods for differentiating instruction

- New "Voices from the Classroom" box with a teacher's experience using innovative instructional methods to help a bilingual student

Chapter 5: What Makes a Teacher Effective?

- New section, "Framework for Professional Practice," describes two ways of measuring effectiveness of teachers, INTASC standards, and Danielson's Framework for Teaching

- New section on personal practical knowledge

Chapter 6: What Should Teachers Know About Technology and Its Impact on Schools?

- Updated examples of software and hardware throughout the chapter

- Updated discussion of teacher technology preparation, including INTASC standards

- Expanded discussion of equity in technological access and "digital divide" issues

- New "Voices from the Classroom" feature on using handheld computers in a third grade class

Chapter 7: What Are the Ethical and Legal Issues Facing Teachers?

- New case study featuring an everyday ethical dilemma

- New extended example to help explain teaching contracts

- New case study example of teacher liability

- Updated legal information throughout the chapter, including summaries of key cases and most recent Supreme Court rulings in liability, academic freedom, school prayer, zero-tolerance policies, student drug testing, and educational privacy.

- New "Open to Debate" on tenure

- New "Voices from the Classroom" feature on ethical dilemmas involved in enforcing school dress code

Chapter 8: What Are the Philosophical Foundations of American Education?

- New major section on romanticism philosophy replaces existentialism

- New "Voices from the Classroom" box on putting a constructivist philosophy into action

Chapter 9: What is the History of American Education?

- New table summarizing educational and curriculum history helps group together history information previously spread throughout the book

- Updated information and statistics on education of minority students

- New "Voices from the Classroom" box on teaching in segregated and desegregated schools

Chapter 10: How Are Schools Governed, Influenced, and Financed?

- Thoroughly updated statistics on school board membership, district superintendents, principals, and school finances

- New information throughout chapter on federal government influence on education through 2002 No Child Left Behind Act, including a box listing key provisions of the Act

- New "Voices from the Classroom" box on teaching in a financially strapped school

Chapter 11: How Should Education be Reformed?

- New section on the role of curriculum standards in educational reform

- New "Voices from the Classroom" box on importance of character education

- Updated discussion of professional development lists qualifications of effective professional development programs

- Updated statistics and information on state-level reform efforts, including increased graduation requirements, increased classroom time, statewide testing, and teacher improvement

- New box, "Letter from a Home Schooling Mother"

- New biography box featuring Marva Collins

Chapter 12: What Are Your Job Options in Education?

- Thoroughly updated statistics on student enrollment, population trends, teacher attrition, and average salaries

- Salary information retained, although most other books do not include state-by-state listings. Annual updates to be placed on Web site

- New "Voices from the Classroom" box comparing teaching in private and public schools

- New mentions of online job listings

Chapter 13: What Can the New Teacher Expect?

- New "Voices from the Classroom" box, "What Can the New Teacher Expect?" written by a new teacher

- New "Policy Matters!" box on zero-tolerance policies and new teachers.

- New case study on teachers' relationships with parents.

Chapter 14: What Does It Mean to be a Professional?

- Section on history of teacher professionalism deleted; history information has been consolidated in history chapter

- New section on levels of professionalism summarizing National Board for Professional Teaching Standards levels

- New section "What Every New Teacher Should Possess: The INTASC Standards"

- New letter from NEA President, Bob Chase, "Those Who Can, Teach" written specially for tenth edition

- New "Voices from the Classroom" box with one teacher's example of demonstrating professionalism through ongoing professional development

- New section on professional development through systematic reflection on practice.

Chapter 15: Why Teach?

- Extensive coverage of recent study of new teachers, *A Sense of Calling*

- New encouragement to work as substitute teachers, as a means of deciding whether to teach and to gain job experience.

- New "Voices from the Classroom" box on deciding if you have what it takes to teach

PART I

Model Syllabi

Note to Instructors: We have provided model syllabi for an introduction to education course, one for a 16-week semester and another for a 10-week semester. It is our hope that these syllabi will give instructors some idea on how *Those Who Can, Teach* can be used in an introductory course. Readings from the companion book *Kaleidoscope* are also included in the syllabi.

Introduction To Education

16-WEEK SYLLABUS

Instructor:

Office:

Telephone:

Office hours:

OBJECTIVES

Students will:

1. deepen their understanding of education by focusing on four themes: schools and students, teachers, foundations and the future, and the teaching profession.

2. improve their academic analytical writing skills through writing assignments and field journals.

3. refine their problem-solving skills in preparation for leadership roles in education.

4. gain knowledge of current educational issues related to the philosophy, history, finance and governance of education in the United States.

5. demonstrate professional behavior in their roles as observers and assistants in field placements.

6. examine their commitment to the teaching profession through reflection on their classroom and field experiences.

COURSE STRUCTURE

Section

Students meet for small group discussions of the readings and of field experiences. Students are expected to have completed the assigned readings and to be ready to discuss ideas and topics found in the readings. Their weekly journal entries based on the readings will be used as discussion starters.

Class

Students meet with the professor—after the section sessions for lectures and other learning experiences. *Regular and punctual attendance is required for section and lecture.*

Field

Each student is assigned a classroom to serve as the apprentice to a cooperating teacher. Students are expected to dress, behave, and speak in a professional manner. They must attend all field visits and should be punctual. Students will keep a field journal in which they will write a weekly entry related to their experiences in the classroom.

Texts (available at the bookstore)

Required

Ryan, K., and J. M. Cooper (2004). *Those Who Can, Teach* (10th ed.). Boston: Houghton Mifflin.

Ryan, K., and J. M. Cooper (eds.). (2004). *Kaleidoscope: Readings in Education* (10th ed.). Boston: Houghton Mifflin.

Grading and Assignments

Semester grades will be based on your knowledge of educational concepts and theories and your ability to express yourself orally and in writing. Knowledge of educational concepts and theories will be evaluated through papers, periodic quizzes and two exams: a midterm and a final. Both exams will consist of multiple-choice, short-answer, and essay questions. The midterm will deal with material covered in the textbooks, discussions, and lectures during the first half of the semester, and the final exam will be cumulative, covering material from both halves of the course.

Because it is so important these days for teachers to communicate their ideas to colleagues, parents, and administrators effectively, writing clear and error-free English is a priority at the School of Education. Therefore, your ability to express your knowledge of educational concepts and theories within the conventions of academic discourse will be assessed through oral presentations and written assignments. Criteria for evaluation will be based on content and mechanics. Integration of information from lectures, readings, discussions, and field experiences will also be taken into consideration. A guide to academic writing as well as specific instructions for each assignment will be distributed.

Assignment	Due Date	Value
An influential teacher		10%
Educational issue investigation: - Introductory paper - Literature review - Position paper		20%
Book critique		10%
Journal and journal summary		10%
Midterm examination		15%
Final examination		20%
Participation: Quizzes Article critique Professional interview		5% 5% 5%
Total		**100%**

Course Schedule

Date	Topic	*Those Who Can, Teach*
Part I:	**Schools and Students**	
Week 1	Introduction	
	Schools	Chapter 1
Week 2	Diverse Students	Chapter 2
	Social Problems and Tension Points	Chapter 3
Week 3	Curriculum	Chapter 4
Part II:	**Teachers**	
Week 4	Effective Teachers	Chapter 5
Week 5	Technology in Education	Chapter 6
Week 6	Legal and Ethical Issues	Chapter 7
Week 7	**Midterm Exam**	
Part III:	**Foundations and the Future**	
Week 8	Philosophy	Chapter 8

Note to Instructors: Although it is probably most effective to keep the chapters of each part together, Parts I through IV can be interchanged to meet your needs.

10-WEEK SYLLABUS

Instructor:

Office:

Telephone:

Office hours:

OBJECTIVES

Students will:

1.   deepen their understanding of education by focusing on four themes: schools and students, teachers, foundations and the future, and the teaching profession.

2.   improve their academic analytical writing skills through writing assignments and field journals.

3.   refine their problem-solving skills in preparation for leadership roles in education.

4.   gain knowledge of current educational issues related to the philosophy, history, finance, and governance of education in the United States.

5.   demonstrate professional behavior in their roles as observers and assistants in field placements.

6.   examine their commitment to the teaching profession through reflection on their classroom and field experiences.

COURSE STRUCTURE

Section:

Students meet for small group discussions of the readings and of field experiences. Students are expected to have completed the assigned readings and to be ready to discuss ideas and topics found in the readings. Their weekly journal entries based on the readings will be used as discussion starters.

Class:

Students meet with the professor—after the section sessions for lectures and other learning experiences. *Regular and punctual attendance is required for section and lecture.*

Field:

Each student is assigned to a classroom to serve as the apprentice to a cooperating teacher. Students are expected to dress, behave, and speak in a professional manner. They must attend all field visits and should be punctual. Students will keep a field journal in which they will write a weekly entry related to their experiences in the classroom.

Texts (available at the bookstore)

Required:

Ryan, K., and J. M. Cooper (2004). *Those Who Can, Teach* (10th ed.). Boston: Houghton Mifflin.

Ryan, K., and J. M. Cooper (eds.). (2004). *Kaleidoscope: Readings in Education* (10th ed.). Boston: Houghton Mifflin.

Grading and Assignments

Semester grades will be based on your knowledge of educational concepts and theories and your ability to express yourself orally and in writing. Knowledge of educational concepts and theories will be evaluated through papers, periodic quizzes and two exams: a midterm and a final. Both exams will consist of multiple-choice, short-answer, and essay questions. The midterm will deal with material covered in the textbooks, discussions, and lectures during the first half of the semester, and the final exam will be cumulative, covering material from both halves of the course.

Because it is so important these days for teachers to communicate their ideas to colleagues, parents, and administrators effectively, writing clear and error-free English is a priority at the School of Education. Therefore, your ability to express your knowledge of educational concepts and theories within the conventions of academic discourse will be assessed through oral presentations and written assignments. Criteria for evaluation will be based on content and mechanics. Integration of information from lectures, readings, discussions, and field experiences will also be taken into consideration. A guide to academic writing as well as specific instructions for each assignment will be distributed.

Assignment	Due Date	Value
An influential teacher		10%
Educational issue investigation Literature review Position paper		20%
Book critique		10%
Journal and journal summary		10%
Midterm examination		15%
Final examination		20%
Participation		5%
Quizzes		10%
Total		**100%**

Course Schedule

Date	Topic	*Those Who Can, Teach*
Part I:	**Schools and Students**	
Week 1	Course Introduction	
	Schools	Chapter 1
Week 2	Diverse Students	Chapter 2
	Social Problems and Tension Points	Chapter 3
Week 3	Curriculum	Chapter 4
Part II:	**Teachers**	
Week 4	Effective Teachers	Chapter 5
	Technology in Education	Chapter 6
Week 5	Legal and Ethical Issues	Chapter 7
	Midterm Exam	
Part III:	**Foundations and the Future**	
Week 6	Philosophy	Chapter 8
	History	Chapter 9
Week 7	Governance and Finance	Chapter 10
	Education Reform	Chapter 11

Note to Instructors: Although it is probably most effective to keep the chapters of each part together, Parts I through IV can be interchanged to meet your needs.

CORRELATIONS FOR *KALEIDOSCOPE*

For those instructors wishing to assign additional readings in conjunction with specific topics, this table correlates topics dealing with various aspects of education with relevant readings (all found in Ryan, K., and J. M. Cooper (eds.). (2004). *Kaleidoscope: Readings in Education* (10th ed.). Boston: Houghton Mifflin).

Topic	Author	Readings from *Kaleidoscope* (Abbreviated Titles)	Relevant chapters in *Those Who Can, Teach*
Accountability	Raywid	*Accountability: What's Worth Measuring*	11
After-School Activities	Hofferth & Jankuniene	*Life After School*	3
Assessment	Guskey	*Making the Grade*	4, 5, 6
	Stiggins	*Assessment Crisis*	4, 10, 11
Bilingual Education	Minicucci et al.	*School Reform and Student Diversity*	2, 9
Brain Research	Hardiman	*Connecting Brain Research with Dimensions of Learning*	
Character Education/Values	Elkind	*The Cosmopolitan School*	11
	Lickona	*The Return of Character Education*	11
	Noddings	*Teaching Themes of Care*	11
	Nord	*The Relevance of Religion to the Curriculum*	7, 11
	Ryan	*Mining the Values in the Curriculum*	11
Child Abuse	Cates, Markell, & Bettenhausen	*At Risk for Abuse*	3, 7
Choice	Carper	*Changing Landscape of U.S. Education*	3, 9, 11
	Levin	*Bear Market*	11
	McDonald	*The False Promise of Vouchers*	3, 11
	Vitaretti	*Coming Around on School Choice*	3, 11
Classroom Management	Wasicsko & Ross	*How to Create Discipline Problems*	1, 5
Constructivism	Perkins	*The Many Faces of Constructivism*	6, 8, 11
Cooperative Learning	Johnson & Johnson	*Making Cooperative Learning Work*	4
Curriculum	Adler	*The Paideia Proposal*	4, 8
	Elkind	*The Cosmopolitan School*	2, 4, 6, 11
	Haycock	*Closing the Achievement Gap*	4, 5, 9, 11
	Hirsch	*Seeking Breadth and Depth in the Curriculum*	4, 8, 11
	Nord	*The Relevance of Religion to the Curriculum*	4, 7, 11
	Peddiwell	*The Saber-Tooth Curriculum*	4
Ethics of Teaching	Strike	*The Ethics of Teaching*	7
Finance	Miles	*Putting Money Where It Matters*	10
Gender Issues	Bailey	*Shortchanging Girls and Boys*	3
	Woods	*Hostile Hallways*	3, 7
	Kirby	*What Does the Research Say About Sexuality Education?*	3
Harassment	Woods	*Hostile Hallways*	3, 7
Home Schooling	Lines	*Home Schooling Comes of Age*	7, 11

Homework	Cooper	*Homework for All*	
	Hofferth & Jankuniene	*Life After School*	3
Inclusion	Kluth et al.	*Our School Doesn't Offer Inclusion*	2
	Merritt	*Clearing the Hurdles of Inclusion*	2
Instruction	Tomlinson	*Mapping a Route Toward Differentiated Instruction*	4
Law and the Teacher	McDaniel	*The Teacher's Ten Commandments*	7
Multicultural Education	Banks	*Multicultural Education in the New Century*	2, 4
	Minicucci et al.	*School Reform and Student Diversity*	2, 4, 11
	Ravitch	*A Considered Opinion*	2, 4
	Stotsky	*Multicultural Illiteracy*	2, 4, 9
Parental Involvement	Finders & Lewis	*Why Some Parents Don't Come to School*	2, 10, 13
	Loveless	*The Parent Trap*	1, 2, 4, 11
Philosophy of Education	Adler	*The Paideia Proposal*	4, 8
	Boyer	*The Educated Person*	4, 8
	Dewey	*My Pedagogic Creed*	1, 4, 8
	Glickman	*Dichotomizing Education*	1, 4, 7, 11
	Hirsch	*Romancing the Child*	4, 8
	Hutchins	*The Basis of Education*	4, 8
	Rogers	*Personal Thoughts on Teaching and Learning*	8
Reforming Education	Cohen	*Schools Our Teachers Deserve*	1, 11, 14
	Darling-Hammond	*What Matters Most*	5, 11, 12, 14
	David	*The Who, What, and Why of Site-Based Management*	10, 11
	Eisner	*The Kind of Schools We Need*	1, 4, 11, 14
	Levin	*Bear Market*	11
	McDonald	*The False Promise of Vouchers*	3
	Miles	*Putting Money Where It Matters*	10
	Vitaretti	*Coming Around on School Choice*	3
Religion and Education	Nord	*The Relevance of Religion to the Curriculum*	4, 7, 11
Schools	Barth	*The Culture Builder*	1, 2, 10, 11, 13, 14
	Cohen	*Schools Our Teachers Deserve*	1, 5, 11, 13, 14, 15
	Cuban	*A Tale of Two Schools*	1, 11
	Elkind	*The Cosmopolitan School*	2, 4, 6, 11
	Wasley	*Small Classes, Small Schools*	1, 11
Sex Education	Kirby	*What Does the Research Say About Sexuality Education?*	3
Site-Based Management	David	*The Who, What, and Why of Site-Based Management*	10, 11
Standards Movement	Haycock	*Closing the Achievement Gap*	4, 5, 9, 11
	Thompson	*The Authentic Standards Movement and Its Evil Twin*	4, 10, 11
Student Motivation and Engagement	Clifford	*Students Need Challenge*	5, 11

	Csikszentmihalyi & McCormack	*The Influence of Teachers*	5, 11, 15
	Dodd	*Engaging Students*	5, 11
Student Needs	Barr	*Who Is This Child?*	2, 3
	Edelman	*Leaving No Child Behind*	2, 3
	Eitzen	*Problem Students*	2, 3
Teacher Development and Qualifications	Barth	*The Culture Builder*	1, 2, 10, 11, 13, 14
	Darling-Hammond	*What Matters Most*	5, 11, 12, 14
	Ducharme	*The Great Teacher Question*	5, 11, 12, 14
	Haberman	*Selecting "Star" Teachers*	2, 5, 11, 12
	Hole & McEntee	*Reflection Is at the Heart of Practice*	5, 13, 14, 15
	Houghton	*Finding Allies*	13, 14
	Wise	*Creating a High-Quality Teaching Force*	5, 11, 12, 14
Teacher Influence and Effectiveness	Csikszentmihalyi & McCormack	*The Influence of Teachers*	5, 11, 15
	Fried	*The Heart of the Matter*	5, 15
	Metzger	*Calling in the Cosmos*	*5, 15*
	Ness	*Lessons of a First-Year Teacher*	12, 13, 14
Teacher Portfolios	Wolf	*Developing an Effective Teaching Portfolio*	12, 14
Teachers, life of	Crowley	*Letter from a Teacher*	13, 14
	Houghton	*Finding Allies*	13, 14
	Ness	*Lessons of a First-Year Teacher*	12, 13, 14
Technology in Education	Healy	*The Mad Dash to Compute*	6, 8
	Means	*Technology Use in Tomorrow's Schools*	6
	Postman	*Making a Living, Making a Life*	6, 8

PART II

Instructional Resources

FOR EACH CHAPTER

Learning Objectives

Chapter Overview

Chapter Outline

Supplementary Lecture and Discussion Topics

Student Study Guide

Additional Resources for Instructors

Media Resources

Student Activities

Student Assignments

    Independent Reading

    Reflective Papers

    Journal Reflections

    Selected Chapters: CD-ROM Video Clips

CHAPTER 1

What Is a School and What Is It For?

LEARNING OBJECTIVES

After studying the chapter, students will be able to

1. distinguish between education and schooling.

2. explain, apply, and analyze the school models described in the text: worker trainer, college prep, social panacea, social escalator, shopping mall, family, human potential developer, acculturator.

3. describe how schools function as transmitters and re-creators of culture.

4. describe how schools can operate as vehicles for social, democratic, and economic reconstruction.

5. identify and give examples of the managerial teacher roles in the classrooms.

6. explain why students in elementary classrooms learn to deny desire, delay gratification, cope with interruptions, and work through social distractions.

7. describe the range of educational experiences for middle-grade students, based on the grade configuration of the school, the size of the school, the administration's and teachers' orientations, the goals of the school, and the staffing patterns.

8. explain how the greater variety of choices secondary students have can result in different high school experiences, based on tracking, the courses in which they enroll, the feedback they receive from teachers, and the tacit agreements they make with their teachers.

9. identify four areas suggested to improve the quality of high schools.

10. list and explain some of the characteristics of schools that are effective with respect to academic outcomes.

CHAPTER OVERVIEW

This chapter highlights some of the more common conceptions of schools. Each model is briefly described, but we also acknowledge that each model is useful only in its ability to explain or describe what exists. No one model, then, can completely explain a school; however, as long as we recognize the limitations of models, we can draw on what the models can offer to form a fuller understanding of schools.

Schools reflect and transmit a culture. This aspect of schooling is one that has come under increased scrutiny in the recent past. Should schools tacitly or overtly support the dominant culture of the society? Should schools be structured so that they are encouraging students to fit into the social structure as it exists, or should schools demonstrate to students how they can be agents of change? Today's public schoolstransmit a community's values, which are imparted through the work of teachers. The ways schools are organized, the content of the curriculum, the methods of instruction—all reflect current norms in the United States.

Chapter 1 also focuses on many different studies that have examined life in classrooms. Research is cited to present to prospective teachers an accurate portrait of what life in school is like. In this way, prospective teachers can broaden their perception of school life beyond their own experiences and can think about their role in the classroom.

The studies reported look at school life at different levels: elementary, middle, and high school. Philip Jackson's study of life in elementary classrooms explains how daily routines shape the experiences of both teachers and students. Student experiences in the middle grades, between sixth and eighth grades, are strongly influenced by the configuration of grades, the size of the school, and the goals and objectives set out by the administration.

Studies of high schools by Boyer and Cuban highlight the unchanging nature of these environments and offer recommendations for change.

Many studies have been conducted regarding the characteristics of effective schools. After choosing a common definition of "effectiveness," the characteristics that have been identified in these studies in schools are described.

Student readers should recognize the range and diversity of schools. For that reason, we encourage them to compare their own experiences of schooling with the ideas and models described in this chapter. We expect that class discussion will highlight differences and similarities in their schooling. For prospective teachers to be effective, reflective instructors as well as participants in renewing schools, it is imperative that they understand the competing conceptions of schools as well as the effects of inertia on school change.

CHAPTER OUTLINE

I.   Education and Schooling
    A.   Education
    B.   Schooling
II.   Four Basic Purposes of School
    A.   Intellectual Purposes
    B.   Political and Civic Purposes
    C.   Economic Purposes
    D.   Social Purposes
III. Models of Schools
    A.   The School as Trainer of Good Workers
    B.   The School as Social Escalator
    C.   The School as Preparer for College
    D.   The School as Shopping Mall
    E.   The School as Developer of Human Potential
    F.   The School as Family
    G.   The School as Social Panacea
    H.   The School as Acculturator
IV.   Schools as Cultures
    A.   Socialization
V.   Schools as Transmitters or Re-creators of Culture
    A.   Transmitting Culture
        1.   Acculturation and Diversity
    B.   Reconstructing Society
        1.   Social
        2.   Democratic
        3.   Economic

VI. What Do Studies Reveal About the Nature of Schools?
  A. Life in Elementary Schools
    1. The Teacher's Role
    2. What Students Experience
  B. Life in Middle and Junior High Schools
  C. Life in High Schools
    1. Multiple Purposes
    2. The Shopping Mall High School
    3. Inside Classrooms
  D. A New Call for High School Reform
    1. Personalization
    2. Coherence
    3. Time
    4. Technology
VII. What Is a Good School?
  A. Characteristics of an Effective School
    1. The Teacher's Expectations
    2. Communication Among Students
    3. Task Orientation
    4. Academic Engaged Time
    5. Behavior Management
    6. The Principal
    7. Parents
    8. The School Environment
VIII. The Unfinished Work of Schools

SUPPLEMENTARY LECTURE AND DISCUSSION TOPICS

1. **Teacher: the creator or transmitter of culture?** In greater detail, present to your class how the teacher can be either the creator or transmitter of culture. Explore the realities of a teacher being either a transmitter or a creator of culture. What obstacles does one face as a teacher fully committed to the cause of reconstruction? To what extent can a teacher be a convincing transmitter of culture? Are the elements of a teaching job and the requirements for social reconstructions too disparate to expect teachers, in general, to work actively to change society? Is there a basic mismatch between those who would continue to teach because of the stability of the profession, and the active participation and risk taking required of those committed to social reconstruction?

2. **Privatization** Discuss how privatization groups like the Edison Project affect the model in the schools they take over. Do they create a new model "School as Business"? Can decisions be too influenced by the economics of the design?

3. **Future instruction in high school** Boyer and Cuban studied high school programs and came up with very different recommendations for change. Boyer advocated revitalizing programs by sweeping changes in teaching. Cuban advocated strengthening teacher-centered instruction. Review the work of these authors, and discuss the implications for students and high schools if either approach were to be adopted.

4. **Tracking in the high school** Although much has been written criticizing the use of tracking in the high school, many, if not most, public high schools still do some tracking. Examine the arguments for and against tracking. Explore some of the common questions surrounding tracking. How does tracking affect a student's self-image? How can a teacher provide enough challenge for a bright student in a mixed-ability class so that he or she won't be held back? How can a teacher effectively teach a classroom of heterogeneous students? What are the differences in class size in the different tracks? How do teachers view teaching "honors" or "general"-level classes? Finally, you may want to share with your students a high school curriculum that uses tracking. Look at the curriculum, for example, of the ninth-grade general science class and the ninth-grade college preparatory science class. What are the differences in activities? Textbooks? Skills to be covered?

5. **Uniforms** Describe the studies on the effects of requiring students to wear uniforms in public schools. Discuss its implications on personal freedom, economics, achievement, school safety, etc. Use schools in your geographical area as examples.

STUDY GUIDE – CHAPTER 1: WHAT IS A SCHOOL AND WHAT IS ITS PURPOSE?

Completing this study guide will help you prepare for the major topic areas on an exam; however, it does not cover every piece of information found in the chapter or the test questions.

1. Define and contrast these terms:

   a. Education

   b. Schooling

2. Describe or give an example of each of the following models:

   a. Trainer of good worker

   b. Social escalator

   c. Preparer for college

   d. Shopping mall

   e. Developer of human potential

   f. Family

   g. Social panacea

   h. Acculturator

3. Give an example of schools functioning as:

   a. Representatives of culture

   b. Transmitters of culture

4. Describe four of the managerial functions of the teacher's role.

5. Name and describe the common experiences of elementary students.

6.   Describe the characteristics that vary in the structure of middle schools.

7.   Name and describe the common characteristics of high schools.

8.   What are four of the areas for improving the quality of American high schools that were suggested in *Breaking Ranks: Changing an American Institution*?

9.   Describe the characteristics of effective schools presented in either the academic outcome or holistic point of view in the chapter.

ADDITIONAL RESOURCES FOR INSTRUCTORS

Boyer, Ernest. *Basic School: A Community for Learning*. Princeton, NJ: The Carnegie Foundation for the Advancement of Teaching, 1995. This is the last book written by one of education's greatest practitioners and spokesmen. It is a statement filled with practical wisdom woven into a clear description of the kind of schools we can and should have.

Freedman, Samuel G. *Small Victories: The Real World of a Teacher, Her Students, and Their High School*. New York: Harper and Row, 1990. The author spent a year with a teacher and her class in a school in the Lower East Side of New York. The book presents a grim portrayal of life in poor, urban schools.

Good, Thomas, and Jere Brophy. *Looking in Classrooms*. 8th ed. New York: Longman, 2000. This classic text offers a popular, class-tested examination of strategies for observing and describing classroom teaching. It contains a concise and authoritative review of classroom research combined with specific teaching recommendations.

Goodlad, John I. *A Place Called School*. New York: McGraw-Hill, 1984. Goodlad and his team of researchers spent several thousand hours collecting data on what schools are actually like. The book is a detailed, scholarly look at the events, forces, and philosophies that shape U.S. schools.

Jackson, Phillip W. *Life in Classrooms*. New York: Teachers College Press, 1990. This classic provides insight into the routines, interactions, and the way students experience life in classrooms.

Lawson, Robert, Val D. Rust, and Susanne Shafer (eds.). *Education and Social Concern: An Approach to Social Foundations*. Ann Arbor, MI: Praeger, 1987. The text explores the social dimensions of schooling, developing in more detail the varying models of schools and their social functions.

Peterson, Ralph. *Life in a Crowded Place: Making a Learning Community*. Portsmouth, NH: Heinemann, 1992. This text discusses how schools struggle with the factors that work against education and how schools can build their own communities.

Pritchard, Ivor. *Good Education: The Virtues of Learning*. Washington, DC: Judd Publishing, 1998. Pritchard's book explores the purpose of education and schooling, giving particular attention to the frequently neglected mission of the schools in character and moral education.

Rottier, Jerry, and Beverly Ogan. *Cooperative Learning in Middle-level Schools*. Washington, DC: National Education Association, 1992. This book provides several sample lesson plans, staff development workshop material, and project planning forms for middle school students.

Siskin, Leslie. *Realms of Knowledge: Academic Departments in Secondary Schools*. Bristol, PA: Falmer Press, 1994. This book explores why teachers find academic departments to be crucial to their high school setting. Departments are seen as boundaries for dividing the school, centers of social interaction, decision-making forums, and knowledge centers.

Sizer, Theodore R. *Horace's Hope: What Works for the American High School*. Boston: Houghton Mifflin, 1996. The third book in Sizer's Horace trilogy, this book embodies the principles espoused by the Coalition of Essential Schools, a reform-oriented association of secondary schools.

Stevenson, Chris, and Judy F. Carr. *Integrated Studies in the Middle Grades: Dancing Through the Walls*. New York: Teachers College Press, 1993. Stevenson and Carr invited middle-level teachers to design and implement innovative teaching units that would be more interesting to the students they teach. They provide the reader with dozens of detailed examples of integrated curriculum units to encourage the reader to try them out or to develop his or her own.

Wexler, Philip. *Become Somebody: Toward a Social Psychology of School*. Bristol, PA: Falmer Press, 1992. Wexler discusses the need to pay attention to students as "whole people" and to be aware of their needs as members of society as well as learners.

Media Resources

The Breakfast Club (MCA, 1985).This movie centers around a Saturday morning detention that a group of students from different cliques must serve. Throughout the morning, they talk and challenge each other's perceptions of who they really are. The movie captures much of the uncertainty teenagers have about their social position, while revealing their aspirations for the future.

Capturing the Essentials: High Schools That Make Sense (Insight Media, 35 min., 1998). Theodore Sizer profiles three exemplary high schools showing how their learning environments are shaped by fundamental ideas that transcend issues of curriculum and standards.

Education (Insight Media, 30 min., 1991). This program examines the role of schools in socializing the young, as well as, historical goals and philosophies of education. It investigates the structure of educational institutions and examines the nature of the teacher-student relationship. The video also probes the relationship between society and schools.

Marshall High Fights Back (Prod: Drew Associates, Dist: Direct Cinema Ltd., 58 min., 1985). An inner-city high school once declared "out of control" makes a crucial turnaround in this story of how a school, a community, and its children find the power within themselves to make changes for the better under a new principal and his successor.

On Tracking and Ability Grouping (AIT, part of *Schools of Thought I*, 28 min., 1992). This video argues that ability grouping is based on flawed suppositions and that alternative strategies would serve all students better.

The Quality School (Insight Media, 207 min., 1993). Dr. William Glasser discusses how reality therapy and control theory can be applied to schools. He provides practical suggestions for creating a quality school where administrators, teachers, counselors, parents, and students work together to provide all students with an education based upon cooperation and established standards.

Successful Schools (Insight Media, 51 min., 1999). This video shows how to raise achievement and support at-risk students with strategies for assessing student needs, reducing discipline problems, structuring a literacy program, and reducing referral to special education.

Teacher, Lester Bit Me! (Lucerne Media, 9 min., 1975). In this animated version of a preschool day, everything seems to go wrong. The teacher arrives at school anticipating a happy and productive day, but mischief and mishaps overturn all her plans. By exaggerating some of the worst fears of people who work with young children, this film provides an opportunity to discuss some common difficulties and ways they might be solved.

Media distributor contact information is available in Appendix I.

Student Activities

School Observation—Rating a School's Effectiveness

It is part of our human nature to make judgments and to gauge people, things, and events according to our preferences. For the moment we would like you to turn off your critical judging capacity to an elementary, middle, or high school with which you are familiar. If you have recently visited a school in connection with your education course, use that school; if not, use a school you personally attended.

After selecting a school, follow these next steps: First, list the criteria you believe contribute to an outstanding school. The list can be composed of both positive items ("The teachers are friendly") and positive items stated negatively ("Children are not fearful while at school"). Second, review the sections in this chapter (pages 44–48) that deal with the research on characteristics of effective schools, and add four or five items to your list. Third, refresh your memory and past impressions of the school you have selected for this exercise. Take a mental journey through the school. Bring to the front of your mind several teachers, staff members, and administrators. Recall what it is like in various classes, the cafeteria, the playground, and other spots around the school that you observed or frequented. Now you're ready to evaluate your school's effectiveness.

   a.   Rate your school on a ten-point scale (with 10 being "truly excellent" and 1 being "very poor") on each of the items on your list.

   b.   Write the strongest bit of evidence for each of your judgments. For example, for the criterion "Teachers are friendly" you might write, "Teachers smile at and talk to students in a friendly way in the halls."

   c.   What are the key factors, such as poor leadership or unsupportive parents, that keep this school from reaching its full potential?

   Finally, if you were given complete control over this school and wished to make it truly outstanding, what are the three changes you would put into effect?

Transmitter of Culture or Social Reconstructionist Debate

Based on the number of students in your class, divide them into groups of four to six. Assign each side as a supporter of the "transmitter of culture" model or the "social reconstructionist" model. Allow each group adequate time to research the theory that it supports. At a scheduled date, conduct a debate between the groups that support the view of schools as transmitting the culture and the groups that support the view of schools as reconstructionist. If you will have more than one debate, stagger the debate times so that no one observes the debate before his or her team debates. After students have conducted their debate, they may sit in on other teams' debates. Videotape each debate, and schedule some time outside of class so that the students can watch the debates they missed. As a class, discuss the issues debated. What are the relative merits of each of the theories? Which points made were particularly strong? Did the debates change or modify people's views on one conception of schools or another?

Case Studies of Student Life

Have each student "shadow" an elementary or secondary school pupil for the duration of the school day. (If necessary, this might be a "day" pieced together from separate short visits.) Be sure students have the pupil's and his or her teacher's permission. . Invite comments and analysis regarding the observations. Suggest using a stopwatch to document the number of minutes the student spends in academic on-task time.

Tracking

Students should interview three or more elementary and/or secondary school teachers to learn their views on tracking or ability grouping. Does the school they teach in track or ability group students? In what subjects? How do they (the teachers) feel about this practice? What effects do they see on their students' affective or cognitive development?

The Role of Rules

Rules and regulations seem to play an important role in our schools. Think back to your elementary, middle, or high school days. Write down some school or classroom rules and regulations that you remember. Make a mark next to those rules/regulations that seemed arbitrary, unfair, or with which you disagreed. Be prepared to state why you marked these rules. Are there reasons for these rules that you understand better now? Share in small groups. Debrief as a whole class.

Create a School Assignment

Students will describe a school of their own creation.

Purpose:

To explore the relationship between philosophy, educational goals, and school models

Assignment:

Select a specific vocation, subject area, or educational goal and create a school to produce students who are equipped to meet the goal or to satisfy the requirements of the vocation. A well-focused goal will help simplify the complexity of the task.

Describe your school's

- goals or purpose.

- philosophy (refer to chapter 18).

- most appropriate model(s) (from this chapter).

- essential skills and/or content.

- necessary resources and materials.

- most effective methods.

Evaluation:

- satisfaction of requirements

- detail and support of ideas

- rationale for decisions

- ability to communicate the model orally or in writing

Note to Instructors: You may want to start this activity in small groups or individually in this chapter with a due date after the philosophy chapter has been presented.

Due Date: _____

Student Assignments

The following activities are suggestions for student portfolio activities. They are a means of providing alternative assessment of students' capabilities.

Independent Reading

Read and respond to any of the selections noted on the chapter/article correlation list found in the front of this manual for Ryan/Cooper, *Kaleidoscope: Readings in Education* (Houghton Mifflin, 2004). You may want to use the Article Review Form in *Kaleidoscope*.

Reflective Papers

Choose one of the following topics to write a reflective paper (2–5 pages). The purpose of the paper is to help you assimilate new knowledge by blending it with your previous knowledge and experiences.

1. Consider your own school experience. Which types and to what degree did your school(s) exemplify the models presented in the text? As a student, how did the purposes of the school become evident to you?

2. Based upon your observation of your field-site school (or another school where you have had experience), write what you perceive to be the school's formal statement of purpose. Consider the range of functions the school serves as you prepare this statement.

3. Schools, historically, have transmitted the dominant culture of society. Describe several instances of cultural transmission in your own schooling or in the school where you observe. Analyze your own reflections.

Journal Reflections

Suggestions for journal topics for students' selection:

1. Pick the school model you would feel most comfortable teaching in and explain why.

2. Name one common practice in schools that you would like to change and describe *how* you would change it.

3. Describe how the routine, methods, or organization in an elementary classroom could be altered to change the students' experience.

CD-ROM Video Clip

View the clip for Chapter 1 and be prepared to discuss the following reflection question:

What was the purpose of schooling for the ancient Sumerians, Egyptians, and Greeks? In which of these ancient cultures did education most resemble schooling today? In what ways? What does this say about present-day American culture?

CHAPTER 2

Who Are Today's Students in a Diverse Society?

LEARNING OBJECTIVES

After studying the chapter, students will be able to

1.   explain the concepts of cultural diversity and cultural pluralism, and their implications in the classroom.

2.   describe the demographic trends of U.S. minorities and describe how ethnic and cultural differences between public school teachers and students may foster misunderstanding.

3.   identify and explain William Glasser's control theory and describe how this theory can influence a teacher's behavior with students.

4.   explain Howard Gardner's theory of multiple intelligences and relate that theory to teaching.

5.   describe the four basic learning styles and their potential influence on instruction.

6.   discuss the opposing positions in the debate on multicultural education.

7.   describe five philosophically different approaches to multicultural education.

8.   describe the salient elements of the IDEA, including the key terms *appropriate public education* and *least-restrictive environment*.

9.   describe the term *gifted and talented* as applied to students, and explain how gifted and talented students are identified and educated.

10.   explain the impact of the *Lau* v. *Nichols* Supreme Court decision on bilingual education.

11.   describe the models of bilingual education.

12.   discuss the implications of California's Proposition 227 on bilingual education.

13.   describe the work of James Comer in the school intervention project of New Haven, Connecticut.

CHAPTER OVERVIEW

This chapter focuses on the students who fill classrooms across the country and the diversity these students represent. The chapter first explores who is being educated in our schools, then seeks to understand what their backgrounds are and what an optimal learning environment looks like for them. The chapter then describes how these students learn and what are some of the programs that exist to facilitate their learning. The chapter closes with a look at who is teaching these students and whether teachers and learners can understand one another. Throughout the chapter, prospective teachers are exposed to the range of ethnic, cultural, and linguistic backgrounds found in our schools; and the challenging and diverse needs, abilities, and learning styles of today's school-age population.

The overwhelming majority of public school teachers continue to be white, middle-class women while the student population becomes more and more diverse. Prospective teachers need to be aware of the wide range of backgrounds represented in a given class. For that reason, we spend considerable time discussing the demographics of the school-age population, which is dominated by a steady growth in the minority population while the white population remains relatively stable. We link this discussion to the concept of cultural diversity and pluralism.

Dr. William Glasser's choice theory provides insight which allows prospective teachers to make sense of their students' behaviors once they understand their students' needs. We hope that teachers will use some of the findings in the planning and implementing of their lessons.

The chapter also presents theories on how students learn. Howard Gardner's theory of multiple intelligences is described and complemented by a discussion of individual learning styles. We strongly believe that teachers should try to incorporate a sensitivity to diverse capabilities and an awareness of learning styles into their lessons so that they can facilitate the learning of all students.

A portion of the chapter is devoted to discussing programs designed to enhance the learning of identified groups of students. We describe multicultural and bilingual education programs that are geared to help students from different cultural or linguistic origins. The special needs of disabled children are served through a variety of individualized programs that strive to provide "free, appropriate public education in the least restrictive environment." We also note that programs for gifted and talented students tend to be underfunded because of the elitist connotation of such programs.

By discussing the diversity of the needs of individual children, we also emphasize that a student is more than a label. It is important for teachers to look beyond the category and teach the person. The most helpful way to teach the individual is by gaining sound knowledge of the students along with strong pedagogical training.

CHAPTER OUTLINE

I.   Sources of Student Diversity
    A.   Racial, Ethnic, and Cultural Backgrounds
    B.   Languages other than English
    C.   Socioeconomic Status
    D.   Sexual Orientation
    E.   Diverse Needs
    F.   Diverse Abilities
II. Racial, Ethnic, and Cultural Diversity
    A.   Not There Yet
        1.   Teaching Implications
III. Diverse Needs
    A.   Glasser's Choice Theory
    B.   Adolescent Subcultures
IV. Diverse Abilities
    A.   Multiple Intelligences
        1.   Teaching Implications
    B.   Differing Learning Styles
        1.   Teaching Implications
    C.   Students with Disabilities
        1.   Teaching Implications
    D.   Gifted and Talented Students
        1.   Teaching Implications
V.   The School's Response to Diversity
    A.   Multicultural Education
        1.   An Ongoing Debate
    B.   Bilingual Education
        1.   The Government Response
        2.   Bilingual Education Models
        3.   Controversies
    C.   Special Education
        1.   Preschool Legislation
        2.   IDEA and ADA
        3.   Controversy over Inclusion
        4.   Assistive Technology
        5.   Implications for Teachers
    D.   Programs for Gifted and Talented Students

SUPPLEMENTARY LECTURE AND DISCUSSION TOPICS

1. **Multiculturalism and cultural diversity** One of the most heated debates in education today concerns multiculturalism and cultural diversity. Those who support these concepts feel that for too long education in America has had a white, Eurocentric bias that minimizes or ignores the contributions of other ethnic and racial groups to the body of knowledge that exists in the world. An additional argument is that including a broader multicultural emphasis in schools will enhance minority children's self-esteem as they learn about important contributions made by members of their own ethnic or racial group. Those who do not ardently support multiculturalism argue that they are not against multiculturalism per se, but that teachers need to help students understand the influential events, people, and thoughts that have shaped the United States. They argue that all students need to know the common roots of the United States and the Western European influence, particularly British, that has had a determining effect on what the country is. In addition, they argue that schools cannot teach everything, so they need to select the most important issues. The debate most likely will rage on. You may want to examine the premises of each argument as well as explore the highly political nature of the debate.

2. **The cost of educating children with special, particular needs** In an ideal world, the cost of education would not be a concern. However, the funding of educational programs has become a looming problem. The federal government is backing away from heavy financial commitments to fund specific programs, and taxpayers repeatedly reject the budget increase requests of their local school districts. Because of budgetary constraints, schools are not able, and probably will not be able in the near future, to meet the needs of all students. What are the actual costs of particular programs for students? How much can a particular program per student cost? In a typical school, how much money is spent on special education programs? Bilingual or ESL programs? Gifted and talented programs? Explain how particular programs, such as special education programs, are mandated by federal legislation, yet federal funding is insufficient to cover the costs of these programs. Speculate on the resentment that these expenditures may cause among residents who see other programs that may serve a large portion of the student body being eliminated due to lack of resources. Explore the various aspects of the problem with your students. You may want to invite a local school board member to discuss the impact of funding difficulties on his or her school district.

3. **Life before PL 94-142** Before special education programs were implemented in the United States, how were children with learning disabilities educated? Trace the history of education for disabled children, and explain the changes and benefits that special education programs have made for children with special needs.

4. **Bilingual education** Invite a colleague (or you, if you are fluent in another language) to teach part of a lesson in a language other than English—perhaps a language spoken at home by a member of the class, if possible. Have the guest speak only in the other language, responding in that language to questions or comments made in English. (This is the immersion model.) After a period of instruction, break to discuss how students feel about the experience. Ask them to project how they might feel in the submersion model, where the instructor responds only to comments made in the instructor's language. If time permits, demonstrate how other models might work. End with a general discussion of *Lau* v. *Nichols* and the implications of bilingual education.

5. **School intervention** Describe in detail Comer's school intervention model in New Haven, Connecticut. What is his underlying philosophy regarding school intervention and reform? How did he create his design? What are the various components of the plan, and how does it all work? Describe the changes in the New Haven schools in which Comer's model has been implemented. You may also compare the Comer model of school intervention with the school intervention developed by Boston University for the schools of Chelsea,

Massachusetts. How does that plan work? What is its underlying philosophy? How is it working? What are the challenges faced by any school intervention model?

6. **Psychological needs of humans** Explore Glasser's theory of human needs and people's motivation for behavior. Describe in greater detail the elements of both and compare them. If those theories were implemented in classrooms, how would that affect the teacher's perception of students' behavior? What are some competing psychological theories of human behavior, and how do they reflect on the work of Maslow and Glasser? Imagine what a classroom would look like if the teacher were a firm believer in the theory of either Maslow or Glasser.

7. **Learning styles and multiple intelligences** How could these two concepts dramatically change the nature of public school education? Explore the possibilities with your students.

STUDY GUIDE — CHAPTER 2: WHO ARE TODAY'S STUDENTS IN A DIVERSE SOCIETY?

Completing this study guide will help you prepare for the major topic areas on an exam; however, it does not cover every piece of information found in the chapter or the test questions.

1.   List at least four different *categories* of student diversity in the classroom.

2.   Define cultural pluralism.

3.   According to Glasser's choice theory, what are an individual's basic needs?

4.   What are the eight areas in Gardner's multiple intelligences?

5.   List and give a one-sentence description of each of the four basic learning styles.

6.   Explain the rationale behind Comer's school intervention program.

7.   Describe or give an example of each of the following models of bilingual education: immersion, submersion, transitional, maintenance-developmental. What does LEP stand for?

8.   Describe PL94-142-IDEA and its major provisions.

9.   Distinguish between the practices of inclusion and mainstreaming.

10.   Why is adjusting instruction for culturally and economically diverse students a special challenge for most teachers?

ADDITIONAL RESOURCES FOR INSTRUCTORS

Cole, Robert W. *Educating Everybody's Children: Diverse Teaching Strategies for Diverse Learners*. Alexandria, VA: Association for Supervision and Curriculum Development, 1995. This text presents research-based but practical instructional strategies for teaching diverse students.

Comer, James. *Child by Child, The Comer Process for Change in Education*. New York: Teacher's College Press, 1999. Comer describes his theory of school intervention and reform.

Crawford, J. *Bilingual Education: History, Politics, Theory, and Practice*. Trenton, NJ: Crane Publishing, 1989. A thorough, yet easy-to-read analysis of bilingual education from a historical, theoretical, and practical perspective.

Delpit, Lisa. *Other People's Children: Cultural Conflict in the Classroom*. New York: The New Press, 1995. Asking why schools have such a hard time making school a happy place for poor children and children of color, the author concludes that most classrooms are dominated by a white perspective and that too many teachers don't acknowledge that children of color have perspectives of their own.

Dyson, Anne Haas. *Social Worlds of Children: Learning to Write in an Urban Primary School*. New York: Teachers College Press, 1993. Dyson's research helps broaden our vision of how language experience contributes to school literacy success. She supports efforts to make literacy more accessible to all children by taking into account the children's cultural background.

Glasser, William. *The Quality School: Managing Children without Coercion*. New York: Perennial Library, 1990. Noted psychiatrist William Glasser presents his vision of how schools could be conducted. He also spends considerable time explaining his control theory and its implications for students.

Grant, Carl (ed.). *Research and Multicultural Education*. Bristol, PA: Falmer Press, 1992. Grant brings together authors who consider the challenges and issues relating to multicultural research. Sixteen articles around three topics are presented: multiculturalism in education, the research process, and the social impact of multiculturalism as reflected in school practice.

Nieto, Sonia. *The Light in Their Eyes: Creating Multicultural Learning Communities*. New York: Teachers College Press, 1999. Draws on research in learning styles, multiple intelligences, and cognitive theories to portray the ways in which students learn; also discusses the social context of learning and the influence of culture on learning.

Pugach, Marleen C., and Cynthia L. Warger. *Curriculum Trends, Special Education, and Reform: Refocusing the Conversation*. New York: Teachers College Press, 1996. Arguing that the reform agenda must address the needs of all children, including those with disabilities, this volume gives practical suggestions for doing so in different curriculum areas.

Ravitch, Diane. "Diversity and Democracy: Multicultural Education in America." *American Educator: The Professional Journal of the American Federation of Teachers* 14 (Spring 1990): 16–20, 46–48. The article discusses the controversy over multicultural education. It contrasts California's pluralistic approach with New York's particularistic approach. Ravitch argues for a multiculturalism that provides students with both an appreciation for America's racial and cultural diversity and a commitment to the common culture that unites us all.

Rothstein-Fisch, Carrie, Patricia Greenfeld, and Elis Trumbull. "Building Cultures with Classroom Strategies". *Educational Leadership* 56:7 (April 1999): 64-67. Presents strategies that address the collectivist orientation of Latino children.

Zehr, Mary Ann. "English-Language Learners Post-Improved California Test Scores" *Education Week* (September 5, 2001): 29. This article provides an update on the success of new bilingual policies in California.

Media Resources

Anything You Can Do, I Can Do Better: Why the Sexes Excel Differently (Films for the Humanities and Sciences, 52 min., 1993). This program debates whether differences in brain architecture lead to a division of talents and aptitudes between the sexes. To illustrate these differences, children are observed in classrooms, on the playground, and at home.

Appreciating Diversity (Insight Media, 22 min., 1992). Educators from around the world share their ideas about how they can instill in their students an awareness of and respect for cultural and ethnic diversity. The video suggests ways to incorporate this multicultural material into the curriculum.

Black America and the Education Crisis (Films for the Humanities and Sciences, 60 min., 1998). This video discusses issues such as why black children score lower on standardized tests, how to improve academic performance, and Ebonics.

Brainwaves (Insight Media, 15 min., 2000). This video presents methods that educators can use to encourage participation and creative thinking including segments on constructivism, multiple intelligences, and learning styles.

Breaking Ties (Pyramid Media, 55 min., 1996). This poignant program offers educators a unique insight into the harsh reality of urban and rural instability. Three teenagers demonstrate that dreams and desires are the first step in breaking the ties of poverty.

The Changing Classroom: Cultural Differences and Similarities (Insight Media, 77 min., 1999). This video examines the different effects of cultural differences and similarities on the group dynamics of a class.

Changing the American School (Insight Media, 2 parts 84 min. each, 1995). Dr. James Comer discusses efforts with at-risk schools and students that reflect his recognition and understanding of such factors as race, economics, class, and school system structure that have successfully transformed dysfunctional schools into constructive, living communities.

Classroom Climate Workshop: Cultural Awareness (Insight Media, 30 min., 1999). This video presents workshops that address classroom dynamics, communication patterns, student orientations, learning styles, and teaching techniques for use with students from different cultures.

Classroom Climate Workshop: Gender Equity (Insight Media, 30 min., 1999). This video depicts a humorous and obvious acceptance of gender-based assumptions; explores the dangers of the subtler problems that typically arise in a classroom; and demonstrates some of the very minor adjustments that can create a more equitable classroom.

Dealing with Diversity in the Classroom (Insight Media, 23 min., 1991). The video examines some of the requisites for effectively teaching, motivating, and evaluating culturally diverse student populations. Leading educational specialists teach how to apply instructional strategies for working with diverse groups in the classroom.

The Demographics of American Education (Insight Media, 25 min., 1991).This video examines the impact of changing demographics on the nation's schools. It presents the views of researchers and demographers, as well as teachers, students, and parents, on such issues as career opportunities and the direction of education in the coming years.

Diversity Issues in the Classroom (Insight Media, 48 min., 1997). This video is made up of four case studies: Confronting Overt Racism, Gender Bias, Diversity as Subject Matter, and Instructor With Language Bias.

Educating Peter (Insight Media, 30 min., 1993). There are 60,000 students being mainstreamed into the public school system in the United States. This program examines how education can prepare for inclusion, showing how Peter, a child with Down's syndrome, was integrated into a "normal" third-grade class.

English Only in America? (Films for the Humanities and Sciences, 26 min., 1995). In this program, advocates for and against the policy examine the topic from social, legal, and educational standpoints.

Giftedness (Insight Media, 30 min., 1991). This video reviews how the concept of giftedness has changed over the last century. Robert Clasen of the University of Wisconsin at Madison explains why the term *able learners* is better than the term *gifted*. The video also differentiates among five types of able learners—intellectually gifted, academically gifted, creatively gifted, artistically gifted, and leadership gifted.

Glasser on Relationships (Insight Media, 5 vols., 25 min. each, 1998). This series presents Dr. William Glasser's ideas on how relationships with teachers, parents, and peers affect student behavior and academic achievement. It explains Choice Theory, which states that behavior is internally motivated, and shows how positive relationships are critical to success in school.

Hello, My Friends (Jon Stoddart Productions, 18 min., 1990). Children with disabilities are seen in primary classrooms as they demonstrate successful integration strategies. Striking simulations allow viewers to share the same frustration, anxiety, and tension that children with learning disabilities face in their daily lives.

Hispanic Education at the Crossroads (Films for the Humanities and Sciences, 44 min., 1996). For members of Hispanic groups, good education may be hard to come by, because of either language barriers or under performing schools. Edward James Olmos presents how Hispanic American children are faring in the educational system, with an emphasis on bilingual education. .

How Difficult Can This Be? A Learning Disabilities Workshop (PBS, 72 min., 1990). Striking simulations allow viewers to share the same frustration, anxiety, and tension that children with learning disabilities face in their daily lives.

The Inclusion Dilemma (Insight Media, 22 min., 1995). Using examples from two schools, this program examines what it means to include special needs children in regular classrooms and discusses how inclusion can be beneficial for all students and teachers.

Learn from the Past, Plan for the Future: Multicultural Value Preference and Dominant U.S. Culture (Insight Media, 34 min., 2000). This video sensitizes viewers to differences between the dominant U.S. culture and other traditions. It highlights issues pertinent to the relationship between instructor and student, such as family relationships, discipline, and perceptions of teachers.

Lost in Translation: Latinos, Schools and Society (Annenberg/CPB, 60 min., 1998). Examines the future of Latino youth, the fastest growing ethnic group in the United States.

Multiple Intelligences in the Classroom (Insight Media, 31 min., 1995). Profiling a program at a Massachusetts elementary school, this video introduces multiple intelligence theory and defines seven kinds of intelligence.

Regular Lives (PBS, 30 min., 1994). This video examines the advantages of mainstreaming children with disabilities and shows typical children playing and working together.

Respecting Diversity in the Classroom (Films for the Humanities and Sciences, 60 min., 1996). Too often educators look upon a multicultural classroom as a problem to be dealt with rather than a resource to be developed. Using actual classroom situations, this program is a "how to" primer offering innovative ideas about exploring the richness of culture and ethnicity.

Step-by-Step: Heather's Story (Insight Media, 65 min., 1996). This program documents the experiences of an eight-year-old girl with Down's syndrome as she moves from a special-education environment to an inclusive classroom. It illustrates how teachers, parents, family, and classmates helped move the inclusion process along.

A Teacher's Culture (Insight Media, 37 min., 2000). This program calls upon teachers to reflect upon their own personal and cultural beliefs and biases, examines various cultural value preferences, and reveals that an instructor's cultural background contributes to the classroom just as much as the students' backgrounds do.

They're Just Kids (Insight Media, 27 min., 1998). This video considers the inclusion of disabled children in and out of the classroom. It examines the fear and apprehension that sometimes accompany experiments in mainstreaming and discusses methods for easing the integration of children and adults into educational programs.

The Under-Represented Gifted (Insight Media, 30 min., 1991).Minorities are underrepresented in programs for the gifted. This video shows how a magnet elementary program has attempted to remedy the problem by offering an extended day, talent area classes, and programs for children as young as three. It examines how the STREAM program helps gifted middle school minority students by identifying them in the sixth grade and offering continuous programming and counseling. The video also profiles a magnet high school.

Understanding Our Frames of Mind: Unique Learning Styles (Insight Media, 2 vols., 60 min., 1989). This two-part program presents an overview of modality and learning-style research. The first part examines the characteristics of visual, auditory, and kinesthetic learners and shows multimodality teaching techniques. The second part describes the right brain and the left brain and shows adaptive teaching techniques that accommodate the right-brained child. It explores the role that color plays in learning and describes the theory of multiple intelligences.

Whisper and Smile: Verbal and Nonverbal Communication Styles (Insight Media, 30 min., 2000). A knowledge of cultural communication styles can facilitate verbal and nonverbal understanding. The video examines the nature of communication styles in the United States and discusses how these styles may be understood by other cultures.

Media distributor contact information is available in Appendix I.

Student Activities

School Observation—Students with Disabilities

In a small group, read and discuss the following:

Imagine you are assigned to visit a middle school classroom in a suburban school district. After you've introduced yourself to the teacher, Debbie, and assumed a seat, you look around the room as the lesson unfolds. Besides Debbie, you observe another teacher working individually with five students. One of these students sits in his seat, rocking back and forth, saying nothing in spite of the teacher's efforts to engage him. Debbie mentioned to you earlier that this boy, Adam, is autistic. Two other students, both girls, are working as a pair on what seems to be a project. The final two students in the five-student group, a boy and a girl, are working individually, using their textbooks to answer questions on a worksheet. Each of them occasionally asks the second teacher for assistance, which she gives them. You notice that while the whole class is working on an assignment, the two teachers meet together and seem to be discussing the five students. Suddenly, one of the two girls who are working together starts yelling at the other girl, throws her project on the floor, and puts her head down and starts crying. All the students in the room stop working to watch her, while both teachers go to her. The second teacher pulls up a chair next to the crying girl's desk and talks to her in a quiet voice. Debbie tells the rest of the class to get back to their assignments, which they soon do. In a brief time, things seem to be back to normal. After class you have a chance to talk with Debbie. You find out that the other teacher is a special education teacher who engages in parallel teaching with the group of five students, each of whom has some type of disability. Besides the autistic boy, two of the students have been diagnosed as learning disabled, one is mildly mentally retarded, and the girl who was crying has been diagnosed as emotionally disturbed. You are filled with questions that you want to ask, both about the students and about the way they are taught in the classroom. Reflect for a moment about the different individual needs that these students might have. Think about the way they are grouped in the classroom, the assignments they were given, and how the teachers responded to them. Jot down four or five such questions that you would ask Debbie if you had a chance. Then compare your questions with those of a few of your peers. What do you learn about your own assumptions?

Learning Styles and Personality Inventory

Get copies of David Kolb's Learning Styles Inventory and the Myers-Briggs Personality Inventory for your class or use the Swassing/Barbe instrument provided at the end of this chapter. Ask your students to work through each inventory, identifying their own learning styles and their personality styles. Then provide time for them to read or listen to descriptions of their learning style and of their personality type.

Field Site Journal Entry

Ask students to review carefully Glasser's choice theory before going to their field site school; tell them to observe the behavior of the pupils in the classroom in light of Glasser's choice theory. Students can focus on the following questions for their observation: To what extent are children motivated by their need for power or self-esteem? Can you come to any conclusions about these pupils based on Glasser's theory? Have students share their observations with one another during class.

Handicap Accessibility

In groups of two, students can investigate the handicap accessibility of educational institutions. Students should visit an institution and note what facilities are available and then arrange an interview with administrative personnel in charge of overseeing compliance with the ADA. In the interview, the students should find out about what facilities must be made available, how the institution complies with these guidelines, and the consequences of noncompliance. Students report their findings to the class.

Case Study

You may want to use the Erica Kaiser, Leigh Scott, or Marsha Warner case studies in Appendix II with the content of this chapter.

Student Assignments

Independent Reading

Read and respond to any of the selections noted on the chapter/article correlation list found in the front of this manual for Ryan/Cooper, *Kaleidoscope: Readings in Education* (Houghton Mifflin, 2004). You may want to use the Article Review Form in *Kaleidoscope*.

Reflective Papers

Choose one of the following topics to write a reflective paper (2–5 pages). The purpose of the paper is to help you assimilate new knowledge by blending it with your previous knowledge and experiences.

1. After completing a learning style inventory (next page), how do you feel about the results? How accurate do you feel the inventory was in describing you? Did you learn anything about yourself that rang true, although you may not have realized it before? Based on your learning style, which methods of learning are most comfortable for you?

2. Consider your position on full inclusion of special needs students in the classroom. How would you feel about it as a regular classroom teacher? What particular challenges do you imagine that managing such an environment would present to you?

3. Present the advantages of each of the models of bilingual education. Which model of bilingual education would you choose? Why do you prefer this model?

Journal Reflections

Suggestions for journal topics for students' selection:

1. As a student, what particular disabilities have you experienced with a peer in your classes?

2. Which type of disability would you find most challenging to adapt for? What can you do to prepare for this?

3. Which area of Howard Gardner's multiple intelligences do you feel is your area of strength? Explain why and give an example.

Swassing-Barbe Checklist of Observable Modality Strength Characteristics			
Area Observed	**Visual**	**Auditory**	**Kinesthetic**
Learning Style	Learns by seeing; watching demonstrations	Learns through verbal instructions from others or self	Learns by doing; direct involvement
Reading	Likes description; sometimes stops reading to stare into space and imagine scene; intense concentration	Enjoys dialogue, plays; avoids lengthy description, unaware of illustrations; moves lips or subvocalizes	Prefers stories where action occurs early; fidgets when reading, handles books; not an avid reader
Spelling	Recognizes words by sight; relies on configuration of words	Uses a phonics approach; has auditory word attack skills	Often a poor speller; writes words to determine if they "feel" right
Handwriting	Tends to be good, particularly when young; spacing and size are good; appearance is important	Has more difficulty learning in initial stages; tends to write lightly; says strokes when writing	Good initially, deteriorates when space becomes smaller; pushes harder on writing instrument
Memory	Remembers faces, forgets names; writes things down, takes notes	Remembers names, forgets faces; remembers by auditory repetition	Remembers best what was done, not what was seen or talked about
Imagery	Vivid imagination; thinks in pictures, visualizes in detail	Subvocalizes, thinks in sounds; details less important	Imagery not important; images that do occur are accompanied by movement
Distractibility	Generally unaware of sounds; distracted by visual disorder or movement	Easily distracted by sounds	Not attentive to visual, auditory presentation so seems distractible
Problem Solving	Deliberate; plans in advance; organizes thoughts by writing them; lists problems	Talks problems out, tries solutions verbally, subvocally; talks self through problem	Attacks problems physically; impulsive; often selects solution involving greatest activity
Response to Periods of Inactivity	Stares; doodles; finds something to watch	Hums; talks to self or to others	Fidgets; finds reasons to move; holds up hand
Response to New Situations	Looks around; examines structure	Talks about situation, pros and cons, what to do	Tries things out; touches, feels; manipulates
Emotionality	Somewhat repressed; stares when angry; cries easily, beams when happy; facial expression is a good index of emotion	Shouts with joy or anger; blows up verbally but soon calms down; expresses emotion verbally and through changes in tone, volume, pitch of voice	Jumps for joy; hugs, tugs, and pulls when happy; stamps, jumps, and pounds when angry, stomps off; general body tone is a good index of emotion
Communication	Quiet; does not talk at length; becomes impatient when extensive listening is required; may use words clumsily; describes without embellishment; uses words such as see, look, etc.	Enjoys listening but cannot wait to talk; descriptions are long but repetitive; likes hearing self and others talk; uses words such as listen, hear, etc.	Gestures when speaking; does not listen well; stands close when speaking or listening; quickly loses interest in detailed verbal discourse; uses words such as get, take, etc.
General Appearance	Neat, meticulous, likes order; may choose not to vary appearance	Matching clothes not so important, can explain choices of clothes	Neat but soon becomes wrinkled through activity
Response to the Arts	Not particularly responsive to music; prefers the visual arts; tends not to voice appreciation of art of any kind, but can be deeply affected by visual displays; focuses on details and components rather than the work as a whole	Favors music; finds less appeal in visual art, but is readily able to discuss it; misses significant detail, but appreciates the work as a whole; is able to develop verbal association for all art forms; spends more time talking about pieces than looking at them	Responds to music by physical movement; prefers sculpture; touches statues and paintings; at exhibits stops only at those in which he or she can become physically involved; comments very little on any art form

From *Teaching Through Modality Strengths: Concepts and Practices* by Walter B. Barbe, Ph.D. and Raymond H. Swassing, Ed.D., with Michael N. Milone, Jr., Ph.D. Used with permission of Zaner-Bloser, Inc.

CHAPTER 3

What Social Problems and Tension Points Affect Today's Students?

LEARNING OBJECTIVES

After studying the chapter, students will be able to

1. identify the impact of poverty, homelessness, and child abuse on children's classroom behavior and learning.

2. describe the structures of U.S. families today, identifying the difficulties that single parents and working parents face in raising children.

3. describe the impact that alcohol abuse, drug abuse, and suicide have had on students in recent years.

4. describe the problems of school violence and vandalism, and summarize some of the aspects that contribute to student aggression.

5. discuss some of the ways that schools, principals, and teachers can reduce the incidence of school violence.

6. understand the reasons for students dropping out and discuss successful preventive measures.

7. describe and discuss several versions of school choice.

8. explain how gender bias leads to unequal educational opportunities for females and how federal legislation, in particular Title IX, seeks to reduce these inequalities.

9. explain the responsibility and liability schools bear in cases of student-to-student sexual harassment.

10. describe the special risks and needs homosexual students face and policies and programs to address them.

CHAPTER OVERVIEW

Social issues and problems in the world impact the operation and effectiveness of public education. In fact, a major portion of the school's work devotes itself to responding, directly or indirectly, to students whose lives are challenged by social ills, such as poverty or violence. Such problems, including homelessness, teen parenting, substance abuse, child abuse, and youth suicide, complicate students' efforts to learn. Other social problems, such as vandalism, school violence, and the dropout rate, are exacerbated when students feel alienated from the school structure. The chapter briefly discusses each of these topics and the ways in which public education is responding as an introduction for prospective teachers, not as a detailed analysis.

In this chapter we also look at family structure in the United States, which has undergone considerable modification in recent years. The traditional family, made up of a working father, a homemaker mother, and two children in school, represents only 6 percent of U.S. households today. Family structures today include single-parent families, blended families, older parents, and working parents. Family structure can play a significant role in a child's school experiences and can affect his or her learning.

The chapter then looks at the tension points in U.S. education, beginning with a key issue in education: equality of educational opportunities in regard to race, social class, and gender. A variety of school choice structures are described as market driven proposals to strengthen educational access and quality.

Inequality in educational opportunities related to the student's gender is a recently recognized problem, and Title IX, an attempt to legislate equality of opportunity based on gender, is described. Although Title IX met with mixed results, new federal legislation that seeks to provide gender equity programs in all phases of society, not just in schools, is currently working its way through Congress. The challenges faced by homosexual students and the schools' responsibility to address these needs is also described.

Finally, the issue of sex education in the schools is revisited in light of the growing concern over the spread of sexually transmitted diseases and the problem of teen pregnancies. The appropriateness of sex education in schools is debated, as is the approach to sex education.

Our purpose in this chapter is not to overwhelm prospective teachers with all the problems affecting schools but to sensitize them to the connections between teaching and social issues of national concern. Although teachers spend a good deal of time absorbed in meeting the challenges of their own classrooms, they must be aware of the conditions outside the classroom which impact their student's lives, in order to participate fully in the advancement of the democratic process.

CHAPTER OUTLINE

I.   Social Problems Affecting Students
    A.   New American Family Patterns
        1.   Family Composition
        2.   Family Relationships
    B.   Poverty
    C.   Homelessness
    D.   Teenage Parenting
    E.   Abused and Neglected Children
    F.   Alcohol and Drug Abuse
    G.   Adolescent Suicide
    H.   School Violence
        1.   Gangs
        2.   Bullying
        3.   Costs of Vandalism and Violence
    I.   School Dropout
        1.   Reasons for Dropping Out
II.   Tension Points in American Education
    A.   Access and Equality of Educational Opportunity
    B.   School Choice
        1.   Parents as Educational Consumers
        2.   Public School Choice
        3.   Magnet Schools
        4.   Charter Schools
        5.   Vouchers
    C.   Gender and Sexuality Issues
        1.   Equality Between the Sexes
        2.   Early Differences in Socialization
        3.   Classroom Interactions
        4.   Implications of Classroom Findings
        5.   Title IX
        6.   Your Role as a Teacher
        7.   Sexual Harassment
        8.   Sexual Orientation
        9.   Sex Education

SUPPLEMENTARY LECTURE AND DISCUSSION TOPICS

1.   **School as one social agency among many** The social problems presented in this chapter are addressed primarily by social agencies that may develop working relationships with the schools. Select a subset of problems, such as poverty-related problems or teen problems, and describe the local agencies that work on them. Explain the relationships that local teachers might have with other agencies, either directly or through

school teams. Invite a local teacher who has been successful in working with the problems to come and describe his or her work.

2. **Crack, gangs, and kids who kill** Each day across the country a dozen or so teens and children are killed on the street. Some may have been involved as drug runners; others may have been walking down the street to a convenience store; still others may have been sitting on their front steps. Their deaths are particularly horrifying because in many instances the killers are themselves children. Not infrequently, the child who pulled the trigger was a member of a gang. Analyze gangs and their philosophy. How do they operate? Why is violence a given? How do drugs play a role in the lives of gang members? What can public schools do for these youth? What do experts think needs to be done to stop the killings and the madness?

3. **Violence in schools** In the past several years, episodes of multiple assaults by students in schools and by adults in families have increased. Columbine High School is just one example. Discuss the contributions of changes in society, family, and community structure, the media, computer technology, and intolerance of those who are different (nerds, trench coat mafia, jocks, etc.) to this problem.

4. **Gender bias in school** Choose two editions of a basal reader, a social studies text, or a math book—one edition somewhat older than the other. For a matched segment of each, tally the number and kinds of characters that are male or female. Present information to the class, and discuss how textbooks can support inappropriate sex-role stereotyping. Reinforce the fact that gender bias not only leads to economic disability for women but also artificially restricts options for both men and women. You may also want to explore other issues concerning sexism in schools: generic use of male pronouns and its effects on shaping the consciousness of both men and women; the representation of women in history, science, and literature; and the hierarchy in schools and its traditionally male dominance.

STUDY GUIDE — CHAPTER 3: WHAT SOCIAL PROBLEMS AND TENSION POINTS AFFECT TODAY'S STUDENTS?

Completing this study guide will help you prepare for the major topic areas on an exam; however, it does not cover every piece of information found in the chapter or the test questions.

1.   What does the term *at risk* refer to?

2.   Name the major social problems affecting education.

3.   How are school choice, charter schools, site-based decision making, and vouchers related?

4.   List the general provisions of Title IX and give an example of each.

5.   What are some of the things that principals and teachers can do to reduce the incidence of violence?

6.   List the major reasons students give for dropping out.

7. Describe the roles of the teacher and school in addressing the needs of homosexual students.

8. What actions can teachers take to eliminate gender bias and gender role stereotyping?

9. What are the pros and cons of private schools receiving public funding?

ADDITIONAL RESOURCES FOR INSTRUCTORS

AAUW Report: *Hostile Hallways: Bullying, Teasing, and Sexual Harassment in School.* Washington D.C.: American Association of University Women, 2001. This report examines the findings of a student survey on bullying, teasing, and sexual harassment in schools.

Burstyn, Joan N., Geoff Bender, Ronnie Casella, Howard Gordon, Domingo Guerra, Kristen Luschen, Rebecca Stevens, and Kimberly Williams. *Preventing Violence in Schools: A Challenge to American Democracy.* Mahwah, NJ: Lawrence Erlbaum Associates, 2001. An in-depth ethnographic analysis of violence prevention programs and an assessment of their effectiveness.

Crosby, Emeral. "The 'At-Risk' Decade." *Phi Delta Kappan* 75 (April 1993): 598–604. Crosby argues that little has been done in the ten years since *A Nation at Risk* to reduce the risks that face American children and threaten their learning.

Donmoyer, Robert, and Raylene Kos (eds.). *At Risk Students: Portraits, Policies, Programs, and Practices.* New York: SUNY Press, 1992. This book explores the circumstances of at-risk students and argues that well-intentioned policymakers and educators run the risk of making matters worse rather than better for these students.

Havinghurst, Robert, and Daniel Levine. *Society and Education.* 8th ed. Boston: Allyn and Bacon, 1992. An examination of many of the social issues touched on in this chapter. The authors summarize recent research.

Lazerson, Marvin, "Access, Outcomes, and Educational Opportunity." *Education Week* (January 27, 1999): 16. This article is a brief overview of several of the issues included in this chapter.

Levine, Daniel U., and Rayna F. Levine. *Society and Education,* 9th ed. Needham Heights, MA: Allyn and Bacon, 1996. The authors summarize recent research that examines many of the social issues presented in this chapter.

Nathan, Joe. *Charter Schools: Creating Hope and Opportunity for American Education.* San Francisco: Jossey-Bass Publishers, 1999. The author, a longtime proponent of charter schools, provides the historical background on the charter school movement, gives examples of successful schools, and offers specific guidelines for people who want to develop and operate their own charter school.

Sadker, David. "Gender Equity: Still Knocking at the Classroom Door." *Educational Leadership* 56:7 (April 1999): 22-27. Explores perceptions about gender equity today and updates the facts about gender bias.

Scherer, Marge. "On Savage Inequalities: A Conversation with Jonathan Kozol." *Educational Leadership* 50 (December 1992/January 1993): 4–9. Kozol describes the conditions that face our nation's urban students and proposes ways to eradicate the inequities.

Stevens, Linda, and Marianne Price. "Meeting the Challenge of Educating Children at Risk." *Phi Delta Kappan* 74 (September 1992): 18–23. Stevens and Price suggest that strategies exist that schools can use to improve conditions for at-risk students. They focus on the curriculum, the context, and the community to ameliorate the plight of these students.

Media Resources

Alternative and Charter Schools: Educating Outside the Box (Films for the Humanities and Sciences, 20 min., 2000). The first half of this program looks at a special breed of alternative school where disruptive students benefit and the second half explores the popularity of charter schools—from just one in 1992 to over 1,700 in 25 states today – and the battles that have arisen over them.

America's Schools: Who Gives a Damn? Part II (PBS video, 60 min., 1991). The problems in America's public schools seem inseparable from our societal diseases—poverty, drugs, crumbling families, and racial tensions. Will a student's difficult environment sabotage his or her success in the classroom or can school save the child?

The Battle Over School Choice (Insight Media, 60 min., 2000). This PBS Frontline analysis explores both sides of the debate, considering proposals ranging from private school vouchers to strategies for transforming failed schools.

Color-Blind: Fighting Racism in Schools (Films for the Humanities and Sciences, 27 min., 1999). In this provocative program, five students from a variety of cultural and ethnic backgrounds speak with candor about racial harassment at their high school in an effort to encourage teenagers to examine their own attitudes and behaviors.

Cultural Bias in Education (Films for the Humanities and Sciences, 28 min., 1991). This program examines roadblocks to Latino academic advancement as well as productive educational models, explores the relationship between standardized testing and cultural diversity and questions whether cultural bias can be eliminated from testing. It also looks at early childhood education programs and the factors that deter Latino families from participating in them.

The Culture of Poverty (Films for the Humanities and Sciences, 26 min., 1991). Many Latino families are caught in the cycle of poverty: unemployment and poor education create a self-perpetuating cycle. The task of educating the children of poverty puts an added strain on school systems. This program explores emerging strategies for meeting the needs of these children.

Dateline on Columbine (subtitles "Killing at Columbine High," "A Time for Healing," "An Ounce of Prevention," "Your Gun Your Fault"). (NBC, 31 min., 1999). This video has segments dealing with the violent incident at Columbine High School, posttraumatic stress, an experimental program to help "out of control" kids before they get violent, and the need for stricter gun control.

Educating the Disadvantaged (Films for the Humanities and Sciences, 30 min., 1990). Born in a poor neighborhood in Los Angeles, Mike Rose was not expected to make it in school. He did and went on to become a teacher, working with people on the edge of society.

Educating to End Inequity (Films for the Humanities and Sciences, 54 min., 2000). This program addresses teachers' efforts to level the educational and social playing fields for their students by examining public school reform and its relationship to social changes. Educators who taught on the western frontier in the late 19th century and in the South during desegregation are spotlighted, along with contemporary instructors working with Native Americans in New Mexico and inner-city youth in New York.

The Lessons of Littleton (Insight Media, 2 vols. 45 min. each, 1999). Looking at the massacre of 15 people by two students at Columbine High School in Littleton, Colorado, William Glasser explains that a lack of good relationships lies at the root of violent behavior and discusses steps teachers and parents can take to help troubled young people.

Out! Making Schools Safe for Gay Teens (Insight Media, 2 vols., 70 min. total, 1999). Laws mandate safe schools and equal treatment. This set shows how to combat homophobia through the sensitization of every member of a school community. Part I features interviews with teachers and counselors, and offers tips for forming a gay-straight alliance. Part 2 presents interviews with gay teenagers who discuss the reactions of their friends and families and how they have coped with harassment.

Over the Edge: Violence in Our Schools (Insight Media, 20 min., 1998). This video of a troubled boy's slide into plans of revenge and death reveals the path from alienation to anger and the failure of friends and family to recognize cries for help. The discussion examines such causal and contributing factors as violence in the media and access to weapons.

The Right Choice? Charter Schools and Voucher Systems (Films for the Humanities and Sciences, 30 min., 2000). This program looks at these alternatives at the Countryside Charter School and elsewhere, demonstrating how they allow concerned parents the option to bypass public schools in favor of institutions with stronger programs and better reputations.

Second Chances (Florida Public Television, 29 min., 1997). This video reports Florida's efforts to reduce the dropout rate and visits a Second Chance school for a look at how educators and law enforcement are working together to give students a second chance.

Shortchanging Girls, Shortchanging America (Insight Media, 19 min., 1992). This program interviews educators and business leaders to illuminate the effects of gender bias in schools. It investigates the loss of self-esteem in girls and shows how they are often tracked away from math and science programs.

A Struggle for Educational Equality: 1950-1980 (Films for the Humanities and Sciences, 52 min., 2000). This program shows how impressive gains masked profound inequalities: seventeen states had segregated schools; 1% of all Ph.D.'s went to women; and "separate but equal" was still the law of the land. *Brown v. Board of Education of Topeka* (1954), the Elementary and Secondary Education Act, Title IX, and the Americans with Disabilities Act are discussed.

Unequal Education: Failing Our Children (Insight Media, 21 min., 1992). This student-produced documentary goes into the classrooms of New York City's public schools to show the disproportionate educational opportunities that exist. Focusing on a school in a middle-class neighborhood and a school in a working-class neighborhood, it contrasts the quality of the staff and the resources available to students. Interviews with teachers, principals, and parents place this local crisis in the context of a nationwide educational crisis.

Vanishing Family: Crisis in Black America (Prod: Ruth Streeter/CBS News, Dist: Carousel and university film libraries, 64 min., video, 1986). *CBS Reports* with correspondent Bill Moyers examines the disintegration of the black family structure. Statistics—that nearly 60 percent of all black children are born out of wedlock—come to life.

When Society's Problems Walk Through the Door (Insight Media, 30 min., 1993). Students do not leave problems such as drug abuse, homelessness, violence, or unrealistic parental expectations at the door when they enter school. In order for instruction to be effective, schools must address the problems faced by students. This video profiles three schools that have instituted programs to address the nonacademic concerns of their students.

Who Needs Boys? (ABC, 15 min., 1992). A John Stoessel report for *20/20* that demonstrates how even in early grades boys dominate classroom participation.

Media distributor contact information is available in Appendix I.

Student Activities

School Observation—A Child Shunned

You're observing some classes at a middle school. As you sit in a seventh-grade language arts class, you particularly notice one boy. Whereas all the other students seem fairly well dressed, in an adolescent sort of way, this young man stands out from the crowd. His clothes are shabby and dirty. His sneakers have holes in them, and some of his toes poke through. His hair looks like it hasn't been washed in days. Some of the kids sitting around him keep looking at him and each other. Making comments that you can't hear, but you can hear them giggling and snickering. The teacher is assigning students to a cooperative learning activity. When Eric, the student you've been watching, is assigned to work with Amy, Raul, and Kim, Amy says out loud, "I don't want to work with Eric, he smells." At this point the whole class erupts in laughter. The teacher quiets the class down and tells everyone that the groups are set and to begin work. Amy, Raul, and Kim pull their seats together and begin working, totally ignoring Eric, who continues to sit by himself. The teacher comes by, talks to Eric, and he slides his desk over closer to where the other group members are working, but still not up close. It's clear that neither Eric nor the other group members want to work cooperatively with one another. On the basis of these observations:

a.   How might you interpret what you've just witnessed? What are some possible explanations for what's going on?

b.   What questions do you want to ask the teacher to help clarify what you've seen?

c.   If you were the teacher, what actions would you have taken during the immediate situation? What long-term strategies and goals would you pursue?

d.   After you've thought about these questions, get together with two or three classmates and compare your interpretations, information needs, and strategies.

The "Normal" Family and Its Variations

First, have the class participate in generating the "normal" family model for itself. Ask each student to indicate on an *unsigned* paper how many parents are now at home, how many siblings there are and whether they are older or younger than the student, how many other adults are at home, and the employment status of the parents. The following form might be provided for their use (sample answers given):

a.   Number of parents at home: 2

b.   Stepparents at home? Yes—father

c.   Siblings (older? younger?) 1 older, 2 younger

d.   Other adults: 1 grandmother

e.   Parents' job(s): Father and mother employed

From these responses, a class "norm" may be determined by taking the most frequently given response to each question. For example, the most common family constellation might be "mother, stepfather, one sibling (younger), both parents working." Using this model as the basis for discussion, break the class into small groups of three to five, and have each group create the set of expectations that might reasonably be held for such a family by a teacher of one of the children. When each group has generated the list of expectations, have members brainstorm ways in which other family constellations (represented by their own real families) might differ in the ability to meet those expectations. Finally, have each group write a list of warnings for a teacher. What kinds of assumptions about families should teachers be aware of making, given the diversity? What ways can teachers facilitate participation, given this diversity?

Social Programs in the Curriculum

As mentioned in the text, schools must face the complexity of educating students challenged by numerous social problems. In groups of four, choose one of the following programs and investigate that program at a given school.

Find out what the curriculum of the program is, what the objectives are, which students are taught the curriculum, why it is taught in that school, and whether the program is perceived as being successful by students, faculty, and the community. If no such program exists, try to find out why.

a.   Substance abuse prevention program

b.   Suicide prevention program

c.   Teen pregnancy prevention program

d.   AIDS education program

e.   Programs for at-risk students or dropout prevention

f.   Conflict resolution and violence prevention

g.   Sex education

Role Stereotyping Simulation (Sex, Age, Ethnicity)

Divide the class into groups of from five to eight members. Be sure the groups are heterogeneous. Supply each group with the following scenario and set of résumés. Direct each group to reach consensus on the three items:

a.   Select the person best qualified.

b.   Select the person with the most executive potential (can be the same person as in item a).

c.   Develop three questions to ask in an interview.

From each group, select an observer who is willing to forgo participation in the group discussion. Give separate instructions to observers, without allowing others in the group to hear, to record any instances of (a) assumptions made by participants about the influence of gender on the suitability of candidates for a position, (b) comments or assumptions about race, (c) comments or assumptions about age, (d) questions or concerns about women that did not arise with respect to men. Observers are not to name group members making comments, only to record comments. At the end of time, compare group findings and observer records.

After the activity, remind the class that it is illegal to ask certain questions in a job interview—for example, one cannot ask questions of a female that would not be asked of a male counterpart. Such questions include plans for marriage, plans for raising a family, and child-care arrangements. Comments on physical attractiveness are also illegal. Have observers report their records. Discuss how assumptions and prejudices may have affected the decisions.

BIG OIL SCENARIO

You are members of the executive personnel committee in the regional office of the Big Oil Corporation. The home office is in New Jersey, with refineries and diversified manufacturing plants throughout the world. Your regional office has an opening for a regional manager of personnel. This is a Level 10 position, the first level with company executive rank. People in Level 10 positions are the first ones to be considered to fill vacancies for such top executive positions as regional manager, vice president, and so on. The position of regional personnel manager carries the following job description:

Manage and assume responsibility for the equitable and efficient conduct of routine personnel activities regarding initial employment, recordkeeping, evaluations for pay increases, promotions, and terminations. In addition, plan, organize, and supervise professional recruitment, orientation, and ongoing training of company employees throughout the region. Salary: $65,000 or commensurate with experience.

The regional office is located in Houston, Texas, and the region encompasses the states of Texas, New Mexico, Arizona, Oklahoma, Kansas, Arkansas, and Louisiana. Employee orientation and training sessions must be conducted periodically in all the regions' branches, and at hours that will not interfere with routine plant or office activities. Recruitment strategies involve establishing recruitment centers on university and college campuses throughout the country. Although the personnel manager is not required to actually conduct training, orientation, or recruiting sessions, it is his or her responsibility to plan and supervise such sessions and to see that they meet the needs of the growing corporation.

Corporation executives are expected to be free to relocate in any of the international branches. They are expected to be loyal to the corporation and to conduct themselves socially in a manner that will enhance the corporate image. People who fill Level 10 positions invariably are promoted to executive positions. It is important that they show dedication to the corporation.

Applicants

- *John P. Morgan, B.S. in general business administration.* Age 43. Married (wife: Jane A. Morgan, homemaker), four children ages 18, 16, 12, 9. NAACP Fellowship. Previous experience: twelve years with a rival company in sales department—seven years as sales agent, five years as area sales manager. Came into the corporation eight years ago in the position of area manager for region. Duties involved recruitment and training of sales agents for all regional branches. Considered stable, good with people, and has executive potential.

- *Mona S. Hickey, B.S. in business management science; M.S. in personnel management.* Age 36. Married (husband: William S. Hickey, physicist, Ph.D., employed by NASA). Three children, ages 14, 8, 5. Previous experience: six years with Exxon USA in New Orleans. Four years as executive secretary to vice president in charge of support personnel. Has been with the corporation three years as assistant personnel manager in charge of support personnel and beginning professional trainees. Came to our office when husband was transferred to NASA. While in our employ, has been taking courses in petroleum engineering at nearby university. Extremely intelligent, very articulate, with excellent organization and management skills. Energetic, in good health, one child (age 14) with chronic illness.

- *Michael J. Martinez, B.S. in business management science.* Age 45. Divorced, single parent, two children, Michael, age 16, and Linda, age 14. Previous experience: ten years in army recruiting and training positions and ten years personnel manager for Texas department of corrections. Efficient, organized, enthusiastic, and well liked.

- *John T. Miller, B.S. in business management science.* Age 28. Second marriage (wife: Sun Li, reporter for CBS local affiliate). One child, age 2. Presently working toward M.S. degree in management psychology. Now employed by family-owned department store chain, in personnel records. Has been with present company since graduation from college three years ago. Previous experience: retail sales with present company, two years while working toward degree; three summers as roughneck in oil fields. Is extremely ambitious and eager for opportunities for advancement, which he feels are limited with present employers. Is mobile, can relocate. Bright, energetic, honor graduate with membership in several professional and civic organizations.

- *James R. Stadtmueller, B.S. in business administration.* Age 58. Widowed, two children—both married. Previous experience: personnel director of small Southwest-area oil company, fifteen years. Responsibilities included planning and conducting executive training programs for company. General office manager of accounting department (same company) nine years. Twelve years experience in billing and accounting departments, with three promotions during period. References from previous employer are excellent.

- *Jaclyn S. Young, B.A. in psychology. M.B.A.* Age 27. Single. Ford Foundation Fellowship. Mary Lyon Scholar. Previous experience: faculty member of Mount Holyoke College Department of Social Science. Youngest appointment; chair of the Presidential Commission on Women and Minorities in Business. Bright, articulate. References are glowing, especially those from the National Feminist Caucus and NOW. Considered a "high flyer."

Educational Current Events Assignment

Purpose: To be able to discuss current controversial issues in education intelligently, the student needs to be able to locate professional resources that shed light on issues reported in the popular as well as professional press. The student will develop the ability to consult research reports and professional literature, using them to analyze the contexts that influence these issues, and to express these ideas orally and in writing.

Requirements: The student will locate _____ current events concerning education in newspapers or popular periodicals during the semester. For each current event the student will do the following:

- Submit a copy of the current event article or a summary of the broadcast report (with a complete bibliographical reference)

- Attach at least one professional source that sheds light on the issues (include complete annotated bibliographical reference and ERIC designation)

- Present an analysis of the issue including the relevant contexts (historical, economical, philosophical, legal, sociological, governance, etc.) and express his or her own informed opinion in no more than 1-1/2 pages typed

Evaluation:

- Satisfaction of all requirements

- Demonstration of use of professional sources

- Depth of analysis

- Completeness of references

- Mechanics of communication

- (Oral presentation)

Due date: _____

Group Controversial-Issue-in-Education Assignment

<u>Purpose</u>: To discuss current controversial issues in education intelligently, the student needs to be able to locate resources to obtain information on all sides of the issue, to recognize the diverse contexts that influence these issues, and then, considering personal values and experiences, to make an informed decision—and if necessary to persuade others.

<u>Requirements</u>: Each group of five students will do the following:

- select an issue and receive instructor approval of the topic
- using ERIC, research the issue in not less than six sources
- present the issue in a 20-minute class presentation

Include the following sections:

- introduction and description of the issue
- discussion of the appropriate historical, social, economical, political, financial, governance, etc., contexts of the issue
- pros and cons of the issue
- various proposed solutions
- current trends
- recognized authorities in the field
- your own opinions and recommendations
- standard bibliography citations, annotated
- one- to two-page summary of the issue, class handout sheets

<u>Sample issues</u>:

Unequal funding	Teacher strikes	Home schooling
Bilingual education	Year-round schools	Charter schools
Inclusion	Sex education	Uniforms
Character education	Censorship	And many others

<u>Evaluation</u>:

- Organization
- Participation
- Satisfaction of all requirements
- Insight into the contexts influencing the issue
- Coherence and detailed support
- Class presentation
- Two-page handout
- Creativity in written and oral presentation

Due date: _____

Student Assignments

The following activities are suggestions for student portfolio activities. They are a means of providing alternative assessment of the students' capabilities.

Independent Reading

Read and respond to any of the selections noted on the chapter/article correlation list found in the front of this manual for Ryan/Cooper, *Kaleidoscope: Readings in Education* (Houghton Mifflin, 2004). You may want to use the Article Review Form in *Kaleidoscope*.

Reflective Papers

Choose one of the following topics to write a reflective paper (2–5 pages). The purpose of the paper is to help you assimilate new knowledge by blending it with your previous knowledge and experiences.

1. Think about your high school experience. What was the ethnic and racial composition of the student body? How did the different groups interact? How did the makeup of the school community affect your experience there?

2. Do you remember a time when you realized that a friend (or a classmate) was "different" from you, that is, when it became clear to you that this friend (or classmate) was being treated differently because of his or her race, ethnic background, or socioeconomic status? Tell about the experience and how it affected you.

3. Have you ever had the opportunity to work with economically disadvantaged youth—for example, in a soup kitchen, a homeless shelter, or a boys and girls club? Describe the experience. What did you learn that will help you as a teacher?

Journal Reflections

Suggestions for journal topics for students' selection:

1. What do you feel will be the most significant social challenge that you will face as a teacher?

2. Pick one of the social challenges and give as many ideas as you can for how a teacher could address its effects in his or her classroom.

3. How would you feel about teaching sex education? Why?

CD-ROM Video Clip

View the two clips for Chapter 3 and be prepared to discuss the following reflection questions:

Clip 1:

   Do you agree that schools should take on the role of surrogate family when students need it? Why or why not? Are you prepared to take on this role in your professional life?

Clip 2:

1. As a student teacher, have you noticed teachers' paying more attention to boys than to girls in class? Do you think you have done or will do the same thing in the classroom? Why or why not?

2. Why do you think teachers favor boys in class? What steps can you take now to prevent yourself from shortchanging girls when you become a full-time teacher?

CHAPTER 4

What Is Taught?

LEARNING OBJECTIVES

After studying this chapter, students will be able to

1. describe what is included in the term *curriculum* and give specific examples.

2. describe recent trends in curriculum reform.

3. describe the influence of the standards movement on curriculum.

4. discuss international comparisons of achievement.

5. summarize current curricular emphases in language arts, science, math, social studies, foreign languages, art, physical education, and vocational studies.

6. explain the relationship between textbook adoption practices, textbook content, and a national curriculum.

7. describe several instructional approaches—interdisciplinary teaching, cooperative learning, critical thinking, writing across the curriculum, differentiated curriculum, and block scheduling.

CHAPTER OVERVIEW

In this text, *curriculum* is defined as not only the intellectual content of the subjects but also as all the organized and intended experiences of the student for which the school accepts responsibility. In addition to content, this includes the methods, interactions among people, and other school-sponsored activities that create the "life experience."

In this chapter we review the growth and effects of the standards-based reform movement, and describe the trend toward and the influence of national standards in the traditionally decentralized U.S. system of education. We also provide an overview of the major curricular emphases in American education and review curricular changes and reforms and present key figures such as Jerome Bruner (discovery method, spiral curriculum). The methods, results, and implications of international achievement comparisons are presented and analyzed. We also explore such hot topics as curricular reform, including block scheduling, cultural literacy, multiculturalism, core curriculum, and tracking. Also discussed are current curricular trends in different subject areas, and other influences on the curriculum, in particular the role of textbooks in curriculum development. We conclude Chapter 4 by presenting some of the innovative instructional techniques now being used in schools.

CHAPTER OUTLINE

I.   What is Curriculum?
II. Standards-Based Reform Movement
III. What Is the Present Curriculum?
   A. Language Arts and English
      1. Issues and Trends
   B. Mathematics
      1. Issues and Trends
   C. Science
      1. Issues and Trends
   D. Social Studies
      1. Issues and Trends
   E. Foreign Languages
      1. Issues and Trends
   F. The Arts
      1. Issues and Trends
   G. Physical Education, Health, and Recreation
   H. Elective Courses
      1. Issues and Trends
   I. Vocational Courses
      1. Issues and Trends
IV. Assessing Student Academic Performance
   A. National Assessment of Educational Progress (NAEP)
      1. International Comparisons
V. Additional Influences on Curriculum
   A. Textbooks
   B. Innovative Instructional Approaches
      1. Interdisciplinary Curriculum
      2. Cooperative Learning
      3. Critical Thinking and Problem Solving
      4. Writing Across the Curriculum
      5. Differentiated Instruction
      6. Block Scheduling
   C. Current Curriculum Controversies
      1. Core versus Multicultural Curriculum
      2. Tracking
VI. Is the Existing Curriculum Relevant to Today's Society?

SUPPLEMENTARY LECTURE AND DISCUSSION TOPICS

1. **Curriculum and values** Analyze a given curriculum and show how it supports particular values. Categorize the course credit requirements for earning a degree in teacher education (what do the addition of academic majors and reduction of hours in education courses signal?), and identify the value system implicit in that distribution of effort. Categorize the activities of a child's school day and identify the social directive implied by those activities.

2. **Multiculturalism and the curriculum** Discuss the impact multiculturalism has had on various curricula at either the elementary or secondary level. Present the arguments of the proponents of multicultural curriculum and those of the opposing view. Then have the students suggest compromise approaches.

3. **Significance of *Sputnik*** Discuss how the U.S. reaction to *Sputnik* affected math and science curriculum in the 1950s. Present how the U.S. Congress and the president reacted to *Sputnik*. Describe the educational projects, movements, and trends that resulted from *Sputnik*. Discuss the "economic" sputnik that had a similar impact on the curriculum in the 1980s. What does this mean for curriculum reform?

4. **Textbooks, publishing, and textbook adoption** Discuss in greater detail the factors that contribute to the writing of a textbook and the factors that publishing companies must consider when developing a textbook. In addition, discuss in more detail the vocal groups, such as those in Texas, that wield power over the contents of textbooks. Provide a background sketch of those involved in these vocal special-interest groups.

5. **International comparisons** Explain the value and cultural differences among modern countries and their conceptions of the curriculum. Present information on a country (Korea, France, and so on) that follows a national curriculum, and discuss that country's goals for the education of its students. Discuss the vocational education and apprenticeship programs other modern countries have for students who want to learn a trade. What are some other countries' ways of preparing all students to become productive citizens?

6. **State standards** Discuss the impact of state standards on the content and methods of delivery of the K–12 curriculums in your state.

STUDY GUIDE – CHAPTER 4: WHAT IS TAUGHT?

Completing this study guide will help you prepare for the major topic areas on an exam; however, it does not cover every piece of information found in the chapter or the test questions.

1. Give a concise description of the curriculum trends in each of the following subject areas:

    a.   Language Arts and English

    b.   Mathematics

    c.   Science

    d.   Social Studies

    e.   Foreign Languages

    f.   The Arts

    g.   Physical Education, Health, and Recreation

    h.   Elective courses

    i.   Vocational courses

2. Summarize American students' achievement in comparison to student achievement in other developed countries. What are some of the possible reasons for this achievement discrepancy?

3. Why are textbooks considered such a powerful force in curriculum?

4. Describe the main advantage of each of the following innovative instructional approaches:

    a.   Interdisciplinary curriculum

    b.   Cooperative learning

    c.   Critical thinking and problem solving

    d.   Writing across the curriculum

    e.   Differentiated curriculum

    f.   Block scheduling

5.   In your own words, explain the contrasting views on each of the following controversies:

     a.   Multicultural curriculum versus core curriculum

     b.   Cultural literacy

     c.   Tracking

ADDITIONAL REFERENCES FOR INSTRUCTORS

Adler, Mortimer. *The Paideia Proposal: An Educational Manifesto.* New York: Macmillan, 1982. This book provides a basis for strengthening the academic curriculum in public schools.

Bracey, Gerald. Tinkering with TIMSS. *Phi Delta Kappan,* 80-1 (September 1998): 32–36. This is an analysis and interpretation of the TIMSS results.

Castenell, Louis A., Jr., and William Pinar. *Understanding Curriculum As Racial Text: Representations of Identity and Difference in Education.* New York: SUNY Press, 1993. This book examines the issues of identity and difference, both theoretically and as represented in curriculum materials. The debates over curriculum are characterized as debates over the American national identity.

Eisner, Elliot W. *The Educational Imagination.* 3rd ed. Upper Saddle River, New Jersey: Prentice Hall, 2001. The author presents a stimulating, controversial book regarding forces influencing today's curriculum.

Hawthorne, Rebecca K. *Curriculum in the Making: Teacher Choice in the Classroom Experience.* New York: Teachers College Press, 1992. The book presents case studies of four English teachers who base their curriculum on the "role of teacher values, beliefs, experience, and expertise." The author discusses the struggle between personal and professional autonomy and obligations to mandated curricula.

Hirsch, E. D., Jr. *Cultural Literacy: What Every American Needs to Know.* Boston, MA: Houghton Mifflin Co., 1987. This provocative treatise asserts that literacy requires the early and continued transmission of specific information—the common knowledge that enables students to make sense of what they read.

Howard, V. A. *Learning by All Means: Lessons from the Arts.* New York: Peter Lang Publishing, 1994. This book presents a modern philosophy of arts education that stresses the personal struggle for competency and creativity.

Johnson, David and Roger Johnson. *Learning Together and Alone: Cooperative, Competitive and Individualistic Learning,* 5th ed. Boston: Allyn and Bacon/Longman, 1999. A comprehensive review of cooperative learning.

Klein, M. F. (ed.). *The Politics of Curriculum Decision-Making.* Albany, NY: SUNY Press, 1991. An edited volume that explores the political processes and issues in centralizing the public school curriculum.

McNeil, John D. *Curriculum: A Comprehensive Introduction.* 4th ed. Glenview, IL: Scott, Foresman/Little, Brown Higher Education, 1990. A comprehensive overview of major curriculum issues, including brief descriptions of new directions in the various subject fields.

Rothstein, Richard. *The Way We Were? The Myths and Realities of American's Student Achievement.* New York: Twentieth Century Fund Press/Priority Press Publications, 1998. An analysis of student academic achievement that concludes that American students are steadily getting better, rather than worse.

Walker, Decker F., and Jonas F. Soltis. *Curriculum and Aims.* 3rd ed. New York: Teachers College Press, 1997. This brief book on curriculum and the aims of education is designed to stimulate thinking about what teachers teach in school and what purposes are served by schooling.

Media Resources

Cross-Subject Teaching (Insight Media, 60 min., 1992). This video considers ways that a teacher, a school, or a community can adopt a general theme for study. It shows how pursuing a theme that includes many subject areas can increase students' appreciation for the scope of learning.

Curriculum (Insight Media, 23 min., 1997). This video discusses how high school curricula are created and established, and examines how curricula differ across states. It looks at who typically makes curriculum decisions and how these decisions are carried out. It also explores issues surrounding the establishment of a national high school curriculum.

Curriculum Innovations (Insight Media, 60 min., 1993). This program explores innovative ideas about how to reach students and how to make the classroom an exciting place.

Developing Student Understandings: The New Direction in Curriculum Part I (ASCD, 40 to 60 min., 1993).This three-cassette series focuses on what schools should be teaching in order to help people be successful in the twenty-first century. #1. - Building a Home for the Mind: How to Design Curriculum that Improves Student Thought and Covers Essential Content by Richard Strong. #2. - Organizing Curriculum Writing Around Essential Questions, Problems, Folio Genres, and Engaging Stories by Grant Wiggins. #3. - Putting It All Together by Bena Kallick.

The Heart of the Nation: Preparing Students to Succeed in the Workplace, (Films for the Humanities and Sciences, 58 min., 1999). This video compares the similarities and differences of preparation of secondary students in Japan, Germany, and the U.S.

New Venues for Learning: Authentic Materials (Insight Media, 22 min., 1993). This video examines school programs that draw on materials from everyday life and surroundings. It visits a Minnesota high school that uses a local river as a source of interdisciplinary learning and a New Mexico middle school where students run businesses and the government in their own simulated city.

Quest for Education (Insight Media, 60 min., 1991). This video contrasts education in the United States and Japan, focusing on the two nations' underlying cultural values. Comparing the American emphasis on individualism with the Japanese emphasis on group participation, it reveals what each nation expects and accepts from its educational system.

Re-Writing/Re-Righting History (Teach It Like It Was) (University of California Extension Center for Media and Independent Learning, 28 min., 1993). This investigative documentary explores the controversy over social studies textbooks and examines the debate over multiculturalism in K–12 history education.

Schools of Thought: Teaching Children in America and Japan (Films for the Humanities and Sciences, 55 min., 1994). This comparison between Japanese and American educational systems examines both the differences in goals between the two and the different ways in which they seek to achieve the same goal and balance creativity and discipline in education.

Media distributor contact information is available in Appendix I.

Student Activities

School Observation: Evaluating School Goals

As part of a field trip to a local school, you have the opportunity to examine the policy manual for the school district. As you thumb through the manual, you come across the following list of educational goals and the curricular emphases they would likely inspire:

Students will:

a.   Develop skills in reading, writing, speaking, and listening.

b.   Develop pride in work and a feeling of self-worth.

c.   Develop good character and self-respect.

d.   Develop a desire for learning now and in the future.

e.   Learn to respect and get along with people with whom we work and live.

f.   Learn how to examine and use information.

g.   Gain a general education.

h.   Learn how to be a good citizen.

i.   Learn about and try to understand the changes that take place in the world.

j.   Understand and practice democratic ideas and ideals.

k.   Learn how to respect and get along with people who think, dress, and act differently.

l.   Understand and practice the skills of family living.

m.   Gain information needed to make job selections.

n.   Learn how to be a good manager of money, property, and resources.

o.   Practice and understand the ideas of health and safety.

p.   Develop skills to enter a specific field of work.

q.   Learn how to use leisure time.

r.   Appreciate culture and beauty in the world.

Now respond to these questions:

a.   Choose the three or four goals that you consider most important.

b.   Compare and discuss your choices with two or three of your classmates. On which choices do you agree? Disagree?

c.   Decide whether each of the goals you have chosen is best achieved in a context of formal courses, informal school experiences, or a combination of the two.

d.   Are there any goals that you would want to add to the above list? Any you think should be deleted from it?

e.   Would you consider your approach child-centered or subject matter-centered? Why?

Note: These eighteen goals were part of a questionnaire given to a sample of Phi Delta Kappans. The results of the questionnaire can be found in the September 1973 issue of *Phi Delta Kappan,* pp. 29–32.

The Saber-Tooth Curriculum

Have students list five social changes they anticipate will occur in the next decade. Next to each prediction, have them write a short explanation of how schools might (or should) respond to these changes. If time permits, have students work in pairs and discuss lists. Using chart paper, make a master list of all the anticipated changes.

The Knowledge Most Worth Having

Have each student select a grade level and write two paragraphs identifying what he or she thinks is the most important knowledge for a student of that age to learn in school and why.

The Little Red Schoolhouse

Copy pages from a *McGuffey Reader* and pages from a current basal reader and have the students compare the content of the two readers. Have them discuss the values and philosophy implicit in each reader.

Curriculum Analysis

Collect several examples of curricula. Divide the class into groups of three or four and provide each group with a distinct curriculum. Ask the students to analyze the curriculum by looking at the goals and the objectives of the curriculum and answering questions such as: What appears to be the underlying educational philosophy governing this curriculum? Are the goals realizable and age-appropriate? To what extent are the goals focused on skills, content, or affective outcomes? Are learning activities specified? Is there any evidence of innovative instructional methods? Then have each group present its findings to the entire class.

Role-Play

Divide the class into groups of seven. Assign one person in each group one of the roles listed below. Have the groups hold simulated meetings for 15 minutes, during which they discuss the "textbook controversy."

At the end of the time period, discuss the following questions:

a.   What pressures were exerted on the superintendent?

b.   Was the group able to reach a consensus?

c.   Is consensus practical or possible in this situation?

d.   What alternatives did the group develop?

e.   Who should have the greatest influence on what a student learns?

f.   How can different values and beliefs coexist in a school setting?

The Textbook Controversy

Scenario: The superintendent of schools has worked in a crisis situation for the past year. The books that were to bring innovation to the school system have resulted in violence and turmoil. Parents are deeply divided over the types of books their children should be using in the class. Many teachers are also divided over the textbook controversy. The "fundamentalist" parents tell the superintendent that they intend to take their children out of the schools unless objectionable textbooks are removed from the classrooms. The "liberal" parents are pressing the superintendent and the school board to keep the books. A meeting has been called that will be attended by representatives of each of the following groups:

Task: The group is expected to resolve the conflict and develop some alternative plans for the remaining three months of school and for the next year. Roles are presented for either sex.

Roles:

a.   Oliver/Olivia Tavares, **superintendent** of schools (chairperson). You have been the head of the school district of 50,000 students for the past year. You have tried to bring some innovations into the system through very realistic and innovative paperback and hardback texts. You want the books to remain in the classroom, but you realize the need to compromise. You are the chairperson for the meeting.

b.   Kim/Kaiser Conrad, **principal** (secondary or elementary school). There has been a great deal of disruption in your school. You have received several belligerent calls from unidentified parents. Absenteeism is about 30 percent higher than normal. The strain is beginning to affect the teachers and the students. Your main concern is to bring the school back to normal.

c.   John/Bonnie Morgan, **teacher**. Most of the turmoil created by the use of the textbooks in the classroom has had little effect on your own teaching. Most parents of students in your classroom favor the new approach to teaching and the use of the controversial books. You feel other materials could be used to avoid the conflict now occurring.

d.   Ray/Rana Bonanno. The **union representative**, who is a teacher in the system, feels the textbook issue has the potential for creating havoc in the classroom. If parents can dictate which texts to use, then they could also dictate what to teach and how it should be taught. You feel the teachers, who have been trained as professionals, should decide educational matters, not the "fundamentalist" or "liberal" parents.

e.   Charles/Charlotte Kravulski, **fundamentalist parent**. You feel that your basic values are being betrayed by "those liberals who dare to bring filth and anti-Americanism" into the classroom. If the books remain in the schools, you will remove your three children and send them to a private school.

f.   Frank/Frannie Scheuer, **liberal parent**. You feel the new books reflect the reality of life in our society. It is better for the students to learn about this life in the classroom than in the streets. You see the textbooks as preparation for the future, while the "fundamentalists" seem to want reality to go away.

g.   Kevin/Lynne McCreanor, **school board member**. You feel the community is being unnecessarily divided by the conflict, and your main aim is to soothe both sides until time passes and heals the rift.

Student Assignments

The following activities are suggestions for student portfolio activities. They are a means of providing alternative assessment of students' capabilities.

Independent Reading

Read and respond to any of the selections noted on the chapter/article correlation list found in the front of this manual for Ryan/Cooper, *Kaleidoscope: Readings in Education* (Houghton Mifflin, 2004 in the front of this manual). You may want to use the Article Review Form in *Kaleidoscope*.

Reflective Papers

Choose one of the following topics to write a reflective paper (2–5 pages). The purpose of the paper is to help you assimilate new knowledge by blending it with your previous knowledge and experiences.

1.   Think back on your own high school experiences and discuss instructional approaches used in your math, science, or English classes (choose one). How would you characterize them based on what you have read in this chapter? How effective were these approaches in helping you learn? How could these approaches have been improved to enhance your learning?

2.   As you observe in your field site, what instructional strategies do you see being implemented? With what degree of success? Do the students respond differently to these strategies? With what results?

3.   Review the curricular changes that have taken place since the 1950s and speculate on the curricular changes that will be implemented in the next 20 years. How will your teaching be affected?

Journal Reflections

Suggestions for journal topics for students' selection:

a.   What do you believe is the greatest challenge to developing a strong curriculum?

b.   What are your thoughts and feelings about the impact textbooks have on the content of he curriculum?

c.   Describe the curriculum philosophy that seemed to be in effect when you were in high school (identify your graduation year).

CHAPTER 5

What Makes a Teacher Effective?

LEARNING OBJECTIVES

After studying the chapter, students will be able to

1. describe the four domains of professional practice.

2. describe the teacher's role as a decision maker.

3. explain how teachers' attitudes toward themselves, their students, their colleagues, their students' parents, and their subject matter affect teaching.

4. identify and explain attitudes that can foster effective teaching and those that can hinder it.

5. describe how knowledge of a discipline, the disciplinary knowledge covered in the curriculum, and pedagogical content knowledge contribute to effective teaching.

6. identify and explain the characteristics of effective teachers.

7. describe what reflective teaching is.

8. describe what is meant by the zone of proximal development.

9. identify and explain the implications of recent cognitive research on teaching and learning.

10. explain the relationship between academically engaged time and learning.

11. define Jacob Kounin's terms (*with-it-ness, smoothness,* and *momentum*) in terms of their meaning in classroom management.

12. summarize guidelines for effective classroom management.

13. explain how questioning, wait-time, and planning contribute to teaching effectiveness.

CHAPTER OVERVIEW

The purpose of Chapter 5 is to introduce the prospective teacher to some current research on teacher effectiveness. The chapter, by its nature, is more theoretical than many other chapters of the textbook, and for this reason it may be more difficult for some students. However, we think that prospective teachers should recognize the importance of a theory of education for every teacher. We agree with John Dewey: "Nothing is so practical as a good theory." Novice teachers, though, often fault their preparation for being too theoretical—a complaint their more experienced colleagues sometimes echo. In our view, the problem is not an oversupply of theory; it lies with an undersupply of how to use theory in the classroom. Reflective teaching involves the use of theory to determine the effectiveness of instruction as well as to find ways to improve it. Teacher education programs need to provide opportunities for beginning teachers to view classroom events and to interpret them by using relevant theories.

We review the findings of research and explore the implications of theory in several areas: teachers' attitudes, subject-matter knowledge, learning and human behavior, instructional strategies, and classroom management. The opening case study about Carol Landis provides a reference point for showing how theory may be applied. This chapter covers a lot of ground; if time permits, you might wish to spend extra time elaborating many of the topics we simply introduce.

CHAPTER OUTLINE

I.   Framework for Professional Practice

II.   The Teacher as a Reflective Decision Maker
    A.   Planning Decisions
    B.   Implementing Decisions
    C.   Evaluating Decisions
III.   Aspects of Reflective Decision Making
IV.   What Attitudes Does the Effective Teacher Possess?
    A.   The Teacher's Attitude Toward Self: Self-Understanding
        1.   Ways to Achieve Self-Understanding
    B.   The Teacher's Attitude Toward Children
        1.   Teacher Expectations
    C.   The Teacher's Attitude Toward Peers and Parents
        1.   Authority/Collaboration
        2.   Competition/Cooperation
        3.   Superiority and Prejudice/Acceptance
    D.   The Teacher's Attitude Toward the Subject Matter
V.   What Subject-Matter Knowledge Does the Effective Teacher Need?
VI.   What Theoretical Knowledge Does the Effective Teacher Need?
    A.   Theories-in-Use
    B.   Why Study Educational Theory?
    C.   How Can Theoretical Knowledge Be Used?
        1.   An Example of Using Theoretical Knowledge
VII.   Personal Practical Knowledge
VIII. What Teaching Skills Are Required of an Effective Teacher?
    A.   Knowing versus Doing
    B.   Classroom Management Skills
        1.   Academic Engaged Time
        2.   Kounin's Research
        3.   Other Research Findings
    C.   Questioning Skills
        1.   Wait-Time
        2.   Effective Questioning Techniques
    D.   Planning Skills

SUPPLEMENTARY LECTURE AND DISCUSSION TOPICS

1.   **Decision making** Using one of your own recent classes as an example, discuss the planning, implementing, and evaluation decisions you made. List the elements that affected your choices: coverage, prior lessons, knowledge of other experiences of the students, and so on. Then describe the interactive decisions you made while teaching—when to pause in a lecture, when to ask for questions, whom to call on, when to stop a small-group activity. After you list the decisions, invite the class to help you generate examples relevant to the grade levels they plan to teach.

2.   **Self-fulfilling prophecy** Elaborate on the research on self-fulfilling prophecies. Describe the early experiments and the later work that established the behavioral connections between expectations and learning.

3.   **The importance of enthusiasm** Most students find the studies of enthusiasm intriguing. Summarize the origins of the research, and describe the organization of the projects designed to measure the effects of enthusiasm. Discuss the need to balance teachers' interests against curricular necessities.

4.   **Classroom management or discipline** One area that beginning teachers (and many others) typically find difficult is classroom management or discipline. You may want to ask your students to recall the management style of their teachers. Which teachers were effective? Which weren't? Summarize their descriptions and help them draw some conclusions regarding classroom management. What do they think they will find difficult in managing a classroom?

5.   **Theory in practice** Choose a set of recommendations about teaching—such as Kounin's on classroom management, Rowe's on wait-time, Wilen's and Clegg's research on effective questioning—and then

review how they work in the classroom. Show a videotape of a teaching episode that illustrates use or nonuse of the recommendations. At the beginning of the tape, stop the tape whenever evidence appears and show students how to spot instances where the theory might have been practiced. As the tape continues, invite students to tell you when to pause so they can practice identifying when theories apply.

6. **Reflective teachers** Elaborate on the importance that reflection has in developing effective teaching. Identify how reflective teachers develop reflection skills and use them to improve their own practice.

STUDY GUIDE – CHAPTER 5: WHAT MAKES A TEACHER EFFECTIVE?

Completing this study guide will help you prepare for the major topic areas on an exam; however, it does not cover every piece of information found in the chapter or the test questions.

1.   List and give an example of each of the three categories of decisions that teachers make.

2.   Name the four categories of specialized skills and attributes necessary for teachers to become effective instructional decision makers.

3.   How does a self-fulfilling prophecy affect the relationship between a student and a teacher, and the student's achievement?

4.   Distinguish between a theory and a theory-in-use.

5.   Explain the theory of the zone of proximal development and describe an example.

6.   How do the authors define classroom management?

7.   Paraphrase the eight characteristic behaviors of effective teachers that David Berliner identified from research studies.

8.   Define and give an example of academically engaged time.

9.   Describe and gave an example of each of the following from Jacob Kounin's research: with-it-ness, smoothness, momentum.

10.   Explain the advantages of using wait-time.

ADDITIONAL RESOURCES FOR INSTRUCTORS

Anderson, Lorin W. *Increasing Teacher Effectiveness*. Paris: UNESCO International Institute for Educational Planning. A fairly concise presentation of the latest research findings on teacher effectiveness and classroom implications.

Bedwell, Lance E. *Effective Teaching: Preparation and Implementation*. Springfield, IL: C. C. Thomas, 1991. Bedwell presents a helpful guide for those practitioners who want to incorporate the principles of effective teaching into practice.

Cooper, James M. *Classroom Teaching Skills*, Boston, MA: Houghton Mifflin Co., 1999. This self- instructional book is designed to help teachers acquire basic teaching skills such as writing objectives, evaluation skills, classroom management skills, questioning skills, and interpersonal communication skills.

Crunkshank, Donald R. *Research That Informs Teachers and Teacher Educators*. Bloomington, IN: Phi Delta Kappa, 1990. This book is a condensed summary of the major findings of thousands of research projects on practices that contribute to successful instruction.

Danielson, Charlotte. *Enhancing Professional Practice: A Framework for Teaching*. Alexandria, VA: Association for Supervision and Curriculum Development, 1996. This useful book, organized around a framework of professional practice, is based on the PRAXIS III criteria, including planning and preparation, classroom environment, instruction, and professional responsibilities.

Gail, Meredith. "Synthesis of Research on Teachers' Questioning." *Educational Leadership* 42 (November 1984): 40–47. This article highlights research on the effects of both factual and higher-level questions; it also suggests reasons for the effectiveness of recitation.

Good, Thomas L., and Jere E. Brophy. *Looking in Classrooms*. New York: Longman, 2000. This excellent book provides teachers with concrete skills that enable them to observe and interpret the classroom behavior of both teacher and student.

Oser, Fritz K., Andreas Dick, and Jean Luc Patry. *Effective and Responsible Teaching: The New Synthesis*. San Francisco: Jossey-Bass, 1992. A scholarly volume detailing recent findings of research on effective teaching.

Ross, Wayne C., Jeffrey Cornett, and Gail McCutcheon (eds.). *Teacher Personal Theorizing: Connecting Curricular Practice, Theory, and Research*. Albany: SUNY Press, 1992. An edited volume of essays illustrating how teachers' own theories are buttressed or contradicted by current theory and research.

Seymour, Daniel, Terry Seymour, and 30 Teachers of the Year. *America's Best Classrooms: How Award-Winning Teachers Are Shaping Our Children's Future*. Princeton, NJ: Petersen's Guides, 1992. A highly readable collection describing how award-winning teachers work with students. The volume includes numerous bibliographical references.

Shulman, Lee S. *Research in Teaching and Learning: A Project of AERA*. New York: Macmillan, 1990. One of the nation's foremost researchers on teaching presents the findings of an AERA research project. A scholarly, dense volume for those interested in the research theory and findings.

Media Resources

Connecting with Kids (Films for the Humanities and Sciences, 26 min., 1994). Teachers talk about how they communicate effectively with students by showing they care and taking an active interest in their students' lives. In the classroom, teachers demonstrate ways of building a team feeling and making students feel successful without compromising standards.

Getting Ready (Films for the Humanities and Sciences, 26 min., 1994). This video shows how teachers plan to create a classroom that is conducive to student learning. Through interviews and classroom demonstration, teachers present how they organize the classroom, introduce themselves to students, define and meet objectives, and address student needs.

I Used To Teach English (Pyramid Media, 20 min., 1994). This program explores the transformation of a teacher who searches for more effective ways to teach and encourage students to listen to their own voices.

Making a Difference: Great Teachers Part I (Films for the Humanities and Sciences, 28 min., 1997). This documentary focuses on three teachers who have made a positive impact—academically or personally—on their students' lives. Selected as a result of an essay contest that asked students to write about the teacher who had most challenged and inspired them, the teachers are shown at work in the classroom.

Making a Difference: Great Teachers, Part 2 (Films for the Humanities and Sciences, 24 min., 1998). This program follows three outstanding teachers throughout the school day to show how they motivate students and the classroom skills that help make them great teachers.

Making a Difference: Great Teachers, Part 3 (Films for the Humanities and Sciences, 28 min., 1999). This is a presentation of three very different educational "styles" that produce the same positive educational results.

Planning for Prevention (Films for the Humanities and Sciences, 26 min., 1994). To stop problems before they start, teachers must clearly define what is expected of students from the outset and establish routines that make the best use of classroom time. Teachers explain and demonstrate unique, effective styles of communicating expectations and initiating class procedures.

Quality Schools (AIT, 28 min., 1992). Glasser argues against traditional coercive management practices in schools. He advocates teaching students in ways that satisfy their needs and convincing them of the importance and significance of what they are learning, making discipline problems disappear and achievement rise.

The Seven Habits of Highly Ineffective Educations (Insight Media, 59 min., 1997). This humorous video presents seven failures characteristic of ineffective educators including anger management skills, blanket instructional methods, cultural discrimination, and the refusal to accept educational change.

Responding to Misbehavior (Films for the Humanities and Sciences, 26 min., 1994). This program examines various classroom disruptions and analyzes some techniques that enable the teacher to deal with misbehaving students without interrupting the class.

The Truth About Teachers (Pyramid Media, 47 min, 1989). Narrated by Whoopi Goldberg, this video is an upbeat look at a few imaginative, inspiring teachers with snapshot videos of them teaching and being interviewed.

Voices From the Classroom: Dimensions of Good Teaching (Pyramid, 24 min., 1999). Classroom scenes and interviews with teachers and their students show the characteristics and qualities of good teaching including high expectations, commitment, effective management, etc.

Media distributor contact information is available in Appendix I.

Student Activities

School Observation—Classroom Management

In a small group, read and discuss the following:

One day while you are observing in a third-grade classroom, a student teacher conducts the lesson. As the student teacher is teaching long division using manipulatives, the students become noisy and inattentive. In response, the student teacher talks more loudly in order to be heard over the noise, and she pays more attention to her materials than to the students. In fact, she seems to ignore the classroom disorder, perhaps because she doesn't know how to handle it. Her students, however, appear to interpret her behavior as an indication that noise is allowed, and the disorder escalates. Finally, the regular teacher steps in and quiets the children.

On the basis of what you know about effective classroom management practices:

   a.   How should the student teacher have behaved?

   b.   Think of at least two different ways to deal with the noise problem that would have been more effective.

   c.   What additional information about this situation would have been useful to you in drafting your approaches to the problem?

d.   Think of a few questions that you would want to ask the classroom teacher or your course instructor that would help you address the problem. Share your approaches to the problem and your questions and information needs with a couple of classmates, and compare your approaches.

Advising Carol Landis

Divide the class into small groups to discuss the case of Carol Landis in the text. Ask each group to identify the decision points used by Carol to plan and react. Have groups either affirm Carol's decision at each point or propose some advice on how she should do things differently or what she should do on the following day. Each affirmation or bit of advice should be supported by the appropriate text citation on sensible practice.

A Gauge of Your Attitudes Toward Teaching

Part of the chapter deals with the significance of a teacher's attitudes toward himself or herself, other teachers, students, and others in the school. To be an effective teacher, she or he needs to know what attitudes she or he has concerning those areas. Ask your students to complete the following gauge of their attitudes about a range of issues. When the students have completed their own, put them in small groups to debrief.

Self-Gauge of Your Attitudes Toward Teaching and Related Areas

Respond to each question as honestly and as thoroughly as you can. This exercise is designed for you to think about your attitudes, especially if they are unexamined ones.

a.   Your ideal class would look like . . .

b.   Your ideal lesson would be . . .

c.   Are you a competitive person? Why? Why not? Are there particular circumstances in which you are more competitive than others?

d.   How easily do you collaborate with your supervisor? How do you respond to someone directing or guiding your actions?

e.   Do you get easily annoyed with or are you judgmental of people? What is your biggest pet peeve about people?

f.   What would make you lose your temper in a classroom?

g.   Are you especially drawn to particular "types" of children? The "underdog"? The class comedian? The earnest, bright student?

h.   What is your attitude toward grading and evaluating student work?

i.   What is your biggest worry about teaching?

j.   How long in your life do you plan to be a teacher? Do you have other possible career goals?

k.   What is your attitude toward classroom management or discipline? What are your underlying thoughts regarding discipline?

The Qualities of an Effective Teacher

Considering what you have learned about the characteristics of an effective teacher, this activity is designed to help you observe these qualities in a real setting. For this activity, you need to observe a teacher in action. You must tell the teacher what this assignment is and ask for permission. When you explain the project, make sure you emphasize that this observation is not to critique his or her teaching style, but to see particular skills in action.

As you observe the teacher over the course of the day, check off the number of times he or she behaves in a certain way. You probably will not be able to use some of the listed abilities. In that case, write "N.A." for "not applicable." Note to yourself what was happening as you made your tally mark. At the end of the day, review your list. You may, if appropriate, want to share your list with the teacher for further discussion.

Qualities of an Effective Teacher

a.   the ability to ask different kinds of questions, each of which requires different types of thought processes from the student

b.   the ability to reinforce certain kinds of behaviors

c.   the ability to diagnose student needs and learning difficulties

d.   the ability to vary the learning situation continually to keep the student involved

e.   the ability to recognize when students are paying attention and to use this information to vary behavior and possibly the direction of the lesson

f.   the ability to use technological equipment, such as microcomputers

g.   the ability to judge the appropriateness of instructional materials

h.   the ability to define the objectives of particular lessons in terms of student behaviors

i.   the ability to relate learning to each student's experience

The Roots of Professional Training

Have the students read the following two accounts of effective teaching. Have them compare each to the advice given in the chapter. Ask them to list similarities and differences and to comment on what things remained the same while others changed. Ask them to write a similar list of do's and don'ts for the year 2004.

How to Keep the Class "On Task"—Advice to Teachers (1867)[1]

a.   The teacher must be well acquainted with the work to be done; must know well how to do it; must be well acquainted with the wants of the class or school and of its individual members; and must be inspired with a love for teaching and filled with the enthusiasm which such love generates.

b.   The capacity of the class or the individual should be so clearly understood and carefully considered that the lesson given may be fully mastered within the limits of proper, healthful exercises. For pupils six to eight years of age, I think the limit may be put at 5 to 10 minutes; from eight to ten, 15 minutes, with 3 to 5 minutes for review at the end of a half hour; from ten to twelve, 20 minutes with a like review; for older pupils, the time of study may be increased until one hour shall not be too long.

c.   THE RECITATION SHOULD NOT BE PROLONGED BEYOND THE PROPER LIMIT OF HEALTHFUL EXERTION. While studying, the pupils should give the whole force of their mental powers to the acquisition of the lesson, so while reciting, they should be thoroughly busy—should perform every mental operation required of anyone. Whatever plan of conducting the recitations is found the best adapted to fix attention should be followed, and any plan that does not secure the undivided attention of every pupil should be discarded or modified at once. The teacher's own

---

[1] Thanks is given to the Education Museum of the Department of History in Education Foundations and Research at The Ohio State University, Columbus, Ohio, for the use of its primary source collection of education materials.

attention should be directed to observing whether the pupils are thoroughly interested and absorbed in the work to be done, and the moment the interest abates the recitation should be closed. Better no recitation at all than one continued while the pupils are thinking of something else or nothing at all—dreaming, as so many do. Many complain of want of time to conduct the recitation. The trouble is not want of time, but want of proper employment of time. More time is wasted than used, if my observations may form a proper basis of judgment.

d.   THE TEACHER SHOULD NEVER ALLOW ANY PORTION OF A RECITATION TO PASS WITHOUT GIVING TO IT HIS OWN PERSONAL AND UNDIVIDED ATTENTION. The habit of assisting individual pupils to do "sums" is hard to find. The habit of assisting individual pupils to do "sums" or to find localities on a map while others are reciting cannot be too pointedly condemned. If the recitation is not worthy of the teacher's attention, how can he expect to command the attention of the pupils?

e.   WHILE THE RECITATION IS IN PROGRESS, THE TEACHER MAY ASK FREQUENT QUESTIONS FOR THE CLASS TO ANSWER IN CONCERT. Let the questions be such as all can answer, and let the teacher see that all do answer.

f.   Many more like suggestions might be added, but I forbear. Enough has already been said to set the LIVE TEACHER to thinking; and more might only serve to harden the plodder to his dullness.

The Art of Questioning—Teacher Training Course, Summer (1918)[2]

Mrs. Boober:

Good questioning is considered one of the greatest achievements of the successful teacher, since this is the only method by which she can get at the best possible results of her work.

In questioning a class, the teacher should first take into consideration the age and intellectual powers of the pupils. Then she should endeavor to adapt her language to their age and understanding. Questions asked in words so difficult as to impede comprehension on the part of the pupils are, of course, useless in stimulating thought. In the lower grades the teacher's language must be very simple, indeed, while in the upper grades the pupils have a larger vocabulary and the teacher may feel that she may use more difficult words. Having this in mind, she should then ask her questions in an encouraging, animated manner. She has, of course, prepared her lesson beforehand, so that her eyes are free from the text, which is used only as a reference book.

Questions should be definite and free from ambiguity. They should be clear, concise, and direct to the point. Indefinite questions lead to indefinite answers; or, if the answer is correct, it is invariably a reproduction of the text, which, in reality, is developing the verbal memory, rather than encouraging the pupil to use his judgment.

One of the teacher's greatest desires should be to stimulate thot [sic]. Text questions lack interest. If the words of the teacher are well chosen they will create pictures in the mind of her pupils, which leads us to inquiry on their part. Thus they result in their understanding the subject. Of course, there are exceptions, but as a rule the teacher should avoid questions that may be answered by a "yes," or "no" as they lead to guessing on the part of the pupil. Of course, if she is developing a lesson, "yes" and "no" questions are permissible, but invariably the pupils will answer offhand without much meditation; thus the teacher is obliged to "pump" her lessons from her class.

Unity and continuity are two important factors in good instruction. The teacher should seek to have one lesson, a continuation of the previous day's, and one question to have some bearing on the one before it. This results in assimilation of the lesson on the part of the pupil.

---

[2]Thanks is given to the Education Museum of the Department of History in Education Foundations and Research at The Ohio State University, Columbus, Ohio, for the use of its primary source collection of education materials.

Student Assignments

Independent Reading

Read and respond to any of the selections noted on the chapter/article correlation list found in the front of this manual for Ryan/Cooper, *Kaleidoscope: Readings in Education* (Houghton Mifflin, 2004). You may want to use the Article Review Form in *Kaleidoscope*.

Reflective Papers

Choose one of the following topics to write a reflective paper (2–5 pages). The purpose of the paper is to help you assimilate new knowledge by blending it with your previous knowledge and experiences.

1. Recall your own experience as a student. Choose one teacher who made a positive impact on you. Write a short description of that teacher, showing what he or she typically did that impressed you. Then analyze your recollections and description. To what extent did that teacher manifest the behaviors and attitudes of an effective teacher?

2. Recent cognitive research suggests that teachers should provide meaningful problem-solving experiences for learners. Assume the perspective of either a teacher or a student. Based upon that point of view, describe what you think would constitute a meaningful problem-solving experience.

3. In the text, Carol Landis had a number of unexamined theories-in-use that determined how she interacted with her students. Reflect upon your own assumptions about learning and teaching. Identify and list several of your own theories-in-use. What does each one reveal about some of your notions about education, about being a teacher, or about how teaching and learning should occur?

Journal Reflections

Suggestions for journal topics for students' selection:

1. In your opinion, what is the *single* most important characteristic of an effective teacher?

2. Who was your most effective teacher? Why?

CHAPTER 6

What Should Teachers Know About Technology and Its Impact on Schools?

LEARNING OBJECTIVES

After studying the chapter, students will be able to

1. describe some of the events in the historical evolution of the audiovisual and computer technologies used in the classroom.

2. identify the sources of pressure on schools to use more technology.

3. discuss a variety of ways that technology can be used to assist student learning.

4. summarize how technology changes the teacher's role in instruction and contributes to the teacher's productivity.

5. explain several ways computers may be organized for use within a school.

6. discuss the financial, technical, and instructional issues surrounding the use of computers in education.

7. explore the equity issues regarding equal access to technology for disadvantaged students.

8. use computer terminology with greater understanding.

CHAPTER OVERVIEW

We believe that educational technology is having an increasingly significant impact on instructional delivery and effectiveness. Because of the fast pace of adoption of technological methods and resources in our schools, it is important to introduce prospective teachers to this information early in their teacher preparation.

In this chapter we briefly review the historical development of the use of educational technology. Varied applications are divided according to subject area (English/Language Arts, Social Studies, Math, Science, Foreign Language, Distance Education, and Special Needs) with acknowledgment that overlap exists. The changes that educational technology makes in instructional methods and the applications that contribute to teacher productivity are described.

Students are introduced to the key issues in educational technology: the infrastructure and budgeting issues, the challenges of integrating technology into the curriculum, parental involvement, the necessity of preservice as well as in-service teacher education, and issues of equity involving students of all genders, races, and socioeconomic classes.

CHAPTER OUTLINE

I.   A Brief Look at Education's Technological Past
II. How Are Schools Being Pressured to Change?
III. How Are Technologies Affecting Student Learning?
   A. English/Language Arts Education
      1. Writing with Word Processors
      2. Communicating with Multimedia
      3. Learning to Read
      4. Combining Technology and Crossing Disciplines
   B. Science Education
      1. Scientific Hardware
      2. Communication with Other Scientists
      3. Enhancing Problem Solving
   C. Social Studies Education
      1. Databases
      2. Online Archives
      3. Simulations
      4. Virtual Fieldtrips
      5. Using Spreadsheets to Connect Disciplines
   D. Mathematics Education
      1. Tutorial Software
      2. Other Math Software
      3. Graphing Calculators
   E. Foreign Language Education
   F. Distance Education
   G. Technology for Students with Special Needs
IV. How Are Technologies Affecting Teaching?
   A. A Different Role for the Teacher
   B. Professional Resources and Communication
      1. Voice Mail
      2. Email
      3. The Web
   C. Management: Teacher Productivity Tools
      1. Gradebooks
      2. Other Teacher Productivity Tools
V.   How Are Computer Technologies Organized for Student Use?
   A. Computer Labs
   B. Single-Computer Classrooms
   C. Classroom Clusters
   D. Laptops and Handheld Computers
VI. What Are the Key Issues in Educational Technology?
   A. Infrastructure and Budgeting
      1. Electrical Problems
      2. Network Wiring
      3. Access
      4. Technology Budgets
      5. Support Personnel

   B. Education of Teachers
      1. Teacher Preparation
      2. Staff Development
   C. Parents
   D. Equity

E.   Integration into Curriculum

SUPPLEMENTARY LECTURE AND DISCUSSION TOPICS

1.   **The Internet** The Internet has vast implications for data access and communication. What possible instructional applications does this type of technology immediately bring to mind for your own teaching? What other possibilities can you envision in other fields of education?

2.   **Extending learning beyond school walls** Connecting schools and classrooms to the Internet will in effect extend learning beyond the confines of the school walls. How might this in fact be true or not true? Under what conditions do you think this vision will be realized?

3.   **The influences of networking** Telecommunication offers educators a new tool, a new technology for advancing learning in exciting ways. The dynamic is that the process of learning will not just be enhanced as a consequence of having this new technology but will evolve into an activity that is more meaningfully enriched. How do you see networking among schools, other institutions, agencies, and corporations influencing the way learning takes place?

4.   **Software and Internet acceptable use and copyright issues** The use of the Internet in education brings to mind additional areas that teachers need to be cognizant of regarding fair use and copyright law. Discuss with students in more detail the stipulations regarding how and under what conditions teachers can use information gained from the various computer on-line services available.

5.   **Computer Technology and Constructivism** Expand the information on how or if technology facilitates constructivist teaching. What are the merits of constructivist teaching? How could the use of technology support or undermine constructivist learning? Does the value or extent of the use of constructivist methods vary by grade level?

STUDY GUIDE – CHAPTER 6: WHAT SHOULD TEACHERS KNOW ABOUT TECHNOLOGY AND ITS IMPACT ON SCHOOLS?

Completing this study guide will help you prepare for the major topic areas on an exam; however, it does not cover every piece of information found in the chapter or the test questions.

1.   Identify the sources of pressure on schools to incorporate more use of technology.

2.   Describe the three stages of application, which new technologies tend to move through as the level of use matures.

3.   List and give examples of how computer technology can serve as a cognitive tool.

4.   List and give examples of how computer technology can serve to develop communication skills in English and Language Arts instruction.

5.   Pick one of the following subject areas (Science, Social Studies, Mathematics, or Foreign Language) and describe the various uses of technology within instruction in that subject.

6.   Describe several different ways computers are used as assistive technology for students with special needs.

7.   Describe the ways technology can change how teachers do their job (include descriptions of professional resources, communication, and teacher productivity tools).

8.   Identify the pros and cons of each of the four common ways of arranging computers for student use within a school.

9.   Give examples of the factors that contribute to the inequities of computer technology between students of affluent and disadvantaged socioeconomic classes.

10. Describe the recommended preservice and in-service teacher preparation that are recommended for the maximum use of technology in the classroom.

ADDITIONAL RESOURCES FOR INSTRUCTORS

Becker, H. J. and J. Ravitz. "The Influence of Computer and Internet Use on Teachers Pedagogical Practices and Perceptions." *Journal of Research on Computing in Education* 31(9) (1999): 356–384. Describes the effect the increasing use of computers has had on the teacher's role and methods.

Cuban, L. *Oversold and Underused: Computers in Classrooms 1980-2000.* Cambridge, MA: Harvard University Press, 2001. The author presents a critical and historical look at the use of technology in education.

Healy, J. M. *Failure to Connect: How Computers Affect Our Children's Minds – for Better and Worse.* New York: Simon and Schuster, 1998. The author explanins how computer use interacts with brain development at different ages.

Jonassen, D. H., C. Carr, and Y. Hsi V-Ping. "Computers as Mind Tools for Engaging Learners in Critical Thinking." *Techtrends* 43 (March 1998): 24–32. Gives concrete examples of technological applications as mind tools.

Means, B., and K. Olson. "The Link Between Technology and Authentic Learning." *Educational Leadership* 51(7) (1994): 15–18. In this article the researchers discuss their observations about effective use of technology in the classroom, and the need for technology to be applied to authentic, meaningful tasks.

Miller, L., and J. Olson. "How Computers Live in Schools." *Educational Leadership* 53(2) (1995): 74–77. This article explores issues relating to how computers are used in schools and how technology can yield unexpected results.

O'Neil, J. "Teachers and Technology: Potential and Pitfalls." *Educational Leadership* 53(2) (1995): 10–11. This short article alludes to the gap between the potential of technology in education and current practice.

Rockman, S. "In School or Out: Technology, Equity, and the Future of Our Kids." *Communication of the ACM* 38(6) (June 1995): 25–29. This article bring up important issues regarding equity of technology resources and use.

Sandholtz, J., C. Ringstaff, and D. C. Dwyer. *Teaching with Technology: Creating Student-Centered Classrooms.* New York: Teachers College Press, 1997. Uses case studies and teachers' voices to address classroom teachers' concerns about technology.

Schofield, J. W. and A. L. Davidson. *Bringing the Internet to School: Lessons from an Urban District.* New York: John Wiley & Sons, 2002. This book discusses the findings of a five-year study of Internet use in schools.

Tapscott, D. *Growing Up Digital: The Rise of the Net Generation.* New York: McGraw-Hill, 1998. This text is a good source for understanding the unique characteristics of the generation that has grown up with digital media.

VanDusen, L. M., and B. R. Worthen. "Can Integrated Instructional Technology Transform the Classroom?" *Educational Leadership* 53(2) (1995): 28–33. Reports the findings of a two-year study of integrated learning systems and discusses key points.

Watson, J. G. "Educational Technology: A Necessity for the 21st Century—Why the Delay?" *Network News & Views* (August 1996): 84–91. An excellent article outlining the justification for using technology in instruction.

(Also see the Web sites listed at the end of this chapter in the text.)

Media Resources

Cyber Classroom—Now and in the Future; Number 6 of the *Imagine II* series (Apple Computer, 30 min., 1996). Combines snapshots of today's technologies with glimpses of what's in store for the future.

Computers and Schools (Annenberg CPB Videos, 30 min., 1990). This video profiles the many ways computers are used at Cincinnati Country Day School.

Distance Learning: The Great Controversy (Films for the Humanities and Sciences, 60 min., 1998). In this program, a literature teacher argues the benefits of online learning, while her department chairperson presents arguments against it. Methods used to conduct an effective online "class" are demonstrated using state-of-the-art software.

Enhancing Curriculum with Technology; Number 4 of the *Imagine II* series (Apple Computer, 30 min., 1996). This video demonstrates that technology works best when it supports what teachers are already doing. This episode chronicles the work of educators integrating technology into their curriculum.

Integrating Technology: More Than an Electronic Blackboard? (Insight Media, 60 min., 1992). This program visits an elementary school that integrates technology into the schoolwide curriculum and a Native American reservation school where technology enhances cross-cultural communication.

Learning From Socrates to Cyberspace (Films for the Humanities and Sciences, 60 min., 1998). This program provides an overview of the history of distance learning including an extensive interview with Professor Neil Postman from the first television classroom of the 1950s *Sunrise Semester* and talks about how teachers can shape the educational environment to include distance learning.

Meeting the Challenges of Information Technology (Insight Media, 70 min., 1999). Willard Daggett describes some of the changes in the offing for information technologies and details their probable influences on education and daily life. He proposes strategies for developing teaching methods that prepare students to live in an increasingly information-based, technological society.

Multimedia in Education (Insight Media, 20 min., 1993). This program shows how educators are using multimedia technology to explore new ways of teaching and learning. It discusses the use of videotapes, laser disks, information networks, virtual reality systems, and computer modeling in education.

The New ABC's: Classrooms of Tomorrow (Films for the Humanities and Sciences, 58 min., 1992). This program visits several "classrooms of tomorrow" to examine how technologies stimulate smart students, involve young children, reduce truancy, aid special education students, and simulate real-world job tasks.

Power Teaching: How to Develop Creative Teaching Techniques Using CD-ROM Technology (Insight Media, 25 min., 1995). Profiling an overview of CD-ROM technology, this video explains how to integrate CD-ROMs into the curriculum. It emphasizes that CD-ROMs not only allow students access to extensive information, but also enable them to adapt the interactive program to their needs and ability levels. The video features samples of CD-ROM programs and demonstrates the use of CD-ROMs by students practicing basic skills.

Technology and the Role of the Teacher: How to Integrate Technology into the Classroom (Insight Media, 20 min., 1996). This fast-paced video addresses technology not as a cure for problems in the classroom but rather as a tool for effective instruction. It shows how to restructure the classroom to incorporate technology and discusses both the pedagogical and emotional issues raised by its growing use in schools.

Technology in the Classroom (Insight Media, 60 min., 1993). This video shows how technology can be used to motivate students and considers how it can make schools and teachers more efficient and effective.

Technology, the Learning Process and a Vision for the Future (Insight Media, 100 min., 1997). This video explains the way in which technology is changing the roles of teachers and students and addresses how teachers can incorporate technology into their curricula.

Your School and the Internet (Films for the Humanities and Sciences, 45 min., 1996). An overview of the effective use of the Internet in the classroom.

Media distributor contact information is available in Appendix I.

Student Activities

School Observations—Educational Technology

As you enter your middle school field placement, you walk down the halls and notice computer labs in every major area of the building. These labs are stocked with current computer models, scanners, projection systems, and various other electronic devices. Students are sitting at each station working on what looks like a spreadsheet. Each student is copying in numbers and formulas from a worksheet provided by the teacher. As you continue to look around the school, you spot a few older computers sitting on teachers' desks, but no other computers in the classrooms.

On the basis of these observations, answer the following questions:

a.   Why do you think the computer resources are distributed in this fashion?

b.   What might you conclude about the use of technology by students in this school?

c.   How do you think the teachers themselves are using the technology?

d.   If you had the opportunity, would you change the way computer resources are distributed and used in this school? Why or why not?

Inventory of Technology Skills

Before you start this chapter, use the technology inventory (included at the end of this section) to assess your students' level of technology background and to raise their awareness of their own skills and needs in this area.

Safe and Effective Use Guidelines

The Internet is a mixed bag for students. It opens up some wonderful resources, but it also exposes students to unverified information and in some cases inappropriate or dangerous materials and opportunities. In small groups, have your students develop guidelines for safe and effective use of the Internet. Each group should also develop at least one teaching activity that could be used with students to teach them these safe and effective skills. Have the small groups share their ideas with the rest of the class.

Debate

Have students research the issues surrounding the restricted or unrestricted use of the Internet. Contact school districts in your area to determine their policies and if they restrict use—how they monitor use. Ask if they use parent information or permission forms. Then stage a debate over restricted and unrestricted use.

Software Review

Use a Liquid Crystal Display (LCD) or other computer projection system and select several pieces of educational software to review with your students. Ask them to evaluate the software's:

Usability

Is it easy to use for both student and teacher? What level of teacher involvement is necessary? Can it be used for students at more than one achievement level? Is the speed or level of difficulty adjustable?

Instructional Design

What audience is it appropriate for? What are the instructional objectives it is designed to achieve? At what level of Bloom's taxonomy does it require the student to operate? How much learner control is there? Is it interesting and motivating for the learner? How much learner interaction does it require? Can work be saved and/or recorded? Is the software designed to be entertaining or motivating for the student?

Evaluation

Does it accomplish what it claims to? Is it worth the time and expense for what it accomplishes?

You may want to select contrasting software: one "good" and one "bad" example, or one elementary and one secondary in the same subject area, or one at a low level of Bloom's taxonomy and one at a higher level.

Telecommunications

Have students use telecommunications technology to research and seek resources for an issue in teacher education or their subject field. This could be done individually but would be of more value if done in small groups. Groups of individuals should produce a two-page outline with an introductory paragraph that describes the topic or issue selected and the telecommunications resources located.

Some of the possible avenues for completing this activity include the use of the following:

Newsgroups:	Post an inquiry to an appropriate newsgroup about the issue or subject field.
Telnet:	Use an online library catalog resource to research your issue or subject field. (At least one reference should be from ERIC— Educational Research and Information Clearinghouse.)
File Transfer Protocol (FTP):	Download and incorporate an existing file into a multimedia report or presentation.
Gopher:	Search for information using a gopher site.
Browser:	Use Netscape, the Internet Explorer, or another browser to find two or three appropriate sources of information.

At this point it is important to develop the idea that technology should support the learning process and should not be the focal point around which the lesson is developed. That is not to say, however, that use of technology shouldn't change some things about how learning takes place. Telecommunications technology places a rich variety of resources in teachers' hands. This activity demonstrates a type of learning in which students are responsible for conducting their own investigations and constructing their own knowledge.

Student Assignments

The following activities are suggestions for student portfolio activities. They are a means of providing alternative assessment of students' capabilities.

Independent Reading

Read and respond to any of the selections noted on the chapter/article correlation list found in the front of this manual for Ryan/Cooper, *Kaleidoscope: Readings in Education* (Houghton Mifflin, 2001). You may want to use the Article Review Form in *Kaleidoscope*.

Reflective Papers

Choose one of the following topics to write a reflective paper (2–5 pages). The purpose of the paper is to help you assimilate new knowledge by blending it with your previous knowledge and experiences.

1.   Trace the development of one type of audio, visual, or computer technology in its use in the public schools. Include information on its purpose(s), advantages, and disadvantages, and any information regarding the documentation of the effectiveness of its use.

2.   Research the gender (or socioeconomic) differences in the use of computer technology. Include information on programs designed to remedy this inequity and give your own ideas about solutions.

3.   Read several articles. Form your own opinion about the probabilities of these predictions coming true and support them with past or present examples.

Journal Reflections

Suggestions for journal topics for students' selection:

1.   Think about your own education. At what grade level did you first encounter computers, CD-ROMs, or the Internet at school or in your classroom?

2.   If you had the opportunity to take a course or all the courses in your degree program over the Internet, would you? Why or why not?

3.   How is technology used at your field-site school? Describe equipment and software, student opportunities, and teacher abilities.

CD-ROM Video Clip

View the clips for Chapter 6 and be prepared to discuss the following reflection questions:

Clip 1:

Do you think technology will prod changes in schooling, or will education reforms determine the way technology is used in schooling? Which will lead the way? Why?

Clip 2:

1.   Can technology in the classroom impede learning? Why or why not?

2.   Assuming you could teach the same lesson or concept with equal effectiveness (in terms of students' meeting a standard) either using computers or without them, which option would you choose? Why?

3.   As a practical matter, how much do you see yourself using computers to teach higher-order thinking skills? For drill and practice? For other purposes? Explain why.

INVENTORY OF PERSONAL TECHNOLOGY SKILLS

Please complete the following inventory of your previous knowledge and experience using technology. If you are not familiar with the terminology in one of the questions, answer in the "never" column.

I own a home computer.   Yes No   Type
I frequently use a computer at work or school.   Yes No   Type
I am connected to the Internet at home.   Yes No

	Frequently	Occasionally	Never
Communication Tools			
I use e-mail.	____	____	____
I use the Internet to find information.	____	____	____
I have participated in a discussion group.	____	____	____
I know how to use hypertext to get more information when I need it.	____	____	____
I have used PowerPoint, Persuasion, or another presentation tool.	____	____	____
I use search engine(s).	____	____	____
I have taken a course online.	____	____	____
I have produced my own computer graphics.	____	____	____
Cognitive Tools			
I use word processing.	____	____	____
I use databases.	____	____	____
I use spreadsheets.	____	____	____
Instructional Tools			
I have reviewed software for use.	____	____	____
I have used tutorial software (as a student).	____	____	____
I have used a computer simulation.	____	____	____
I have used interactive multimedia (e.g.: a multimedia encyclopedia).	____	____	____
I have generated a test or worksheet using software designed for that purpose.	____	____	____
I have created multimedia presentations.	____	____	____

I am familiar with the following types of assistive technologies for students with special needs:

_____

_____

_____

CHAPTER 7

What Are the Ethical and Legal Issues Facing Teachers?

LEARNING OBJECTIVES

After studying the chapter, students will be able to

1. distinguish between ethics and the law and explain the proper province of each.

2. list, explain, and apply the six dimensions of ethical teaching, as defined by Kenneth Howe.

3. give examples of some ethical and legal problems that teachers commonly face and explain how to think about resolving them.

4. define due process, liability, assault, and battery as they relate to teaching.

5. explain in general terms the laws relating to copyright, self-defense, and religion in the classroom, lifestyle choices, and academic freedom.

6. describe the rights of students regarding due process, corporal punishment, free speech, sexual harassment, and access to their own school records.

CHAPTER OVERVIEW

Teaching is full of ethical and legal issues, and all teachers need to know how both ethics and the law play an integral part in their work. This chapter explains the difference between ethics and law, and it begins to explore the particular ethical and legal questions teachers must answer. It presents to prospective teachers ethical guidelines as they begin their career and also highlights particular laws that are germane to the classroom teacher. The purpose of this chapter, then, is to examine both the ethical and the legal aspects of teaching.

We begin with a discussion of ethics: the system of morality that people adopt to help them develop productive relationships with others in their communities. Because teachers can powerfully influence their students, trainees ought to be aware of the formal statements of ethics developed by the profession. We also recount several stories, right from the experiences of practicing teachers that illustrate the variety and intensity of ethical dilemmas.

Next we discuss the legal issues that teachers need to know for their own protection and for the protection of their students. Without attempting to cover all aspects of the law and teaching, we introduce some of the most common problems and sketch the implications of recent court decisions on: due process, tenure, liability, abuse, copyright, religious practices, freedom of speech, etc.

Our aim in this chapter is to stimulate students to think about how their own moral imperatives will mesh with the code of the profession. We want them to know something about the ways in which the law encumbers with responsibilities, protects, and restricts them.

CHAPTER OUTLINE

I.   Laws and Our Ethics
II. The Ethics of Teaching
    A.   The Characteristics of Ethical Teaching
        1.   Appreciation for Moral Deliberation
        2.   Empathy
        3.   Knowledge
        4.   Reasoning
        5.   Courage
        6.   Interpersonal Skills
    B.   Ethical Dilemmas in Teaching
        1.   Big Deal or a Little Fudge?
        2.   Righting Wrongs?
    C.   The Everyday Ethics of Teaching
    D.   Codes of Professional Ethics
        1.   Boston University Educator's Affirmation
III. The Teacher and the Law
    A.   The Teacher and Due Process
        1.   Two Types of Due Process
    B.   Contracts, Tenure, and Dismissal
        1.   Contracts to Teach
        2.   Tenure
        3.   Dismissal
        4.   Reduction in Force
    C.   The Teacher and Liability
        1.   Liability Precautions
    D.   Reporting Child Abuse
    E.   Self-Defense
        1.   Assault and Battery
    F.   Freedom of Expression
        1.   Symbolic Expression
        2.   Academic Freedom
    G.   Copyright Laws
        1.   Videotapes, Software and the Internet
    H.   Lifestyle and the Teacher
        1.   Personal Appearance: Hair, Clothes, and Weight
        2.   Private Sexual Behavior
        3.   Conduct with Students
    I.   Law, Religion, and the School
        1.   Prayer and Scripture in the School
        2.   Religious Clubs and Prayer Groups
        3.   Religion and Secular Humanism
        4.   Guidelines for Religious Neutrality
IV. Students and the Law
    A.   The Student and Due Process
    B.   Suspension and Expulsion
        1.   Major Court Cases
        2.   Pregnancy, Parenthood, and Marriage
        3.   Guidelines for Educators

    C.   Corporal Punishment
    D.   Search and Seizure
        1.   Reasonableness and Probable Cause
        2.   Drug Tests as Searches

    E.   Freedom of Speech
        1.   Students' First Amendment Rights
        2.   A Shift in Legal Direction: Restricting Student Speech
        3.   School Newspapers and Freedom of the Press
        4.   Implications of the Court Cases
    F.   Sexual Harassment
    G.   Records and the Students' Right to Privacy

SUPPLEMENTARY LECTURE AND DISCUSSION TOPICS

1. **Formal ethical codes** Discuss the terms of the NEA's Code of Ethics, the AFT Bill of Rights, and the Boston University Educator's Affirmation. Compare and contrast their contents. Describe how each came to be written.

2. **The "everyday ethics of teaching" and the everyday ethical conflicts in teaching** Discuss with students in greater detail how ethics permeates the life of the teacher. Discuss in detail some of the everyday ethics of teaching, such as taking a "mental health day" to spend a day in solitude out-of-doors. For example, is there a difference between taking a "mental health day" because a teacher needs some time to rest and "regroup" and taking a "mental health day" because it is the first day of deer-hunting season? Are ethical differences involved when teachers comment hastily on papers because they want to give immediate feedback to students or when they do so because they just want to finish grading? Teachers are human, too, so how should teachers respond if they realize that they truly delight in a particular student? How can teachers make sure they aren't "playing favorites"? What should teachers do if they just cannot get along with another teacher on their team? How can they hide the friction they feel toward certain colleagues from the students that they share? There are numerous everyday, but important, ethical aspects of a teacher's job that you may want to discuss in more detail with students.

3. **Teachers and the law** Explain the way the courts have defined teachers' rights in recent decisions. Show how certain broadly defined rights—for example, due process—come to have specific meaning in professional situations. Also discuss how particular legal issues, such as reporting suspected child abuse, have influenced the job of teaching. In addition, you can discuss the impact the Buckley Amendment has had on the role of teachers. To what extent has the Buckley Amendment created positive change? To what extent has it inhibited teachers and their autonomy?

4. **Students and the law** Explore the reasons for a change from an *in loco parentis* position to a due process orientation regarding student rights. Review court decisions that protect the rights of students.

5. **Religion, secular humanism, education, and the law** Although public schools are not allowed to establish any religion, some influential groups decry the secular humanist bias they see in textbooks, teaching materials, and classroom procedures. Explain to students what secular humanism is and show some instances of texts in which a secular humanist bias is said to be found. Is secular humanism a religion? Is there an anti-religion bias in public schools? Have public schools reacted too strongly against any hint of religion in their environment? Explore and consider these questions with your students.

6. **Technology and copyright laws** The advent of the information superhighway raises additional areas that teachers need to be cognizant of regarding fair use and copyright law. Discuss with students in more detail the stipulations regarding how and under what conditions teachers can use information gained from the various computer online services available.

STUDY GUIDE – CHAPTER 7: WHAT ARE THE ETHICAL AND LEGAL ISSUES FACING TEACHERS?

Completing this study guide will help you prepare for the major topic areas on an exam; however, it does not cover every piece of information found in the chapter or the test questions.

1.   Explain the difference between "the law" and ethics.

2.   What are the six characteristics of ethical teaching?

3.   Define the following terms:
    a.   Due process
    b.   Tenure
    c.   Liability
    d.   Academic freedom
    e.   Corporal punishment
    f.   Probable cause
    g.   Sexual harassment

4.   What does the Buckley Amendment establish?

5.   How do a school administrator's search and seizure rights differ from those of a law enforcement officer?

6.   What guidelines would you give to a new teacher based on recent Supreme Court rulings on teachers' rights regarding personal appearance, right to free speech, and personal sexual behavior?

7.   What are a licensed teacher's responsibilities regarding the reporting of child abuse?

8.   Briefly summarize copyright provisions for print, video, and software resources.

9. Describe the three guidelines teachers should keep in mind when dealing with student behavior that might lead to suspension or expulsion.

10. Describe three or four basic guidelines for the interface between religion and education.

11. Give examples of how students' rights may be abridged by their status as students.

ADDITIONAL RESOURCES FOR INSTRUCTORS

Edwards, Jane. *Opposing Censorship in the Public Schools: Religion, Morality, and Literature*, Mahwah, NJ: Erlbaum Associates, 1998. This book not only summarizes a number of the debates surrounding censorship, but also reports on several of the controversies related to specific works of recent literature.

Fischer, Louis, David Schimmel, and Cynthia Kelly. *Teachers and the Law.* 5th ed. New York: Longman, 1999. This book, written by scholars who are lawyers and professors of education, bridges the worlds of the courts and the classroom with great detail and clarity.

LaMorte, Michael W. *School Law: Cases and Concepts.* 6th ed. Boston: Allyn and Bacon, 1999. This current text covers both key legal opinions and dissenting opinions, and adds valuable commentary and explanation.

Mills, Cheryl D. "Important Education-Related U.S. Supreme Court Decisions." In *Challenges and Achievements of American Education.* Edited by Gordon Cawalti. Association for Supervision and Curriculum Development, Alexandria, Va. (1993): 187–191. This brief article summarizes changes in school law.

Simpson, Carol. "Copyright 101," *Educational Leadership* (59) 4 (Jan. 2002): 36-39. This article explains when educators can claim "fair use" and when they are violating the law.

Strike, Kenneth, and Jonas Soltis. *The Ethics of Teaching.* New York: Teachers College Press, 1998. This short book gives an illuminating discussion of practical ethics and is filled with illustrations of the types of moral problems classroom teachers regularly encounter.

Strike, Kenneth, and P. Lance Ternasky (eds.). *Ethics for Professionals in Education: Perspectives for Preparation and Practice.* New York: Teachers College Press, 1993. This volume is particularly practical for use with prospective teachers.

Taylor, James and Richard Baker Jr., "Discipline and the Special Education Student," *Educational Leadership* (59) 4 (Jan. 2002): 28-29. Article includes suggestions for creating discipline policies that apply to all students.

Zirkel, Perry Alan, and Sharon Nalbone Richardson. *A Digest of Supreme Court Decisions Affecting Education.* Bloomington, IN: Phi Delta Kappa Press, 1993. Zirkel, who also has an educational law column in the educational journal *PDK*, and Richardson present a concise, highly readable digest of the court cases that have affected education. A useful reference for teachers.

Zirkel, Perry A., "Decisions That Have Shaped U.S. Education," *Educational Leadership* (59) 4 (Jan. 2002): 6–12. This article reviews some of the most significant recent legal rulings.

Media Resources

Censorship or Selection: Choosing Books for Public Schools (PBS video, 60 min., 1982). This video still has currency. It describes the censorship controversies that have erupted in America's public schools. Who should determine what goes on the shelves of libraries and in the textbooks of public schools? Learn the complex issues with this recorded-live debate among authors, librarians, educators, and legal experts. Panelists include Kurt Vonnegut, Judy Blume, Judith Krug from the American Library Association, and the Moral Majority vice president, Ronald Godwin.

Child Abuse: It Shouldn't Hurt to Be a Kid (Insight Media, 27 min., 1985). Educators, school personnel, and day care providers are required by law to report suspected child abuse. This video advises these mandated reporters of these legal responsibilities. It defines child abuse, teaches how to recognize it, and explains where to report suspected abuse.

Classrooms, Courtrooms, and Common Sense (Insight Media, 3 parts, 30 min. each, 1991). This series on administrative liability helps teachers understand the legal implications of their actions. An attorney who has defended educators explains school law using on-site simulations.

Copyright Law (Insight Media, 90 min., 1998). This video provides information about copyright law as it applies in applies in educational and library settings. It discusses photocopying, the use of videotape, computer software, and information obtained from online sources as well as methods for obtaining permission to use copyright-protected work.

How to Tell If a Child Is Being Abused (Insight Media, 15 min., 1988), This video examines the four major types of child abuse: neglect, physical, emotional, and sexual.

Professional Ethics: A Guide for Educators (Insight Media, 22 min., 1990). Explains that legal behavior is not necessarily ethical behavior. Describes sensitive situations and how to make ethical choices.

The Scopes Monkey Trial (Insight Media, 52 min., 1998). This video presents the landmark 1925 trial in which John Scopes, a young biology teacher, was charged with teaching evolution in his classroom—an act prohibited by law in the state of Tennessee.

Student Rights (Insight Media, 23 min., 1997). This primer on student rights explores how first and Fourth Amendment rights relate to schools. It examines such issues as freedom of expression, school prayer, dress codes, and drug testing.

Toward an Ethical Learning Community (Insight Media, 35 min., 1994). This video considers the importance of regarding relationships with students as essential elements in the creation of an effective learning environment. Faculty and students discuss ethical teaching.

Media distributor contact information is available in Appendix I.

Student Activities

School Observation—Who Is Being Tested?

You have enjoyed assisting a good teacher. Now, though, you are concerned. She is unexpectedly ill today, the day of her freshman algebra class's midterm exam. You like these students and know that most of them have worked hard, but now they are struggling with and being stumped by these test questions, some of which the teacher let you write. You were so sure they were going to be too easy for most of the class. To your surprise, the students who have coasted all year appear to be gliding right through the exam as if it were so much whipped cream. In the midst of your musing, you glance across the room and see Floyd stuffing what looks like a crib sheet up his sleeve. He has been trouble all semester. You are certain he copied 90 percent of his homework assignments on the bus; he was mouthy and disruptive in class; and you are fairly sure he cheated on two of the other major tests. Now, finally, you've got the drop on him. But as you move quickly across the room toward Floyd, you see that Judith is copying formulas from a ribbon-like spool of paper. You cannot believe it! Judith is your favorite student, and she recently was elected secretary of next year's sophomore class. She is a very conscientious, diligent girl who gets good grades, but not out of natural brilliance. She gets them the old-fashioned way—through hard work. She has very high standards and puts a good deal of pressure on herself. Although you cannot imagine what has led her to cheat today, you suspect that the pressure for good grades she puts on herself is the root cause. You stand in the middle of the room, trying to decide what to do.

On the basis of these observations, how would you answer these questions?

a.   What are you going to do about Floyd? What are you going to say to him?

b.   What are you going to do about Judith? What are you going to say to her?

c.   Is there any difference between how you have responded to these two students? Why? Or why not?

d.   Do you believe that teachers who give overly difficult tests bear some responsibility for students' cheating? Again, why or why not?

Legal Issues and Teaching

Select one area of legal decisions in education, such as free speech, or a current event with educational/legal ramifications and research it in more depth. What were the underlying conditions that gave rise to this particular legal issue? If you are researching a topic such as free speech, explore how the courts' decisions have developed over time. What has the impact of these legal rulings been upon education? What are the ramifications for future educational practice regarding some of the more recent court cases? Students may present their work either as a paper or as a presentation to the entire class.

Tenure

Review the provisions for tenure in local districts. Then assign students to a "pro" team and a "con" team to argue the merits of having tenure. Give each team time to pull together arguments for its position. Assemble a panel of judges, using students. Have each team make an opening statement and then debate the issue. Announce a winner on the basis of logical argument.

Legal Case Studies

Ask students in groups or individually to consider one or more of the following case studies to demonstrate their ability to recognize the applicable law(s) and plan their actions. For each case the students should:

- identify the applicable law(s)
- describe the teacher's and/or student's rights and/or responsibilities
- describe a legal course of action for their classroom
- identify ways the situation could be avoided in the future

(Several probe questions are also included with each case.)

Law Case Study 1

Your school has had significant gang problems over the last few years. Last semester alone, there were five students who were expelled for bringing guns to school. There were physical fights between different gangs on school grounds. One gang member was arrested for dealing drugs out of her school locker.

In response to the gang problems on campus, the School Board has prohibited students from wearing or bringing gang symbols, clothes, and colors to school. If a student violates this prohibition, he or she is immediately suspended from school and is subject to further and more severe discipline.

Four months after the School Board's ban goes into effect, a new student transfers into your school. The student and his family have just moved to the United States from Israel. On the student's first day in your class, he proudly displays his Star of David necklace. When the principal sees the necklace, she wants to suspend the student immediately.

What legal issues do you need to consider?

Is there a way to avoid this situation?

What should you do as the classroom teacher?

Law Case Study 2

You are the faculty advisor for the student run newspaper at your high school. The end-of-the-year issue of the paper includes articles on drug addiction and drug treatment programs. The authors of the articles put a semester's worth of work into them. The articles are well researched and factually accurate. They include interviews and advice from doctors, nurses, and counselors. The articles also include anonymous interviews with other students at the school who are taking drugs now or who have taken drugs in the past.

Just before the newspaper is distributed throughout the school, your principal reviews it. She does not like the articles on drug addiction, especially the interviews. She threatens to forbid distribution of the newspaper unless these articles are removed.

What legal precedents should you consider?

As the sponsor what should you do?

Is there a way to avoid this problem?

Law Case Study 3

A boy in your sixth grade class was just elected class president. During his acceptance speech, he said, among other things, "I am a person who is firm . . . firm in character and firm in my clothing . . . I will go to the very end, even the climax, for each and every one of you." When students (both boys and girls) in your class heard this, some giggled, some just sat still and some paid no attention.

Which law(s) should you consult to decide what your responsibility is in this situation?

What are the consequences teachers face if they ignore these statements?

Law Case Study 4

Sandi's parents have been divorced since she was five years old. She is now seven. She lives with her mother and visits her father every other weekend. He brings her to school on Monday mornings following his weekend visitations. Last year, Sandi was diagnosed with diabetes. She is required to stick to a very strict diet. You noticed that on Mondays following her weekend visits with her father, Sandi is hungry, tired, and unable to concentrate and has even passed out at her desk. Upon talking to Sandi, you learn that when she is with her father, he feeds her all kinds of food, like candy and soda pop, which is not on her diabetic diet.

What is the teacher's responsibility in this situation?

What are the consequences to the teacher for not acting appropriately?

Law Case Study 5

You have just completed a summer school course on using poetry in the classroom. You are really excited about what you have learned and want to incorporate it into your classes. You decide that instead of using your usual textbooks, you will download poems off of the Internet, copy poems from various books and magazines, and put them into a packet for your students to read and study. Your colleagues see the packet and ask if they can make copies as well. You all decide to make this a regular unit and use the packet every year.

What law(s) do you need to consider when doing this?

What guidelines do you need to follow?

Law Case Study 6

A family who has a child with severe communication and mobility disabilities from cerebral palsy moves into your attendance area. When her parents come to school to enroll their child the principal explains to them that the school does not have adequate adaptive equipment or teacher aid resources to meet their child's needs and suggests that they check out the private special education schools in the area.

Which law(s) address this situation?

What should your school do?

Law Case Study 7

The principal at your school decides to retire and several well-qualified teachers on the staff apply for the position. Mr. England has been teaching for four years and has his administrator's license. Mrs. Boyer has taught for eight years, has her administrator's license, and has been the area coordinator for her grade level. When Mr. England is appointed, Mrs. Boyer asks for an explanation and is told that the committee felt that Mr. England would have more time to do the job and that it was a tough job dealing with irate parents, etc.

Which law addresses this situation?

What options does Mrs. Boyer have?

Law Case Study 8

For many years the composition of your community has been very homogeneous, Christian and conservative, but in recent years more and more families of different faiths and beliefs have been moving to your attendance area. One of your students brings in a children's Bible storybook for show and tell and begins to retell some of the stories.

How do you respond?

What laws do you need to be aware of?

Law Case Study 9

Recently students at your elementary school have been caught with forbidden weapons (knives, brass knuckles, and num-chuks) on school property. The school has a zero tolerance policy and expels any student found with an item that could be used as a weapon and is not appropriate to have in school. To address this problem, faculty decide to conduct a surprise backpack and desk check where every student will be required to dump the contents of their desk and backpack on the floor in the presence of the teacher who will do the inspection.

What laws should you consult to conduct this search legally?

What other responses might accomplish the same purpose?

Ethical Deliberation

Kenneth Howe discusses how teachers must have the capacity for moral deliberation. Have your students consider the following scenarios to help them enhance their ability for ethical deliberation. Divide the students into small groups of no more than five. Have each group do the following:

- Define the problem

- List the relevant moral or legal imperatives

- Brainstorm a few solutions

- Determine the pros and cons of each proposed solution.

Resolving ethical dilemmas involves applying three time-tested principles for deciding ethical dilemmas: *ends-based, rule-based,* and *care-based.*

Ends-based thinking is best captured in the phrase: "Do whatever provides the greatest good for the greatest number."

Rule-based thinking asks, "If everyone in the world were to do what I am about to do—to follow the rule that I am about to follow—is that the kind of world I would want to live in?" Rule-based thinking is opposed to ends-based thinking. It challenges the idea that we can ever really know what the consequences of our actions will be. Instead, the rule-based thinker says, we must always stick to our principles and let the chips fall where they may.

Care-based thinking commands that we do to others what we would want others to do to us, most commonly known as the Golden Rule.

An ethical dilemma is a conflict between two right courses of action. Ethical dilemmas tend to fall into four different patterns or paradigms.

a.   Individual vs. Community. The needs of the self or the small group are pitted against the claims of the larger society.

b.   Truth vs. Loyalty. Personal honesty or integrity is at odds with responsibility and promise keeping.

c.   Short-term vs. Long-term. Real and important requirements of the present come up against foresight, stewardship, and deferred gratification.

d.   Justice vs. Mercy. Fairness, expectations, and an equal application of the rules are opposed to empathy, compassion, and a desire to make exceptions.

Have the groups try to reach a consensus on one solution. Ask each group to present its findings to the class. Compare strategies used by each group. Students should identify which of the three principles for deciding ethical dilemmas is most applicable to their case and which of the four patterns above provides the most insight.

Ethics Case 1: To Strike or Not to Strike

You are a tenured, first-grade teacher who has been teaching in an urban area for five years. You, like many of the other teachers, are frustrated and angry at the city's and the school board's treatment of teachers. You have seen oceans of the taxpayers' money going toward civic projects (a domed athletic stadium, a newly renovated city hall and downtown area), while teachers' salaries and the conditions in the schools have deteriorated. Like your colleagues, you are desperate to get the attention of the citizens, so you support your professional association's decision to strike.

The teachers walked out three days ago, and gradually you are realizing that the real losers in this strike are your twenty-eight first-graders, most of who come from disorganized, poverty-ridden homes. Whereas many children in other parts of the city, and especially older children, can probably afford to lose the time in school, you believe yours cannot. They are at a critical point in their basic skills development. Also, they have just learned to settle down and really become engaged in their work. You are sure that prolonging the strike will mean disaster for the students. Then, on the strike's fourth day, several of your students' parents approach you, saying that they have secured a church basement and, if you will only come and teach, classes can go on there. However, such action might undermine the strike and would appear to be a betrayal of your coworkers. What do you do?

Ethics Case 2: Pressure to Perform

You are a fourth-grade teacher in a suburban elementary school, which caters to the children of a largely professional population. Most parents are quite interested in the school's keeping to high academic standards and expect good performance from their children. It is late in the school year, and the parents of a third-grade boy named Derek have approached you. They would like you to tutor their son for the rest of the spring and possibly during the summer. You tell the parents that you would like to think it over for a week. Since Derek's current third-grade teacher is a close friend, you speak to her.

She seems to know Derek well, and a picture emerges of a pleasant, cooperative, and hard-working boy who is performing right up to his capacities. He is a slow reader, has trouble with abstractions, and experiences difficulty with instructions when they become at all complex. His second-grade teacher says basically the same things. The school psychologist tells you that Derek's performance and these difficulties are confirmed in his test data. Everyone who knows Derek says that if there is a problem, it is the unrealistic expectations of his rather intense parents. One is a lawyer and the other is an accountant. They are convinced that Derek is performing at "C level," as they call it, simply because he is being lazy and not applying himself. They dismiss the psychologist's views as "just so much silly psychobabble" and claim that Derek simply needs to be given more work to do and to be held to higher standards. Further, they feel that if Derek doesn't "catch fire" soon, he will get accustomed to mediocrity and will lose all chance of attending a good college. They have not asked you for your opinion, but you support the professionals: Derek is working well up to his capacities.

Derek's parents want you to tutor him after school two days a week and for five hours on Saturday. They have offered you $250 a week to do so. You have the time, and the money would mean that you could buy a dependable car to replace the clunker you currently drive. You also are aware that if you do not accept the assignment, there are several other teachers who will, teachers who are not as skilled and conscientious as you are. What is the right thing to do?

Ethics Case 3: The Games Children Play

Four months ago you began your first year of teaching in a fairly rural part of the state. The community is spread out, but the people are closely knit, which you soon discover has pluses and minuses. Newcomers like you are noticed by all and welcomed by most. As the new fifth-grade teacher in a strange community, you were naturally sympathetic to Denise, a shy young girl who transferred in from out of state a few weeks after the school year started. After the students' initial curiosity wore off, they left Denise to herself. At lunch and on the playground, she was always alone, and, from her appearance, she was not happy about it. You made efforts to weave her into different cliques of girls, but nothing seemed "to take." Twice you tried to speak to her about it privately, but the first time she clammed right up, and the second time she cried and fled the room. Not sure what to do, you had this problem on the back burner and were watching it when things began to boil.

First, Denise started missing a good deal of school, and she apparently was not sick. Then, for no visible reason, she would sometimes burst into tears or turn and yell at her classmates, "Leave me alone!" Some students seemed surprised; others laughed at her.

Yesterday as school was letting out, Denise came up to you with a reproachful look on her face and said, "I found my gloves," and showed you what seemed to be new gloves with the fingers cut off. You called her mother last night, and she said that Denise is convinced all the kids hate her and are trying to punish her for something.

You think the apparent hazing is the work of a very popular, strong-minded girl with whom you have had your own struggles of will this year. The girl is a natural leader, as is her mother, the president of the Parent-Teachers Association. The mother has let you know in half a dozen ways that she is not thrilled with her child having "an inexperienced teacher."

Now, you have finally decided that you are going to send Denise to the library and talk to the entire class about whatever is going on. However, when the children come back from lunch and begin to take out their books, you first hear Denise gasp and then see her staring wide-eyed into her desk. After a moment, she lets out a terrifying scream. You rush over and discover the cause. In her desk is a large paper bag inside of which is a dead rat caught in a trap. There is also a note saying, "You're next!!!" You recognize the handwriting as belonging to your chief suspect who, when you glance her way, is looking very pleased with herself. What should you do?

Ethics Case 4: Academic Moonlighting

You are just beginning your third year of teaching in a school district you like a great deal. Your first two years of teaching were hectic but by and large successful. Your principal has recently asked you to move from the fifth grade, where you were comfortable, to the third grade, where you are not. However, he has confidence in you, and you are coming up for tenure at the end of this year. You are also working toward a master's degree in education at the state university, and you need to take a course this semester. If you get three more graduate credits during this fall semester and three next semester, you will not only be closer to the degree but will also have a total of fifteen credits, automatically moving you up $900 on the district's salary scale.

The only graduate course open to you this semester is a very demanding and time-consuming educational statistics course, about which you have heard nothing but bad news. You have to take the course sometime, but this semester could not be worse. You know very little about the third-grade curriculum or, for that matter, about third-graders. You think that even without the course, you will be scrambling to prepare and stay a jump ahead of the children. You are sure you can bluff your way through, but you are worried about shortchanging the students. Still, the course is part of your graduate requirements. What do you do?

Ethics Case 5: For the Good of the Team

You teach in a city in which many of the students drop out of school, and the only type of job they are qualified for is unskilled work. The city also struggles to keep its youth off the streets and out of criminal activity. You are a history teacher in senior high, and most of your students are seniors. One student you particularly admire is Bruce. One of four children, he was raised by his mother. His father left when he was eight, and Bruce has been treated like the "man of the family" ever since. You think he has borne his responsibility admirably. He is a kind and mature young man.

Bruce is also a star athlete. In fact, as captain of the football team and as quarterback, he led his team to the state championship, the most positive news for the high school in twenty years. Bruce's coach has told you that college scouts are quite interested in Bruce, and that all he needs to do is graduate from high school with a C average and he will be admitted to any one of the major universities that have nationally ranked athletic programs. Bruce could be heading for a professional football career.

As much as you admire Bruce, he never has been a strong student. He is courteous in class, participates in discussions frequently, but his writing and test-taking ability are weak. He has not been identified as having any learning disabilities. You have worked with him individually after class several times, and his improvement has been slight. In your class, he has been running a C-minus average, and U.S. history is a requirement for graduation. You have figured that he needs a least a C-plus to earn a C for the year.

When you correct Bruce's exam, you see he earned a 68, which is a D. Both the coach and Bruce have said they will stop by later in the day to find out his grade. You check over his exam twice to see if you made any mistakes in correcting. You didn't. Then you consider curving the exam, even though the grades seem to be evenly distributed. When Bruce and the coach arrive, what will you do?

Ethics Case 6: Social Promotion

You are a first-year teacher in a poor, urban public middle school. Some of your students, despite all your hard work, have remained beyond your reach. Consequently, a number of your eighth-graders still cannot read near grade level and have mastered only the most elementary computing skills. You and several other eighth-grade teachers are reviewing the students' files to see who will be promoted to ninth grade. During the middle of the meeting, the principal enters. His agenda, you learned quite early, is far different from yours. Central office judges his performance not on the students' real academic achievement but on the percentage of students promoted and on the number of student suspensions and expulsions. His goal is to keep students quiet and out of trouble. He listens to the teachers' recommendations for a moment without comment and then interrupts.

"Look," he says bluntly. "I would strongly encourage you to promote your students if they have met state attendance requirements." He continues on for several minutes, talking about how important it is for the eighth-graders to feel successful and to go to the high school.

You look at him dumbfounded. Essentially, he's telling you to pass all of your students, whether they are literate or not. What will you do?

Ethics Case 7: Sex Education

You have taught for several years in Greenpond, a small rural town, and have developed a good rapport with most of your students, especially those students who seem to need a caring adult in their lives. One such student is Jessye. At thirteen, she is already sexually mature and looks to be nineteen to twenty, rather than just beginning her teen years.

Several months into the school year, Jessye lingers in your room after school. Without speaking, she starts to help you straighten the room, and after you finish, you sit down to share some cookies for a snack. You let Jessye speak. It's just small talk at first; then she tells you details about her family life. Then she says she wants to know what form of contraception you use.

You look at her and say nothing for a moment. Jessye continues unselfconsciously: "I figured you're about my mom's age, and you don't have any kids. So either there's something wrong with you or you do something so you don't have kids."

You ask Jessye why she is so curious, and she tells you that she has slept with "four or five guys," and she has just started going out with Pete, an eighteen-year-old who graduated last year. She hasn't "gotten caught" so far, but she's "not dumb." "I figure sooner or later, I'll get pregnant, but I'd rather it come later," she tells you with a chuckle.

You mention to Jessye that she should talk to her mom about her questions, but Jessye looks at you and snorts, "Are you kidding? She's never around, and she said she'd kick me out if she found out I was doing anything." What should you do?

Note to Instructors: Two additional cases are included in Chapter 7 of the text.

The following more detailed, extensively developed case studies in Appendix II are appropriate for use with this chapter.

Leigh Scott

Erica Kaiser

Karen Washington

Student Assignments

The following activities are suggestions for student portfolio activities. They are a means of providing alternative assessment of the students' capabilities.

Independent Reading

Read and respond to any of the following selections noted on the chapter/article correlation list found in the front of this manual for Ryan/Cooper, *Kaleidoscope: Readings in Education* (Houghton Mifflin, 2004). You may want to use the Article Review Form in *Kaleidoscope*.

Reflective Papers

Choose one of the following topics to write a reflective paper (2–5 pages). The purpose of the paper is to help you assimilate new knowledge by blending it with your previous knowledge and experiences.

1. Consider the information that has been presented in Chapter 12 concerning the ethics of teaching. What are some of the ethical imperatives that you see as vital in teaching and in being a teacher?

2. What experiences have you had—either as a student or as an observer in schools—that especially underscored the ethical dimensions of teaching?

3. Select several of the legal rulings presented in the chapter. Explain how they would apply in your work as a teacher. You may wish, instead, to discuss how they apply to the field-site school in which you are observing.

Journal Reflections

Suggestions for journal topics for students' selection:

1. What do you think will be one of the toughest ethical challenges for you as a professional and why?

2. Do you think recent interpretation of the law has infringed on the teacher's civil rights? Why or why not?

3. Do you think the laws regarding discipline in schools have made classroom management easier or harder? Why?

CHAPTER 8

What Are the Philosophical Foundations of American Education?

LEARNING OBJECTIVES

After studying this chapter, students will be able to

1. describe the role of philosophical knowledge in clarifying questions of educational decision making in policy and practice.

2. explain how the four branches of philosophy—metaphysics, epistemology, logic, and axiology—relate to the work of the teacher.

3. describe and distinguish among four philosophies of education—perennialism, progressivism, essentialism, and existentialism—and explain the implications of each for schooling.

4. explain how psychological theories especially constructivism have influenced practices in modern education.

5. identify the key contributions of John Dewey to U.S. education.

6. apply the information they have learned about educational philosophy to analyze existing school curricula.

7. begin to formulate and articulate their personal philosophy.

CHAPTER OVERVIEW

Chapter 8 introduces prospective teachers to the four major branches of philosophy—metaphysics, epistemology, logic, and axiology—and demonstrates how those branches apply to education. It also provides examples of how each branch of philosophy affects decisions about education. When a faculty decides, for example, what constitutes knowledge, their goals in educating students, the content of their curriculum, or the methods their teachers will use, they are making educational decisions rooted in philosophy. The chapter presents the various implications philosophy has for education and invites readers to apply this information to their own lives as prospective teachers.

The chapter also traces the development of four major philosophies of education: perennialism, progressivism, essentialism, and existentialism. The chapter highlights the similarities and differences in each of these schools of philosophy and demonstrates how each philosophy would be manifested in schools. The chapter also includes an overview of the work and philosophy of John Dewey as it relates to U.S. education.

Perennialism. Perennialism views human nature as constant over time, asserting that people's rationality sets them apart from animals. Applied to education, perennialists maintain that the development of the intellect is the sole purpose of schooling. Perennialists believe that the best way to develop one's intellect is through rigorously studying the enduring truths of humankind contained in the classics of Western culture.

Essentialism. Essentialism views the mind as the central element of reality and holds that knowing requires the ability to observe and measure the physical world accurately. Essentialists claim that there is a core body of knowledge, including both classical and contemporary disciplines, that all people need to have in order to function productively in society, and that the overwhelming majority of students can learn this core. In essentialism, the worth of any knowledge is measured by how much an individual needs that knowledge to become a productive member of society.

Romanticism. Romanticism views reality as stable and asserts that the meaning of life is derived primarily through self development uncontaminated by society. Values are determined by the individual and knowledge is gained through sensory experiences with the environment. Romantics believe that education is a natural process that grows out of children's innate curiosity. Teachers are to respond to children's questions, not impose the learning of subjects the child has no interest in. The approaches to learning are individualized and self directed.

Progressivism. Progressivism views nature as being ever-changing, so knowledge must be continually redefined and rediscovered. Progressive education views learners as problem solvers who naturally develop by exploring questions of interest to them. Progressives contend that no knowledge is privileged over another and that the knowledge of most value is the knowledge that the learner wants to know.

*Romanticism shares a lot of values with the existentialist philosophy in previous editions.

CHAPTER OUTLINE

Our philosophy of education (values and goals) influences the decisions we make regarding education whether we are teachers, parents, students, or legislators.

I.   What is Philosophy?
    A.   Fundamental Questions of Existence
    B.   Sources of Our Philosophy
    C.   The Philosopher's Method and Language
II.   The Terrain of Philosophy
    A.   Metaphysics
        1.   Metaphysics and the Curriculum
    B.   Epistemology
        1.   Teaching and Ways of Knowing
    C.   Axiology
        1.   Ethics and Aesthetics
    D.   Logic
        1.   Deductive Reasoning
        2.   Inductive Reasoning
III. Schools of Educational Philosophy
    A.   Perennialism
        1.   Perennialism in the School
        2.   The Paideaia Proposal
        3.   Education as Preparation for Life
        4.   Personal Point of View: A Perennialist Teacher
    B.   Essentialism
        1.   The Roots of Essentialism
        2.   Essentialist Goals and Practices
        3.   Personal Point of View: An Essentialist Teacher
    C.   Romanticism
        1.   The Education of Emile
        2.   Implications for Education
        3.   Personal Point of View: A Romantic Teacher
    D.   Progressivism
        1.   Progressive Education
        2.   The School as a Training Ground for Democracy
        3.   Personal Point of View: A Progressive Educator
IV.   The Influence of Psychological Theories

    A.   Behaviorism: Conditioning Students or Setting Them Free?
    B.   Cognitive Psychology: Students as Makers of Meaning?
        1.   Implications of Constructivism for Teachers
V.   Your Philosophy of Education
    A.   Eclecticism: Not an Excuse for Sloppy Thinking
    B.   Philosophy and the Liberal Education

SUPPLEMENTARY LECTURE AND DISCUSSION TOPICS

1.   **Philosophy of education in other countries** The text mentions that essentialism and progressivism are two educational philosophies that are distinctly American. They also have had considerable influence on the U.S. educational system. How do those philosophies compare with other countries' philosophies of education around the world? Describe and explain the educational philosophies of countries such as France, Korea, Kenya, or Brazil. What are they? What are the philosophical assumptions about the role of the teacher? The learner? The curriculum? If you have students in your class from other countries, you can invite them to participate in the lecture.

2.   **Current issues in education and their philosophical roots** Often even the best-informed students fail to look behind educational controversies or ideas to see their philosophical origins or bases. Particular terms used in education—such as *diversity, equity, PC (politically correct), core curriculum, excellence, back-to-basics, outcomes-based education, authentic assessment, inclusion,* and *effective schools*—have philosophical as well as political roots. Choose a few of the current educational terms and analyze them in terms of the implicit educational philosophy they reflect.

3.   **Schools choose eclecticism** The text mentions that many teachers are eclectic in their philosophy of education. Many schools are, too, for a variety of reasons. Some consciously choose elements of different philosophies; others demonstrate various philosophies in their educational practice because they have never clearly identified their own philosophy of education. Still others are eclectic because it is far too difficult to adhere completely to one philosophy. For example, most schools would find it quite difficult to implement a wholly existentialist philosophy of education. Explain and describe the forces that may result in an eclectic philosophy of education for a school, and explain its ramifications.

4.   **Multiculturalism and educational philosophy** Examine the philosophical underpinnings of the various manifestations of multicultural education. Present the various associated educational schools of thought, such as global education, Afrocentrism, and ethnic studies, and describe the distinctions among them. In multicultural education, what are the core issues? What is the core concept of knowledge, and how do various people learn it? What significance do the terms *knowledge* and *curriculum* have for those engaged in multicultural education? To what degree is multicultural education complementary to the educational philosophies discussed in this chapter?

STUDY GUIDE – CHAPTER 8: WHAT ARE THE PHILOSOPHICAL FOUNDATIONS OF AMERICAN EDUCATION?

Completing this study guide will help you prepare for the major topic areas on an exam; however, it does not cover every piece of information found in the chapter or the test questions.

1.   Define the word *philosophy*.

2.   List and define the four branches of philosophical study.

3.   Compare and contrast inductive and deductive reasoning.

4.   List and describe the characteristics of the four educational philosophies. Be able to recognize examples of each (goals, methods, teacher role, student role, key ideas, etc.).

5.   Describe the fields of aesthetics and ethics.

6.   Who is John Dewey, and with which educational philosophy is he most closely associated?

7.   Describe how behaviorism and cognitive psychology have influenced educational practice.

8.   What is an eclectic philosophy, and what are the hazards associated with it?

ADDITIONAL RESOURCES FOR INSTRUCTORS

Adler, Mortimer. "The Paideia Proposal: Rediscovering the Essence of Education." *The American School Board Journal* 169 (July 1982): 17–20. This article summarizes Adler's *The Paideia Proposal, An Educational Manifesto* (New York: Macmillan, 1982), which is a reformulation of perennialism.

Ayers, William. "Rethinking the Profession of Teaching: A Progressive Option." *Action in Teacher Education* 12 (Spring 1990): 1–5. This article discusses Dewey's concept of progressive education and states the experientialist assumptions that characterize progressive education as a guide in the movement toward teacher professionalism.

Bloom, Allan. *The Closing of the American Mind: How Higher Education Has Failed Democracy and Impoverished the Souls of Today's Students.* New York: Simon and Schuster, 1987. A trenchant intellectual attack on what the author sees as the collapse of the liberal arts tradition in U.S. higher education.

Broudy, Harry S. *The Uses of Schooling.* New York: Routledge, 1988. Well-known educational philosopher Harry S. Broudy argues that schools should provide only a general, or liberal arts, education. He defines the types of knowledge that he thinks constitute a general education.

Gutek, Gerald L. *Historical and Philosophical Foundations of Education: A Biographical Introduction.* 2nd ed. Upper Saddle River, NJ: Prentice-Hall/Merrill, 1997. This textbook is a comprehensive and up-to-date account of the competing schools of educational philosophy and their application to schooling. Gutek provides thumbnail sketches of key figures and leads the reader in investigating their thought.

Holtz, Harvey (ed.). *Education and the American Dream: Conservatives, Liberals, and Radicals Debate the Future of Education.* Granby, MA: Bergin and Garvey, 1989. This volume contains essays written from differing perspectives regarding the goals and future of education.

Knock, Gary H. "Our Philosophical Heritage: Significant Influences on Professional Practice and Preparation." *NASPA Journal* 27 (Winter 1989): 116–22. The article examines the influence on student affairs of four philosophical perspectives: rationalism, neohumanism, pragmatism, and existentialism.

Noddings, Nel. *Philosophy of Education.* New York: HarperCollins, 1995. This book is a brief, clear review of the basics in educational philosophy. It would be especially helpful for instructors who don't have a strong background in this topic.

Peddiwell, J. Abner. *The Sabertooth Curriculum.* New York: McGraw-Hill, 1939. Peddiwell was the pseudonym of Harold Benjamin who wrote this caveman parody of philosophical influence in education.

Postman, Neil. *The End of Education.* New York: Alfred Knopf, 1995. Postman describes the influential narratives in education—past, present (misguided), and proposed narratives—as guidelines for the future.

Media Resources

A Teacher's Story includes 1. *The Butterflies of Zagorsk,* 2. *Out of the Wilderness,* 3. *Socrates for Six Year Olds* (Films for the Humanities and Sciences, 30 min., 1993). In so many lives, a great teacher makes all the difference. Under the guidance of a patient teacher, a frightened child begins to open up; an abused girl learns to trust; a boy written off as unteachable takes the first steps toward learning. These are the triumphs that make teaching special.

The Americans (Insight Media, 21 min., 1988). This video discusses Noah Webster's work to improve American education, foster patriotism, and promote American literature and uniformity of speech. It explores the influence of Horace Mann's belief that a just society must educate all of its citizens, covers the contributions of Henry Barnard's *American Journal of Education,* and examines Robert Owen's emphasis on character formation and early childhood education.

The Critics (Insight Media, 25 min., 1988). Maria Montessori, John B. Watson, Margaret Naumburg, and W. E. B. Du Bois are the subjects of this video, which discusses critiques of educational orthodoxy.

Cultural Illiteracy (Films for the Humanities and Sciences, 28 min., 1987). Cultural illiteracy among today's teenagers threatens the very fabric of society, according to Professor E. D. Hirsch, Jr., author of *Cultural Literacy.* Hirsch and moderator Robert MacNeil are joined by poet Maya Angelou; Patrick Welsh, a teacher; and Dr. Robert Coles.

The End of Education (Into the Classroom video, 50 min., 1996). A presentation of Neil Postman's analysis of the narratives that have guided educational philosophy in the United States. It covers the past, the present, and proposals for the future. An ideal demonstration of philosophical thought in education.

John Dewey: An Introduction to His Life and Work (Insight Media, 40 min., 2001). This video examines John Dewey's life and philosophy, and considers his critical studies of education and the implications of democracy for individuals and communities.

Perennial Philosophy: The Themes That Bind Us Together (Hartley Film Foundation, 30 min., 1985). The film maintains that the world's great spiritual traditions are strikingly similar. It uses dance, music, and poetry to illustrate the common core of perennial philosophy.

The Progressives (Insight Media, 24 min., 1988). This program explores the lives and views of four key figures in progressive educational theory: G. Stanley Hall, Francis W. Parker, John Dewey, and Ella Flagg Young.

The Sudbury Way (CBS Video, 20 min., 2001). A 60 Minutes segment that is an excellent example of a K-12 private school organized around the romantic philosophy,

Summerhill at 70 (Films for the Humanities and Sciences, 52 min., 1994). Summerhill, the first and last bastion of totally permissive, anti-authoritarian education, has been going strong for over seven decades. This video shows how Summerhill children, left entirely to their own devices, behave. A fascinatingly close look at an educational community that appears constantly on the edge of anarchy and at the method underlying the apparent chaos.

Too Good to Be True (CBS video, 20 min., 1995). A *60 Minutes* segment that revisits Chicago educator Marva Collins and her students. Excellent example of a perennialist philosophy at the elementary level.

Transformation (Insight Media, 25 min., 1995). Designed to help teachers develop a personal philosophy of education, this program provides an overview of the history of educational philosophy, presenting observations from Darwin, Skinner, Piaget, Parker, Dewey, and Chomsky.

Media distributor contact information is available in Appendix I.

Student Activities

School Observation—Determining a School's Philosophical Orientation

While occasionally private school educators are explicit about the philosophical orientation of their schools, public school educators rarely identify their schools as following a particular educational philosophy. The lack of a label (e.g., The Richard M. Nixon Essentialist Elementary School or the Isadora Duncan Progressive Middle School) does not mean that philosophy is absent from a school. Quite the contrary. What makes schools different is typically their ideas-in-action and the ways the schools' educators are acting on various philosophical tenets.

Therefore, on your next school visit, try to look below the surface activity of the schools to see the philosophical ideas in action. Start by concentrating on one classroom and "ask of that classroom" a number of the questions raised in this chapter:

    a.   What is most important in this classroom? The subject matter from the curriculum? Or the curiosities and interests of the children?

    b.   Is the teacher a teller, a demonstrator, a questioner, a guide, or a coinvestigator?

    c.   How is the room physically organized? For students to "receive" information from the front of the room? Or to create their own information?

    d.   Do the students work independently or in groups? What is valued—cooperation or competition?

    e.   Are the students active or passive?

Few classrooms are a philosophical open book, or completely consistent with one of the philosophies studied in this chapter. However, after careful observation and careful reflections, you will begin to see these ideas in action.

Educational Philosophy Survey

Before the students read the chapter, have them complete the short E.P.—educational philosophy test (at the end of this section of the IRM)—to discover if they have already acquired a strong affinity for one philosophy or another. Emphasize that all of the answers are "right" for one of the philosophies. Reassure students whose answers are evenly spread across philosophies that with more experience their own philosophy will develop and emerge.

School Analysis

A number of individual schools have become well known for their educational philosophy. More generally, numerous schools adopt a particular philosophy and operate on the basis of its principles. Through text or video, provide opportunities for your students to see these various types of schools. As they find out more about particular schools, as a class, analyze each school's educational philosophy and discuss the implications of this type of schooling for students. Some suggestions include Summerhill; the Boston Latin school; various Quaker schools; the Waldorf schools; Montessori schools, the Bronx High School of Math and Science; and Stuyvesant High. More general suggestions include single-sex schools, magnet schools, schools adopting the Paideia approach, and charter schools in your own area, which tend to have strong philosophical underpinnings.

Teacher Interview

Have students interview a teacher to discover his or her philosophy of education. Suggest the following probes to use to follow up this general question: "What is your philosophy of education?"

- "What are your learning goals?"
- "What do you believe are the most effective methods for teaching?"
- "What values do you try to foster in your teaching?"
- "How do you try to foster them?"
- "What do you think is the role of the teacher?"
- "What is the role of the student?"
- "What factors may sometimes keep you from acting in strict accord with your beliefs?"
- "What about your philosophy would you like to pass on to a new teacher?"
- "As you've gained experience, has your philosophy of education changed?"

Minilessons

Design a minilesson exemplifying one of the educational philosophies presented in this chapter (perennialism, progressivism, essentialism, existentialism). You may select a topic of your choice. After you present this minilesson to your class, analyze it. What were the elements within it that exemplified that particular philosophy? (This activity could easily be used in cooperative learning groups.)

Create a Charter School (group activity)

You and your colleagues have just been granted a charter to create your own school. Your school will operate under one of the four philosophies presented in the chapter. Given those conditions, you and your colleagues will prepare some important documents for your school. (1) Write your school's mission statement. What will your mission be, and how will your educational philosophy be reflected in your mission? (2) Construct general curricular goals/competencies—or select a particular grade and academic subject and create a more specific curriculum. (3) Provide a brief description of the topics covered (in elementary grades) or the course offerings provided for middle or high school. Present and discuss your documents with the whole class.

Student Assignments

The following activities are suggestions for student portfolio activities. They are a means of providing alternative assessment of students' capabilities.

Independent Reading

Read and respond to any of the selections noted on the chapter/article correlation list found in the front of this manual for Ryan/Cooper, *Kaleidoscope: Readings in Education* (Houghton Mifflin, 2004). You may want to use the Article Review Form in *Kaleidoscope*.

Reflective Papers

Choose one of the following topics to write a reflective paper (2–5 pages). The purpose of the paper is to help you assimilate new knowledge by blending it with your previous knowledge and experiences.

1. Select any current controversy in education and demonstrate how philosophical differences inform the analysis of the issue.

2. Imagine you have been named superintendent of schools in a brand-new school district. Everything—from buildings to faculty to students—is new to this school district. You have been hired because of your vision for education, including your educational philosophy. What would your guiding philosophy be for this new school district? Describe and give examples of how it would be carried out.

3. Imagine you are interviewing now for a teaching position. One part of your interview includes writing your educational philosophy as a teacher. Describe your educational philosophy and how you see it influencing your work with students.

4. As you observe in your field-site school, think about the educational undergirding of what you observe. Based upon the activities, lessons, and interactions between students and teachers and teachers and colleagues, what educational philosophy emerges? What seems to be the general conception of what knowledge is and how it is best acquired? Give specific examples to support your ideas.

Journal Reflections

Suggestions for journal topics for students' selection:

1. Indicate which of the four philosophies of education seems closest to your own and tell what in your life may have contributed to developing your philosophy.

2. Tell what philosophy you think your instructor holds most strongly and describe what evidence you have for this.

3. Pick one person or group of people (state legislators, the president of the United States, a political party, parents, yuppies, etc.) and indicate which philosophy they seem to be acting from and why you think so.

4. Write your own philosophy of education.

5. See copy-ready assignment sheet on the following pages.

CD-ROM Video Clip

View the clip for Chapter 8 and be prepared to discuss the following reflection questions:

1. Which is a more important emphasis for U.S. education today: student self-discovery or the needs of society? Why?

2. Does U.S. public education currently resemble Rousseau's concept of education? Does it resemble the colonial model discussed in the clip? In what ways?

3. What sort of "wells" do American students need to learn how to "dig" today? Is this knowledge more or less important than intellectual development for its own sake? Why?

HOW TO WRITE YOUR PHILOSOPHY OF EDUCATION

<u>Assignment:</u>

Your own philosophy of education is very important because it provides focus and emphasis for your teaching. Working to communicate your philosophy helps you to become aware of your own goals and values, which prepares you to integrate them with the goals and values espoused by your district and your community.

Your statement of philosophy is a description of your own goals and beliefs as a teacher. There is no "right" philosophy. Some fit into certain settings better then others. You will refine, augment, and develop your philosophy for the rest of your career. Usually it is not successful to "change" your whole philosophy to meet the expectations of someone else.

Below are some guidelines to keep in mind to produce a well-written, focused, and articulate statement of your philosophy.

- Your philosophy should be no longer than two typed, double-spaced pages. Somewhere in your statement of philosophy answer the following questions:

  - What is the purpose of education? (What goals do you want your students to achieve?)

  - What is the student's role? (What are students' responsibilities?)

  - What is the teacher's role?

  - What is the teacher's role as a bridge to the community? (optional)

  - What is the teacher's role in educational renewal and reform? (optional)

- This statement of philosophy should rely on your personal beliefs and experiences. Your philosophy will be influenced by the knowledge and experience you acquire as you proceed through your licensure/certification program.

- You may want to "try on" a metaphor to more clearly and vividly describe your philosophy. Growing plants, filling a pitcher, and molding clay are some common (but stereotypical) metaphorical vehicles. You may want to create a new one to avoid previous connections associated with these three. Successful use of a metaphor may depend on using a skill, hobby, or activity you have experience with and also on knowing when to step outside the metaphor and show a contrast (e.g., unlike a bicycle, education has more than two wheels).

Due date: _____

THE EDUCATIONAL PHILOSOPHY TEST (E.P.)

BY PATRICIA D. JERSIN

INSTRUCTIONS:

Please check the answer under each item that best reflects your thinking.

1.   What is the essence of education?

    a.   The essence of education is reason and intuition.

    b.   The essence of education is growth.

    c.   The essence of education is knowledge and skills.

    d.   The essence of education is choice.

2.   What is the nature of the learner?

    a.   The learner is an experienced organism.

    b.   The learner is a unique, free, choosing and responsible creature and is made up of intellect and emotion.

    c.   The learner is a rational and intuitive being.

    d.   The learner is a storehouse for knowledge and skills, which once acquired, can later be applied and used.

3.   How should education provide for the needs of man?

    a.   Students need a passionate encounter with the perennial problems of life: the agony and joy of love, the reality of choice, the anguish of freedom, the consequences of actions, and the inevitability of death.

    b.   Education allows for the needs of man when it inculcates the child with certain essential skills and knowledge, which all men should possess.

    c.   The one distinguishing characteristic of man is intelligence. Education should concentrate on developing the intellectual needs of students.

    d.   Since the needs of man are variable, education should concentrate on developing the individual differences in students.

4.   What should be the environment of education?

    a.   Education should possess an environment in which the student adjusts to the material and social world, as it really exists.

    b.   The environment of education should be life itself, where students can experience "living" . . . not prepare for it.

    c.   The environment of education should be one that encourages the growth of free, creative individuality, not adjustment to group thinking or the public norms.

    d.   Education is not a true replica of life; rather, it is an artificial environment where the child should be developing his or her intellectual potentialities and preparing for the future.

5.   What should be the goal of education?

    a.   Growth, through the reconstruction of experience, is the nature and should be the open-ended goal of education.

    b.   The only type of goal to which education should lead is the goal of truth, which is absolute, universal, and unchanging.

    c.   The primary concern of education should be with developing the uniqueness of individual students.

    d.   The goal of education should be to provide a framework of knowledge for the student against which new truths can be gathered and assimilated.

6.   What should be the concern of the school?

    a.   The school should concern itself with man's distinguishing characteristic, the mind, and concentrate on developing rationality.

    b.   The school should provide an education for the "whole child," centering its attention on all the needs and interests of the child.

    c.   The school should educate the child to attain the basic knowledge necessary to understand the real world outside.

    d.   The school should provide each student with assistance in his or her journey toward self-realization.

7.   What should be the atmosphere of the school?

    a.   The school should provide for group thinking in a democratic atmosphere that fosters cooperation rather than competition.

    b.   The atmosphere of the school should be one of authentic freedom where a student is allowed to find his or her own truth and ultimate fulfillment through nonconforming choice making.

    c.   The school should surround its students with "Great Books" and foster individuality in an atmosphere of intellectualism and creative thinking.

    d.   The school should retain an atmosphere of mental discipline, yet incorporate innovative techniques that would introduce the student to a perceptual examination of the realities about him or her.

8.   How should appropriate learning occur?

    a.   Appropriate learning occurs as the student freely engages in choosing among alternatives while weighing personal responsibilities and the possible consequences of his or her actions.

    b.   Appropriate learning takes place through the experience of problem-solving projects by which the child is led from practical issues to theoretical principles (concrete to abstract).

    c.   Appropriate learning takes place as certain basic readings acquaint students with the world's permanencies, inculcating them in theoretical principles that they will later apply in life (abstract to concrete).

    d.   Appropriate learning occurs when hard effort has been extended to absorb and master the prescribed subject matter.

9.   What should be the role of the teacher?

    a.   The teacher should discipline his or her pupils intellectually through a study of the great works in literature in which the universal concerns of man have best been expressed.

    b.   The teacher should present principles and values and the reasons for them, encouraging students to examine them in order to choose for themselves whether or not to accept them.

    c.   The teacher should guide and advise his or her students, since the children's own interests should determine what they learn.

    d.   The teacher, the responsible authority, should mediate between the adult world and the world of the child, since immature students cannot comprehend the nature and demands of adulthood by themselves.

10.   What should the curriculum include?

    a.   The curriculum should include only that which has survived the test of time and which combines the symbols and ideas of literature, history, and mathematics with the sciences of the physical world.

    b.   The curriculum should concentrate on teaching students how to manage change through problem-solving activities in the social studies, empirical sciences, and vocational technology.

    c.   The curriculum should concentrate on intellectual subject matter and include English, languages, history, mathematics, natural sciences, the fine arts, and also philosophy.

    d.   The curriculum should concentrate on the humanities—history, literature, philosophy, and art—where greater depth into the nature of man and his conflict with the world is revealed.

11.   What should be the preferred teaching method?

    a.   *Projects* should be the preferred method whereby the students can be guided through problem-solving experiences.

    b.   *Lectures, readings,* and *discussions* should be the preferred methods for training the intellect.

    c.   *Demonstrations* should be the preferred method for teaching knowledge and skills.

    d.   *Socratic dialogue* (drawing responses from a questioning conversation) should be the preferred method for finding the self.

Scoring the Test

This test is self-scoring. Circle the answer you selected for each of the questions checked on the test. Total the number of circles below each column. The more answers in one column, the stronger your inclination toward that philosophy.

Test #	Progressivism	Perennialism	Essentialism	Existentialism*
1	b	a	c	d
2	a	c	d	b
3	d	c	b	a
4	b	d	a	c
5	a	b	d	c
6	b	a	c	d
7	a	c	d	b
8	b	c	d	a
9	c	a	d	b
10	b	c	a	d
11	a	b	c	d
Total				

If your answers are more evenly distributed, your philosophy has not yet fully evolved through your education and experience. As you continue your program, your experiences will influence the development of your philosophy.

Excerpted from "What Is Your E.P.?" by Patricia D. Jersin, *Clearinghouse* 46, (January 1972): 274–278.

*Similar to romanticism.

CHAPTER 9

What Is the History of American Education?

LEARNING OBJECTIVES

After studying the chapter, students will be able to

1. identify, explain, and analyze the six key forces that have shaped the history of American education: local control of schools, universal education, public education, comprehensive education, secular education, and the changing ideas of the basics.

2. identify and describe the purposes of the various types of elementary schooling available during the colonial period and be able to associate particular types of schooling with the geographical region in which it was most common.

3. identify and describe the purposes of various types of secondary schooling available, from the colonial period through the present.

4. locate on a time continuum the introduction of the following major developments in U.S. education: grammar schools, public (common) schools, academies, kindergarten, middle schools, and secondary schools.

5. identify, explain, and apply the educational ideas and methods of several key European educators.

6. identify, explain, and apply the educational ideas and methods of several key American educators.

7. articulate the major arguments supporting and opposing the establishment of common schools in the United States.

8. define and explain the impact that several key rulings or laws have had upon expanding education: the Old Deluder Satan Act, the Northwest Land Ordinances, the *Kalamazoo* case, the Morrill Acts, *Plessy* v. *Ferguson*, and *Brown* v. *Board of Education*.

9. explain and apply the general principles of the Progressive Education Association.

10. describe the evolution of education for women, for African Americans, for Hispanic Americans, for Asian Americans, and for Native Americans.

CHAPTER OVERVIEW

The history of American education spans more than 350 years. In this chapter on the history of American education, we paint in broad brush strokes to provide prospective teachers with the general landscape of educational history. In this way, we hope that future teachers will become familiar with significant ideas, events, and people that have shaped American education. Moreover, we also hope that prospective teachers can gain perspective on contemporary educational practices and their relationship to earlier practices. Tracing the growth of public education from the dame schools of colonial New England to the advent of middle schools in the mid-twentieth century, this chapter highlights how access to educational opportunities has gradually widened over the course of U.S. history. In that vein, we identify and discuss significant events that have helped educational institutions include a greater number and variety of people.

We identify six forces that have had an impact on shaping education in this country: local control of schools, universal education, public education, comprehensive education, secular education, and the changing ideas of the basics. Each of the subtopics we present can be related to those broad forces.

CHAPTER OUTLINE

I.   Themes in American Education
II. Elementary Education
    A.   Colonial Origins
        1.   New England Town and District Schools
            a.   Old Deluder Satan Act
        2.   Education in the South
        3.   Education in the Middle Colonies
    B.   The Common School
        1.   Arguments for the Common School
        2.   Arguments against the Common School
        3.   Victory of the Common School
    C.   Other Developments in Elementary Education
        1.   European Influences
            a.   Kindergarten—Froebel
            b.   Children's Interests—Pestalozzi
            c.   Moral Development—Herbart
            d.   Direct Experience—Montessori
        2.   Curriculum Changes
        3.   Consolidation
        4.   Progressive Education Association
        5.   Since World War II

III.   Secondary Education
    A.   Early Forms
        1.   Latin Grammar Schools
        2.   Alternative Forms of College Preparation
        3.   English Grammar Schools
        4.   Secondary Education for Females
    B.   The Academy
        1.   Growth of Academies
    C.   The Public High School
        1.   Debate Over the Secondary Curriculum
        2.   The Comprehensive High School
    D.   Growth of Junior High and Middle Schools
    E.   Secondary Education Today
IV.   Private Education
V.   Education of Minorities
    A.   Education of African Americans
        1.   Morrill Act
        2.   *Plessy* v. *Ferguson*
        3.   Segregation – de jure and de facto
        4.   *Brown* v. *Board of Education*
        5.   Desegregation Efforts
    B.   Education of Native Americans
    C.   Education of Hispanic Americans
    D.   Education of Asian Americans

SUPPLEMENTARY LECTURE AND DISCUSSION TOPICS

1.   **Historical textbooks** Assemble a sample of textbooks used in various periods of our nation's history from a local library collection. The *New England Primer* and McGuffey readers are widely available. Compare the features of these books to the features of modern textbooks. Or assemble comparable samples of old and modern teacher education texts. What do the old teacher education texts emphasize? What qualities did they say a teacher should have? What are the differences between training then and now?

2.   **Private and parochial education** Trace the development of private or religious schools in the United States, paying particular attention to the nineteenth and twentieth centuries. Include discussions of contemporary religious fundamentalist schools.

3.   **Charter schools and home schooling** Discuss the historical development of these two movements as well as their relationship to the six major themes in American education.

4.   **Higher education** Trace the development of American higher education from colonial days to the present. Include changes in the student body, relevant legislation, curriculum, and accessibility. Explain how your own institution was affected by these factors.

STUDY GUIDE – CHAPTER 9: WHAT IS THE HISTORY OF AMERICAN EDUCATION?

Completing this study guide will help you prepare for the major topic areas on an exam; however, it does not cover every piece of information found in the chapter or the test questions.

1.   List and describe the six themes in American education.

2.   Describe the location, time period, and characteristics of dame schools, town schools, moving schools, district schools, and common schools.

3.   List the pros and cons of establishing common schools.

4.   Identify the European educators that have made significant contributions to American education and briefly describe each of their contributions.

5.   Indicate how the ruling in each of the following legal cases affected education in the United States: Old Deluder Satan Act, the *Kalamazoo* case, *Plessy* v. *Ferguson,* and *Brown* v. *Board of Education.*

6. Describe the significant changes in education that have taken place since World War II.

7. Describe Latin grammar schools, English grammar schools, and academies. Distinguish between their purposes.

8. Identify the significant characteristics of true middle schools.

9. Indicate the percentage of students who attend private schools and analyze the significance of this option in the United States.

10. For women and for each group of minority students in American schools, briefly describe the historical evolution of their participation in the American school system.

ADDITIONAL RESOURCES FOR INSTRUCTORS

Cuban, Larry. *How Teachers Taught: Constancy and Change in American Classrooms: 1890–1990*. New York: Teachers College Press, 1993. A respected educational historian, Cuban presents a scholarly account of the teaching methods of the last one hundred years. His findings are striking.

Curti, Merle. *The Social Ideas of American Educators*. New York: Littlefield, Adams, 1959. Curti examines the ideas of educational thinkers such as Thomas Jefferson, Benjamin Franklin, and Horace Mann.

Lessons of a Century. Education Week, January 27, 1999–October, 1999. Ten monthly installments examining aspects of the educational landscape of twentieth century America, including the people, trends, historical milestones, enduring controversies, political conflicts, and socioeconomic forces that have shaped education in the twentieth century. Available online at **http://www.edweek.org**.

Power, Edward J. *A Legacy of Learning: A History of Western Education*. Albany: SUNY Press, 1991. This comprehensive volume provides important events and their analyses for anyone interested in understanding the major themes and goals of Western education.

Pulliam, John P. *History of Education in America*. 5th ed. Columbus, OH: Merrill, 1991. A clearly written history of the major events in American education.

Ravitch, Diane. *The Troubled Crusade: American Education 1945–1980*. New York: Basic Books, 1983. Ravitch traces the history of U.S. education from directly after World War II to the beginning of the 1980s. She analyzes the fall of progressive education, the *Brown* v. *Board of Education* decision, the controversies surrounding public education during the 1960s, and the politicization of education during the second half of the twentieth century.

Rippa, S. Alexander. *Education in a Free Society: An American History*. New York: Longman, 1992. This book presents educational history through a political framework, interpreting key events in educational history.

Spring, Joel. *The American School: 1642–1990*. New York: Longman, 1990. Spring writes a history of the social, political, and ideological forces that have shaped American education from the 1600s to the present.

Tyack, David B., and Larry Cuban. *Tinkering Toward Utopia: A Century of Public School Reform*. Cambridge, MA: Harvard University Press, 1995. These authors argue that utopian policy talk about school reform has usually only involved incremental policy action —"tinkering with the system." An important book on school reforms in the United States.

Urban, Wayne J., and Jennings L. Wagoner. *American Education: A History*. 2nd ed. New York: McGraw-Hill, 2000. This book is a relatively brief overview of American education.

Media Resources

As American as Public Schools: 1900–1950 (Films for the Humanities and Sciences, 52 min., 2000). This program recalls how massive immigration, child labor laws, and the explosive growth of cities fueled school attendance and transformed public education, and explores the impact of John Dewey's progressive ideas as well as the effects on students of controversial IQ tests.

The Bottom Line In Education: 1980 to the Present (Films for the Humanities and Sciences, 52 min., 2000). Following the *A Nation At Risk* report, this program explores the impact of the "free market" experiments that ensued-from vouches and charter schools to privatization-and looks at how the debate over education continues to rage.

Brown v. Board of Education (Insight Media, 19 min., 1997). This video traces the history of educational opportunities for black Americans examining the social and political context of the watershed Brown case, which declared segregation in public schools to be unconstitutional.

The Common School: 1770-1890 (Films for the Humanities and Sciences, 52 min., 2000). This program profiles the passionate crusade launched by Thomas Jefferson and continued by Noah Webster, Horace Mann, and others to create a common system of tax-supported schools that would mix people of different backgrounds and reinforce the bonds of democracy.

Common Threads (Insight Media, 20 min., 1995). This video chronicles the history of education in the United States from the colonial period to the present. It examines how curricula have evolved, how the purposes of education have changed over time, and how technology affects modern education.

A Day in the Life of the One-Room School (Insight Media, 16 min., 1988). This program gives an overview of daily life in a one-room school at the turn of the century. It considers both academic and non-academic daily activities.

Education in America: The 19th Century (Insight Media, 16 min., 1998). This program discusses the development of free public school systems, westward movement, the change to secular education, the rise and decline of the district school, the struggle for tax support, compulsory attendance laws, the influence of American textbooks, and the contributions of Webster, McGuffey, Hawley, and Mann.

Education in America: 20th-Century Developments (Insight Media, 30 min., 1998). This video examines changes in education in the first half of the twentieth century. It discusses the effects of the industrial revolution on education, the appearance of the junior high school and graduate education, and the building of central consolidated schools. It describes the influence of Herbart, Binet, Dewey, and Thorndike, and considers the G.I. Bill of Rights and Supreme Court decisions affecting education.

The Evolution of Our Education System (International Center for Leadership Education, 76 min., 1999). This video shows how the American education system has evolved from the agricultural age through the industrial age into the technological/information age. Conflicts with present structures including tenure, contracts, certification, testing, school bells, and schedules are discussed by William R. Daggett.

Eyes on the Prize (Prod: CCBlackside Inc., Dist: PBS and Boston University, 6-part series, 60 min. each, 1986). The civil rights struggle between 1954 and 1965 is covered by this documentary series. Included in the series: *Fighting Back* (1957–1962). The law has been used both to promote change and to resist change, particularly educational change. This episode explores the lawsuits brought by parents on behalf of their children, with special emphasis on the crucial 1954 Supreme Court *Brown* v. *Board of Education* decision.

The Fateful Decade: From Little Rock to the Civil Rights Bill (Films for the Humanities and Sciences, 27 min., 1994). This program begins at Little Rock's Central High School, when soldiers had to provide safety for black children exercising their legal right to go to school. Martin Luther King, Jr., appears in 1958 at a meeting of black leaders with President Eisenhower. The civil rights movement accelerated: marches, clashes with the police and the jailing of demonstrators, the murder of Medgar Evers, the bombing of the Baptist church in Birmingham, sit-ins and protests, the Montgomery march, the Mississippi Freedom march, King's famous "I Have a Dream" and "I Have Been to the Mountaintop" speeches, his funeral, and President Johnson's signing of the Civil Rights Bill of 1968.

A History of Education (Films for the Humanities and Sciences, 52 min., 1999). This program traces the evolution of education through the ages, from oral traditions to its role in today's ever-changing society, where the need to learn new job skills is a constant necessity.

The Middle School: Why and How (Insight Media, 126 min., 1993).John H. Lounsbury, "father" of the middle-school movement, conducts this seminar on designing a school to match students' needs. He discusses developmental attributes of early adolescents, explaining how middle-school curricula should complement this stage of development.

The Road to Brown (California Newsreel, 47 min., 1990). This video dramatizes the events and legal rulings that preceded the desegregation decision in *Brown* v. *Board of Education.*

Saviors (Films for the Humanities and Sciences, 47 min., 1994). This program provides insight into the role of the federal government in legislating and enforcing rights for African Americans. It tells the story of the Supreme Court's decision in *Brown* v. *Board of Education of Topeka*, a landmark in the battle to end segregation in public schools.

Teaching Indians to Be White (Films for the Humanities and Sciences, 30 min., 1994). Schools are where children are taught to integrate into society, and schools represent a major problem for native children—whether they are religious schools with native teachers; residential schools that tear children away from their families and traditional values; or public day schools, where native children find it nearly impossible to balance the white view they are taught in school with the language and values they learn at home. The results are that the Seminole of Florida resist being integrated, the Miccosukee decided not to fight but to join, and the Cree took back their own schools.

Media distributor contact information is available in Appendix I.

Student Activities

School Observation—How Have Schools Changed?

Compared to today's classrooms, those of the nineteenth century were similar in some ways and different in others. Look at two photos of high school classes, one from the late 1800s and one from today. Study the pictures and then respond to the following items:

a.   Make a list of the things you notice about the nineteenth-century picture, and then another list for the modern photo.

b.   In what ways are your two lists similar and different?

c.   Aside from the people's dress, would you say that the photos are more alike or more dissimilar? Why?

d.   Share your impressions with three or four other students in your class. Think about the reasons why the classrooms appear similar or dissimilar.

Analysis of Key Issues in Education

Ask students to collect news articles on local schools. These should be articles about educational issues (the introduction of a new curriculum, the school budget, a push for school vouchers, etc.) rather than articles about educational personnel. After the students have collected and read these articles, ask them (either individually or in small groups) to analyze the stories in terms of the historical forces discussed in Chapter 11. To what degree are these news articles implicitly or explicitly linked to some of the key educational issues throughout American educational history? What conclusions can the students make?

Historical Research

Teams of three or four students can choose or be assigned different historical periods on which to do research on schooling. Each group makes a class presentation in which the members describe some important features of the larger society that affected schools. For example, presentations could answer questions such as: Who was in the student body (immigrant waves might affect this)? What developments of science and technology were influencing school life? What great artists were affecting the cultural climate? How was the shape of the country changing, and how, therefore, were geography lessons changing? What heroes or heroines of the time were functioning as role models for students?

Historical Research of a School or School District

Have students, either individually or in small groups, research the history of a particular school or a particular school district. Have students visit local libraries to discover when formal schooling first took place in the community and what type of schooling it was. How did formal education change over the years in the district? What were some of the major events in the district? If they are researching a school, find out when it was built and what purpose(s) it has served over the years. What were the plans when the school was built? What was the structure of the district? Were there particular reasons why it was designed as it was? What does the structure of the school building reveal about the community's philosophy of education? Is the building named after someone? Who is the person, and what is his or her significance? How would the same school be different if it was built in the same place today?

Oral History (individual or group work)

Ask each student to interview the oldest person he or she knows or can contact. (It would be best if all the interviewees were older than sixty.) Ask that person his or her memories of school. Sample questions might include the following: What did the school look like? What was the inside like? What subjects did you study? What was a typical day like? What do you remember about your teachers? What were some of the school's rules? Present to the class and discuss. An interesting whole-group project might be to construct a chart of commonalities found among the people interviewed or to look at the different experiences women had from men, various ethnic groups had from each other, or the college-bound student had from the commercial or vocational student.

Student Assignments

The following activities are suggestions for student portfolio activities. They are a means of providing alternative assessment of the students' capabilities.

Independent Reading

Read and respond to any of the selections noted on the chapter/article correlation list found in the front of this manual for Ryan/Cooper, *Kaleidoscope: Readings in Education* (Houghton Mifflin, 2004). You may want to use the Article Review Form in *Kaleidoscope*.

Or select three recent articles (those written within the past five years) on any of the following topics and write a short summary of the main ideas for each article.

the common school

the education of American women

secular education

the education of minority students

comprehensive high schools

the education of minorities

the history of the curriculum

Reflective Papers

Choose one of the following topics to write a reflective paper (2–5 pages). The purpose of the paper is to help you assimilate new knowledge by blending it with your previous knowledge and experiences.

1.   Considering your background (race, gender, ethnicity), imagine that you are living in the 1700s, 1800s, or early 1900s in a particular region of the United States. Write about the kind of education you probably would have received. What would have been the kinds of knowledge you would have been expected to possess? Compare that to your own education.

2.   The history of American education can be viewed from a number of different perspectives. As discussed in the text, one underlying reason that public schools came about was that many believed public education would build national unity and increase economic productivity. From that vantage point, education's purpose is primarily for the common economic good of the society. At other points in the text, the authors indicate that many people believed that the purpose of education was for humanitarian reasons: so the individual would be enriched. Think about those vantage points and respond. What do you see as important considerations for either or both of those positions? What do you see as the primary purpose of education?

3.   Visit two schools in your area—one built within the last ten years and the oldest one that you can find that is still in use. Compare the differences in the architectural form and function and link these to historical changes in education.

Journal Reflections

Suggestions for journal topics for students' selection:

1.   Discuss a current school practice you consider to be the result of a historical relic (like an agrarian calendar).

2.   Select a period in the history of education and tell why you would or would not want to be a teacher during this period.

3.   Predict what will have changed about today's schools by the year 2020.

CD-ROM Video Clip

View the clip for Chapter 9 and be prepared to discuss the following reflection questions:

1. Could technology become the ground for the new civil rights movement of the future? Can equal access to technology be the key to eliminating racial inequality in American society? Why or why not?

2. What do you think will be the ultimate effect on inequality of an increased emphasis on technology in education? Why?

CHAPTER 10

How Are Schools Governed, Influenced, and Financed?

LEARNING OBJECTIVES

After studying the chapter, students will be able to

1. define the source of authority and particular responsibilities of the governor, state legislature, state board of education, the chief state school officer, the state department of education, the local school board and superintendent, and the school principal.

2. describe the demographic data relating to school superintendents, principals, and school board members and explain the significance of those data.

3. identify and describe other groups that exercise informal influence in education.

4. describe and explain the advantages and disadvantages of the influence business has had upon public education.

5. discuss the educational impact of Supreme Court rulings in areas such as desegregation, rights of the disabled, gender equity, etc.

6. explain the role of standardized tests as measures of school effectiveness.

7. explain the implications of several Supreme Court cases regarding equitable state and local funding of education, including the *Serrano* case and the alternative plan to finance public education in Michigan.

8. describe the typical pattern of school funding by local, state, and federal agencies, and explain the relationships among the local economy, tax structure, and the quality of education.

9. describe the trends in federal support of education from the 1960s through the 1990s.

10. discuss the philosophy supporting and the effectiveness of compensatory education programs.

CHAPTER OVERVIEW

Few prospective teachers probably think at length about the governance, forces of influence, or finance of public schools. To someone enthusiastically learning how to become a teacher, such issues may seem far removed from life in classrooms. Yet issues involving the governance, influence, or finance of schools directly and indirectly affect a teacher's job because they define the parameters of public education and the roles of those involved in public education. For that reason, we describe some of the features of formal school governance that are common to all the states, as well as some aspects that may differ. We think prospective teachers should know how the organizational structure of a school works and how they, as teachers, will fit into that structure. Their effectiveness as teachers and possible reformers can be enhanced by the knowledge of the forces that shape other formal roles.

In addition, we want student readers to be cognizant of the ways informal influences affect school operation. As teachers, they will assume informal authority daily through the decisions they make about their classes. Department chairs, supervisors, and other teacher-administrators will exercise informal authority, often out of necessity. What beginning teachers may be less aware of is the informal influence that parents, business groups, and political organizations will try to exert in running the schools. New teachers ought to know what to expect and what limitations are set by law and custom.

We also discuss the sources of funding for education. We describe the local, state, and federal contributions to education, also pointing out the historical changes in the federal funding of education. It is important to explain where money for school budgets comes from and what services each funding source has agreed to finance. Because of recent court cases finding that funding schemes in some states were unconstitutional, public funding, and educational equity will be linked tightly in the near future. Such court cases and their implications could have a powerful influence on public education in the near future.

CHAPTER OUTLINE

I. Who Legally Governs Public Education?
    A. State Offices and Administrators
        1. The Governor and Legislature
        2. The State Board of Education
        3. The Chief State School Officer
        4. The State Department of Education
    B. The Local School District
        1. The Local School Board
        2. The Superintendent of Schools
        3. The School Principal
II. Who Influences American Public Education?
    A. Professional Education Organizations
    B. Parents
    C. Business
    D. Standardized Testing
        1. Privatization Efforts
    E. The Federal Government
        1. The Federal Courts
        2. The U.S. Department of Education

III.   How Are Schools Financed?
    A.   School Spending
    B.   State and Local Funding
    C.   School Finance Reform and the Courts
    D.   Federal Funding
        1.   Funding in the Past
        2.   No Child Left Behind "Act of 2001"
        3.   Compensatory Education

SUPPLEMENTARY LECTURE AND DISCUSSION TOPICS

1.   **Changes in financing schools** Discuss in more detail the recent court cases determining that the existing system of school financing is unconstitutional. Describe the differences among school support structures in two states—one state with an equation that equalizes resources among districts, another state with an equation that allows significant per-pupil variations in expenditures. Explain something about the cost-of-living differences that may account for some of the variations in expenditure among states and the differences in the quality of education. Explain in more detail what "redistribution" of funds would mean. What are the advantages? Any disadvantages? How would you explain the inequity in school funding to a low-income parent who hopes that his or her child will have an opportunity to succeed? How would you explain the court decisions to middle- or upper-income parents whose decision to move to a particular town was based on the reputation of its school system?

2.   **An international comparison** Compare the federal government's role in U.S. education to the government's role in education in several other industrialized countries. Compare the similarities and differences in financing and in governing the public schools.

3.   **Superintendent/principal/school board member** Invite a local superintendent, principal, and school board member to your class to discuss their roles and their perspectives on being a superintendent, principal, or school board member. If possible, have each person come from a different school district so that each can talk about his or her position and answer students' questions without any awkwardness. What are some of the speakers' greatest satisfactions in their role? What are some of their greatest frustrations? What do they spend most of their time doing on the job? Ask your students to prepare some questions beforehand for each speaker.

4.   **Role of the state education agency** Describe the role of the state education agency in your state. Name the chief school officer and tell something about the people and programs that are particularly relevant to the students—for example, the teacher certification or licensure office or the staff development office. Many states are currently offering beginning teacher induction programs. If yours is, perhaps a person from that program could be invited to discuss it.

5.   **Site-based management of schools** Educational journals and research have discussed the benefits of site-based management of schools. Describe this concept in more detail to your students, outlining the changes in school hierarchy and the changes in roles and functions.

6.   **Role of the PTO** Invite the president of a local parent-teacher organization to describe the responsibilities and activities of the group.

7.   **U.S. Department of Education** Describe the budget of the department—the size of the budget in relation to the budgets of other cabinet-level departments and the programs it funds. Identify any programs that affect your college or community. Explain some of the arguments made for and against the continued existence of the department.

8.   **Property tax** If you live in a community that funds schools through property taxes, use the following Property Tax Chart and Formula to walk your students through the calculations that determine mill levy and property tax amount.

JEFFERSON COUNTY COLORADO
Property Tax Statement

Tax Dist 7015   Schedule No. 408809   1996 TAXES PAYABLE 1997

DOING BUSINESS AS: **BLDG 4 UNIT 102**	PROPERTY LOCATION		FIN. INST. RD
SEC.TWN.RNG.QTT SQ,FT. LAND BLK LOT KEY BOOK PAGE	TAX AUTHORITY	TAX LEVY*	TAX AMOUNT
JEWELL LAKE CONDOS 4TH SUPP	SCHOOL	39.6610	344.65
28 04 69 NE 004 0102 91093779	SCHOOL GEN	10.3000	89.51
RESIDENTIAL	SCHOOL BND		
	COUNTY	14.2220	123.57
	CNTY GEN'L	.5000	4.35
	DEV DISABL	3.4130	29.66
	R&B SRVCS	2.1160	18.39
	SOC SERVCS	2.2040	19.15
	CAP'TL EXP	3.5000	30.42
	LIBRARY	.0230	.20
	CNTY OTHER	4.7110	40.94
	LKWD	1.7460	15.17
	B-CLW&SD	4.0680	35.35
	FR&PD	.7800	6.78
	UDFCD	11.4130	99.18
	WMFPD		
PROPERTY VALUATION	DUE FIRST HALF DUE SECOND HALF	TAX LEVY* 98.6570	FULL AMOUNT DUE APRIL 30 857.32
ACTUAL LAND AND BUILDING.... 83,900	FEB 428.66		
ASSESSED LAND AND BUILDING 8,690	28		
ASSESSMENT PERCENTAGE	------------------------		
RESIDENTIAL PROPERTY 10.36% ALL	DUE SECOND HALF		
OTHER PROPERTY 29.00%	JUNE 428.66		

Example

$83,900 x 10.36% x f(98.657/1,000) =

Assessed	Legislatively	Mill Levy Formula: 1 mill = 1/1000 of a dollar
Value of	set/assessment	or
A House	percentage	1/10 of a cent

$83,900 x .1036 x .098657 = 857 = Tax

STUDY GUIDE – CHAPTER 10: HOW ARE SCHOOLS GOVERNED, INFLUENCED, AND FINANCED?

Completing this study guide will help you prepare for the major topic areas on an exam; however, it does not cover every piece of information found in the chapter or the test questions.

1. Describe the roles, responsibilities, and relationship between the state board of education, the state department of education, and the chief state school officer.

2. Describe the role of the district superintendent of schools.

3. Identify and describe six other informal but powerful influences that affect the decisions made in education.

4. Indicate the three levels of governance that contribute to school funding, the relative amounts they contribute, and their source for these funds.

5. Give an example of privatization in education.

6.   Distinguish between the appropriate uses for categorical grants and block grants.

7.   Define site-based decision making and give an example.

8.   To which level of government is the legal responsibility for the governance of schools delegated, and what legal document states this?

9.   Describe several ways in which business influences education.

10.   Compare and contrast the pros and cons of year-round schools.

11.   Describe the purpose of compensatory education, the students who qualify to participate, and two examples of compensatory programs.

ADDITIONAL RESOURCES FOR INSTRUCTORS

Burke, Fred G. *Public Education: Who's in Charge?* New York: Praeger, 1990. An account of the different forces that control public education. A readable book that details the issues of control and governance in public schools.

Brimley, Vern Jr., and Rulon R. Grafield. *Financing Education in a Climate of Change.* 8th ed. Boston: Allyn and Bacon, 2002. This comprehensive text examines how schools are financed in this country, the role of the federal government, and significant court cases affecting school finance.

Campbell, Roald, et al. *The Organization and Control of American Schools.* 6th ed. Columbus, OH: Macmillan, 1990. A good overview of the American educational system, including both governance and control issues.

Chubb, John E., and Terry Moe. *Politics, Markets, and America's Schools.* Washington, DC: Brookings Institute, 1990. A critical analysis of the ways in which politics, the market, and choice affect the public schools. This book captured immediate attention from the education community when it was published.

Fuller, Bruce, and Richard Rubinson (eds.). *The Political Construction of Education: The State, School Expansion, and Economic Change.* New York: Praeger, 1992. A detailed account of the intricacies and political complexities of funding schools.

Giroux, Henry A., "Education Incorporated?" *Educational Leadership* 56(2) (1998). Examines commercialization's increasing inroads in the public schools.

Karp, Stan, Robert Lowe, Barbara Miner, and Bob Person. *Funding for Justice: Money, Equity, and the Future of Public Education.* Milwaukee: Rethinking Schools Ltd., 1997. This book gives the facts and opinions of leading researchers and thinkers in the area of school finance. It also features an overview of major court cases on state funding.

Kozol, Jonathan. *Savage Inequalities: Children in America's Schools.* New York: Harper Perennial, 1992. A portrait of the schooling provided for children in some of America's most financially depressed cities. A disturbing account and highly recommended reading.

LoVette, Otis K. "You Ask, 'Why Have School Costs Increased So Greatly During the Last 20 Years?'" *Phi Delta Kappan* (October 1995): 169–172. LoVette lists the reasons under the general headings of court decisions, federal legislation and regulations, state legislation and regulations, and social expectations and demands.

Turnbull, Brenda, Megan Welsh, Camilla Heid, William Davis, and Alexander C. Ratnofsky. *The Longitudinal Evaluation of School Change and Performance (LESCP) in Title I Schools. Interim Report to Congress.* Washington, DC: Policy Studies Associates, Inc., 1999. This interim report provides findings on Title I services and policies and on instructional practices and their impact on student performance over the first two years of the Longitudinal Evaluation of School Change and Performance conducted in seventy-one elementary schools in seven states and eighteen school districts that moved early to implement standards, align assessments, and adopt other elements of reform policy.

Verstegen, Deborah A. "Financing the New Adequacy: Towards New Models of State Education Finance Systems That Support Standards Based Reform." *Journal of Education, Finance* 27 (Winter 2002): 749–782. This article reviews proposals for new educational funding schemes.

Media Resources

Changing Schools Through Shared Decision Making (ASCD video, 30 min., 1994). This video shows the benefits of a shared approach to decision making on curriculum, instruction, and management policies. It shows how schools and districts successfully seek input from teachers, school support staff, parents, and students.

Children in America's Schools, with Bill Moyers (South Carolina ETV Marketing, 2 hrs., first 60 min. most informative, 1996). Using Jonathan Kozol's book, *Savage Inequalities: Children in America's Schools,* as a starting point, this video depicts the undeniable inequities in American schools today.

The Crafting of America's Schools: The Power of Localism (Insight Media, 40 min., 1997). Theodore Sizer argues for national quality of education through redesign of curriculum, assessment, and instructional practice through the exercise of local responsibility and control.

Inner City vs. Suburban Schools (Films for the Humanities and Sciences, 28 min., 1993). This specially adapted Phil Donahue program provides a platform for parents as well as for Jonathan Kozol. Both the parents and Kozol claim that America's educational system is savagely unequal and discriminatory.

It's Your Money (Annenberg/CPB Videos, 60 min., 1995). This video compares the vastly varying conditions in schools from one community to the next and examines how educational budgets are spent.

Unequal Education (Films for the Humanities and Sciences, 60 min., 1992). This video examines the political rhetoric versus the reality of American schooling. A video profile of students at two different public schools in the Bronx points out the inequities of our current system and how the discrepancies affect the quality of education. Includes comments from John Chubb and Jonathan Kozol.

Media distributor contact information is available in Appendix I.

Student Activities

School Observation—A School Board Meeting

As part of your field experiences, you're assigned the task of attending a local school board meeting, which will be your first such meeting. You arrive early at the school auditorium where the meeting is taking place. After the Pledge of Allegiance is said and a few housekeeping details are addressed, the chairman of the school board invites the public to comment on a proposed redistricting plan under consideration. You think this is a reasonable way to solicit public opinion; but you are completely shocked by the comments and the high emotions displayed. One African-American man denounces the school board for creating a school attendance plan that will require children living in a mainly black neighborhood to ride more than 40 minutes each way on the bus to attend their assigned school. Many other African-Americans in the audience shout loud support for the speaker's comments. A white woman then gets up and criticizes the school board and the superintendent because her daughter has to attend a new school even though most of her friends will continue to go to the old one. A white man then denounces the board for its proposed plan because of the additional transportation costs that will be incurred. Finally, two high school students complain that the new school they'll be required to attend doesn't have a swimming pool and their competitive swimming program will be ended. By the end of the meeting, you are exhausted by the rancor, shouting, and strong feelings of the 2 1/2-hour meeting.

    a.   What points raised in this textbook can you find illustrated in this vignette?

    b.   Have you experienced a similar situation in any school or school board meetings you've attended? If so, describe the issues raised and the various positions taken.

    c.   Write another vignette that you think might realistically illustrate a point made in this chapter. Exchange your vignette with three other students' vignettes and discuss the various perspectives that the writings reveal.

Budget Role Play

The purpose of this exercise is to simulate the problems that school boards and educators deal with annually to balance the budget. Divide students into groups of two or three.

A student or group of students will be given an assignment that requires a presentation to the school board in order to retain or improve the current level of services for various program areas. Ask the students to assume the role of one of the influence groups (students, parents, taxpayers, professional education organizations, etc.) for their rationale and presentation.

BOARD OF EDUCATION (one group of three)

    a.   Elect a chair for the board.

    b.   Evaluate the various presentations to the board.

    c.   Recess, discuss, and vote on the proposals.

    d.   Final decisions must allow only a $6 million increase in the budget.

        Note to Instructors: Adjust the budget amount if you don't use all the requests.

PRESENTATIONS TO THE BOARD

a.   Plan a 2-minute presentation that gives the best rationale for keeping a program or increasing the services of that program.

b.   Present alternatives that indicate that you are trying to save the board money or are willing to compromise.

COMPUTER LABS

Need $0.7 million to keep programs at current levels, or the district will have to halt plans for putting a computer lab in each elementary school and for adding IBM computers at each high school to go with the current Macintosh computers.

INSTRUMENTAL MUSIC

Need $0.5 million to maintain elementary music teachers, or the district will have to

a.   Eliminate one-half of the current music teachers at the elementary school level.

b.   Eliminate elementary band and orchestra for this year.

DROPOUT PROGRAMS

Need $0.75 million to retain this program at the current level, or the district will have to

a.   Cut the dropout prevention staff by 50 percent.

b.   Eliminate this year's purchase of additional materials for the high school retention programs.

c.   Cut the elementary bilingual staff by 25 percent.

d.   Eliminate the community liaison position.

TEACHER SALARY INCREASES

Need $2 million to grant the increase, or the district will have to cut the 3.5 percent salary raise that was approved at the last board meeting provided that funds were available at this last round of cuts. If there is no salary raise, this will be the second year in a row.

SPORTS

Need $0.75 million to maintain remaining services, or the district will have to

a.   Eliminate all varsity sports. Community would assume financial support of all continuing sports programs.

b.   Cut back 15 percent in high school P.E. teachers.

c.   Cut back 25 percent in elementary P.E. teachers.

d.   Operate intramurals on a volunteer basis.

ARTS

Need $0.5 million to keep remaining programs, or the district will have to

   a.   Eliminate all elementary art teachers.

   b.   Cut back 35 percent in secondary art teachers (7–12).

FOREIGN LANGUAGE PROGRAMS

Need $0.75 million to continue this program, or the district will have to

   a.   Cut junior high teachers by 25 percent.

   b.   Not replace any senior high teachers who leave their positions.

GIFTED AND TALENTED

Need $0.75 million to

   a.   Establish a part-time pullout program in each elementary school.

   b.   Hire traveling gifted and talented specialists to operate the pullout programs.

ELEMENTARY TEACHER AIDES

Need $1 million to retain the current ratio of 2 hours a day per teacher, including paperwork, student assistance, and lunch and recess supervision.

ELEMENTARY CLASS SIZE REDUCTION

Need $1 million to reduce the primary ratio of 1:25 to 1:22, and the intermediate ratio of 1:30 to 1:26.

INCLUSION/MAINSTREAMING SUPPORT

Need $1.5 million to provide support for the classroom teacher.

   a.   Add teacher aides to assist inclusion of pupils in their regular classrooms.

   b.   Institute a weighing system to reduce pupil-teacher ratios in relation to the additional time and attention required by the number of mainstreamed students in each classroom.

Allow students to prepare for a few minutes in class or to research their issue from one class period to the next. Allow the board members to study the issues ahead of time and develop a plan or philosophy for decision making. After the presentations, while the board is deliberating, discuss the rationales and tactics used by the various groups. Point out current points of view and issues that students may have omitted. Have the school board members present their decisions, their rationale, and the decision-making process they developed and chose to use.

Mini-Debates

Debate the relative pros and cons of the examples of commercialization described in the "Reading, Writing, and Purchasing" box in the text.

Channel One Analysis

Obtain permission for your students to watch several segments of Channel One. As they watch, ask them to note what strikes them. You may want to direct your students to the following issues. How many and what kind of commercials are included? How frequently are these commercials shown? What are the underlying messages promoted by the commercials? What kinds of informational programming does Channel One provide? How is it edited and presented for the viewers? After you finish watching, discuss with the students their insights and analysis. The discussion could also include commercialization of school buses, sporting events, and offerings in the school cafeteria.

Analysis of School Funding and Per-Pupil Spending (for individual or group work)

This project is ideally suited to those students in field-site schools. Collect economic and budgetary data from your field-site school. Try to collect the following information: per-pupil expenditure, teachers' salary scale, and a district graph of split of funds for materials, personnel, capital costs, etc. Find out what percent of the students receive free or reduced lunches. Collect reports on student academic achievement (standardized test scores, percentage who graduate, percentage who attend and who complete postsecondary education, drop-out rate, absenteeism rate)? Also collect information on the residential and commercial property tax rate. Ask what the percentage of the school district budget is supplied through other sources: corporate taxes, state and federal funding, and so on. What kinds of grants has the school applied for? What other fund raising projects are being pursued by student or parent groups? What kinds of programs will they support? What kinds of findings do you have? How does your field-site school compare to neighboring districts? Present your findings to the class in a chart or table form.

Alternative Funding Schemes for Schools (for individual or group work)

Research in greater detail the court cases concerning school funding in New Jersey, Kentucky, Texas, or, most recently, New Hampshire. What is the background of the state's school funding? What were the results? Based upon the court ruling, what are the alternative funding schemes being proposed or implemented? Or look at the public school funding in Michigan more closely, examining the background of this issue and how Michigan has chosen to fund its public schools.

Report on School Board Meeting (for individual or group work)

The school board plays an important role in local government. Each school district has different priorities, and they often reflect the interests of the school board members. Meetings are open to the public and are usually held monthly. Find out when the local school board meets and attend one meeting. If a printed agenda is provided, ask students to add to it their own notes on any hidden agenda items. After the meeting, analyze the various concerns raised, the issues presented, and the factions (if applicable). Also try to assess the relationship between the school board and the superintendent. Present your analysis to the whole class.

Student Assignments

The following activities are suggestions for student portfolio activities. They are a means of providing alternative assessment of the students' capabilities.

Independent Reading

Read and respond to any of the selections noted on the chapter/article correlation list found in the front of this manual for Ryan/Cooper, *Kaleidoscope: Readings in Education* (Houghton Mifflin, 2004). You may want to use the Article Review Form in *Kaleidoscope*.

Reflective Papers

Choose one of the following topics to write a reflective paper (2–5 pages). The purpose of the paper is to help you assimilate new knowledge by blending it with your previous knowledge and experiences.

1. Select a recent example of commercialization in the schools in your community and present your understanding of the issues involved and explain your position.

2. Consider yourself both as a student and as a prospective teacher and describe your views on year-round schooling. If you are observing in a school now, consider the impact year-round schooling would have on your school setting.

3. In many respects, local control is guaranteed over public schools as long as property taxes fund such a large percentage of the school budget. Any attempt to equalize educational spending across districts, some argue, diminishes local control and ultimately parents' freedom to select schooling for their own child. Others vehemently disagree, claiming that the per-pupil spending disparity among school districts is grossly unfair; therefore, the funding of schools needs to be dramatically changed. What do you think?

Journal Reflections

Suggestions for journal topics for students' selection:

1. Describe how you think the inequities in school funding could be resolved.

2. What do you think is the relationship between school funding and student achievement? Why?

3. Outside of a teacher position, in which of the governing roles (legislator, principal, superintendent, school board member) would you most like to serve? Why?

CD-ROM Video Clip

View the clip for Chapter 10 and be prepared to discuss the following reflection questions:

1. In your opinion, where should the locus of control for funding, curricula, standards, and instructional methods be in the public schools: at the site level, the district level, the state level, or the federal level? Why?

2. Which problems facing the public schools today could be eased by the charter school model, where the locus of control is at the site level? What new problems might this model introduce?

CHAPTER 11

How Should Education Be Reformed?

LEARNING OBJECTIVES

After studying the chapter, students will be able to

1. recognize the complexity of educational reform in the United States.

2. identify and describe seven elements that are essential to true and lasting school reform.

3. explain national efforts to bring about educational reform.

4. describe state reform efforts, identifying common elements found in these efforts.

5. identify successful state efforts to bring about educational reform.

6. explain the constraining factors that restrict local reform efforts.

CHAPTER OVERVIEW

Chapter 11 looks at the school reform movement, discussing both what it should be and what it has been. We preface our discussion on the reform of education by reminding prospective teachers of the complexity of trying to reform public education in America, especially in light of the range of views about what constitutes a "good" education.

We introduce the reform movement by reminding prospective teachers of the three aims of education: to develop the democratic citizen, the good worker, and the private person. With these three aims as an ideal, we propose seven components that we feel are essential to true and lasting school reform. These components, present to varying degrees in successful reform projects, include a call to high standards, accountability, active learning, community, lifelong learning, character education, and professional development. Each of these elements is described to provide prospective teachers with an understanding of what each element incorporates and how we feel it can improve the quality of education in our schools.

The second part of the chapter discusses the actual reform initiatives that are being carried out. We present reform efforts from the national, state, and local level. At the national level, proposals are being formulated by the federal government, such as the Goals 2000: Educate America Act. National groups of scholars in different disciplines and fields are developing curriculum frameworks, standards, or in some cases entire curriculum plans that attempt to identify essential skills and knowledge that students should possess in these disciplines. State reform efforts have emphasized structural change, promoting more time in schools, higher graduation requirements, statewide testing, and higher standards and salaries for teachers. We also note that state reform efforts tend to involve top-down reform with changes that may be more cosmetic than effective and that have led primarily to a loss of local autonomy and authority. Local efforts have been limited primarily because of lack of funding, not lack of interest.

We close the chapter with a reminder that educational change is a slow, demanding process, but one that cannot be successful without the involvement of teachers, who are at the very heart of the educational process.

CHAPTER OUTLINE

I. What Ought to Be the Elements of Educational Reform?
    A. A Call for Excellence
    B. High Standards
    C. Accountability
    D. Active Learning: The Constructivists' Approach
    E. A Sense of Community
        1. Schools-Within-Schools
    F. Life-long Learning
        1. Tools for Learning
    G. Reclaiming Character Education
        1. Arguments Pro and Con
        2. Character in the Curriculum
        3. Service Learning
    H. Professional Development
II. Current Reform Initiatives
    A. National-Level Reform Efforts
        1. National Goals for the Year 2000
        2. National Standards
        3. National Voluntary Networks
    B. State Educational Reform
        1. Common Elements in State Reforms
    C. Local-Level School Reform
III. The Current State of School Reform

SUPPLEMENTARY LECTURE AND DISCUSSION TOPICS

1. **State educational reform** What has been done in your state in the way of educational reform? Present the reform efforts that are being discussed or have been implemented in your state. What is the focus of these reform efforts? Ask the students to identify which of the nine essential principles are evidenced in the state reform proposal.

2. **Goals 2000: Educate America Act** Explain in greater depth the history of this act. Discuss the Education Summit of 1989, explaining why it was held, who attended, and what the outcome of the summit was. Relating back to Chapter 9, you may want to evoke the idea that the federal government has no authority over education in the United States. How then, can the Goals 2000 act be constitutional? Have the students identify the overriding goals of the act and ask them to discuss whether these goals have been achieved.

3. **Values in schools** Explain in greater depth the debate around character education. Present the historical perspective of character education, highlighting the 1960s and 1970s, when values clarification became the most widely practiced approach to teaching values in school. Compare that period to the renewed interest in character education. Ask students to identify factors that affect the teaching of values in schools.

4. **Local reform efforts** Try to locate a school or school district in your area that has successfully implemented reform efforts. Ask a well-informed participant, a teacher, principal, or superintendent, to come to class and talk about the reform proposal. Your guest could talk about the content of the reform proposal and the process for implementing the proposed changes.

5. **Community building** If there is a middle or high school in your area that has instituted houses, ask someone who is familiar with the structure to come and talk to the students. The guest speaker should focus on the rationale behind creating houses and what the effect of these houses has been on the school environment. Has he or she seen any improvement in the academic performance of the students? How have the social and emotional climates of the school been affected?

6. **Site-based management and total quality management (TQM)** Introduce your students to the concepts of site-based management and TQM. Explain that these ideas originally came from business and are being

tried out in the school setting. Discuss the principles behind them and how they are to affect school effectiveness, at least from a theoretical standpoint. As more research is carried out on the effectiveness of these approaches, a more solid position can be formulated.

STUDY GUIDE — CHAPTER 11: HOW SHOULD EDUCATION BE REFORMED?

Completing this study guide will help you prepare for the major topic areas on an exam; however, it does not cover every piece of information found in the chapter or the test questions.

1. What are the "three people" in each student that need to be educated?

2. List and describe the seven elements of education reform.

3. Explain the constructivist theory of learning.

4. Compare and contrast authentic assessment with the traditional model of assessment.

5. Describe the components of character education.

6.   Explain the genesis and significance of the *A Nation at Risk* report.

7.   What are six common components of state reform efforts?

8.   List and give an example of each of the three initiatives to improve teacher quality.

9.   Identity the five principles suggested to guide reform.

ADDITIONAL RESOURCES FOR INSTRUCTORS

Clark, David, and Terry Astuto. "Redirecting Reform. Challenges to Popular Assumptions About Teachers and Students." *Phi Delta Kappan* 75 (March 1994): 512–20. Clark and Astuto maintain that responsibility for reforming schools must be a grassroots effort. They examine the assumptions underlying reform efforts and show why these efforts have been unsuccessful to date.

Fine, Michelle. *Chartering Urban School Reform.* New York: Teachers College Press, 1994. This book is designed to provoke a radical rethinking of educational practice and research for school-based change in urban America. A series of essays written by school reformers, it presents the development of a reform movement in an urban district.

Finn, Chester E., Jr., and Diane Ravitch. *Education Reform 1995–1996.* Indianapolis, IN: Hudson Institute, 1996. Two scholars, veterans of the school wars, lay out a clear and detailed blueprint for the reform of American schools.

Fullan, Michael. *Changing Forces: Probing the Depths of Educational Reform.* Bristol, PA: Falmer Press, 1993. Drawing on research from successful organizations in business and education, Fullan identifies eight basic lessons about why change is seemingly chaotic and what to do about it.

Hirsch, E. D. *The Schools We Need and Why We Don't Have Them.* New York: Doubleday, 1996. This long-time advocate of "cultural literacy" describes what is right and what is wrong with our schools in a wide-ranging, scholarly, and highly readable book on educational reform.

Hirsch, Eric, Julia E. Koppich, and Michael S. Knapp, *Revisiting What States Are Doing to Improve The Quality of Teaching: An Update on Patterns And Trends.* Seattle, Washington: Center for the Study of Teaching and Policy. University of Washington, 2001. This is a compilation of information on trends in state efforts at education reform.

Likona, Thomas. "The Return of Character Education." *Educational Leadership* 51 (November 1993): 6–12. Likona presents a historical overview of character education in the United States and explains why character education has received a groundswell of support in the last ten years.

Moffett, James. "On to the Past: Wrong-headed School Reform." *Phi Delta Kappan* 75 (April 1994): 584–90. Moffett questions the assumptions of the business world that educational reform based on free-market competition can bring about effective change in American schools. He argues that educators need to look at what works best in education, not in business or bureaucracy, to reform schools.

Rossi, Robert. *Schools and Students at Risk.* New York: Teachers College Press, 1994. This book provides an examination of reform efforts aimed at students at risk for failure in our schools. The four parts of the book cover the historical perspective of the reform efforts, the context in which reform must take place, current reforms, and a new framework for change.

Ryan, Kevin and Karen Bohlin. *Building Character In Schools: Practical Ways to Bring Moral Instruction to Life.* San Francisco: Jossey-Bass, 1999. This book offers to teachers both a theory and a set of practical steps to infuse their teaching with core moral values. In addition, the book has many pages of practical lists and materials to promote character in classrooms and schools.

Sizer, Theodore, and Nancy Sizer. *The Children Are Watching.* Boston: Beacon Press, 1999. This short book, by two veterans of the school reform wars, focuses on the personal side of the reform effort. The Sizers describe schools and students the way they currently are and then suggest ways teachers need to respond.

Tanner, Daniel. "A Nation 'Truly' at Risk." *Phi Delta Kappan* 75 (December 1993): 288–97. Tanner responds to the proposals in America 2000 and reproduced in Goals 2000, contending that some of them need to be challenged in light of the other reports of studies carried out by different groups, in particular the Sandia Report. Tanner compares the findings and recommendations of the two reports and concludes that the priorities of educational reform must be clearly focused on improving the educational quality of our schools, not meeting the political goals of diverse groups.

Toch, Thomas. *In the Name of Excellence: The Struggle to Reform the Nation's Schools, Why It's Failing and What Ought to Be Done*. New York: Oxford University Press, 1991. Toch presents a critical analysis of the quest to make the nation's schools "excellent" by analyzing some flaws within the existing reform movement. He also proposes some alternative approaches that would improve the nation's schools.

Wiggins, Grant. "Assessment: Authentic, Context, and Validity." *Phi Delta Kappan* 75 (November 1993): 200–14. Wiggins suggests that test makers recognize their obligation to link their tests to the tasks, contexts, and "feel" of real-world challenges.

Media Resources

America's Schools: Who Gives a Damn? Part I (PBS video, 60 min., 1991). The role of the teacher is examined as one factor in the continuing dilemma of a failing public school system. The "bureaucracy" and the "system" are also suspected culprits.

Capturing the Essentials: High Schools That Make Sense (Insight Media, 35 min., 1998). Theodore Sizer profiles three exemplary high schools, showing how their learning environments are shaped by fundamental ideas that transcend issues, curriculum, and standards thereby creating learning environments that are simple, flexible, and humane.

Character 101: Reading, Writing, and Respect (Films for the Humanities and Sciences, 21 min., 1995). This program focuses on the issue of character education and shows what some schools are doing to combat vandalism, violence, and cheating: to teach good citizenship and moral behavior; and to answer the questions that students themselves are asking about what it means to be a good person.

Character Education: Application in the K–6 Classroom (Insight Video, 40 min., 1998). This video explains what character education is and describes the importance of creating a moral culture in the school community, and teaching such virtues as responsibility and respect.

Character Education: Restoring Respect and Responsibility in Our Schools (Character Education Partnership (CEP), 44 min., 1999). Dr. Thomas Lickona presents the argument for the role schools can play in helping students develop responsibility and strong ethics.

Commitment to Character (CEP, 10 min., 1996). An overview of the history and philosophy supporting character education with brief site visits to schools.

In Schools We Trust (Annenberg/CPB Videos, 60 min., 1996). The history of public school reform from the "Americanization" movement to the current drive to raise standards is portrayed.

Lessons for the Future: Today's Schools (Films for the Humanities and Sciences, 46 min., 1993). In this urgent wake-up call to American society, journalism icon Walter Cronkite interviews principals, teachers, educational experts, parents, and students to reveal why educational reform is so hard to implement and showcases three schools where innovations have proved that change is possible.

Liberating America's Schools (PBS video, 60 min., 1993). This documentary shows the school choice movement through the eyes of parents, students, teachers, administrators, and community activists who have tried choice as a means to achieving better schools.

Predicting the Future of Education (Insight Media, 70 min., 1999). In this video, Willard Daggett analyzes a series of technological, economic, workplace, demographic, and social trends that will have a dramatic impact on schools in the immediate future. He makes a series of bold predictions of fundamental changes that will occur in and around schools over the next several years.

Teaching Values in Schools (Insight Media, 60 min., 1992). This video features a debate by educators, business people, and government officials on whether or not values should be explicitly taught in school and, if so, how they should be presented.

There's No Place Like Home: The Return to Homeschooling (Films for the Humanities and Sciences, 30 min., 2000). Recent statistics indicate that more than two million students in the U.S. are taught at home. This program examines the homeschooling phenomenon through the eyes of those involved in homeschooling.

What Should We Do in School Today? (Insight Media, 22 min., 1992). This video explores some of the most pressing issues facing educators today. It examines problems with curriculum, discipline, teacher evaluation, and children at risk, and visits innovative programs around the country that aim to improve the quality of education.

Why Do these Kids Love School? (Pyramid, 60 min., 1990). This documentary visits schools around the country that have introduced bold, innovative programs in which students, teachers, parents, and administrators join together to create a vibrant and supportive educational environment. The video underscores the strong student and faculty morale and the improved test scores that have resulted from these programs.

Why Is Change So Hard? (Insight Media, 22 min., 1995). Systematic school change is a difficult process, even when staff members are committed to it. Designed to help school administrators facilitate change, this video shows the change process as a "work in progress."

Will School Reform Ever Work? (Insight Media, 90 min., 1999). This video features a panel discussion on the question of the utility of school reform. It features the commentary of Linda Darling-Hammond, John Goodlad, Ann Lieberman, Peter Senge, and Theodore Sizer.

Media distributor contact information is available in Appendix I.

Student Activities

School Observation—Reform Ideas for a Specific School

As a nation, the United States has been rather complacent about its schools during the last half of the twentieth century. Once the envy of the world, our elementary and secondary schools have become the focus of serious criticism from both inside and outside our borders. However, for the last fifteen years, with growing energy and commitment, we have been trying to reform our schools. As a new teacher, you will be a part of school reform. And, as a professional, you should consider yourself a person who will contribute to the reform agenda.

With this in mind, select a school you know well—one you attended yourself, or one in which you've been spending a good deal of time as a student teacher. Think about various aspects of that school, from curriculum to teaching methods, from the physical facilities to the extracurricular life of the students. Then develop a list of reforms that you believe the school should adopt.

On the basis of your observations and reflections, answer the following questions:

a. How does your list of reforms for your particular school compare with this chapter's discussion of the "oughts" of schools reform: Are your school's needs similar to those we have been describing for American schools in general? Why or why not?

b. Why do you believe your suggested reforms have not yet taken place in your school? Lack of money? Lack of leadership? Are your ideas too radical?

c. From your list of possible reforms, which do you favor most? That is, if you could implement only one idea, which would it be and why?

d. Review your list of reforms and identify which group would be the major beneficiary. Students? Teachers? Taxpayers?

State and National Curriculum Reform

Have the students form groups according to their subject area of interest to investigate what has been done in that subject area or discipline by professional associations and state governing bodies to standardize and harmonize the learning of essential skills and knowledge. In some areas like science, there is more than one group developing curriculum guides or frameworks. (Elementary education majors should focus on the elementary goals and established state or national standards in the subject area of their choice.)

The students can also look at the feasibility of the standards that have been set. Based on their experience and on the textbooks available or other instructional materials, do the students believe that the proposals developed or the standards set can be realized?

Have each group present its findings to the class.

Keys to Educational Reform

Students are divided into seven groups, with each group assigned one of the key elements of true educational reform from the text. The students can think about the specific desired effects that these elements seek to bring about. For example, how will authentic assessment or active learning help improve the quality of education? Students may find a flow chart a helpful way of organizing their thinking.

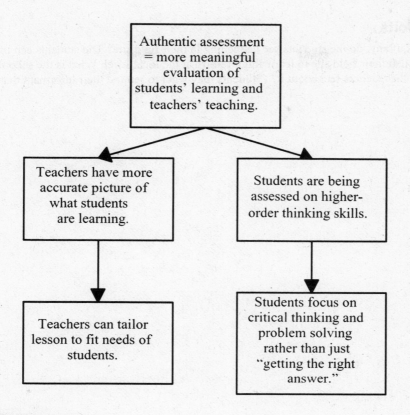

Model Reform Projects

Although national or state reforms have brought about limited improvement in public education, there are a number of success stories in individual schools or districts. The Comer School, Sizer's Essential Schools, Slavin's Success For All Schools, and Levin's Accelerated Schools are examples of successful reform projects. Have students research a successful reform project carried out at either the school or the district level. In their research, they would want to consider the following questions:

- Who initiated the project?

- What kind of support was there for the project—from the faculty, administration, central office administration?

- Who participated in the development and implementation of the project?

- Where did the funding for the project come from?

- What did the project focus on? What were its goals? Why was there a need for this reform project?

- What have been the effects of the project on student learning and school climate?

- Have any attempts been made to replicate the project in another school or district? With what results?

Local Reform Efforts

What reform projects, if any, do the students see happening in their field site? The students can interview a knowledgeable person at their field site to learn about reform at the local level. What is the school doing? Who is initiating it? How do the teachers feel about it? (Students may want to remind their informant that all information is confidential.)

Student Assignments

The following activities are suggestions for student portfolio activities. They are a means of providing alternative assessment of students' capabilities.

Independent Reading

Read and respond to any of the selections noted on the chapter/article correlation list found in the front of this manual for Ryan/Cooper, *Kaleidoscope: Readings in Education* (Houghton Mifflin, 2004). You may want to use the Article Review Form in *Kaleidoscope*.

Reflective Papers

Choose one of the following topics to write a reflective paper (2–5 pages). The purpose of the paper is to help you assimilate new knowledge by blending it with your previous knowledge and experiences.

1.   Think about your own education and what values and morals you were taught in school either explicitly or implicitly through the teachers' behaviors, the school climate, or district funding of educational activities. What behaviors were encouraged and consequently valued among the students? Between the students and teachers? Between teachers and administrators? How would you describe the moral environment of your high school?

2.   You have no doubt had the experience of hearing someone recount an event that you were present at or participated in, yet that person's retelling of the event diverges significantly from your recollection of the event. Taking a constructivist's approach to learning, how can we explain these differences? Is it that one person is telling the truth and the other isn't?

3.   Have you ever been evaluated through portfolio assessment? What was the experience like? How did you react to the portfolio process? Did you feel that the portfolio accurately conveyed your ability in that subject area? Was that approach to assessment more or less stressful than a final exam? Why?

Journal Reflections

Suggestions for journal topics for students' selection:

1.   Into which of the seven elements of educational reform would you put the most effort to achieve the greatest improvement? Why?

2.   Do you feel the initiatives to improve the quality of education will be successful? Why or why not?

3.   How will you go about teaching character education in your own classroom?

CHAPTER 12

What Are Your Job Options in Education?

LEARNING OBJECTIVES

After studying the chapter, students will be able to

1. describe the current and projected job market in education.

2. explain factors that affect the supply and demand of teaching positions.

3. identify and explain effective job search strategies.

4. describe the purpose of both traditional-route and alternative-route licensure.

5. identify competencies and areas of specialized knowledge that may enhance their employment opportunities.

6. identify other occupations for which they may be qualified on completion of a teacher education program.

CHAPTER OVERVIEW

As prospective teachers begin to contemplate a career in teaching, they are plagued by many questions. Two of the more crucial ones are "Where will I find a job?" and "How will I find a job?" This chapter attempts to answer these questions by presenting a portrait of the current job market in education, discussing the factors that influence that job market, and then providing prospective teachers with some advice about job hunting.

The chapter first describes the current job market in education, which we see as very promising because the number of new teachers needed for elementary and secondary schools is projected to rise until at least 2008 due to increasing student enrollments and teacher retirements.

We expect to see the number of teachers increase by 9.4 percent between 2000 and 2008 to keep up with projected increases in student enrollment and teacher retirements. The greatest need for teachers continues to be minority teachers, who represent only 9 percent of the teaching population, even though the minority student population is near 36 percent.

The second part of the chapter discusses the various factors that influence the supply and demand of teachers in the job market. While the unpredictability of the job market is highlighted, factors that impact the availability of teaching positions, such as subject area, geographic location, community demographics, and type of school (public or private) are explained. Trends in teachers' salaries and benefits as well as salary schedules are described to help prospective new teachers understand the financial complexities of teaching.

We give prospective teachers some helpful job search strategies, recommending that they develop a plan for their search and that they campaign actively for teaching positions. Skills necessary for job applicants include preparation of a résumé, cover letter, credentials, and interview skills. We also suggest that prospective teachers construct a teaching portfolio to be presented to possible employers.

The chapter also presents important information on licensure, both in traditional and alternative routes. We make note of the wide range of requirements for either route of licensure, depending on the state. We also acquaint prospective teachers with the Teach for America program as one alternative program. We remind prospective teachers of the reciprocity agreements for licensure that exist between many states, but also encourage them to pursue more than one licensure area in order to make themselves more attractive candidates.

Finally, we explore options for those teacher candidates who are unsuccessful in finding a teaching position or decide that teaching is not for them. We identify some of the teaching skills that are transferable to other jobs, making teachers attractive candidates for those jobs as well.

CHAPTER OUTLINE

I.   Will There Be Job Openings in Education?
- A.   Factors Influencing Teacher Supply and Demand
  1.   Student Enrollment
  2.   Class Sizes
  3.   Enrollment in Teacher Education Programs
  4.   Geographical Location
  5.   Subject Matter and Grade Levels Taught
  6.   Retiring Teachers, Teacher Turnover, and Returning Teachers
  7.   Economic Conditions
- B.   The Severe Shortage of Minority Teachers
- C.   Employers Besides the Public Schools
  1.   U.S. Government
  2.   Private Schools
- D.   What Are Teachers Paid?

II.   How Do You Obtain a Teaching Position?
- A.   Campaign Actively
- B.   Prepare Materials
- C.   Develop Interview Skills
- D.   Determine Job Availability
- E.   Gain Experience Through Substitute Teaching

III.   How Do You Become Licensed?
- A.   Traditional Licensure Programs
- B.   Alternative Licensure

IV.   If You Don't Teach, What Then?
- A.   Transferable Skills
- B.   Other Jobs

SUPPLEMENTARY LECTURE AND DISCUSSION TOPICS

1. **Merit pay for teachers** This concept, promoted as a way to retain and reward expert teachers, is by no means universally hailed. The National Education Association was and is opposed to the concept because of the difficulty of implementing it fairly. Because of its potential to change fundamental aspects of the teaching profession and because it provokes such heated debate, this is a topic well worth exploring with your class.

2. **Public school versus private school teaching** The advantages and disadvantages of teaching in private schools, as opposed to public schools, can be examined. Discussion can include salaries, job availability, licensure, personal rewards, discipline, student motivation, and parental support.

3. **Job interviews** Invite one or more personnel officers from local school districts to visit your classes to describe what they look for when hiring new teachers. They can also discuss the kinds of teaching positions that are most in demand.

4. **Information on your state's requirements** You may want to detail for students the licensure/certification procedures and requirements in your state.

5. **Alternative and traditional teaching licensure** Since the mid-1980s, alternative routes to teaching licensure have been gaining strength. A class lecture devoted to further explanation of this change in teaching licensure is helpful. The text mentions that these licensure programs vary widely. It is a useful exercise to examine several states' alternative teaching licensure programs to discern their underlying notions of what constitutes adequate preparation to teach. You can also devote some time to the traditional licensure requirements and explain the recent changes in many states' licensure procedures.

STUDY GUIDE — CHAPTER 12: WHAT ARE YOUR JOB OPTIONS IN EDUCATION?

Completing this study guide will help you prepare for the major topic areas on an exam; however, it does not cover every piece of information found in the chapter or the test questions.

1.　What are the major factors influencing the demand for new teachers?

2.　What are beginning teacher salaries and average teacher salaries on the national level and at your state level?

National:

Beginning _____

Average　　_____

Your state:

Beginning _____

Average　　_____

3.　Describe the purpose and procedures for alternative licensure.

4.　What are the advantages and disadvantages of teaching in a private school?

5.   What are some other job options open to teachers besides classroom instruction?

6.   What are the components of a successful job search?

7.   Licensure requirements are enacted by states to accomplish what purpose?

8.   Why is there a shortage of minority teachers?

9.   Why is it important to have minority teachers (for white students as well as minority students)?

10.   What are the advantages of substitute teaching while you are looking for a full-time position?

11.   Distinguish between the terms *licensure* and *certification*.

ADDITIONAL RESOURCES FOR INSTRUCTORS

"Alternative Certification." *Kappa Delta Pi Record* 36(l) (Fall 1999): 8–30. This edition contains a collection of articles discussing alternative certification teaching internships in California, alternative certification programs, and mature teaching candidates.

ASCUS Annual: A Job Search Handbook for Educators. Evanston, Ill.: Association for School, College and University Staffing. An annual publication designed to assist both new and experienced educators in their job searches, and the single most important reference in this topic. The *Annual* is usually distributed through career planning and placement offices in colleges and universities, but it may also be obtained from the ASCUS Office, 1600 Dodge Ave., S-330, Evanston, IL 60201-3451, (847) 864-1999.

Edelfelt, Roy A. *Careers in Education*. 3rd ed. Lincolnwood, IL: NTC Contemporary Publishing, 1998. This book explores various educational careers in teaching, administration, higher education, business, and industry.

Feistritzer, C. Emily, and David T. Chester. "Alternative Teacher Certification: A State-by-State Analysis 1996." *Washington, D.C. National Center for Education Information*. This analysis provides information on requirements and procedures in each state that has alternative licensure.

Feldman, Sandra. "Two Million Teachers." *American Teacher* 83(3) (November 1998): 5. There are fears that efforts to recruit 2.2 million new teachers over the next ten years will be hampered by inadequate pay and working conditions. With serious shortages already hitting many districts, some boards of education are offering signing bonuses as a means of attracting new teachers.

Galuzzo, Gary. "Will the Best and the Brightest Teach?" *Education Week* 18(34) (May 5, 1999): 56+. The writer discusses how the real teacher shortage is in attracting people who have not been attracted to teaching before, preparing them in a professional culture, employing, supporting, and retaining them.

Hussar, William J., and Debra E. Gerald, *Projections of Education Statistics to 2008*. Washington, DC: National Center for Education Statistics, 1998. Presents current projections for the next decade.

Lewis, Anne C. "Just Say No to Unqualified Teachers." *Phi Delta Kappan* 80(3) (November 1998): 179–80. The article presents ideas from America's leading researcher on teacher quality, Linda Darling-Hammond, who says school districts ought not to recruit unqualified teachers. According to conservative estimates, the demand for extra teachers will reach around 200,000 a year for the next decade, and between half and two-thirds of these people will be first-time teachers.

Meek, Anne. "America's Teachers: Much to Celebrate." *Educational Leadership* 55(5) (February 1998): 12–16. Presents a positive review of the current teaching force.

Pipho, Chris. "A Real Teacher Shortage." *Phi Delta Kappan* 80(3) (November 1998): 181–2. It is unclear whether the present lack of teaching staff in America will become a full-blown teacher shortage. The lack of teachers is acute in a number of states and in urban areas, and the problem is just now coming to the attention of the public.

Salaries Paid Professional Personnel in Public Schools, 1996–1997. Arlington, VA: Educational Research Services, 1997. This document presents the results of a survey of the annual salaries of people in professional and support positions in over a thousand school districts. The data are reported separately for large, medium, small, and very small school districts, and for eight different geographical regions.

Media Resources

The Endangered Teacher (Films for the Humanities and Sciences, 29 min., 1996).Educators around the country are leaving their field because of inadequate salaries, working conditions, and budget cuts. Is the future of the teaching profession at risk? What can be done to attract and keep excellent teachers in our schools? This program explores the role of the teacher in our society today.

Teacher Shortage False Alarm? (Learning Matters, 57 min., 1999). This program explores the issue of teacher shortage, which may be more an issue of appropriate education, training, mentoring, and administrative support for prospective teachers, rather than actual shortage of teachers graduating from the nation's colleges and universities.

Who Will Teach for America? (PBS video, 60 min., 1993). This documentary is about Teach for America, an organization that is modeled to bring 500 college graduates who deferred their careers to teach for two years in urban schools.

Media distributor contact information is available in Appendix I.

Student Activities

School Observation—Teaching Salaries

After observing a classroom for an hour, you stop in the teachers' lounge to pick up a soft drink. As you sit, sipping your drink, you overhear a conversation between two teachers seated close to you. Teacher #1 says that she is thinking about getting out of teaching and going to work in an advertising agency because she's afraid that as a single mother she can't save enough money on her teacher's salary to send her two children to college. Teacher #2 is very sympathetic, confessing that she can afford to teach only because she and her husband both work.

Both teachers admit that they love their jobs, especially working with the kids in their school, but they don't think the community really appreciates all the work they do as teachers. If the community did appreciate them, they say, their salaries would be higher. The raises they've received over the last few years have barely kept even with inflation, and they just don't seem to be able to gain any ground. The two teachers exit the room, leaving you thinking about their conversation.

a. If you overheard such a conversation, how would it affect your own plans about teaching?

b. What are your expectations regarding your beginning teacher's salary? Do you think you will make enough money as a teacher to satisfy your needs? How do you know?

c. For school districts in your area, at what salaries do you think beginning teachers start? If you don't know, do some research to find out.

d. Talk to some beginning and experienced teachers to determine if lack of money is a problem for them, and how they manage to make a living. Do they work at other jobs during the summer? Do they feel they are making financial sacrifices?

e. Compare your findings with those of other students in your class. Is this an area of concern to them?

Writing Your Résumé (out-of-class activity)

Have students write their own résumé out of class and then bring it in for review and discussion with classmates. They may refer to the résumé in the text and the one included here as models. They should also contact the career center on their campus regarding available resources and services.

The Job Interview

This activity allows students to experience a simulated job interview. Allow 25 minutes for it. Have one person role-play the personnel director and the other the prospective teacher. Identify the grade level or content area for the job opening. *After 10 minutes, reverse the roles.*

Instructions: You are the personnel director of a medium-size school district. A few job openings are available because teachers have retired and left the school system. Here are your main criteria for hiring new teachers:

a.   The prospective teacher must have only a bachelor's degree and little or no teaching experience (because you can hire almost two new inexperienced teachers for the price of each veteran teacher retiring from the system).

b.   The prospective teacher must be able to handle classroom discipline.

c.   The prospective teacher should be able to discuss many of the recent innovations in education.

d.   The prospective teacher should be a model for the students.

Here are some questions you may ask the prospective teacher:

a.   Why did you choose this school district over others?

b.   What would you do on the first day in class?

c.   What are some advantages and disadvantages of ability grouping or tracking?

d.   What do you think is the mission of the public schools? What abilities and competencies should they emphasize?

e.   What should be the role of the teacher in establishing moral standards?

f.   What is your philosophy of education?

g.   How do you visualize your classroom? What will you and the students be doing on a typical day or during a typical period?

h.   What are your views on discipline?

i.   We start our teachers at $25,000 and prohibit them from taking other jobs. How will this affect your decision on taking a position in our district?

j.   Where do you see yourself in five years? Ten years? What are your career goals?

k.   Why should we hire you?

Salary Schedules

Given the nature of school financing, teachers' salaries will vary. Have students determine the beginning salary for a B.A. or B.S. teacher in the school district in which they (a) reside, (b) intend to teach, or (c) graduated.

a.   Students should also compare at other points on the scale, for instance: MA and 5 years experience; maximum salary possible on the scale and requirements to receive it.

b.   Are there years in which no raise is given for experience?

c.   What effect do additional hours of education have on the amount of the salary?

d.   Does the district use any kind of merit system?

e.   Are school funding or salaries tied to student test scores?

f.   What other benefits are included in compensation?

Discuss differences in salary and other benefits.

Local School District Data

Much of the chapter has been devoted to discussing the statistical data concerning teaching. Have students collect data from different school districts in your area or from their home district so that they can compare statistical information from region to region.

Instructions for Students

Make an appointment with a local school personnel office and ask them to supply you with statistical information regarding the teaching demand or surplus they have experienced. Here are some suggested questions:

a.   What is the median age of teachers employed in this district?

b.   What is your pupil-teacher ratio? Do you expect it to change?

c.   How many students are in your district? Has this number been increasing or decreasing?

d.   If you will be hiring, are there any types of teachers for which you anticipate a particular demand? (examples: ESL, elementary, or physics teachers)

e.   If you do not expect to be hiring in the next few years, what are the reasons? Shrinking school enrollment? Stable supply of teachers? Economic constraints?

f.   What percentage of teachers will be eligible for retirement in the next five years?

g.   (If speaking to a personnel officer) Which factors make a teaching candidate appealing to this school district? (examples: years of teaching experience, dual certification, coaching or advising ability) What factors do you actively seek in a candidate, if any?

h.   Have any recent federal or state regulations affected the number of teachers hired?

Conclude with a class discussion comparing information.

Teacher Demographics

Ryan and Cooper speak of an aging teaching force, but is that the case in your community? Have the students form groups, and assign each group a school to investigate. Each group will describe the faculty of that school. How many teachers are in their 20's, 30's, 40's, 50's? Average number of years of teaching experience? How many teachers have been in the district fewer than five years? More than twenty years? How many male teachers are there? How many teachers of color are there?

Students are encouraged to chart their information, and then each group can present its findings.

Student Assignments

The following activities are suggestions for student portfolio activities. They are a means of providing alternative assessment of students' capabilities.

Independent Reading

Read and respond to any of the following selections noted on the chapter/article correlation list found in the front of this manual for Ryan/Cooper, *Kaleidoscope: Readings in Education* (Houghton Mifflin, 2004). You may want to use the Article Review in *Kaleidoscope*.

Reflective Papers

Choose one of the following topics to write a reflective paper (2–5 pages). The purpose of the paper is to help you assimilate new knowledge by blending it with your previous knowledge and experiences.

1.   What are your views on alternative-route licensure? Should it exist? For whom? Under what conditions? Keeping in mind that you are following the traditional route to licensure and learning a great deal about

education, do you think that a person who has not had a similar educational experience can be as effective a teacher as someone who has studied in the field of education?

2.   What strengths (and weaknesses) do you bring into teaching? Think about your own personality and describe the qualities that can help you be an effective teacher.

Journal Reflections

Suggestions for journal topics for students' selection:

1.   What are the factors that favor you to get a job in the district of your choice?

2.   Would you become a substitute teacher? Why or why not?

3.   Answer at least three of the sample interview questions from the chapter.

SAMPLE RÉSUMÉ

Glen P. Stewart

School Address: *Home Address:*
3413 Chestnut Street   15 Sea Mist Boulevard
Philadelphia, PA 19104   Stone Harbor, NJ
(215) 555-1234   (609) 555-9876

PROFESSIONAL OBJECTIVE
To obtain an English or language arts teaching position in middle or high school

EDUCATION
TEMPLE UNIVERSITY, Philadelphia, PA
    Bachelor of Arts. Majors: Theater Arts and English; minor: Education
    Cum laude. May 1999

OCEAN HIGH SCHOOL, Stone Harbor, NJ
    June 1993

EXPERIENCE
STUDENT TEACHER   Springfield High School
                                                     Springfield, PA
Taught ninth- and eleventh-grade English classes. Designed a thematic unit on "Heroes in Literature" and taught it to ninth grade. Taught *Macbeth* and SAT–vocabulary building skills to eleventh-graders. Conducted writing conferences for all students. Volunteered as assistant director for student production of *The Glass Menagerie.*

                                                     February–April, 1999

LITERACY TUTOR   West Philadelphia High School
Volunteered to help high school students and adults learn to read. Also assisted others in strengthening their reading abilities.

                                                     September 1993–April 1995

LIFEGUARD   Stone Harbor, NJ
Employed as lifeguard at town beach. Assisted in several rescues.

                                                     Summers 1993–1994

SWIMMING INSTRUCTOR   Stone Harbor Y.M.C.A.
                                                     Stone Harbor, NJ
Instructed several levels of swimmers, from beginner to advanced. Also instructed an advanced lifesaving course.

                                                     Summers, 1989–1992

ACTIVITIES
The Temple Players
Member of Temple University's acting troupe that performed on campus and at other locations throughout the city. Acted in *Long Day's Journey into Night, One Flew over the Cuckoo's Nest,* and *Waiting for Godot,* September 1996–May 1997

References available on request

CHAPTER 13

What Can the New Teacher Expect?

LEARNING OBJECTIVES

After studying the chapter, students will be able to

1. define and discuss the culture shock experienced by first-year teachers.

2. identify and explain the role of the principal and the principal's relationship to the teacher.

3. identify and explain supervisors' roles in the school.

4. summarize the authors' recommendations for the first day of teaching.

5. identify the most reliable indicator of a teacher's success with students.

6. describe the impact that other teachers can have on the first-year teacher's experience.

7. describe and analyze the potential difficulties inherent in parent-teacher communication.

8. identify and analyze the change that many first-year teachers undergo in their attitude toward children.

9. explain and analyze the concept of "social distance" between teacher and student.

10. identify and apply the practical teaching tips the authors supply for surviving the first year of teaching.

11. recognize the role and value of induction programs and the roles of mentors.

CHAPTER OVERVIEW

Because everyone has spent considerable time in schools, one might think that a prospective teacher's introduction to school life would be smoother than, say, that of a young trainee learning the culture of a large corporation. That sounds reasonable, but it is wrong. Our own experiences as teachers and educators of teachers have convinced us that most new teachers are surprised by the experience of becoming a teacher. The life of a teacher, they immediately discover, is worlds apart from the life of a student. Unexpected problems as well as unexpected pleasures confront every teacher during the first year of teaching.

The first year of teaching, many claim, is the most stressful of the teacher's career. *Everything*—from the school building to the teachers to the students to the job of teaching—is new. The new teacher can't refer to previous experience; so every lesson, every morning is uncharted territory. The first year is an awkward time of figuring out how to put theory into practice, how to put into effect all those good ideas collected during teacher education, and how to turn educational dreams into classroom realities.

Our purpose in this chapter is to have future teachers "walk in the shoes" of some teachers who have gone before them. There are two main reasons for taking this approach. First, if they do have a difficult time as beginning teachers, we want them to realize that "I am not alone. Others have had this problem." One of the worst adjustment difficulties many beginners face is their sense that no one else is having problems. Second, we believe that having them confront common problems at this stage in their preparation helps develop the breadth of awareness that may keep them from being undone by the nature and extent of the challenges they face. Our expectation is that such preparation will enhance their experience as new teachers.

CHAPTER OUTLINE

I.   The School Milieu: The Shock of the Familiar
    A.   Culture Shock
II.   Administrators: Mixed Bag and Many Hats
    A.   The Multiple Roles of the Principal
III. Peers: A Mixed Blessing
IV.   Instruction: So Much to Learn
V.   Students: Friends or Fiends?
    A.   Sources of a Distorted View
    B.   Classroom Management
        1.   Unaccustomed to Being in Charge
    C.   Social Distance
    D.   Sex
VI.   Parents: Natural Allies with Different Agendas
    A.   Reasons For Parent–Teacher Problems
VII. Surviving the First Year of Teaching
    A.   Begin Now
    B.   Keeping a Teaching Journal
    C.   The Proper Frame of Mind
    D.   Find a Mentor
    E.   Make Your Students' Parents Your Allies
    F.   Take Evaluation Seriously
    G.   Take Care of Yourself

SUPPLEMENTARY LECTURE AND DISCUSSION TOPICS

1.   **School structure and new teachers** Many schools have either brief orientation programs or induction programs designed for new teachers. Some systems have a mentor system where an experienced teacher is paired with a new teacher to provide support. The new teacher can talk to the mentor for special advice, feedback, and instructional ideas. Invite a mentor or a first- or second-year teacher to address your class. Discuss some of the practices available to help new teachers in schools in your area.

2.   **The role of the principal** Describe the roles and functions of a principal. Show how the principal's roles and functions that relate to the beginning teacher fit into the total picture. Invite a principal to address students regarding principal/teacher roles and relationships.

3.   **Sociology and school relations** Explain the way sociological variables affect relationships between teachers and their colleagues or their students' parents. For example, the location of a classroom in the building to some extent predicts its place in teachers' "traffic patterns" and perhaps creates greater or lesser likelihood that teachers will pass the classroom often and thus have frequent opportunities to extend friendship. Colleagues or parents who speak with the same accent as the teacher or come from the same part of the city or attended the same church or school may be given the warmest welcome in return for friendly comments. The teacher in the next room may become a mentor just because of proximity.

STUDY GUIDE — CHAPTER 13: WHAT CAN THE NEW TEACHER EXPECT?

Completing this study guide will help you prepare for the major topic areas on an exam; however, it does not cover every piece of information found in the chapter or the test questions.

1.   Give a brief description of at least six of the roles principals play.

2.   What kinds of help can new teachers expect from principals or supervisors?

3.   According to the authors, what accounts for the very idealistic views of children and classrooms that most new teachers have when they begin teaching?

4.   List and describe the reasons new teachers may experience discipline problems according to the authors.

5.   What are the two extremes of behavior new teachers may adopt when trying to establish appropriate social distance? Describe the problem with this.

6.   Identify and give an example of each of the five reasons for parent-teacher problems.

7.   What are the seven recommendations the authors make for surviving the first years of teaching?

8.   List the authors' six recommendations for getting off to a good start on the first day of school.

9.   What are the authors' seven additional rules for surviving the first year of teaching?

10.   What are induction programs and what roles do mentors play?

ADDITIONAL RESOURCES FOR INSTRUCTORS

Codell, Esme Raji. *Educating Esme: Diary of a Teacher's First Year*. Chapel Hill, NC: Algonquin Books, 1999. This book is the account of a new fifth-grade teacher in a Chicago inner-city school. Hip, imaginative, and irreverent, the book takes the reader through the triumphs and travails with students and a particularly dense administrator.

Grossman, Pamela. *The Making of a Teacher: Teacher Knowledge and Teacher Education*. New York: Teachers College Press, 1990. Grossman analyzes the skills and knowledge of the beginning teacher and offers recommendations for future teachers.

Kellough, Richard D. *Surviving the First Year of Teaching: Guidelines for Success*. Columbus, OH: Merrill/Prentice Hall, 1999. Designed specifically as a survival guide for beginners, this manual is filled with practical tips from first lessons to conducting conferences with parents.

Kronowitz, Ellen. *Beyond Student Teaching*. New York: Longman, 1992. This volume explores the stages and transitions that new teachers go through to move beyond their conceptions as a student teacher and into the role of a teacher.

Moran, Carol. *Keys to the Classroom: A Teacher's Guide to the First Month of School*. Newbury Park, CA: Corwin Press, 1992. This is a helpful, practical guide for establishing a successful year through the patterns and activities established during the first month.

Palonsky, Stuart. *900 Shows a Year: A Look at Teaching from a Teacher's Side of the Desk*. New York: Random House, 1986. The author recounts his experiences as a high school teacher in a small, suburban community outside New York City. The descriptions of his encounters with students, fellow teachers, and administrators are fresh and vivid.

Ryan, Kevin (ed.). *The Roller Coaster Year: The Stories of First-Year Teachers*. New York: HarperCollins, 1991. This book contains the accounts of 12 first-year teachers as they give an honest account of the events and feelings that fill their lives as they begin their teaching careers.

Ryan, Kevin, et al. *Biting the Apple*. New York: Longman, 1980. This book is a collection of stories of first-year elementary and secondary school teachers. The stories are told by the researchers with the collaboration of the new teachers. The accounts are candid pictures of the problems and joys of beginning a career in teaching.

Supporting New Teachers, Educational Leadership (special issue) 56(8) (May 1999). This special issue has several articles, which focus on the plight of first-year teachers and how schools can help them get over their initial difficulties.

Media Resources

Conquering the First Day, First Week, and First Month (Insight Media, 32 min., 1999). Using mentoring, this video details initial acclimation to the school environment, how to help new teachers get their bearings, create a positive learning environment in their classrooms, understand their students as individuals, and establish strong relationships with parents.

Harry Wong: Inducting New Teachers into the Profession (AIT, 30 min., 1992). Harry Wong is a self-described "plain old classroom teacher" who has taught and served as director, advisor, or consultant to many professional science education agencies. Wong argues that what happens within the first several days of class each fall is critical to the success of the school year for both teachers and students. He recommends conducting induction programs for new teachers to introduce them to the school's culture and to establish classroom discipline, procedures, and routines from the first day.

How to Start the School Year Right (Insight Media, 15 min., 1998). Using scenes from classrooms, this video details the steps of planning a school year. It shows how to involve students in classroom administration and curriculum development and teaches methods for dividing students into groups.

Room 109: Elementary Education (Insight Media, 15 min., 1987). Illustrating some of the unique management situations facing an elementary classroom teacher, this program provides an opportunity for teachers in training to practice making decisions about disruptive situations they are likely to face.

Room 309: Secondary Education (Insight Media, 14 min., 1987). This two-volume set depicts vignettes of scenes from a teacher's day to stimulate discussion of how to manage problematic situations. Volume 1 features situations typical of a junior high or middle school classroom, and Volume 2 focuses on senior high students.

Success and Failure at P.S. 27, Part 1 (Films for the Humanities and Sciences, 60 min., 2000). Ted Koppel tracks the progress of Lesley-Diann Jones' combined class of fourth and fifth grades, from opening day in September to February 1st, when the students re-took the state English exam that they had failed the previous year. Amidst Ms. Jones' efforts to help her students improve their learning and test-taking abilities, other dramas unfold involving stubborn parents, disruptive classroom behavior, and deadline pressure.

Success and Failure at P.S. 27, Part 2 (Films for the Humanities and Sciences, 60 min., 2000). How does a teacher develop the skills, courage, and stamina to teach disadvantaged youth, the children given up on by virtually everyone else? In this program, Ted Koppel reports on Lesley-Diann Jones and her class, covering January to graduation day in June. In addition to her concerns over chronic absenteeism and the future prospects of her students, Ms. Jones is forced to deal with one student who made a death threat against a classmate and another who alleged that Ms. Jones had publicly humiliated her.

Teaching:The First Year (Annenberg CPB Videos, 60 min., 1993). Following the highs and lows of the first year for three new teachers this video shows how inadequate supervision hinders professional development.

Who Will Teach for America? (PBS video, 60 min., 1991).This documentary about 500 college graduates who deferred their careers to become teachers offers a stirring portrait of young people who are making a difference. Their organization, Teach for America, the brainchild of Wendy Kopp, who has formed a domestic teacher corps modeled on the Peace Corps, is designed to bring the best young minds to teaching.

Media distributor contact information is available in Appendix I.

Student Activities

School Observation—Observing the New Teacher Yourself

This chapter has tried to lay out the major trouble spots or pitfalls awaiting you as a new teacher. We know from experience, though, that many students breeze right through this chapter, dealing with the information in a very impersonal manner. (Oh, this would never in a million years happen to me!) They walk into teaching with the best of intentions, high idealism, and good preparation only to crash and burn. Although it is improbable that you can anticipate all potential difficulties and thus guarantee your success, there is much that you can do to lessen the potential for real trouble. However, it takes imagination and serious reflection. And it must start with some genuine self-observation.

First, begin to do a serious self-inventory. What is your basic personality type? Are you comfortable in a leadership role (realizing that much of teaching is, in fact, leadership)? Are you organized or disorganized? Do you rattle easily? What do you do when you are upset or thrown off stride? Get a clear picture of your vulnerable areas, and then start overcoming them or, at least, get yourself prepared to deal with them in the following ways.

a. Write a list of your vulnerabilities, and keep it in a place where you will encounter it often.

b. Talk to experienced teachers about their experiences as first-year teachers and what they did to overcome their problems.

c. Get advice from people who know you well (your parents, former teachers, and perhaps a long-time roommate). Ask them what they think are your potential vulnerabilities as a teacher.

d. Using both your understanding of yourself and the knowledge you have gained from observing in classrooms, start now to catalog things you will do as a teacher to keep from falling into the predictable traps for new teachers.

Planning for Culture Shock

One way to decrease culture shock is to learn as much as possible about a situation from a safe distance. Some of the surprising bits of information that flood in during the first few weeks of teaching can be discovered by asking the right questions before school even begins. Here is a list of questions about some mundane and some substantial aspects of daily school life. Have students, individually or in pairs, visit a teacher or a school and get answers to as many of them as possible. if possible, have students give their teacher-interviewee a copy of the questions before the scheduled interview to facilitate the conversation. When students have completed the assignment, have them meet in groups of five or six and compare answers.

The Nitty Gritty School Fact Sheet

a. How do teachers notify the school when they will be absent? Do teachers have a sub folder? What do they keep in it?

b. What kinds of teacher-parent communication are expected?

c. Where is the copy machine? Are there copy limits? What cannot be copied?

d. Where do teachers eat? How much time do they have for lunch? Breaks? Planning?

e. Are there teachers' aids? What is their title? What are their duties?

f. How is attendance taken? How are tardies handled? What are the makeup work policies?

g. Who dispenses supplies? What are the policies about amounts?

h. What do you do if a student faints or has some other medical problem in class?

i. Is there a formal or unstated, but expected dress code for teachers?

j. Where do you find the school, district and/or state curriculum standards or guidelines?

k. Where can teachers park?

l.   Which doors are open to get into the building?

m.   What kinds of things do the custodians do, and what should you take care of yourself?

n.   Is there a media center? How do you order equipment?

o.   Is there an active professional organization? Should you join?

p.   Are there computer labs? How do you schedule a class to use one?

q.   Are there hall passes or student rules that you should know about on the first day?

r.   Who has the keys to unlock the things that are locked?

s.   Can you get a copy of the school's teacher, student, or parent handbook?

t.   What kinds of extracurricular activities are expected of teachers?

u.   How often does the faculty meet and what do they talk about?

Teachers' Memories

Have your students survey or interview experienced teachers, working or retired, about their memories of their first year of teaching. Many students will benefit from hearing how veteran teachers "toughed it out" the first year. You may even compile a list of questions for the whole class to use or a short form such as the following:

I now teach _____ (grade/subject/courses)

As a first-year teacher, I taught _____

I started my teaching career in the 1920s, 1930s, 1940s, 1950s, 1960s, 1970s, 1980s.

(Circle one.)

(If applicable) My greatest anxiety about becoming a teacher was _____

My worst teaching moment was
_____

My best teaching moment was
_____

Before I started teaching, I wish I had learned _____

My biggest challenge as a first-year teacher was _____

If I had one piece of advice for any entering teacher, it would be
_____

If I had to do it all over again, I
_____

After students talk to other teachers, discuss their findings in class. Were there any themes that emerged? How did the advice correlate with the information presented in the text?

Faculty Orientation/Faculty Handbook

Collect some faculty handbooks from schools. Pass the handbooks out to students, asking them to read one of the handbooks. Compare the handbooks to one another. Have your students focus on the following questions:

a.   What kind of information makes up most of the handbook? Is there any particular emphasis, such as classroom management or bureaucratic procedures?

b.   To what degree are the handbooks similar to one another?

c.   To what degree does the handbook answer the kinds of questions raised on the "Nitty Gritty School Fact Sheet"? (In activity #1)

d.   Based on the handbook, what theories can you derive about the atmosphere of the school and the teacher's position in the organization?

Teaching Tips File (individual or group work)

This activity could be done in conjunction with the teacher interview project. Talk to at least ten teachers. Ask them the following question: "Can you describe one or two of the most helpful teaching tips you would share with beginning teachers?" Collect their responses and create a file presenting their "tips." The file could take on a wide variety of styles and forms, including photographs and sayings about teaching. Divide the tips into sections for particular areas, such as grading, starting a new unit, classroom management, and the like. Also, include file tips that you read in teaching journals or books. Present several of your favorite file ideas or particular subject areas or topics to the class. An additional very helpful idea is to compile all "tips," print them up, and distribute them for students' future reference. Add to your file throughout your program.

Teacher Evaluations

Imagine the shock of a first-year teacher thinking he or she is doing a "good job," only to see on the written evaluation from the principal that several areas "need improvement." Collect sample evaluation forms from schools. You may also want to include your college's evaluation for student teachers. Duplicate them so each student in class has several to analyze. Allow students to work individually analyzing them, and then place students in discussion groups.

Ask them to look for the following: What is the relative weight given to different aspects of teaching? (How many questions deal with classroom management? How many with the instructional technique?) What are some of the most surprising elements that are included on the teaching evaluation form for students? (How many forms include questions on the appearance of the room—noting, for instance, if shades were drawn evenly, or if papers were organized neatly?) What appears to be rewarded? What is censured? After the discussion groups have identified and analyzed some trends, debrief with the whole class.

You may also want to ask several evaluators—principals, curriculum coordinators, department chairs, and others responsible for evaluating teacher performance—to visit your class. What do they look for in their evaluations? What are the "red flags" for them? What do they see as the indicators of a successful teacher?

Student Assignments

The following activities are suggestions for student portfolio activities. They are a means of providing alternative assessment of students' capabilities.

Independent Reading

Read and respond to any of the selections noted on the chapter/article correlation list found in the front of this manual for Ryan/Cooper, *Kaleidoscope: Readings in Education* (Houghton Mifflin, 2004). You may want to use the Article Review Form in *Kaleidoscope*.

Reflective Papers

Choose one of the following topics to write a reflective paper (2–5 pages). The purpose of the paper is to help you assimilate new knowledge by blending it with your previous knowledge and experiences.

1. In Chapter 13, the authors suggest that prospective teachers "begin now" to analyze their own personality and its match with teaching. Specifically, they encourage you to make a systematic study of your strengths and weaknesses that you can articulate. Think about your personality and write a reflective paper describing what you identify as your biggest strength and your biggest weakness. To what degree do you see your personality characteristics advancing or possibly impeding your teaching? After you've written your paper, share it with your cooperative learning group. Are there any suggestions the group can provide? To what extent do you share similar traits?

2. After observing in your field-site school, see if you can identify a situation where the teacher's perception of a child and a parent's perception may differ. Observe the child and his or her interaction with the teacher over several visits. Then write two "letters," one from the perspective of the teacher about the child and one from the perspective of the parent, describing the child. Share your "letters" with your cooperative learning group. What are the possible implications of regarding a child's behavior through the lens of a teacher or of a parent?

Journal Reflections

Suggestions for journal topics for students' selection:

1. Of the challenges for new teachers reviewed in the chapter, which do you think will be the most difficult for you? Why?

2. What is your greatest "fear" in becoming a teacher? What can you do about this?

3. What part of a teacher's job or tasks do you most look forward to doing? Why?

CD-ROM Video Clip

View the clip for Chapter 13 and be prepared to discuss the following reflection questions:

1. Do you agree that discipline should be taught in school, like any other subject? Why or why not?

2. Do you feel that your teacher preparation program has adequately prepared you to deal with classroom discipline? How much emphasis has your teacher training placed on discipline? What questions do you have about discipline that remain unanswered?

CHAPTER 14

What Does It Mean to Be a Professional?

LEARNING OBJECTIVES

After studying the chapter, students will be able to

1. identify the defining characteristics of a profession.

2. identify and describe arguments that support the position that teaching is a profession and those that support the contention that it is not.

3. describe the role of the National Board for Professional Teaching Standards (NBPTS) in setting high standards for the profession.

4. discuss the role of the two major professional organizations in education, the National Education Association, and the American Federation of Teachers.

5. explain continuous learning opportunities available to teachers.

CHAPTER OVERVIEW

This chapter focuses on the status of teachers in American society in order to clarify the debate over teaching as a profession. It begins with a brief overview of the history of teaching and teacher education, and then looks to identify the defining characteristics of a profession. This discussion serves as a basis for an examination of the current status of teaching. Other factors that affect the status of teaching, such as professional associations, are also discussed.

We begin the chapter with some anecdotes in order to point out the vulnerability of teachers, because most prospective teachers are so preoccupied with the act of teaching that they may not be aware of the many issues surrounding their actual work. We then trace the history of teaching and teacher education in the United States, highlighting the periods of substantial change in teaching and the events that helped to bring about these changes. The second half of this century marks a significant shift in teacher preparation: from teacher *training* to teacher *education*.

Next, we present Myron Lieberman's classic definition of a profession and make use of these eight criteria to present the debate over whether teaching is a profession. We discuss the arguments supporting the contention that teaching is a profession and those that maintain that it is not. We also propose a third option—that teaching is a semi-profession or is *becoming* a profession. The effects of the National Board for Professional Teaching Standards (NBPTS) on the development and perception of the profession are described. We strongly encourage prospective teachers to take part in this debate, which could affect their career choice.

We help preservice teachers consider the importance of continuing education as part of teacher professionalism. As the social landscape becomes more complex and new knowledge and skills more abundant, teachers need to keep abreast of these changes to maintain their effectiveness and "professional" status. We describe five types of continuous learning opportunities for teachers.

We close the chapter with a look at the role of professional organizations—one of the criteria of a profession—in the teaching-as-a-profession debate. We introduce the two main teachers' organizations: the National Education Association (NEA) and the American Federation of Teachers (AFT), presenting the history of each association and the kinds of issues they choose to support or defend. Traditionally, the NEA has been more conservative than the AFT; however, changes are occurring in both organizations that make clear delineation between the two more difficult to maintain. We also present the position of those educators who are opposed to these associations, who see them as unions that are only protecting the interests of their members rather than promoting professional growth. This image of teachers, they feel, diminishes their status and professionalism. We end the debate by eliciting the potential benefits and abuses of teacher professionalism and suggest that the new teacher empowerment movement may play a key role in the professionalism debate.

The overriding purpose of this chapter is to help prospective teachers feel that they are joining an occupation with a history—one that is embedded in a particular social context. We hope that prospective teachers recognize their responsibility to the profession.

CHAPTER OUTLINE

I.   The Status of Teaching: A Profession or Not?
   A.   The Case *against* Teaching as a Profession
      1.   A Child's Many Teachers
      2.   Limited Training
      3.   Constraints on Autonomy
      4.   Responsibility for Their Profession
      5.   Job Security and Salary
   B.   The Case *for* Teaching as a Profession
      1.   Teachers' Commitment to Service
      2.   The Teacher's Unique Skills
      3.   The Teacher's Autonomy
   C.   A Third Possibility: An Evolving Profession
      1.   Greater Self-Determination
      2.   Better Preparation
      3.   Recognizing Excellence in Teaching
   D.   Levels of Professionalism
      1.   The Level One Teacher
      2.   The Level Two Teacher
      3.   The Level Three Teacher
   E.   The National Board for Professional Teaching Standards
      1.   Core Propositions and Characteristics
      2.   Advantages to Board Certification
      3.   Criticisms of NBPTS
   F.   What Every New Teacher Should Possess: The INTASC Standards
II. Professional Associations
   A.   The National Education Association
      1.   Services to Members
      2.   The NEA and Political issues
   B.   The American Federation of Teachers
      1.   The AFT's Stance on issues
   C.   A Possible Merger?
   D.   Other Professional Associations
   E.   Professionalism at the Crossroads
   F.   Wanted: A New Professionalism
III. Your Own Professional Development
   A.   Types of Continuous Learning Opportunities
      1.   Independent Study
      2.   Group Study
      3.   Graduate Study

4.   In-Service Programs
5.   Supervision
6.   Mentoring
7.   Systematic Reflection on Practice

SUPPLEMENTARY LECTURE AND DISCUSSION TOPICS

1.   **The history of teacher education** Trace the history of teacher education with your class (found in previous editions of this text). Focus on the minimal education teachers received in the colonial period, and discuss how the normal schools prepared teachers. Discuss how teacher training changed its direction in the twentieth century to teacher education. Include a review of fifth-year programs, early field experiences, and the extension of teacher education into the first year of teaching with induction programs and mentorships. Has the shift made a difference in the professionalism of teachers?

2.   **What would teaching be like today without its professional organizations?** You may wish to do your own hypothesizing here, or you may find it illuminating to invite a superintendent who is unsympathetic to teachers' associations, a teachers' association representative, and teachers with strong views on the subject to speak in your class. In colleges and universities where faculty are not allowed to be represented by a professional organization a comparison of salaries, working conditions, and benefits between professors of education and K–12 teachers may be revealing.

3.   **The continuing growth of teachers** One part of the chapter deals with the ways in which a teacher can develop professionally. You may want to elaborate on how teachers can continue to develop professionally. It is particularly effective to invite veteran teachers who have maintained their love of teaching to talk to the class. How did they continue their professional development throughout the years? What advice would they give to prospective teachers?

STUDY GUIDE — CHAPTER 14: WHAT DOES IT MEAN TO BE A PROFESSIONAL?

Completing this study guide will help you prepare for the major topic areas on an exam; however, it does not cover every piece of information found in the chapter or the test questions.

1. List the eight criteria that must be satisfied for teaching to be considered a profession and indicate which of these criteria teaching meets.

2. Describe the characteristics of teachers at each of the three levels of professionalism.

3. Compare and contrast the characteristics of the NEA and the AFT.

4. Describe what the National Board for Professional Teaching Standards is and how it could affect your career in teaching.

5. List and give examples of the types of continuing education opportunities for teachers.

ADDITIONAL RESOURCES FOR INSTRUCTORS

Berube, Maurice. *Teacher Politics: The Influence of Unions.* New York: Greenwood Press, 1988. Looking at unions from a critical perspective, Berube analyzes the effect that unionization has had on teaching as a whole.

Darling-Hammond, Linda. "Teachers and Teaching: Signs of a Changing Profession," in the *Handbook of Research on Teacher Education*, ed. Robert Houston. New York: Macmillan, (1991): 267–290. This article summarizes recent research on various factors and trends affecting the teaching profession, from the demographic composition of the teaching force to supply-and-demand factors.

Grant, Gerald, and Christine Murray. *Teaching in America: The Slow Revolution.* Boston: Harvard University Press, 1999. This book traces the progress of two groups—college professors and pre-collegiate teachers, pointing out the similarities and differences of the evolution of professions. Drawing lessons from the development of the professoriate, the authors point out the steps teachers need to make to continue their progress.

Lieberman, Ann, and Lynne Miller. *Teachers—Their World and Their Work.* New York: Teachers College Press, 1992. This book explores the affective world of teachers. The authors tie the social realities of school life to the process of instructional improvement.

Lortie, Dan. *School Teacher: A Sociological Study.* Chicago: University of Chicago Press, 1975. This classic study treats many of the factors implicit in school teaching that work against teaching becoming a profession.

Murphy, Marjorie. *Blackboard Unions: The AFT and NEA, 1900–1980.* Ithaca: Cornell University Press, 1990. Murphy examines the history of the two major teachers' associations, describing their origins, their philosophies, and their impact on teachers.

Shanker, Albert. "The Making of a Profession." *American Educator* 9 (Fall 1985): 10–17, 46, 48. Proclaiming the second revolution in U.S. public education, the president of the American Federation of Teachers outlines a bold new plan for our children and their teachers. Furthermore, Shanker offers four recommendations for improving professional standards.

National Educational Association, *Status of the American Public School Teacher: 1995–96.* Washington, DC: National Educational Association, 1996. This report is one in a series of studies conducted every four years. It contains a massive amount of information on who teachers are, what is on their minds, and the conditions of their work.

Provenzo, Eugene F., and Gary McCloskey. *Schoolteachings and Schooling: Ethoses in Conflict.* Norwood, NJ: Ablex Publishing Corp., 1996. This short book is a thoughtful and detailed picture of how teaching has changed in the last third of the twentieth century and the forces at play in a teacher's life.

Media Resources

Introduction to the Foundations of American Education (CNN video, min. vary by segment, 1993). Includes segments on teacher burnout, teacher salaries, and teacher strikes.

Inducting New Teachers into the Profession (AIT, 28 min., 1992). Harry Wong is a self-described "plain old classroom teacher" who has taught and served as director, advisor, or consultant for over 30 years. Wong, author of *The First Days of School*, argues that what happens within the first several days of class each fall is critical to the success of the school year for both teachers and students. He recommends conducting induction programs for new teachers to introduce them to the school's culture and to establish classroom discipline, procedures, and routines from the first day.

New Schools, New Teachers Part II (Phi Delta Kappa, 57 min., 1994). Part 2 explores the connection between teacher preparation and school reform, and describes Goodlad's version of teacher preparation.

Partnership in Education: Helping New Teachers Succeed (Kappa Delta Pi, 20 min., 1994).This video is designed to support the interaction of experienced educators and new teachers in a mentorship relationship.

Teacher as Learner: Lifelong Learning (National Louis University, 90 min., 1993). In the first segment, Stephen Brookfield talks about continuing education for the teacher. The second features Rita Weinberg who talks about using metaphors as an indirect method for personal change.

Teacher, Teacher (PBS video, 59 min., 1990). Originally a Frontline segment, teachers discuss issues and problems of their profession and the role and value of teachers in society.

Those Who Can . . . Teach (Films for the Humanities and Sciences, 56 min., 2000). This video traces the evolution of teaching as a profession, honoring educators who risked everything to stand up for teachers' rights, and presents issues such as training, unionization, standards, bureaucracy, and professional growth, while four teaching interns share the lessons of their baptisms of fire.

Media distributor contact information is available in Appendix I.

Student Activities

School Observation—The Role of Professional Associations

It is quite likely that when you begin teaching you will be asked to join an association or union. In many places, association dues are automatically deducted from one's paycheck. Though any good professional group of teachers should be convinced that it is helping to improve education for all involved, certain issues promoted by the group may make you, or some of the other members, uncomfortable. For instance, there are teachers' association members who are deeply opposed to seniority in hiring and firing. There are those who are deeply opposed to strikes.

To prepare for becoming a member of a professional association, you can take the following steps, among others:

    a.   Talk to former teachers or to the teachers you encounter in your field experience about their attitudes toward teachers' associations or unions. Ask them what they believe has been improved by the associations or unions, and what (if anything) has been lost.

    b.   Interview a school administrator, asking her or him about the pluses and minuses of teachers' associations.

    c.   Keep a special eye out for news and reports on teachers' associations and unions. Attempt to understand what they are standing for and who is being served by their efforts.

    d.   Reflect on whether you anticipate any conflicts between your own professional values and those advanced by teachers' associations.

Debates

Present two debate topics: "Are teachers' associations necessary?" and "Is teaching a profession?" Ask your students to select a position, either pro or con, for each debate topic. If the numbers are unbalanced, assign students to one side to provide for each position approximately the same number of people. Allow students adequate time to prepare for the debate, and tell them they will have 45 minutes to debate the issue. On the designated day, invite guests—perhaps other education students and professors—to observe and judge their arguments.

Who Has the Power? A Simulation [1]

Divide the class into groups of nine students. Reproduce enough of the following role descriptions so that each group has a complete set of nine different roles. The groups should spend 20 to 30 minutes in a role-played discussion to determine the answers to the following questions:

- Who will evaluate teacher classroom competency?

- How will the evaluation be done?

---

[1] Adapted from a paper presented at the American Association for Supervision by Emily Feistritzer, H. Jerome Freiber, and Frank Kunstel, March 14, 1976. Used by permission.

At the end of the small-group discussions, the class as a whole should discuss the frustrations and successes felt in their own groups, the answers they reached, and the problems inherent in being the spokesperson for a "position."

The Setting

Metro City schools serve a large urban area with a decreasing school population. In fact, enrollment is expected to decline 5 percent over the next two years, which will probably lead to a reduction of the teaching personnel. At the beginning of the current school year, a dynamic new superintendent was brought in to get the system moving again after several years of stagnation. It is now March, and the superintendent is trying to improve the quality of instruction in the schools. As part of this process, a committee has been assigned the task of revamping the teacher evaluation process for tenured and nontenured teaching staff. Due to a high rate of faculty turnover in these challenging schools, most of the teachers in the Metro City district are not tenured.

In an attempt to ensure a fair evaluation process and to incorporate as many ideas as possible, the superintendent has appointed the following people to serve on the committee:

- the assistant superintendent for instruction
- the coordinator of staff development
- one representative from the state department of education
- two professors from the city's university (drop one if groups are smaller)
- two principals (drop one if groups are smaller)
- two representatives from the local teachers' union (drop one if groups are smaller)

The committee is currently deliberating about the component of the evaluation process that focuses on teacher classroom competency. Three questions are of primary concern at this stage:

- Who will evaluate teacher classroom competency?
- What will be evaluated to determine level of competence?
- How will the evaluation be done?

The purpose of the current meeting of the committee is to outline answers to these two basic questions so that subcommittees can proceed to work on the details.

Roles

1. *Teachers' union representatives: Nick DeLiberato* (collective bargainer for the union) *and Lisa Liu* (math teacher and union representative from one of the high schools in the Metro City schools). You each have your own view about the proper procedures for teacher evaluation, but your union has taken a look at what has happened in other states and the executive board has given you two mandates:

   a. Don't allow student achievement scores to play any part in the criteria for evaluation. This would be a gross misinterpretation of the whole concept of accountability, because teachers do not control all the factors that influence student achievement.

   b. Push for a procedure that includes evaluation by several people, including union reps, rather than allowing just principals to do the evaluation.

2.   *Principal A. Lee Diamond.* You have talked many hours with your associates in the principals' association and have reached the consensus that this is a chance to strengthen the quality of teaching in the Metro schools. The principals want a procedure that will finally allow them to weed out the incompetent teachers, who in some buildings represent a substantial portion of the staff. The procedure should be fair but should not require an inordinate amount of time, because most principals are already overworked. The principal must be the one to do the evaluating, because he or she knows the teachers best.

   a.   *Principal B. Dale Callaghan.* You are afraid that this whole task could strain teacher-administrator relations, which are already poor. You don't want the principals to get stuck with the dirty work of evaluating the teachers. It would take too much time from an already busy schedule, and it would make the principals the "bad guys." You do want to see the quality of teaching in the district upgraded, however.

   b.   *Community representative: B. J. Rosario.* You have for some time been actively concerned with the quality of the schools and have supported the tax levies in an attempt to improve the schools. Nevertheless, you are continually hearing about bad teachers in the system. Although these are a minority, they do a lot of damage to boys and girls every year. When the new superintendent was hired, he pledged to improve school-community relations but originally neglected to appoint any community representatives to the evaluation committee. This has upset you, because you have been so active in supporting the schools. Also, you feel that community people must have some input into the teacher evaluation process, because your taxes pay their salaries.

   c.   *Assistant superintendent for instruction: Pat Kavanaugh.* You are trying to maintain harmonious relations on the committee, because you are the highest-ranking school official on the committee and have an overall view of the system. You sincerely want to help the committee reach a consensus so that every group feels ownership of the final product.

   d.   *Coordinator of staff development: Lou Gonzalez.* You have a small, overworked staff of your own with which to plan, organize, and help conduct the district's in-service program. The final evaluation procedure will have an important impact on how your department functions in the next few years, because you will have to help teachers develop competence in those areas deemed important enough to include in the evaluation process. You need to maintain good relations with all the parties because you work so closely with all the people in the system. In particular, it is important that the teachers not feel defensive about the evaluation process.

   e.   *State department of education representative: Sandy Lee.* This is an opportunity for you to make some real contributions to education in the state. Metro is the largest and most influential school district in the state; if you can come up with an evaluation procedure that works here, other districts will be likely to adopt similar procedures. The superintendent of instruction for the state has clearly pushed for competency-based teacher education and evaluation, and she is especially strong on behavioral objectives as the way to improve education. Discrete, observable skills, coupled with an emphasis on actual student achievement, are the key to teacher evaluation.

   f.   *Professor Denny Kravulski.* You believe that the current emphasis on systems approaches and behavioral objectives is pushing education into the industrial model more than ever before, and you strongly object to it. You believe that teachers, as well as students, need to be treated as human beings first.

   g.   *Professor Leslie Lane.* You believe that education would improve greatly if only educators would start thinking about being more efficient. You support a well-planned evaluation procedure that focuses on specific teacher competencies. Because the principal is the instructional leader in his or her building, the principal must be the one to do the evaluating. This is also an opportunity for the university to have more influence and input into the public schools, a role the dean has been pushing.

Playing by the Rules

This can be either a whole-class or small-group discussion. It is designed to develop the concept of teacher power while offering an opportunity to expand the issue. The power of teachers is realized in their rule-making capabilities. Often this power is limited to the managerial functions within their classrooms.

1. Which of the following rules have been established for the entire district? Which ones are school rules? Which are classroom rules determined by the teacher?

   a. No papers or notebooks will be accepted late.

   b. All papers must be dated and show the section number.

   c. All written work must be in ink.

   d. Pencils may not be sharpened after the bell rings.

   e. Students who arrive after the bell starts to ring must report to the principal's office for a pass.

   f. Students must get permission to open-enroll at a school outside their attendance district.

   g. Parents must sign a student's papers if a failing grade has been assigned.

   h. A student may not chew gum in class.

   i. Any student in possession of a weapon will be automatically and immediately suspended.

   j. No student may speak without being recognized by the teacher.

   k. Everyone must sit in his or her assigned seat.

   l. Boys must have their hair neatly combed.

   m. Textbooks must be covered.

   n. Fourth-graders have to pass a writing sample to be promoted to fifth grade.

   o. A student may not go to the water fountain during class.

   p. When the bell rings, students will sit quietly and wait for the teacher's instructions.

   q. A student who fails the final exam fails the course.

   r. The school day will not be started with a prayer over the P.A. system.

2. Have students discuss what changes they perceive in teachers' power from earlier decades.

Student Assignments

The following activities are suggestions for student portfolio activities. They are a means of providing alternative assessment of students' capabilities.

Independent Reading

Read and respond to any of the selections noted on the chapter/article correlation list found in the front of this manual for Ryan/Cooper, *Kaleidoscope: Readings in Education* (Houghton Mifflin, 2004). You may want to use the Article Review Form in *Kaleidoscope*.

Reflective Papers

Choose one of the following topics to write a reflective paper (2–5 pages). The purpose of the paper is to help you assimilate new knowledge by blending it with your previous knowledge and experiences.

1.   Do you see yourself joining one of the professional associations when you become a teacher? Why would you join one? Discuss your perceptions of these associations and what you feel they contribute to teaching.

2.   What effect do you think the National Boards certification process will have on the profession? Will you plan to "take the boards" when you are eligible? Why or why not?

3.   Ryan and Cooper have traced the history of teaching and teacher education in the United States up to the present. How do you see the future of teaching and teacher education? Keeping in mind that many of the changes made in schools were *in response* to societal changes, what do you anticipate will be the most influential social factors affecting education in the next century, and how will teaching and teacher education be affected?

Journal Reflections

Suggestions for journal topics for students' selection:

1.   Do you think you will join the NEA or AFT (whichever one is the collective bargaining agent in your district)? Why or why not?

2.   Will it make a difference in how you do your job if teaching is perceived as a profession?

3.   Describe how you think teacher education programs will change over the next twenty years.

CHAPTER 15

Why Teach?

LEARNING OBJECTIVES

After studying the chapter, students will be able to

1. identify several personal motivations for wanting to become a teacher.

2. identify and discuss common motivations for people wanting to teach.

3. identify the most common reasons teachers give for leaving the profession.

4. identify and explain both extrinsic and intrinsic rewards in teaching.

5. list and explain sources of useful experience regarding teaching.

6. explain a potential difficulty faced by teachers whose primary motivation is to teach a particular content or subject matter.

7. explain the potential difficulty of using teaching as a means to work out one's own problems.

8. explain how teachers can aid in the renewal of society through their teaching.

9. apply the concepts introduced to their own perspective on teaching.

10. think, speak, and write with greater clarity and insight about why they are considering (or not considering) a career in teaching.

CHAPTER OVERVIEW

Everyone has gone to school, so everyone knows what it must be like to be a teacher. Right? Wrong. Although recalling one's own experiences in school may be helpful, prospective teachers need to base their career choice on more than just memories. Prospective teachers need to explore their desire to teach in more depth, and Chapter 15 encourages them to do just that. Teaching is a very satisfying career for thousands of people, yet to be satisfied in the career, prospective teachers must think about why they are becoming a teacher and whether their career aspirations can be fulfilled in teaching.

Chapter 15 presents factual data as well as case studies for prospective teachers to mull over as they begin their teacher education program. Too often, students are willing to rely on outside information without testing it against their own knowledge or frame of reference. This textbook's intent is to engage the students so that reading it becomes a more reflective experience than just reading and memorizing.

Basic facets of the teaching profession are highlighted in the chapter. One part discusses the rewards of teaching. We point out that teaching yields both extrinsic and intrinsic rewards, yet the extrinsic rewards are often downplayed. Intrinsic rewards, because of their highly individualistic nature, vary in degree from teacher to teacher. The authors suggest that considering the personal value of both the extrinsic and intrinsic rewards of teaching is a realistic way for students to assess if they would be content as a teacher.

Four sources of experience, as well as case studies depicting common motivations for people to teach, are included for students to consider as they begin their teacher education programs.

CHAPTER OUTLINE

I. Motivations for Teaching
    A. Motivations of Current Teachers
    B. Examining Your Own Motives for Teaching

II.   The Rewards of Teaching
    A.   Extrinsic Rewards
        1.   Salaries
        2.   Status
        3.   Power
        4.   Work Schedule
    B.   Intrinsic Rewards
        1.   Students
        2.   Performance of a Significant Social Service
        3.   Stimulation and Support from Fellow Teachers
        4.   The Work of Teaching
    C.   Rewards in perspective
III.   Sources of Useful Experience
    A.   Real Encounters
    B.   Vicarious Experiences
    C.   Guidance
    D.   Reflection
IV.   Case Studies In the Motivation to Teach
    A.   The Desire to Teach a Particular Subject
        1.   Comment
    B.   The Desire to Aid in the Renewal of Society
        1.   Comment

SUPPLEMENTARY LECTURE AND DISCUSSION TOPICS

1.   **Mixed motives for teaching** In Chapter 15 we examine a few motives for teaching and list others. Students may get the wrong impression that most teachers have a single and clear reason for doing certain things. Point out that people engage in most activities for a mixture of motives and that having mixed motives is not a moral failing. Also, forewarn them that motives for teaching tend to change over time. The article by Fuller and Bown listed in the "Additional Resources for Instructors" for this chapter may help here.

2.   **Pitfalls in choosing teaching** We are convinced that many people simply "slide" into teacher education programs. Teaching represents a non-choice. People "know" schools, they can meet the standards, and teaching doesn't look overly taxing and has plentiful vacations distributed throughout the year. So why not give it a try? The personal cost of a casual approach to such an important decision should be spelled out.

STUDY GUIDE — CHAPTER 15: WHY TEACH?

Completing this study guide will help you prepare for the major topic areas on an exam; however, it does not cover every piece of information found in the chapter or the test questions.

1. Name several of the most common motives for becoming a teacher.

2. Name the extrinsic rewards of a career in teaching.

3. Name the possible intrinsic rewards of a teaching career.

4. List and describe three alternative kinds of sources of information on a career in teaching.

5. Describe the drawbacks of using media representations as sources of vicarious experiences.

ADDITIONAL RESOURCES FOR INSTRUCTORS

Bogue, Ernest Grady. *A Journey of the Heart: The Call to Teaching.* Bloomington, IN: Phi Delta Kappa Education Foundation, 1991. This short volume explores the reasons and the motives attracting people to teaching.

Fuller, Frances F., and Oliver Bown. "Becoming a Teacher." In *Teacher Education: The Seventy-fourth Yearbook for the Study of Education*, ed. Kevin Ryan. Chicago: University of Chicago Press, 1975. Fuller and Bown discuss research on the personal context of becoming a teacher, including their own theory of the stages of teaching.

Jersild, Arthur T. *In Search of Self.* New York: Teachers College Press, 1955. This classic in the field provides much insight into why people become teachers.

Johnson, Susan Moore. *Teachers at Work: Achieving Success in Our Schools.* New York: Basic Books, 1990. Johnson provides an analysis, based on interviews with teachers, of why the best teachers are leaving the classroom.

Joseph, Pamela Bolotin, and Gail E. Burnaford (Eds.). *Images of School Teachers in Twentieth-Century America: Paragons, Polarities, Complexities.* New York: St. Martin's Press, 1994. This book makes explicit those things that most often are implicit in the common cultural experiences of teachers and students.

Perrone, Vito. *A Letter to Teachers: Reflections on Schooling and the Art of Teaching.* San Francisco: Jossey-Bass, 1991. This respected scholar on teaching articulates his understanding of schooling and the importance of teaching.

Schubert, William, and William Ayers (Eds.). *Teacher Lore: Learning from Our Own Experiences.* White Plains, NY: Longman, 1992. This edited volume contains essays by various teachers discussing what they have learned from their teaching experiences and the myths and lore surrounding teaching.

A Sense of Calling: Who Teaches and Why. Public Agenda (2000). This is an insightful, in depth study of the characteristics of teachers in the first five years of their career and their opinions.

Swetnam, Leslie A. "Media Distortion of the Teacher Image." *The Clearing House* (September/October 1992): 30–32. This article describes some of the most common representations of the "stereotypical" images of teachers.

Weber, Sandra, and Claudia Mitchell. *That's Funny, You Don't Look Like a Teacher: Integrating Images and Identity in Popular Culture.* Washington, DC: Falmore Press, 1995. This is a book about the images of teachers and teaching that infiltrate our lives, shaping in important but unrecognized ways our notions of who teachers are and what they do.

Non-Fiction Accounts of Teachers (sources of vicarious experiences for students)

Ashton-Warner, Sylvia. *Teacher*. New York: Simon and Schuster, 1963.

Ayers, William. *To Teach: The Journey of a Teacher*. New York: Teachers College Press, 1993.

Codell, Esme Raji. *Educating Esme*. Chapel Hill, N.C.: Algonquin Books, 1999. This book is an inspiring, irreverent, and hilarious diary of a teacher's first year.

Collins, Marva, and Civia Tamarkin. *Marva Collins' Way*. Los Angeles: Tarcher, 1982. This book takes the reader inside the world of one of America's most inspiring and controversial teachers. Marva Collins describes her method of educating the children others forgot.

Finnegan, William. *Crossing the Line*. New York: Harper and Row, 1986.

Freedman, Samuel G. *Small Victories*. New York: Harper and Row, 1990. This book chronicles life in a New York City high school and its staff in the late 1980s. The highs and lows of teaching in urban schools are pictured, and the major problems affecting life in these schools are vividly presented.

Greenstein, Jack. *What the Children Taught Me: The Experience of an Educator in the Public Schools*. Chicago: University of Chicago Press, 1983.

Herndon, James. *Notes from a Schoolteacher*. New York: Simon and Schuster, 1985.

Hohler, Robert. *I Touch the Future . . . The Story of Christa McAuliffe*. New York: Random House, 1989. The story of the first teacher in space.

Kammeraad-Campbell, Susan. *Teacher: Dennis Littky's Fight for a Better School*. New York: Plume, 1991. The book chronicles the work of Dennis Littky in a rural New Hampshire high school and the changes that his innovative methods as an administrator brought to a poor, rural, troubled school.

Kane, P. R. (ed.). *My First Year as a Teacher*. New York: Penguin Books, 1991. This book is a collection of accounts by twenty-five teachers of their first year in teaching, describing their struggles and triumphs as they grappled with their new profession.

Keizer, Garret. *No Place But Here: A Teacher's Vocation in a Rural Community*. New York: Penguin, 1988. Keizer writes evocatively of his experience teaching in a rural high school in northern Vermont. His faith in the students and the people of that rural Vermont town is countered by his skepticism toward the values and driving force of U.S. society at large.

Kidder, Tracy. *Among Schoolchildren*. Boston: Houghton Mifflin, 1989. Kidder spent the entire school year in Chris Zajac's classroom, observing her teach every day. His account shows the demands, rewards, and realities of teaching elementary children in an urban, distressed environment by one teacher, and her impact on the children.

Lathrop-Hawkins, Frances P. *Journey with Children: The Autobiography of a Teacher*. Boulder, CO: University Press of Colorado, 1996. This autobiography integrates personal experiences in the classroom with educational teaching practice and theory.

Marquis, David Marshall (ed.). *I Am a Teacher: A Tribute to America's Teachers*. New York: Simon and Schuster, 1990. The book presents in photographs and interviews why people became teachers and why they stayed in the profession. A moving tribute to real teachers across the United States.

Mathews, Jay. *Escalante, Best Teacher in America.* New York: Holt, 1990. This is the biography of Jaime Escalante, an inspiring math teacher who is the subject of the film *Stand and Deliver.* Escalante wins his students, largely urban Hispanics, with a combination of challenges to pride, demands of dedicated hard work, and demonstrated love.

Millstone, David H. *An Elementary Odyssey.* Portsmouth, NH: Heinemann, 1995. Millstone outlines his successful thematic integrated teaching of social studies and his interdisciplinary weaving of the arts, writing, and storytelling.

Natkins, Lucille. *Our Last Term: A Teacher's Diary.* Landem, MD: University Press of America, 1986.

Paley, Vivian Gussin. *White Teacher.* Cambridge, MA: Harvard University Press, 1989. Paley describes her progress in learning to deal more openly with her own perceptions of race.

Palonsky, Stuart. *900 Shows a Year.* New York: Random House, 1986.

Parkay, Forest. *White Teacher, Black School: The Professional Growth of a Ghetto Teacher.* New York: Praeger, 1983.

Rofes, Eric. *Socrates, Plato, and Guys Like Me: Confessions of a Gay Schoolteacher.* Boston: Alyson, 1985.

Ryan, Kevin (ed.). *The Roller Coaster Year: Stories of First Year Teachers.* New York: HarperCollins, 1991. This book presents the stories of twelve first-year teachers and their struggles and triumphs as they discovered who they were as teachers and why they taught.

Twiss, Ruth. *Morning, Noon, and Night.* Smithtown, NY: Exposition Press, 1982.

Welsh, Patrick. *Tales Out of School.* New York: Viking, 1986.

Wigginton, Eliot. *Sometimes a Shining Moment: The Foxfire Experience.* Garden City, NY: Anchor Press/Doubleday, 1985.

Media Resources

Career Close-Ups: School Teacher (Insight Media, 27 min., 1994). As classrooms become more dangerous and crowded, teachers are challenged to find creative ways to motivate their students. This video, hosted by Whoopi Goldberg, profiles extraordinary teachers who entertain as they educate, tailoring their lessons to fit their students' interests.

Career Encounters: Teaching (Insight Media, 28 min., 1992). This documentary-style program looks at the career of teaching and includes practical information about educational and certification requirements. Teachers explain what they do, how they became involved in education, and what they find most rewarding about their careers.

Celebrating Teachers (Annenberg CPB Videos, 30 min., 1992). This video is a salute to inspiring educators with classroom memories from Jesse Jackson and actors Edward James Olmos and Phylicia Rachad.

Educating Educators (Insight Media, 20 min., 1989). What are the challenges facing teachers today? What challenges will teachers face in the future? Prominent educators join host Dr. John Goodlad to explore ideas that will help to set the agenda for reform in teacher education.

Making a Difference: Great Teachers Part I (Films for the Humanities and Sciences, 28 min., 1994). This documentary focuses on three teachers who have made a positive impact—academically or personally—on their students' lives. Selected as a result of an essay contest that asked students to write about the teacher who had most challenged and inspired them, the teachers are shown at work in the classroom.

A Teacher Affects Eternity (Films for the Humanities and Sciences, 56 min., 2000). This program explores the importance of educators in the lives of their students, emphasizing their influence as role models, as upholders of society norms, and even as agents of social change. Dedicated women who spent their careers teaching newly freed slaves and turn-of-the-century teachers of immigrants are profiled, as well as exemplary instructors of today's struggling teenagers.

Wanted: A Million Teachers (PBS video, 60 min., 1989). This program looks at some of the crises in teaching today, including "burnout," poor pay, low morale, and an overload of administrative duties. These elements in the school work environment may contribute to the sharp decline in the number of teachers entering the profession at a time when attracting talented individuals to the field may be more important than ever.

What is a Teacher? (Insight Media, 30 min., 1987). This program presents three views of teachers: as knowledgeable decision makers, as executives who share many of the traits and functions of business executives, and as interpersonal facilitators. It emphasizes the need to define what a teacher is in order to increase both the status and efficacy of teachers.

Media distributor contact information is available in Appendix I.

Student Activities

School Observation—Why Teach?

In a small group read and discuss the following: Schools are much in the news these days. Newspapers, magazines, and television are filled with reports of school troubles and controversies. In recent years there have been many films (some good and some not so good) about life in schools. Teachers are usually a major part of theses real and fictional stories. The images that come through are of extremes: heroic or villainous; courageous or cowardly; dedicated or selfish; idealistic or cynical; energized or burnt out. When you visit schools as part of your field experiences, look very closely at the teachers. Probably you will encounter a few teachers and administrators who fit the extreme categories portrayed by the media, but you will probably also see people very much like your parents and neighbors, people going about their work in a purposeful, somewhat low-key manner. As you get to know these people, try to engage them in discussions of their work. Without getting too personal, try to discover what they are giving to teaching and what they are getting in return. Ask about what they enjoy most about teaching and what bothers them. Inquire about what has changed for them over the years. What motivations for teaching have changed? How have their career expectations been altered? Find out the important lessons they have learned. Having talked with hundreds of teachers over the years, we have discovered that most teachers are eager to discuss their careers and what they have learned and are more than willing to talk with aspiring teachers.

On the basis of our observations and conversations with teachers, answer the following questions.

1. How do these "real-life" teachers differ from the teachers you have encountered through the media?

2. What are the "surprises" you picked up from your conversations with teachers?

3. How do your motives for considering teaching compare with those of seasoned, experienced teachers?

4. How have these contacts with teachers altered your thoughts about teaching as a career?

The Teacher and Schools in Media

Have students rent and view any of the films (television teachers could also be used) available on the following list. Using the chart provided, have them analyze the portrayal of the teacher in the film. Follow up with a class discussion of the similarities and differences they found in the portrayals and the similarities and differences between the portrayals and the reality in classrooms.

Miss Bishop
The Dead Poet's Society
Mr. Holland's Opus
Stand and Deliver
Teachers
Music of the Heart
Goodbye Mr. Chips
The Paper Chase
Rachel, Rachel
The Karate Kid (I)
Water Is Wide
The Prime of Miss Jean Brodie
Ferris Buehler's Day Off

Principal
Up The Down Staircase
How Green Was My Valley
Summer School
Children of A Lesser God
The Blackboard Jungle
To Sir With Love
The Marva Collins Story
The Corn Is Green
Good Morning Miss Dove
Man With No Face
Miracle Worker
Crisis at Central High

My Fair Lady
Hoosier
Lean on Me
Kindergarten Cop
Fame
Chalk Garden
Children's Hour
Christie
Teacher Teacher
Dangerous Minds
A Lesson Before Dying

To determine availability in your area call 1-800-800-6767.

Teacher Portrayal Analysis Form

Film title Teacher Name (sex/race/age)	Motivation to Teach Classroom Goals	Apparent Educational Philosophy	Visible Management & Instructional Style	Classroom Demographic Characteristics	"Message"
Example: "The Paper Chase" Prof. Kingsfield (Male, White, Elderly)	Dedication to law profession	Perennialist	Authoritarian Information Processing Socratic Questioning	Graduate School, mainly men, few women or students of color, middle and upperclass, large lecture hall.	"Teacher's job is to make students think." (Work)

Real Teachers and Real Schools

An additional topic that may be presented is the real experiences of actual teachers. The accounts of real teachers in such books as *Educating Esme, Small Victories, Among Schoolchildren, Marva Collins' Way*, and *No Place But Here* present vivid accounts of teaching. The lecture could also touch on local news about teachers. As an additional presentation for class, the lecturer can invite several local teachers to discuss with students their motivations for teaching and their experiences as teachers. (See references under *Non-Fiction Accounts of Teachers* in "Additional Resources for Instructors.")

A Few Thoughts on Teaching and Education

In this activity, students consider various statements regarding teaching and education, compare those perceptions with their own, and share their reflections on the quotations with the class.

Instructions

Divide students into small groups, and distribute a sheet with the quotations about teaching listed below to each group. Have each group select several quotations to consider. Ask students to choose which of the following statements *most* reflects their thoughts about education and teaching. Ask them which of the statements *least* reflects their notions of teaching and education. What are the implications of their selections for education as a whole?

List of Quotations

- "You cannot teach a man anything; you can only help him find it within himself." (Galileo)

- "One good schoolmaster is worth a thousand priests." (Robert Green Ingersoll)

- "A child . . . must feel the flush of victory and the heart-sinking of disappointment before he takes with a will to the tasks distasteful to him and resolves to dance his way through a dull routine of textbooks." (Helen Keller)

- "That type of scholarship which is bent on remembering things in order to answer people's questions does not qualify one to be a teacher." (Confucius)

- "The teacher is one who makes two ideas grow where only one grew before." (Elbert Hubbard)

- "Her job [the teacher's] is limited to offering the materials and suffices if she demonstrates their use; after that, she leaves the child with his work. Our goal is not so much the imparting of knowledge as the unveiling and developing of spiritual energy." (Maria Montessori)

- "The man who can make hard things easy is the educator." (Ralph Waldo Emerson)

- *More:* Why not be a teacher? You'd be a fine teacher. Perhaps—a great one.

  Rich: And if I were, who would know it?

  More: You, your pupils, your friends, God—not a bad public, that.

  (Robert Bolt, A Man for All Seasons)

- "I see the mind of the five-year-old as a volcano with two vents: destructiveness and creativeness." (Sylvia Ashton-Warner, *Teacher*)

- "A poor surgeon hurts one person at a time. A poor teacher hurts 130." (Ernest Boyer, president, Carnegie Foundation for Advancement of Teaching)

- "We have inadvertently designed a system in which being good at what you do as a teacher is not formally rewarded, while being poor at what you do is seldom corrected nor penalized." (Elliot Eisner, professor, Stanford School of Education)

- "I have one rule—attention. They give me theirs and I give them mine." (Sister Evangelist, RSM, teacher in Montana)

- "The most important function of education at any level is to develop the personality of the individual and the significance of his life to himself and to others. This is the basic architecture of a life; the rest is ornamentation and decoration of the structure." (Grayson Kirk, president, Columbia University)

- "What a teacher doesn't say . . . is a telling part of what a student hears." (Maurice Natanson, professor of philosophy, Yale University)

- "I cannot join the space program and restart my life as an astronaut, but this opportunity to connect my abilities as an educator with my interests in history and space is a unique opportunity to fulfill my early fantasies." (Christa McAuliffe, teacher, Concord, N.H.; from her winning essay in NASA's nationwide search for the first teacher to travel in space)

- "I had learned to respect the intelligence, integrity, creativity, and capacity for deep thought and hard work latent somewhere in every child; they had learned that I differed from them only in years and experience, and that as I, an ordinary human being, loved and respected them, I expected payment in kind." (Sybil Marshall, on eighteen years as a teacher in a one-room schoolhouse in rural England)

- "A teacher must believe in the value and interest of his subject as a doctor believes in health." (Gilbert Highet, *The Art of Teaching*)

- "Teaching is an instinctual art, mindful of potential, craving of realization, a pausing, seamless process." (A. Bartlett Giamatti, president, Yale University)

- "Much that passes for education . . . is not education at all but ritual. The fact is that we are being educated when we know it least." (David P. Gardner, president, University of Utah)

- "A primary reason for my success in the classroom was that I couldn't forget that schooling was changing me and separating me from the life I enjoyed before becoming a student." (Richard Rodriguez, writer, scholar, in his autobiography, *Hunger of Memory*)

- "I didn't know anything about educational theory, and I have often thought that worked in my favor. Without preconceived ideas and not bound by rules, I was forced to deal with my students as individuals, to talk to them, to listen to them, to find out their needs. I wasn't trying to see how they fit into any learning patterns or educational models. I followed my own instincts and taught according to what felt right." (Marva Collins)

- "I believe the impulse to teach is fundamentally altruistic and represents a desire to share what you value and to empower others." (Herbert Kohl)

- "The function of education is to teach one to think intensively and to think critically. Intelligence plus character – that is the goal of true education." (Martin Luther King Jr.)

- "Education is not filling a bucket, but lighting a fire." (William B. Yeats)

- "Education is not preparation for life, it is life itself." (John Dewey)

- "The best education for the best is the best education for all." (Robert Maynard Hutchins)

- "Only three things are important to the teacher. First, to have command of your subject; Second, to know how to motivate the different ethnic groups we have in this country in order to preserve the unit – because the unit, or team, will give you success; And last, to understand your kids and keep a good relationship with them. A good relationship will be a giant step to success." (Jaime Escalante)

- "The great aim of education is not knowledge but action." (Herbert Spencer)

- "I still argue that . . . while there are ways to teach that are more efficient, more effective, more pleasant, exciting, and so on – children will learn, no matter what method you use, if they feel wanted, valued, and accepted in an environment in which they can interact with caring people they trust." (James Comer)

- "Give a man a fish and you feed him for a day. Teach a man to fish and you feed him for a lifetime." (Chinese Proverb)

- "The love of nurturing and observing growth in others is essential to sustaining a life of teaching. This implies that no matter what you teach or how you present yourself to your students, you have to be on the learner's side and to believe that they can and will grow during the time that you are together." (Herbert Kohl)

Student Assignments

Independent Reading

Read and respond to any of the selections noted on the chapter/article correlation list found in the front of this manual for Ryan/Cooper, *Kaleidoscope: Readings in Education* (Houghton Mifflin, 2001). You may want to use the Article Review Form in *Kaleidoscope*.

Reflective Papers

Choose one of the following topics to write a reflective paper (2–5 pages). The purpose of the paper is to help you assimilate new knowledge by blending it with your previous knowledge and experiences.

1. Many people who choose to teach have vivid, warm memories of one (or several) teachers. Choose one memorable teacher from your schooling and write a descriptive paper about him or her. What made that teacher memorable to you? Are there any key events that made you remember this teacher? From your perspective, what made him or her such a good teacher?

2. Conversely, many people choose to teach, in part, because they had a terrible teacher at one point in their education. Choose a teacher who made a negative impression on you and write a description of this person. How did that teacher behave with students? What was his or her teaching style? Why do you have negative memories of that teacher? From your perspective, what were some of the person's attributes that made him or her a poor teacher?

3. Select any of the Non-Fiction Accounts of Teachers listed in "Additional Resources for Instructors" or others approved by the instructor. Analyze the teacher's motive for entering teaching, his or her philosophy, and the theme(s) reflected in the story. Include your reaction to the story.

Journal Reflections

Suggestions for journal topics for students' selection:

1. Articulate your own reasons, as you understand them, for becoming a teacher.

2. Indicate your thoughts and feelings after observing in a classroom like one in which you will teach.

3. Describe the characteristics of your own most significant teacher.

CD-ROM Video Clip

View the clip for Chapter 15 and be prepared to discuss the following reflection questions:

1. Which do you believe teachers do more: impact our culture, or react to it? Which of these paths do you see yourself following as a teacher? Why?

2. Do you see your most basic role as a teacher as one of introducing students to humanity? If so, why? If not, what else do you see as your most basic role?

PART III

Sample Chapter Quizzes

Many student users of this text are in their first or second year of college and are inexperienced with college-level material and the demands of their new, independent status. Study guides and practice quizzes may provide them with the help they need to get the most out of the text and your course. These quizzes can be photocopied directly and given to students.

CHAPTER 1

What Is a School and What Is It For?

MULTIPLE CHOICE QUESTIONS AND ANSWERS

Read each item carefully. Select the letter of the choice that represents the best answer.

Ans: c

1. Schooling can best be described as

    a. a process of human growth that leads to greater self-control.
    b. an informal arrangement made for the benefit of students of all ages.
    c. a specific, formalized process.
    d. an experience over a set period of time spent in an institution.

Ans: c

2. When a student is able to exist productively in a rule-bound system and can read, write, and compute, it is probably the result of his or her

    a. education, defined broadly.
    b. vocational training.
    c. schooling.
    d. directed study.

Ans: b

3. A curriculum designed to teach people how to be effective learners, able to master complex academic content, is characteristic of schools of the

    a. trainer of good worker model.
    b. college preparatory model.
    c. human development model.
    d. acculturator model.

Ans: d

4. The "product" of schools run on the trainer model is students who

    a. become crafts people.
    b. work quickly.
    c. fit into the dominant culture.
    d. become good workers.

Ans: a

5. In one high school, students are given freedom to choose from a broad selection of courses in the fine arts, sciences, literature, vocational areas, and athletics. This high school probably represents the

    a. shopping mall school.
    b. college prep school.
    c. acculturator school.
    d. social escalator school.

Ans: a

6. By the end of the first year, a student knows how to behave in class, on the playground, and in the lunchroom, and as a result is well liked by the teachers. This appropriate behavior is probably a result of successful

   a. socialization.
   b. achievement.
   c. peer-group influence.
   d. immersion in an interactive environment.

Ans: b

7. Jackson's study of elementary classrooms found that

   a. students learn to be aggressive and loud.
   b. students learn to wait and repress desires.
   c. teachers learn to wait and take turns.
   d. students learn to follow directions.

Ans: a

8. Boyer's study of modern high schools showed that a major problem that most experience is

   a. an accumulation of contradictory purposes.
   b. the absence of written goals.
   c. the inability to offer relevant courses.
   d. an unwillingness to provide something for everyone.

Ans: d

9. In *The Shopping Mall High School*, which group of students may be neglected?

   a. gifted athletes
   b. underachievers
   c. special needs students
   d. average students

Ans: d

10. Which one of the following was *not* suggested as a way to improve quality in American high schools?

    a. more technology
    b. personalization
    c. flexible scheduling
    d. more variety

SHORT-ANSWER QUESTIONS

Answer each of the following questions briefly, but specifically, in complete sentences.

1. Explain the concept of a school as a social panacea. To what degree do you think this model is appropriate for schools?

2. What changes can be noticed in the organization and instructional practices in high schools over the past one hundred years?

ANSWERS TO SHORT-ANSWER QUESTIONS

1. The school as a social panacea model sees the schools as doing whatever is necessary to relieve the social problems of society. If students are threatened with AIDS, then the school should provide AIDS instruction. If the community has a problem with widespread alcohol abuse, then the schools should provide instruction or training in resisting substance abuse. The school as an institution is used as a vehicle for combating social ills and problems.

2. Most studies show that little has changed in either the organizational patterns or the instructional practices in most high schools in the recent past.

CHAPTER 2

Who Are Today's Students in a Diverse Society?

MULTIPLE CHOICE QUESTIONS AND ANSWERS

Read each item carefully. Select the letter of the choice that represents the best answer.

Ans: c

1. The anticipated student population trend for the next ten years is

   a. significant increases in all populations.
   b. an increase in the white population percentage while the minority population remains stable.
   c. an increase in the minority population while the white population percentage declines.
   d. zero growth for any population.

Ans: b

2. Before laws regarding bilingual education were passed, the most frequent model for teaching non-English-speaking students was likely to have been

   a. immersion.
   b. submersion.
   c. transition.
   d. maintenance.

Ans: c

3. Mrs. Blazer has been strongly influenced by William Glasser's choice theory. Unlike most teachers, she never puts "happy face" stickers on her students' work or provides them with other rewards like bonus points for work well done. Why would she avoid such practices?

   a. Because they exert a form of control on students by encouraging them to desire external rewards
   b. Because the external rewards such as stickers have no intrinsic relationship to the work itself
   c. Because she wants students to develop their own internal standards for judging the quality of their work
   d. Because she believes the competition spurred by handing out stickers encourages her students to exert psychological control over each other.

Ans: a

4.   What previous legislation does IDEA build on?

a.   PL 94-142, which established special education for students
       with disabilities
b.   The *Lau Remedies* for non-English-speaking students
c.   The Head Start program, an early intervention program
d.   Title I for disadvantaged children

Ans: b

5.   Dominic is a basketball player, and he has the ability to run quickly,
      jump high into the air, and easily make a basket from the three-point
      range. Which of the following theorists identifies Dominic's ability as
      a form of intelligence?

a.   John Goodlad
b.   Howard Gardner
c.   Jean Piaget
d.   Erik Erickson

Ans: d

6.   Which way of implementing learning-style theory in classrooms
      would be the most educationally sound?

a.   Test the students in the classroom, and then individually
       determine their learning styles.
b.   Design monthly units featuring a particular learning style, and
       emphasize it with your class.
c.   Have teachers identify their learning styles, and then have them
       teach in the ways in which they feel most comfortable.
d.   Integrate as many learning styles as possible in activities and
       lessons so that all students will have the opportunity to perform
       well.

Ans: c

7.   Generally, white women constitute the majority of teachers. In the
      near future, the teaching profession is expected to

a.   gain a significant increase in the number of female minority
       teachers.
b.   attract more men to the profession; nearly 40 percent of the
       teaching force will be men within the next twenty years.
c.   continue to be a profession where white women will be the
       majority.
d.   see a marked decrease in the dominance of white women in the
       field.

Ans: a

8.   The goal of multicultural education is to

a.   reduce prejudice and foster tolerance for other cultures.
b.   academically support ethnic minority students.
c.   provide a nurturing environment for children who have been
       abused.
d.   teach students to speak other languages.

Ans: d

9. The decision of *Lau* v. *Nichols* provided for

    a.   the free and appropriate education of children with disabilities.
    b.   the creation and maintenance of programs for the gifted and talented.
    c.   the early intervention for education of children with special needs who are between three and five years old.
    d.   the establishment of bilingual education programs for all limited English students.

Ans: a

10. Inclusion refers to

    a.   including students with disabilities in the regular classroom.
    b.   including students with disabilities in after school sports.
    c.   including non-English speakers in the regular classroom.
    d.   including parents in their child(ren)'s education.

SHORT-ANSWER QUESTIONS

Answer each of the following questions briefly, but specifically, in complete sentences.

1. Why do some educators oppose multicultural education in the schools?

2. How will the changing student population affect teaching?

ANSWERS TO SHORT-ANSWER QUESTIONS

1. Educators who oppose multicultural education in schools do so because they are concerned that a focus on multiculturalism will destroy any sense of common tradition, values, and beliefs in American society. They recommend that cultural pluralism be limited.

2. Because the student population is expected to become more diverse while the teaching population remains heavily white female, the two groups (minority students and white teachers) may have difficulty relating to one another, thus limiting the effectiveness of the learning environment.

CHAPTER 3

What Social Problems and Tension Points Affect Today's Students?

MULTIPLE CHOICE QUESTIONS AND ANSWERS

Read each item carefully. Select the letter of the choice that represents the best answer.

Ans: a

1. Are teenage mothers particularly vulnerable to poverty?

   a. They do not usually complete their education to get marketable skills.
   b. They usually demonstrate a lack of commitment to any job.
   c. They usually expect that social service agencies will be able to meet their needs.
   d. They don't set attainable goals.

Ans: a

2. The psychological effects of abuse on a child can lead to

   a. serious learning difficulties for the child.
   b. a dislike for school.
   c. free breakfast and lunch in school.
   d. more study hall time.

Ans: d

3. The U.S. family structure is changing. Today, it would not be unusual to find

   a. a single-parent family.
   b. a blended family with children from previous marriages.
   c. children living with grandparents or other relatives.
   d. All of these are quite likely.

Ans: b

4. Magnet schools are

   a. private schools that receive public support because they resolve some problems of segregation.
   b. public schools with high-quality, special-interest, cost-effective programs.
   c. private schools that attract minority and white students equally.
   d. public schools that are expensive and enroll students from a narrowly defined geographic area.

Ans: c

5.   A basal reader has fifty stories about people. Thirty-five of the stories involve males having adventures in which they always succeed. Fifteen of the stories are about females who have either of two roles: a "damsel in distress" or a parent in a two-parent family. The stories featuring females are mysteries, romances, or stories about families. This text might be called sexist because

a.   male role models are successful in their pursuits.
b.   the stories concerning males involve adventure.
c.   the stories are about females who are shown as weak or able to succeed only in partnerships.
d.   the stories featuring women emphasize mysteries or stories about families.

Ans: a

6.   Ms. Juniper suspects that one of the students in class is being abused at home. When she asks the student about it, he first denies it, then reluctantly tells her the truth, but begs her not to say anything or he'll "really get in trouble." What should Ms. Juniper do?

a.   Report it to the proper authority right away.
b.   Respect the boy's wishes and not say anything.
c.   Go to see the boy's father and tell him to stop or she will have to report him to the police.
d.   Wait a while to see if he continues to be abused.

Ans: c

7.   The practice of gender bias in any school activity that is funded in part or wholly by federal dollars is forbidden by provisions of

a.   Chapter I of ESEA.
b.   Brown v. Board of Education.
c.   Title IX of the Educational Amendment Act.
d.   Title I.

Ans: d

8.   All of the following are risk factors contributing to the high rate of children living in poverty *except*

a.   family headed by a female.
b.   household where no parent has a job.
c.   full time jobs that pay minimum wage.
d.   school systems built by and for the wealthy.

Ans: c

9.   Which of the following is the largest factor in the growing number of children living with a single parent?

a.   Teen mothers
b.   Deaths
c.   Divorce
d.   Working parents

Ans: d

10. Research seems to indicate that high school principals can help reduce violence and vandalism in schools by

    a.   maintaining a stern, watchful eye and punishing misbehavior consistently.
    b.   being a good friend to all students.
    c.   cultivating the support of student leaders for programs to subdue troublemakers.
    d.   establishing high expectations for student behavior and performance.

SHORT-ANSWER QUESTIONS

Answer each of the following questions briefly, but specifically, in complete sentences.

1. Why is it important to provide a stable class for an abused child?

2. Why have schools not been very successful in reducing poverty?

ANSWERS TO SHORT-ANSWER QUESTIONS

1. Children who have been abused need to be able, more than anything else, to learn to trust people again. For that reason, it is vital that a teacher be a positive, trustworthy role model. The teacher should set the tone for the class, and much of the teacher's time should be spent in creating an environment in which children can expect or trust certain things to happen. That doesn't mean that the teacher can never change the routine of the day; rather, it means that children will know that the teacher will maintain a consistently fair atmosphere in the class.

2. Although many educators and social scientists see education as a way out of poverty, schools are middle-class institutions with middle-class values and as such they may cause poor children to begin to believe they are losers. These poor students become more and more disengaged with school and are not very successful. The cycle of poverty remains.

CHAPTER 4

What Is Taught?

MULTIPLE CHOICE QUESTIONS AND ANSWERS

Ans: c

1. According to E. D. Hirsch, a culturally literate person in the United States

   a. speaks English and one other language fluently.
   b. moves into new and culturally different environments easily and graciously.
   c. is knowledgeable of the historical events and notable persons in this culture.
   d. has attended a liberal arts college and has taken courses emphasizing multiculturalism.

Ans: c

2. Given recent trends in art education at the elementary and secondary levels, the course that is most likely to be offered now is

   a. oil painting.
   b. modern dance.
   c. art appreciation.
   d. dramatic storytelling.

Ans: d

3. For both teachers and students, most of the content in any lesson is probably taken from

   a. district curriculum guides.
   b. research reports on each subject.
   c. school scope-and-sequence charts.
   d. published textbooks, manuals, worksheets, and tests.

Ans: d

4. Studies of effective ways to teach writing have led to the belief that

   a. writing is most efficiently taught within the regular language arts program.
   b. writing is best learned in the context of a course focused only on writing.
   c. writing cannot be taught directly but can be learned only with practice and feedback.
   d. writing achievement as well as content area mastery is enhanced when writing instruction is spread over several content areas.

Ans: b

5. A teacher who uses a social studies or science lesson to show students how to find and evaluate evidence is teaching

    a. mastery of content knowledge.
    b. critical thinking.
    c. Socratic dialogue.
    d. data analysis.

Ans: a

6. According to the Third International Mathematics and Science Study (TIMSS), U.S. students performed

    a. below average in both math and science.
    b. above average in math but below average in science.
    c. above average in both math and science.
    d. below average in math but above average in science.

Ans: c

7. Based on the newer trends in math instruction, which of the following will most likely occur in math classes?

    a. a decreased use of calculators and computers in classes at the high school level.
    b. greater emphasis on drill and practice to reduce errors at the elementary level.
    c. an increased compartmentalized emphasis on reason and argument when using manipulatives at the elementary level.
    d. an increased number of diverse math courses offered at the high school level.

Ans: c

8. Successful cooperative learning strategies include

    a. group goals and individual work.
    b. individual goals and group accountability.
    c. group goals and individual accountability.
    d. homogeneous grouping and individual accountability.

Ans: d

9. An important reason for emphasizing reading in the curriculum is that

    a. most people like to read, once they become skilled.
    b. reading is not very hard to teach.
    c. success in reading raises students' pride.
    d. success in reading contributes to success in all areas of curriculum.

Ans: a

10. Detracking high school students (eliminating the separation of academic, general, and vocational tracks) had which of the following effects?

    a. Detracking raised the performance of low achieving students.
    b. Detracking raised the performance of high achieving students.
    c. Detracking had the most positive effects for average students.
    d. Detracking erased social distinctions among students.

SHORT-ANSWER QUESTIONS

Answer each of the following questions briefly, but specifically, in complete sentences.

1. Explain the differences between instruction based on core curriculum and multicultural curriculum with regard to goals and content.

2. How does interdisciplinary teaching lead to enhanced learning?

ANSWERS TO SHORT-ANSWER QUESTIONS

1. A core curriculum presents a shared understanding of our national culture, history, and traditions (i.e. cultural literacy): a Eurocentric curriculum. A multicultural curriculum involves cultural pluralism. The curriculum should reflect the contributions and experiences of American people of all ethnic backgrounds.

2. Interdisciplinary teaching allows students to experience coherence in the curriculum and connections to real-world situations. They see that all knowledge is related, so that what they learn in one subject is reinforced in another.

CHAPTER 5

What Makes a Teacher Effective?

MULTIPLE CHOICE QUESTIONS AND ANSWERS

Read each item carefully. Select the letter of the choice that represents the best answer.

Ans: a

1. Angela Herrera is a sixth-grade teacher. She spends many days during August visiting the school library, reviewing material, and creating lessons for her class in September. During this time, Angela makes

   a. planning decisions.
   b. reflective decisions.
   c. implementing decisions.
   d. evaluating decisions.

Ans: c

2. Teacher A argues that professional training ought to focus mainly on the content to be taught. Teacher B responds that pedagogical knowledge about learning and human behavior is more essential. Which teacher does the text support?

   a. Teacher A
   b. Teacher B
   c. Both teachers
   d. Neither teacher

Ans: a

3. Dana was in the middle of teaching a lesson he had worked hard preparing when he realized that many students did not understand it. He immediately changed the direction of the lesson to help them understand. In this instance, Dana made a(n)

   a. implementing decision.
   b. reflective decision.
   c. evaluating decision.
   d. planning decision.

Ans: a

4. According to the text, one reason for studying theoretical knowledge is that it

   a. equips the teacher to interpret the complexities of the classroom.
   b. has been shown to discipline the teacher's mind to make learning easier.
   c. is part of the rite of passage of teacher education.
   d. enables a teacher to cover more material with students.

Ans: c

5.   According to the text, which of these factors is likely to contribute to students' high achievement? A teacher who is

     a.   well educated in a subject.
     b.   strict in discipline.
     c.   involved in research on the subject.
     d.   impersonal and professional.

Ans: a

6.   The explanation that people refer to when choosing a course of action is called

     a.   theory-in-use.
     b.   a theory.
     c.   a discipline.
     d.   knowledge about knowledge.

Ans: d

7.   When the principal comes in unannounced to ask the teacher a question, the principal notices that several students are creating a model together. Other students are reading science books, and the rest are writing. They all seem immersed in their task. These students are demonstrating

     a.   cooperative learning.
     b.   classroom management.
     c.   group process.
     d.   academic engaged time.

Ans: b

8.   Which of the following teacher behaviors is properly classified as classroom management?

     a.   Using a student team learning approach
     b.   Defining routines for the use of class supplies
     c.   Having a spelling bee to make spelling more interesting
     d.   Assigning a timed test in math

Ans: b

9.   The three major categories of decisions that teachers make in the course of instructing are

     a.   planning, management, and environment.
     b.   planning, implementing, and evaluating.
     c.   instructional, management, and evaluating.
     d.   planning, environment, and instructional.

Ans: b

10.   Every morning during math, your class seems to go haywire. At most other times, the students are not a problem. What do "Kevin and Jim's Management Rules" tell you to do first?

     a.   Go straight to your mentor for help.
     b.   Check your instruction.
     c.   Try a threat of calling home.
     d.   Ask a colleague to come in and observe the class to give you some pointers.

SHORT-ANSWER QUESTIONS

Answer each of the following questions briefly, but specifically, in complete sentences.

1.   In what ways is theoretical knowledge vital for an effective teacher? Explain.

2.   What are the defining characteristics of a reflective teacher?

ANSWERS TO SHORT-ANSWER QUESTIONS

1.   Theoretical knowledge gives one the ability to interpret situations, solve problems, and avoid pat solutions to problems in the classroom.

2.   A reflective teacher is one who has developed the attitudes and skills to become a lifelong student of teaching. A reflective teacher examines his or her teaching practices and asks questions like "What am I doing and why?" "How can I meet my students' needs better?"

CHAPTER 6

What Should Teachers Know About Technology and Its Impact on Schools?

MULTIPLE CHOICE QUESTIONS AND ANSWERS

Read each item carefully. Select the letter of the choice that represents the best answer.

Ans: a

1. The sources of pressure on schools to increase their use of technology tools include

   a. parents and teachers.
   b. students and legislators.
   c. businesses and citizens.
   d. all of these.

Ans: c

2. When did technology that helped teachers use more pictures in the classroom first become available?

   a. Early 1800s
   b. Late 1800s
   c. Early 1900s
   d. Late 1900s

Ans: d

3. Test generators, lesson-planning software, and grade books are examples of

   a. teacher-generated software.
   b. teacher communication tools.
   c. teacher instructional tools.
   d. teacher productivity tools.

Ans: a

4. According to the text what was one of the earliest technological devices used in classrooms?

   a. Chalkboard
   b. Television
   c. Radio
   d. Filmstrip

Ans: d

5. Acceptable use policies for technology result in all of the following benefits *except*:

   a. reduce a school's liability.
   b. solicit parental input and permission.
   c. make expectations and consequences clear.
   d. prevent all inappropriate uses of technology.

Ans: d

6. The educational advantages of using technology to assist students with special needs are

 a. presentation for a variety of learning styles.
 b. individualization.
 c. enhanced communication.
 d. all of these.

Ans: b

7. Which of the following is *not* an example of assistive technology?

 a. remote control units
 b. Internet
 c. voice output device
 d. computer to enhance communication

Ans: b

8. All of theses are examples of using the computer as a cognitive tool *except*

 a. word processor.
 b. e-mail.
 c. database.
 d. spreadsheet.

Ans: a

9. Which of the following was *not* created specifically to facilitate instruction?

 a. World Wide Web
 b. Drill-and-practice software
 c. Simulation software
 d. Interactive multimedia

Ans: c

10. Which arrangement of computers is a more expensive investment for schools?

 a. Single-computer classroom
 b. Computer labs
 c. Classroom clusters
 d. All of these require equal investments.

SHORT-ANSWER QUESTIONS

Answer each of the following questions briefly, but specifically, in complete sentences.

1. Describe at least three ways that educational technology affects teaching today. Give examples.

2. Identify the major contributors to unequal access to computers for students across schools or districts.

ANSWERS TO SHORT-ANSWER QUESTIONS

1. Answers should include references to using the computer for communication, for instruction, for presentation, to enhance productivity, and so on.

2. Answers could include lack of funding in low socioeconomic areas, inadequate electrical systems, lack of access to the Internet, and poorly trained teachers.

CHAPTER 7

What Are the Ethical and Legal Issues Facing Teachers?

MULTIPLE CHOICE QUESTIONS AND ANSWERS

Read each item carefully. Select the letter of the choice that represents the best answer.

Ans: d

1. A teacher is notified on the day before school begins that no contract will be offered to him for that year. On hearing the teacher's objection, the principal announces that the teacher may plead the case for employment at the end of the school board meeting that night, at about 11 p.m. What violation of rights has the teacher suffered ?

   a. Violation of the everyday ethics of teaching
   b. Violation of Fourteenth Amendment rights
   c. Violation of professional courtesy
   d. Violation of the right to due process

Ans: a

2. The case that resulted in a decision to permit teachers to discuss the theory of evolution in science classes was the

   a. *Scopes* case.
   b. *Nichols* case.
   c. *Pickering* case.
   d. *Kalamazoo* case.

Ans: d

3. In a public elementary or secondary school setting, *academic freedom* refers to a teacher's right to

   a. select any published course textbook that seems appropriate.
   b. use any reading in class that bears on the general subject of the course.
   c. determine the content of their courses.
   d. use a reading for class if it is age-appropriate and directly relevant to the goals of the course curriculum.

Ans: b

4. The Family Educational Rights and Privacy Act, also known as the Buckley Amendment, guarantees the right of

   a. students to see teachers' personnel files.
   b. parents to see school files kept on their own children.
   c. teachers to see the files of students in the whole family.
   d. parents to see personnel files of their children's teachers.

Ans: c

5. Under current copyright laws, a teacher may

    a. copy a published article for use in preparing for class.
    b. tape off-the-air copies of special broadcasts for student viewing the next day.
    c. copy a published article for use in preparing for class and tape off-the-air copies of special broadcasts for student viewing the next day.
    d. neither copy a published article for use in preparing for class nor tape off-the-air copies of special broadcasts for student viewing the next day.

Ans: a

6. The rights protected under due process include

    a. the right to timely notice of dismissal.
    b. the right to wear one's hair in any style.
    c. the right to take public positions on policy.
    d. the right to take public positions on policy and the right to wear one's hair in any style.

Ans: d

7. A student accuses a teacher of having used profanity when she reprimanded him the hall. The teacher is guaranteed by due process that when this incident comes under investigation,

    a. she will have an impartial decision maker in the investigation.
    b. free representation by a school district lawyer.
    c. the school district will pay her legal fees.
    d. she may cross-examine witnesses.

Ans: c

8. Knowledge of the professional code of morality is particularly helpful for cases in which the teacher

    a. must decide whether to sign the contract offered for the following year.
    b. is asked to drive some students to a math contest.
    c. needs to decide how to handle his or her own conflict with another teacher.
    d. suspects that one of the children in class is abused at home.

Ans: a

9. A teacher should understand the professional code of morality that applies to education because

    a. teachers help children learn about the place of moral codes in society.
    b. teachers have an ethical role in the lives of children.
    c. teachers must protect themselves from unjust court actions.
    d. teachers must protect children from unwarranted legal actions.

Ans: c

10. A tenured teacher is dismissed from her teaching position. According to the text, for which of the following reason(s) could a tenured teacher legally be dismissed?

   a. She had not volunteered for extracurricular duties during the past several school years.

   b. She had written a letter to the editor of the local newspaper sharply criticizing the policies of the school board.

   c. There was a reduction in force in the school district.

   d. She had not demonstrated professional growth during the past several school years, and she had written a letter to the editor of the local newspaper sharply criticizing the policies of the school board.

SHORT-ANSWER QUESTIONS

Answer each of the following questions briefly, but specifically, in complete sentences.

1. What is the distinction between ethics and law in teaching? Give an example demonstrating each.

2. What is meant by the "everyday ethics of teaching"? Provide some examples.

ANSWERS TO SHORT-ANSWER QUESTIONS

1. Ethics is the code of morality followed by a particular group of people. For professional groups, there is frequently a code of ethics that the professionals agree to follow. The National Education Association, for example, has a code of ethics for educators. The laws are agreed-on rules that a community must follow. The law is part of the system of rules governing the community. Examples of ethics and law in teaching will vary, but the examples should be clear indications of ethics or law. Examples of an ethical act by a teacher are encouraging a discouraged student to do the best he or she can on an activity and treating each child fairly. Examples of laws are the laws regarding reporting suspected child abuse and regarding the procedures for search and seizure of students' lockers.

2. The everyday ethics of teaching, according to the authors, involve teaching every day in the manner in which it ought to be done. That means doing the job to the best of one's professional ability. Every day, a teacher has to make hundreds of small ethical decisions, and if a teacher is observing the everyday ethics of teaching he or she will approach each of these decisions in a consistent, thoughtful manner with goodwill. Some examples include not taking a "sick" day unless one really is ill; spending time carefully responding to students' work and returning work within a reasonable time; putting care into the daily planning of lessons; treating all students fairly; and not gossiping about colleagues, students, or administrators.

CHAPTER 8

What Are the Philosophical Foundations of American Education?

MULTIPLE CHOICE QUESTIONS AND ANSWERS

Read each item carefully. Select the letter of the choice that represents the best answer.

Ans: d

1. Philosophers try to find answers to fundamental questions about existence by using

   a. historical patterns.
   b. human experience.
   c. intuition.
   d. reasoning.

Ans: c

2. An advanced placement biology class is discussing if physicians should transplant tissue and organs from aborted fetuses to patients diagnosed with various diseases. The discussion centers on the physician's conduct in performing such procedures. This discussion is focusing on

   a. aesthetics.
   b. epistemology.
   c. ethics.
   d. logic.

Ans: c

3. Asked why she taught history, Mrs. Wong replied that the study of history revealed the universality of human nature and that by studying the constancy of human nature, we could best learn how to approach contemporary issues. She is a(n)

   a. romanticist.
   b. progressive.
   c. perennialist.
   d. agnostic.

Ans: b

4. When students study Latin and also learn about the Roman values and Roman art, their instruction is in the field of

   a. epistemology.
   b. axiology.
   c. logic.
   d. metaphysics.

Ans: b

5. Making choices about whether knowledge comes from collective wisdom or from the individual's intuition represents which aspect of philosophy?

    a. Axiological
    b. Epistemological
    c. Metaphysical
    d. Phenomenological

Ans: b

6. A group of teachers met to decide if a newly created standardized test of mathematics should be administered to the students in their school. One teacher was opposed to administering the test because she claimed the test could *not* demonstrate *how* the students knew the mathematical concepts. Her concerns were of a(n) _____ nature.

    a. aesthetic
    b. epistemological
    c. ethical
    d. metaphysical

Ans: a

7. Which of the following lists of content is most representative of a perennialist curriculum?

    a. *The Odyssey*, by Homer, *Introduction to European History*, and *Biology: The Science of Living Things*
    b. *The Grapes of Wrath*, by John Steinbeck, *The Elements of Keyboarding*, and *Money Management for the '90s*
    c. *The Joy Luck Club*, by Amy Tan, Bruce Catton's volumes on the Civil War, and *Introduction to Psychology*
    d. *A Catcher in the Rye*, by J. D. Salinger, *Introduction to Mechanical Drawing*, and *Geometry*

Ans: b

8. In the essentialist school of education, the worth of any knowledge is measured by

    a. the stimulation and curiosity it provokes on the students' part.
    b. the degree to which an individual needs that knowledge to be a productive member of society.
    c. its potential to be verified, observed, and proven to be the truth.
    d. its usefulness in helping someone in his or her quest for personal meaning.

Ans: d

9. In a progressivist school, which of the following would most likely be evident? An emphasis on

    a. student choice and individuality.
    b. the usefulness of the curriculum content.
    c. students' self-discipline to sustain and propel them through the rigors of academic work.
    d. the cooperative and problem-solving capacities of the students.

Ans: c

10. A teacher is working with individual students to discover their interests and help them develop plans to investigate them and later choose how to communicate their learning about their chosen topics. This is an example of

    a.   behaviorism.
    b.   essentialism.
    c.   romanticism.
    d.   progressivism.

SHORT-ANSWER QUESTIONS

Answer each of the following questions briefly, but specifically, in complete sentences.

1. Why is essentialism considered an "American" philosophy? What facets of it indicate that it reflects America?

2. Why is it important to recognize the philosophies of education and identify your own?

ANSWERS TO SHORT-ANSWER QUESTIONS

1. Essentialism is a highly pragmatic philosophy of education. It looks to what one will need to function in society and includes those skills and subjects in the curriculum. In that respect, it is closely linked to the demands of the market, because functioning in society is typically understood to be working and contributing to the country.

2. Understanding the philosophy of education transforms a teacher from being merely a skilled or technical deliverer of information to being a professional educator. With the understanding of different philosophies of education, a teacher will know more clearly his or her goals, his or her methods for teaching, and the reasons behind all the decisions he or she will make. The teacher will also be able to spot more easily any inconsistencies in practice.

CHAPTER 9

What Is the History of American Education?

MULTIPLE CHOICE QUESTIONS AND ANSWERS

Read each item carefully. Select the letter of the choice that represents the best answer.

Ans: c

1. Private, family-based education, generally relying on tutors, was characteristic of colonial

    a. New England.
    b. mid-Atlantic communities.
    c. communities of the South.
    d. agricultural centers.

Ans: a

2. Common schools were founded on the belief that

    a. democracy required a well-educated citizenry.
    b. all students needed to have a moral education.
    c. students needed to develop workplace skills in school.
    d. all students had a right to a free education.

Ans: b

3. The purpose of the Old Deluder Satan Act, passed in Massachusetts in 1647, was to

    a. encourage religious instruction in the schools.
    b. require towns to provide education for children.
    c. set up a system of secular schools.
    d. set aside land for schools in every township.

Ans: a

4. Friedrich Froebel is best known for

    a. developing kindergarten.
    b. developing a hands-on approach to science.
    c. initiating bilingual education in the United States.
    d. proposing writing across the curriculum.

Ans: a

5. Horace Mann argued in favor of the common school because he believed that

    a. the common school would help forge a national identity.
    b. all people should receive a religious education in the schools.
    c. the common school would train better workers.
    d. common schools would allow for greater harmony of thoughts and ideals.

Ans: d

6. In the late 1600s, who would most likely have been a student in an elementary school?

    a.   A white female
    b.   A white male or white female of the middle class
    c.   A male of any race
    d.   A white, upper-class male

Ans: c

7. The main difference between the Latin and English grammar schools in the 1700s was that

    a.   Latin schools were for boys and English schools were for girls.
    b.   Latin schools were just early, primitive forms of English schools.
    c.   Latin schools prepared students for college and English schools prepared them for work.
    d.   Latin schools had higher status but did not differ from English schools in goals or curriculum.

Ans: c

8. The Progressive Education Association maintained that schools should help to

    a.   train teachers.
    b.   develop the students' interests in working.
    c.   make the connection between school and the real world.
    d.   end poverty and homelessness.

Ans: c

9. The Morrill Acts of 1862 and 1890 provided for the establishment of

    a.   multicultural education in the public schools of the north.
    b.   the common school in the New England colonies.
    c.   land grant colleges if they did not discriminate in admission.
    d.   segregated but equal schools in the southern states.

Ans: b

10. Female academies to teach women how to be intelligent and productive companions for men or to be qualified teachers were established in the 1800s by

    a.   Willa Cather, Laura Ingalls, and Catherine Stowe.
    b.   Catherine Beecher, Emma Willard, and Mary Lyon.
    c.   Harriet Beecher Stowe and Maria Montessori.
    d.   Jane Addams, Mary Lyon, and Dorothea Dix.

SHORT-ANSWER QUESTIONS

Answer each of the following questions briefly, but specifically, in complete sentences.

1. Describe the impact that one of the following people had on American education: Horace Mann, W. E. B. Du Bois, or Noah Webster.
2. How did religion influence the development of the early schools and how do today's practices differ?

ANSWERS TO SHORT-ANSWER QUESTIONS

1. See text for brief biographies.

2.   Some type of religious instruction, whether it was reading the Lord's Prayer or learning moral and religious values from a primer, made up much of early American education. During the early to mid-nineteenth century, however, the emphasis on religious instruction diminished as the demand for students skilled in practical trades or possessing functional knowledge for life after school drove the formal curriculum. More emphasis was placed on practical subjects and less on religious instruction.

CHAPTER 10

How Are Schools Governed, Influenced, and Financed?

MULTIPLE CHOICE QUESTIONS AND ANSWERS

Read each item carefully. Select the letter of the choice that represents the best answer.

Ans: d

1. Control of schools was made the legal responsibility of the individual states by the

   a. verdict in *Brown* v. *the Board of Education.*
   b. individual states in their Constitutions.
   c. federal government in the Declaration of Independence.
   d. the Tenth Amendment of the U.S. Bill of Rights.

Ans: d

2. In practice, which body has the most responsibility for carrying out the majority of educational policies?

   a. Federal government
   b. State legislature
   c. State department of education
   d. Local school board

Ans: c

3. State authorities usually delegate to local school boards the responsibility for

   a. certifying or licensing teachers.
   b. setting guidelines for elementary education.
   c. setting policy and administering schools.
   d. advising teacher-training institutions on professional programs.

Ans: a

4. Talia Lopez is meeting with the teacher education faculty at Shelburne State College to approve the changes in their teacher licensure program that were made to meet the new teacher licensure requirements. Based upon this description, Ms. Lopez most likely represents

   a. the state department of education.
   b. the state board of education.
   c. the governor's office.
   d. the U.S. Department of Education.

Ans: b

5.   Which of the following is *not* a characteristic of compensatory education programs?

a.   They are federally funded.
b.   They are focused on students with disabilities.
c.   They serve low-income students.
d.   They serve students at risk of failing.

Ans: b

6.   Bob Moorehead was the district superintendent of a small city's public school system for twenty years. Bob's longevity in this nontenured position was most likely due to

a.   his ability to assess student achievement.
b.   his ability to resolve conflicts among groups that make competing claims on the schools.
c.   his ability to rejuvenate the faculty through his strong program in staff development.
d.   his ability to restrict spending and to manage finances creatively.

Ans: a

7.   Which one of the following is *not* one of the responsibilities of the local school superintendent?

a.   Certifying qualified teacher applicants
b.   Constructing and maintaining buildings
c.   Selecting and promoting personnel
d.   Setting educational policy

Ans: a

8.   Professional educators exercise their strongest control in schools through

a.   daily decision making about program implementation.
b.   policy-setting powers shared by school boards.
c.   activities of professional associations.
d.   input and decision making about school finances.

Ans: a

9.   Education budgets are funded through contributions from federal, state, and local agencies, with the amount from each varying over time and from state to state. Which agencies *never* contribute the greatest proportion of funds?

a.   Federal agencies
b.   State agencies
c.   Local agencies
d.   All agencies contribute equally.

Ans: c

10.   The court decision ruling that a child is entitled to an education of the quality most reflective of the state's wealth is the

a.   *Brown* decision.
b.   *Kalamazoo* decision.
c.   *Serrano* decision.
d.   *Rodriguez* decision.

SHORT-ANSWER QUESTIONS

Answer each of the following questions briefly, but specifically, in complete sentences.

1. Compare and contrast the responsibilities of the state board of education and the state department of education.

2. Why have so many state systems for financing education been declared unconstitutional?

ANSWERS TO SHORT-ANSWER QUESTIONS

1. The state department of education's responsibilities include the accreditation of college and university educational certification/licensure programs, certifying or licensing of teachers, and carrying out of policies established by the state board of education and the state legislature. The state board of education exercises general control and supervision of schools in the state, establishes academic standards and assessments, and sets policy. The state board makes decisions and the state department carries them out.

2. Many school systems depend on local property taxes to raise funds to run the schools, so the wealthier towns have more money to run their schools than the less affluent towns. Therefore, the children who live in wealthier towns have better educational opportunities, and those in the less affluent towns receive unequal educational opportunities, which is in conflict with state constitutions that guarantee equal educational opportunities.

CHAPTER 11

How Should Education Be Reformed?

MULTIPLE CHOICE QUESTIONS AND ANSWERS

Read each item carefully. Select the letter of the choice that represents the best answer.

Ans: d

1. Which one of the following is *not* a recommendation to improve staff development?

   a. Teachers should see staff development as part of their workday.
   b. The definition of staff development should be broad.
   c. The costs should be paid by the district or state.
   d. Teachers should be required to earn a masters degree.

Ans: b

2. Ryan and Cooper identify seven essential elements of true school reform. Which of the following is *not* one of these elements?

   a. Excellence
   b. Consensus
   c. Authentic assessment.
   d. Character education

Ans: c

3. In the call-to-excellence movements, students are expected to

   a. feel good about themselves.
   b. appreciate the importance of education.
   c. achieve high levels of academic performance.
   d. speak more than one language fluently.

Ans: a

4. Reformers advocate for smaller schools because students

   a. feel a sense of belonging and become more engaged in their work.
   b. can get lost in the crowd and feel isolated.
   c. can see the chalkboard and hear the teacher better.
   d. do not have to walk as far to get from one class to the next.

Ans: d

5. A summary of research on reducing class size yields the following results.

   a. large gains in student achievement.
   b. lower student achievement.
   c. inconclusive results.
   d. small gains in achievement.

Ans: d

6. Joe's school requires that he complete twenty hours of community service in order to graduate. This requirement reflects a commitment to

    a.   basic skills testing.
    b.   teaching students life skills.
    c.   improving the local economy.
    d.   character education.

Ans: c

7. The most recent wave of educational reform efforts began with

    a.   Desert Storm.
    b.   Woodstock II.
    c.   *A Nation at Risk* report.
    d.   the end of the Vietnam War.

Ans: c

8. Common among state reform proposals are

    a.   higher teacher salaries and easier licensure criteria.
    b.   fewer graduation requirements and longer school years.
    c.   stricter graduation requirements and higher teacher salaries.
    d.   longer school days and larger class sizes.

Ans: b

9. State reform efforts have been largely characterized by

    a.   grassroots efforts coming from the teachers.
    b.   top-down reform from state legislatures.
    c.   collaborative efforts of teachers and administrators.
    d.   federal mandates.

Ans: a

10. Local reform efforts have been limited by lack of funds and

    a.   directed by state mandates.
    b.   driving the reform movement.
    c.   almost nonexistent because of a lack of interest on the part of the teachers.
    d.   most effective in bringing about change.

SHORT-ANSWER QUESTIONS

Answer each of the following questions briefly, but specifically, in complete sentences.

1. Why do Ryan and Cooper maintain that change is a slow process?

2. Describe the pros and cons of the federal government establishing national educational standards.

ANSWERS TO SHORT-ANSWER QUESTIONS

1. Ryan and Cooper explain their position by noting the size of American education, which involves 15,000 centers of decision and 50 million people, and influences from many quarters of society. More important, it has a standard operating procedure that is very hard and slow to alter.

2. Proponents cite the mobility of the K–12 population and the success of federal education programs in other countries to support establishing national standards and assessment. Opponents fear a power grab by the federal government, loss of local control, a lack of recognition of cultural diversity, and less support for disadvantaged students.

CHAPTER 12

What Are Your Job Options in Education?

MULTIPLE CHOICE QUESTIONS AND ANSWERS

Read each item carefully. Select the letter of the choice that represents the best answer.

Ans: d

1. According to the text, the strategy most likely to prepare a prospective teacher for a successful job search is

    a. specializing in physics and chemistry.
    b. moving to a community where teachers are in great demand.
    c. planning to work in a private school.
    d. acquiring exceptional competence, knowledge, and experience during pre-service training.

Ans: a

2. General reports on the demand for teachers indicate the following trends

    a. a shortage of teachers in certain subjects and geographical areas.
    b. an oversupply of teachers in most areas.
    c. a shortage of elementary and middle school teachers.
    d. a shortage of teachers in the northeastern and mid- Atlantic states.

Ans: d

3. The factor that makes it most difficult to predict how large a teacher shortage might occur are

    a. unknown teacher retirement rate.
    b. unpredictable student population growth rate.
    c. unknown number of teacher education graduates.
    d. unknown number of teachers not currently teaching who could re-enter teaching.

Ans: a

4. Which of the following plays the most significant role in determining if a school district hires new teachers?

    a. Student enrollment
    b. National economy
    c. Number of alternative-route teaching candidates in the area
    d. Size and space of the physical plant

Ans: c

5. Traditionally a public school teacher's base salary is determined by his or her level of education and

   a. any additional coaching or advising.
   b. the grade level taught.
   c. years of experience.
   d. the quality of teaching.

Ans: a

6. The shortage of minority teachers is problematic because

   a. minority students do not have enough positive minority role models.
   b. white students do not have enough positive white role models.
   c. educated minorities are going into other, higher-paying fields.
   d. many minority teachers are expected to retire in the next ten years.

Ans: a

7. Alternative teaching licensure programs are based on the premise that

   a. subject matter knowledge is more important to good teaching than courses in methods of teaching.
   b. competency in teaching requires more field experience than does subject-based knowledge.
   c. this route to certification is less costly and more efficient than traditional teacher education programs.
   d. the state needs to have greater control over who becomes certified to teach.

Ans: d

8. States establish licensure requirements in order to

   a. attract the best to teaching.
   b. maintain authority over teachers.
   c. collect licensure fees.
   d. ensure that teachers meet a minimum standard of excellence.

Ans: a

9. Alternative licensure programs become more popular when

   a. there is a shortage of teachers
   b. there are salary negotiations for teachers.
   c. tests scores decline.
   d. the economy is slow.

Ans: b

10. The components of an effective job search includes

    a. an academic rating of public schools.
    b. an individually typed cover letter for each school district.
    c. the names and addresses of current superintendents of area schools.
    d. the application to a very limited number of schools, thereby concentrating one's efforts.

SHORT-ANSWER QUESTIONS

Answer each of the following questions briefly, but specifically, in complete sentences.

1.   Describe several factors that are contributing to an expected increase in the shortage of teachers.

2.   How can prospective teachers best prepare themselves for a job search?

ANSWERS TO SHORT-ANSWER QUESTIONS

1.   The factors are

- Growth in student enrollment.

- Changes in pupil/teacher ration (class size).

- Shortages are bigger in some geographical locations than other and teachers tend to be more place bound.

- Teacher education programs are not producing enough graduates.

- There are shortages in certain subject areas and all teachers are not interchangeable.

2.   First, prospective teachers should attempt to get the most thorough training and extensive education that they can. When looking for a job, they should prepare a job file that includes their college transcript, several letters of recommendation, a resume, and individually written and typed letters to school districts.

CHAPTER 13

What Can the New Teacher Expect?

MULTIPLE CHOICE QUESTIONS AND ANSWERS

Read each item carefully. Select the letter of the choice that represents the best answer.

Ans: d

1. The feeling of dislocation people experience when they initially encounter a foreign culture is called

   a. alienation.
   b. ennui.
   c. anxiety.
   d. culture shock.

Ans: b

2. The principal's role is to act as a liaison between the central office administration and his or her school. This is done by

   a. being the scapegoat for parental disgruntlement.
   b. guiding teachers in achieving the district's curriculum goals.
   c. frequently visiting the teachers in their classrooms.
   d. keeping abreast of current research and reform efforts.

Ans: a

3. A mentor helps a new teacher by

   a. giving the new teacher professional and pedagogical advice.
   b. inviting the new teacher to lunch.
   c. giving the new teacher job postings from other districts.
   d. officially evaluating the new teacher.

Ans: c

4. Beginning teachers can look to colleagues in the school for

   a. little practical help, but strong moral support.
   b. support, friendship, and evaluation recommendations.
   c. support, ideas, and information.
   d. information about the school climate and students, and theoretical ideas about pedagogy.

Ans: a

5. After a typical first year, in which both victories and disasters abounded, two new teachers decide to grade their own performance. To what evidence should they give the greatest weight?

   a. Student achievement gains, considered in light of reasonable expectations
   b. Gains in evaluation ratings from the teachers' first to last formal administrative observations
   c. The number of students who indicated by word or action that they liked the teachers
   d. The number of supportive comments received from parents

Ans: d

6. According to the text, from the start of pre-service training to the end of the first year of teaching, how does the attitude of most new teachers toward their students change?

    a. At first they find students intimidating, but later they get more comfortable.
    b. At first they think students are really interesting, and by the end of that first year they are even more positive.
    c. At first they think students are naturally bad, but they come to see them as innately good.
    d. At first they have a warm positive attitudes toward students, but then there is a sharp drop in their positive perceptions.

Ans: b

7. Kayla is concerned about her knowledge of Spanish as she begins teaching it at the middle school level. However, after the first month, she realizes that a great concern may be

    a. her salary.
    b. classroom management.
    c. the workload.
    d. her unfriendly colleagues.

Ans: c

8. The recommendations made by the text for the teacher's first day include

    a. assigning some sort of homework activity, for those who teach above grade 2.
    b. acknowledging to students that the teacher "intends to make them work"—let the students know that the teacher is serious.
    c. learning and using the children's names.
    d. reviewing information and skills from the previous year.

Ans: c

9. A frequent factor in the ineffectiveness of parent-teacher communication is that

    a. American parents believe that teachers are low-status people.
    b. teachers do not believe that parent involvement is necessary in children's education.
    c. parents and teachers have a different view of the strengths and weaknesses of the child.
    d. parents disagree with the curriculum being taught and refuse to talk with the teachers.

Ans: a

10. One of the most important reasons to maintain the social distance between student and teacher is that

    a. once the teacher loses that distance, it becomes increasingly difficult to assume authority again in the class.
    b. it is inappropriate for a teacher and student to have a warm relationship.
    c. it is the traditional way students and teachers have interacted.
    d. too many people would misinterpret informality between student and teacher.

SHORT-ANSWER QUESTIONS

Answer each of the following questions briefly, but specifically, in complete sentences.

1. Explain the role of the principal in a school.

2. What is the greatest source of beginning teachers' problems?

ANSWERS TO SHORT-ANSWER QUESTIONS

1. Principals play a number of different roles in the school. They are the liaison between the teachers and the superintendent; they are reward dispensers; they act as buffers between angry parents and teachers. They can be helpers and evaluators of teachers. Because they play so many different roles, it is not unusual for them to be in conflict.

2. The source of many beginning teachers' problems is their unrealistic expectations. Teachers think they know what schools are like after many years in them as students, but the view is different from the other side of the desk. They develop a rosy, over optimistic view of students during their teacher education programs. Reality can be a surprise and coping with it is an unexpected challenge.

CHAPTER 14

What Does It Mean to Be a Professional?

MULTIPLE CHOICE QUESTIONS AND ANSWERS

Read each item carefully. Select the letter of the choice that represents the best answer.

Ans: c

1. A teacher who focuses on student interests, is reflective about their own institutional practices, and sees diagnosis as one of their roles is at which level of professionalism?

   a. Meditative level
   b. Mastery level
   c. Generative creative level
   d. Imitative maintenance level

Ans: d

2. The INTASC Standards focus on

   a. content standards for K–12 students.
   b. selecting master teachers based on meeting professional criteria.
   c. standards for accrediting school districts.
   d. standards prospective (new) teachers must meet to be licensed or certified.

Ans: c

3. To be defined as a professional, workers must

   a. provide a public service, and be well compensated for their work.
   b. have considerable autonomy and be accountable to a superior for the consequences of their work.
   c. provide an essential service, relying on intellectual skills, with autonomy and accountability for their work.
   d. be well respected, well educated, and accountable for their work.

Ans: a

4. One could argue that teaching is *not* a profession because

   a. teachers have limited power.
   b. teachers do not provide an essential skill.
   c. teaching does not particularly require intellectual skill.
   d. teachers do not earn high salaries.

Ans: c

5. What is one reason there is a need for continuous education for teachers?

   a. Teachers forget what they learned in college.
   b. Teachers do not know how to teach very well when they finish college.
   c. New information and skills become available, like the increasing use of technology.
   d. Teachers need to be challenged.

Ans: b

6. The National Board of Professional Teaching Standards has developed a board certification for teachers in order to

   a. make it easier to become a teacher.
   b. raise the expectations for effective teaching.
   c. relieve the states of the burden of licensure.
   d. create a career ladder for administrators.

Ans: a

7. The teacher organization that represents about three out of four public elementary and secondary teachers and that takes a relatively conservative stand on school reform issues is the

   a. National Education Association.
   b. American Federation of Teachers.
   c. Association for Curriculum and Development.
   d. American Educational Research Association.

Ans: d

8. A difference between the NEA and the AFT is that the AFT

   a. is much older than the NEA.
   b. is more conservative than the NEA.
   c. is more concerned with teacher autonomy and the NEA is concerned with national issues.
   d. has been more aggressive in pursuing teachers' benefits and salaries.

Ans: a

9. The AFT is best known for its:

   a. active support for bread-and-butter issues for teachers.
   b. strong support of teacher competency exams.
   c. support for greater control of schools by neighborhood groups.
   d. representation of a broad group of people associated with education: teachers, aids, administrators, and clerical staff.

Ans: c

10. Ryan and Cooper contend that teaching is an evolving profession because

   a. new teachers coming in are more professional than the ones currently teaching.
   b. Congress will pass legislation soon on the status of teaching.
   c. it meets some but not all of the criteria to be considered a profession.
   d. teachers frequently take part in professional development activities.

SHORT-ANSWER QUESTIONS

Answer each of the following questions briefly, but specifically, in complete sentences.

1. Do you plan to join one of the professional organizations (NEA or AFT)? Support your answers with the advantages or disadvantages of joining either organization.

2. Describe the purpose of INTASC standards on teacher education programs.

ANSWERS TO SHORT-ANSWER QUESTIONS

1. Answers will vary.

2. INTASC attempts to establish a common core of teaching skills and knowledge for beginning teachers across the country and to be compatible with the requirements of the National Board of Professional Teaching Standards, which teachers may wish to meet later in their career to become board certified.

CHAPTER 15

Why Teach?

MULTIPLE CHOICE QUESTIONS AND ANSWERS

Read each item carefully. Select the letter of the choice that represents the best answer.

Ans: a

1. Working as an aide or volunteer in a school is one of the best ways to

    a. test your interest in and aptitude for teaching.
    b. get sound advice about a range of career choices.
    c. learn about subject areas such as history or math.
    d. earn money for college expenses.

Ans: c

2. The most often cited extrinsic reward of teaching is primarily

    a. the high salary.
    b. the power of the position.
    c. the work schedule, which allows for a lot of flexibility.
    d. the prestige of being a teacher.

Ans: d

3. Which of the following is a *false* statement according to the study of teachers in the first five years of their career?

    a. The majority reported loving teaching.
    b. Most said they intended to continue teaching.
    c. Most teachers would choose teaching again.
    d. Many individuals fell into teaching "by chance".

Ans: b

4. Which of the following is an intrinsic reward of teaching?

    a. Promotion to Administration
    b. Making a positive contribution to society
    c. Respect of the community
    d. Vacation schedule

Ans: a

5. Teachers can help in renewing society by

    a. teaching students to be good citizens.
    b. having students do service projects as part of their classwork.
    c. going with the students to register to vote.
    d. teaching critical pedagogy in the class.

Ans: c

6. The work schedule in teaching that allows for personal time is a(n)

    a.   monetary reward.
    b.   status symbol.
    c.   extrinsic reward.
    d.   intrinsic reward.

Ans: a

7. Among the motivations for teaching given by those at work in the profession, which was the least cited response?

    a.   "I want to make a good salary."
    b.   "I enjoy working with children."
    c.   "I think teaching is important and honorable work."
    d.   "I want to make a contribution to the community."

Ans: b

8. One motivation that might jeopardize your effectiveness as a teacher is

    a.   to be enthusiastic about your content or subject matter.
    b.   to use teaching as a way of meeting your personal needs.
    c.   to advise students after school about their education.
    d.   to maintain a formal tone in your classroom.

Ans: a

9. Melinda has a particular fondness for geography and does more of it in her elementary class than any other subject. If she continues to focus so narrowly on geography, what might happen?

    a.   The students can lose interest and become disengaged.
    b.   Students will win state geography bees.
    c.   She will burn out.
    d.   She will become disengaged.

Ans: d

10. One way to predict what we will accomplish as teachers is to ask ourselves this question:

    a.   "What subjects most interest me?"
    b.   "What are my personal skills?"
    c.   "What do my trusted advisors say to me about teaching?"
    d.   "Why should I teach?"

SHORT-ANSWER QUESTIONS

Answer each of the following questions briefly, but specifically, in complete sentences.

1. Identify three methods that you could use to explore if teaching is right for you.

2. What are intrinsic rewards? How do they apply to teaching?

ANSWERS TO SHORT-ANSWER QUESTIONS

1. The ways in which a person can explore whether teaching is a suitable match for him or her is through real experience, vicarious experience, reflection, and counsel. Real experience entails working with students in a school or school-like setting. Vicarious experience is gained from reading books, talking to other teachers, and watching movies. Reflection entails carefully thinking about why you want to be a teacher and what you hope to accomplish. Counsel is the considered advice from those who know you.

2.   An intrinsic reward is something that exists within the work itself. For example, the pleasure of working with children is an intrinsic reward of teaching; working closely with children is an integral part of a teacher's job. Other intrinsic rewards in teaching include the performance of an important social service, the contribution to one's community, working in a collegial atmosphere, and the teaching itself.

PART IV
Assessment Materials

FOR EACH CHAPTER
- Multiple-Choice Items with Answer Key
- Short-Answer Questions with Suggested Answers
- Essay Questions with Key Answer Points

CHAPTER 1

What Is a School and What Is It For?

MULTIPLE CHOICE QUESTIONS

(An additional ten multiple-choice items and two short answer items are available in the sample quiz for this chapter.)

Read each item carefully. Select the letter of the choice that represents the best answer.

1. Which of the following is the best definition of education, according to the text? Education is
    a. technical proficiency in skills and knowledge that allows one to maneuver throughout the world.
    b. a continual growth process whereby a person gains greater understanding of himself or herself and the world.
    c. extensive knowledge of several discrete areas that allows one to become a productive member of society.
    d. a formal process of instruction and learning by which one learns to read, write, compute, problem-solve, and think critically about issues.

2. Schooling is most generally defined as
    a. a process of human growth that leads to greater self-control.
    b. a formal arrangement designed so that students will achieve their creative potential.
    c. a specific, formalized process aimed mostly at the young.
    d. an experience over a set period of time spent in an institution.

3. "The biggest mistake our schools ever made was in encouraging these kids to become 'individuals.' They need to learn how to work with each other efficiently and to take pride in the work that they do. I urge the board to move toward the redesign of our schools' mission," commented one school board member. This school board member is advocating the model of schools as
    a. acculturators.
    b. trainer of workers.
    c. developers of human potential.
    d. social panaceas.

4. A typical student in her high school, Keisha is enrolled in physics, trigonometry, Spanish IV, English, and U. S. history. Her school would most likely be described by the model of school as
    a. social escalator.
    b. preparer for college.
    c. acculturator.
    d. trainer of workers.

5. Hildi has selected her courses for the academic year, but she finds, after one week, that two of the courses do not interest her. She plans a meeting with her guidance counselor to rearrange her schedule. If this school is accurately represented by the "shopping mall" model, her guidance counselor will most likely
    a. provide her with a series of forms to fill out and steps to complete so that her registration will be accurate.
    b. tell her that it is a poor habit to switch courses so early in the year, she should learn to work hard and develop good work habits for her future.
    c. show her the course listings of numerous other courses available at the times she requested and sign her drop-add sheet to expedite the process.

    d.   encourage her to take courses that will best further her goals.

6.   Ben Franklin, with his great range of talents and notable curiosity, might well be a role model for which type of school?

    a.   College prep type
    b.   Human development type
    c.   Social escalator type
    d.   Acculturator type

7.   Which of the following programs would be well suited to a human development model of a school?

    a.   An individual reading program designed to stimulate a lifelong interest in reading
    b.   A career education course designed to inform high school students of the careers available and the requirements for each one
    c.   A math program designed to boost every student's math scores on standardized tests by 15 to 20 percent
    d.   A personal keyboarding and computer course designed to help students strengthen their skills on the computer

8.   Sophie Kao urges her working-class students to learn all they can and to work hard, for if they do well in school, they will have wider choices concerning where and how they want to live. Sophie is promoting the vision of a school as

    a.   a preparer for college.
    b.   a source of human development.
    c.   a social panacea.
    d.   a social escalator.

9.   Horace Mann ardently believed that education provided the means for people to rise out of poverty and to live a more personally satisfying life. He most likely would have agreed with the model of a school as

    a.   a social escalator.
    b.   a developer of human potential.
    c.   a bureaucracy.
    d.   a preparer for college.

10.   A city is distressed by the number of unwed teenage pregnancies handled by the local hospital. City officials loudly proclaim that the schools are not doing their jobs because they are not teaching students about sexual restraint or, at least, reliable birth control methods. Their vision of school is one of

    a.   an acculturator.
    b.   a social panacea.
    c.   a social escalator.
    d.   a source for human development.

11.   The parents and school board of Williamsport are having a heated debate about sex education and condom distribution in schools. Although one group is vehemently opposed to condom distribution, a slightly larger group, "Citizens for Informed Education," argues that the schools must provide students with adequate and up-to-date information to make informed choices about their sexual lives. "Citizens for Informed Education" would support the notion of a school as

    a.   social panacea.
    b.   family.
    c.   acculturator.
    d.   human developer.

12.   During the early 1900s, America accepted millions of immigrants from various countries. The model that best represents the model of schooling demonstrated by the schools of the time would be

    a.   the trainer model.
    b.   the human development model.
    c.   the acculturator model.

    d.   the social panacea model.

13.   The acculturator model of schools is best explained by

    a.   the statement that schools should direct their attention to helping students accept the values of and blend into the dominant culture of the society.
    b.   the statement that schools should provide students with courses that will enable them to become cultured: courses in music, art, and literature.
    c.   the statement that schools should emphasize the benefits of democracy and capitalism.
    d.   the statement that schools' major purpose is to help students advance out of their social and economic class if they are needy and to maintain their class status if they are affluent.

14.   Several teachers are having a team meeting. They discuss whether Jimmy, one of their students, is getting enough positive reinforcement during class and how he is adjusting to his new reading buddy. These teachers support the notion of school as

    a.   acculturator.
    b.   trainer of good workers.
    c.   bureaucracy.
    d.   family.

15.   Principal Alma Juliana described the work of Howell Elementary School to a member of the press: "Most of our students don't live with both parents, and their grandparents, aunts, and uncles often are scattered in different parts of the country. They don't have roots the way we did growing up. We need to teach them how to act, how to treat each other, how to care for one another. And we need to discipline them when they make mistakes." Alma's comments demonstrate what model of schooling?

    a.   School as bureaucracy
    b.   School as family
    c.   School as developer of human potential
    d.   School as social panacea

16.   Reid Conrad firmly believes that the purpose of schools is to transmit dominant American culture. What might he do in class to further his educational goals?

    a.   Emphasize the benefits of competition and consistently reward students who perform better than their classmates
    b.   Take his students on field trips to museums, theaters, and music halls
    c.   Frequently tell students that they must create their own meaning and must search for their purpose in life
    d.   Emphasize cooperative learning and peer tutoring

17.   One drawback of using schools as vehicles for cultural transmission is that

    a.   time limitations will prevent students from studying all the important works necessary for them to understand the culture.
    b.   students may then not be able to recognize the merits of any other culture but the dominant culture of their society.
    c.   teachers cannot both prepare students to go to college and impart the benefit of the culture to the students.
    d.   schools have achieved limited success in cultural transmission.

18.   John believes that schools can help students become actively involved in alleviating the problem of homelessness. John personifies the view of

    a.   cultural transmission.
    b.   human development education.
    c.   social reconstructionism.
    d.   the acculturator model of schooling.

19. Which of the following would an educator who is a democratic reconstructionist support?

    a.   Student involvement in local government with the expressed intention of maintaining the security and the stability of the status quo
    b.   The perspective that social problems are best solved by government officials whom citizens select
    c.   Students single-mindedly preparing for their own individual success
    d.   The notion that change happens most effectively when citizens are actively involved as change agents

20. Lou Parker harshly criticizes public schools, claiming that they reinforce the inequities that exist in the current system. Furthermore, he claims that the values taught by public schools are the values of IBM, Dow Chemical, Exxon, and the other corporations that dominate America. Lou is most likely a

    a.   supporter of cultural transmission in schools.
    b.   supporter of schools as developers of human potential.
    c.   supporter of the economic reconstructionist conception of schooling.
    d.   supporter of schools as the social panacea for society.

21. Socialization is an important element of schooling. As a result of socialization, children learn how to

    a.   succeed academically.
    b.   become acceptable members of society.
    c.   pursue their own interests.
    d.   become more popular.

22. In his study, Philip Jackson noted that teachers engage in hundreds of interchanges a day. He found that most of these interchanges were

    a.   the teacher directing and controlling the discussion.
    b.   the teacher sharing responsibility for the flow of the discussion with selected students.
    c.   the teacher speaking to colleagues and administrators.
    d.   the teacher seeking information from the students.

23. What could one reasonably conclude from Jackson's observations of elementary classrooms?

    a.   The structure of the elementary classroom requires students to develop self-restraint and patience.
    b.   Elementary classrooms are structured to fulfill the needs of every child.
    c.   Classrooms are designed to make children resourceful with their time.
    d.   The elementary classroom structure caters to precocious children, generally ignoring the particular needs of the other children.

24. A consistent similarity that emerges from schools teaching students in the middle school grades is that

    a.   teachers work in teams, sharing the same body of students.
    b.   those who teach students in grades between five and eight emphasize their students' personal growth and developmental issues.
    c.   staffing for schools serving students in the middle grades is overwhelmingly departmentalized.
    d.   few consistent similarities exist; the schools vary widely based on the grades included in the school and the goals of the administration.

25. Research has shown that each of the following school characteristics are influenced by the grade configuration of the "middle school" *except*

    a.   school goals.
    b.   course offerings.
    c.   instructional practices.
    d.   school size.

26. Which of the following students' experiences support Ernest Boyer's findings about life in high school?

    a.   Barbara entered high school placed in the general studies track. However, after her sophomore years, she was able to switch rather easily into the college preparatory track upon the advice and encouragement of several of her teachers.

b. Keisha is in the academic track at high school and wants to go to college. She consults with her friends about which courses to take rather than consulting with her guidance counselor or a teacher.

c. Ellen is in the general studies track. Her teachers are well equipped to teach, but are uninterested in the students in the general-level courses.

d. Despite low scores on the achievement test, Juanita is encouraged by her teachers to pursue the academic track.

27. Which of the following statements captures the findings of Ernest Boyer's research on high schools?

a. Despite small problems, high schools generally have and follow a clear vision of their purpose.

b. In the effort to be all things to all people, high schools are burdened by many contradictory goals.

c. High schools have streamlined their objectives since earlier times; however, their ability to translate those objectives into real instructional practices is weak.

d. High schools in affluent areas have clear visions shared by both the administrators and the faculty alike.

28. According to Larry Cuban's analysis of high schools, which of the following practices is likely to remain the same in the future?

a. The amount of time teachers teach through the lecture method and directed question and answer

b. The heavy use of cooperative learning and peer tutoring

c. Tracking students by academic ability

d. The strong emphasis on sports to the neglect of academic achievement

29. According to *The Shopping Mall High School*, how do many teachers deal with classroom management?

a. They strictly monitor their classes, ruling their classes with an iron fist.

b. They make tacit agreements with their students that neither will push the other too hard.

c. They have little classroom management. The students rule the classes.

d. They provide, for the most part, engaging lessons with plenty of student involvement so that there is little time for students to become bored or distracted.

30. According to the authors of *The Shopping Mall High School*, average high school students

a. are encouraged to achieve.

b. enjoy a variety of school options.

c. are ignored and poorly served.

d. embody the lively spirit of the "mall."

31. Which one of the following is *not* one of the Carnegie Foundation's recommendations for improving high schools?

a. Personalization by breaking the students into groups of no more than 600 with a specific group of teachers.

b. Scheduling of time should be flexible and schools should operate twelve months a year.

c. Long-term plans should be developed to use all types of technology in all aspects of teaching and learning.

d. High schools should put more emphasis on individualization, cooperative and hands-on learning to meet diverse student needs.

32. Among the characteristics of schools with records of great success in academics are

a. high teacher expectations, strong instructional leadership, and orderly environments.

b. strict rule enforcements, high levels of funding, and enthusiastic teachers.

c. low-key teacher ambitions, a cooperative administration, and good textbooks.

d. supportive parents, strict rules, and few extracurricular activities.

33. The characteristics of teachers in effective schools include:

a. high student expectations, methods focusing on individualization, and safe environment.

b. high percentage of academic engaged time, effective communication with the principal, and an orderly environment.

c. high task orientation, high rates of parent participation, and principals as instructional leaders.

    d.   high expectations of students, communication among teachers, and effective behavior management skills.

34.   Research on the effects of students wearing school uniforms found all of the following as reasons why requiring students to wear uniforms restores order and discipline *except*

    a.   they establish an appearance of economic equality.
    b.   they are associated with private and parochial schools, which are perceived as more orderly.
    c.   they are visible evidence of the administration's authority over students.
    d.   they increase structure thereby improving attitudes.

SHORT-ANSWER QUESTIONS

Answer each of the following questions briefly, but specifically, in complete sentences.

1.   What are the limitations of assigning a model for any school?

2.   The author of *The Shopping Mall High School* concludes that "average" students are basically left to their own devices in high schools. They are benignly ignored, apparently, by both the teachers and the administration. If this is, in fact, a common phenomenon among high schools, what does this mean for the quality of education that these students are receiving?

3.   Describe two characteristics of a school that is effective in promoting achievement measured in traditional terms.

ESSAY QUESTIONS

Read each of the following questions, and respond by composing an organized essay that includes an introduction, fully developed paragraph(s), and a conclusion.

1.   Explain the distinction made in this chapter between *education* and *schooling*. Give some examples of each. Describe the limitations of schooling, and explain its advantage over less formal education for some purposes.

2.   Schools have been defined as socialization agents that can teach children to be compliant, competitive, creative, cooperative, or curious. Define *socialization*, and give examples of school routines or practices that might nurture the development of the traits just listed.

3.   Identify and analyze the model or models of schooling that were prevalent in the high school or elementary school you attended. Name and describe the model(s) citing specific examples to demonstrate how the models accurately describe your school.

ANSWERS TO MULTIPLE CHOICE QUESTIONS

1.   b

2.   c

3.   b

4.   b

5.   c

6.   b

7.   a

8.   d

9.   a

10.   b

11.   a

12. c
13. a
14. d
15. b
16. a
17. b
18. c
19. d
20. c
21. b
22. a
23. a
24. d
25. d
26. c
27. b
28. a
29. b
30. c
31. d
32. a
33. d
34. c

ANSWERS TO SHORT-ANSWER QUESTIONS

1. *(suggested answer)*

    Although learning about particular models of schools can be very helpful to understand various types of schools and the pressures and expectations they meet, a model does not capture every complexity or nuance of a school. Schools could, in fact, match the requirements of several models. The power of a model lies in its ability to make sense of what we perceive; however, we must analyze and assess the school and then see how well the model describes what we see. A model is helpful in organizing our perceptions, not replacing them.

2. *(suggested answer)*

    The quality of education is most likely mediocre. Teachers negotiate a peaceful coexistence with these students in which each group causes little difficulty for the other. These students then are not receiving a challenging or demanding education and are consequently not learning to their potential. The potential for a large segment of the population to be minimally educated with little motivation or drive is significant.

3. *(suggested answer)*

    Criteria include high expectations of student success, high task orientation, lots of academic engaged time, good behavior management, strong instructional leadership from the principal, effective collaboration with parents, and a safe and orderly school environment. Students should identify and describe two of these criteria clearly.

ANSWERS TO ESSAY QUESTIONS

1. *(suggested answer)*

    The broad term *education* refers to the process of human growth by which one gains greater control over oneself and one's world. Education involves mind, body, and relations with others and with the world. Its end is learning. The term *schooling* refers to the specific, formal process by which one gains certain limited bits of knowledge. Schooling is more reliable in transmitting essential content and skills than is education, which is less formal. Education can include many experiences that lead to learning. Schooling usually involves enrolling for credit and following the course set by a teacher.

2. *(suggested answer)*

    Socialization is the general process of social learning whereby a person learns what must be known in order to be an acceptable member of society and learns what rules must be followed and how to follow them. Compliance can be nurtured by offering rewards to children who follow rules and cooperate with orderly behavior.

    Competitiveness is nurtured by grading or recognition systems that honor students at the top only, rather than all who meet the standard of excellence. Creativity is nurtured in activities that call for divergent thinking and brainstorming. Cooperation is nurtured by reward systems or task structures that are most productive when students help each other. Curiosity is nurtured by lessons that end with questions, by research activities, and by attention to critical thinking.

3. (Answers will vary.)

CHAPTER 2

Who Are Today's Students in a Diverse Society?

MULTIPLE CHOICE QUESTIONS

(An additional ten multiple-choice items and two short answer items are available in the sample quiz for this chapter.)

Read each item carefully. Select the letter of the choice that represents the best answer.

1. Which one of the following is *not* one of the different approaches to multicultural education?

   a. Human relations
   b. Democratic pluralism
   c. Multicultural and social reconstructionist
   d. Single group studies

2. The Allen Elementary School is in the midst of revising its curricula. Some community members are asking that the school pay more attention to cultural pluralism. What would the residents like to see in the curriculum?

   a. More attention given to the contributions of nonwhite, non-Europeans to the development of the United States
   b. A two-pronged curriculum with two social studies texts, one written from an Anglo perspective and one from an African-American perspective
   c. New emphasis on anthropology as part of the social studies curriculum
   d. Greater focus on classical literature

3. If cultural pluralism were part of a U.S. school, how would that affect a group of immigrant students from Portugal?

   a. They would mingle together during school, but teachers would encourage them to become Americanized and make U.S. friends.
   b. The school they attended would hold a "Portugal" month with banners and posters of Portugal in the hallways.
   c. The teachers would treat the Portuguese students warmly and would make sure that the U.S. students treated the Portuguese students nicely, too.
   d. The Portuguese would be encouraged to treasure their culture, and teachers would provide ways for the U. S. students to learn about life in Portugal.

4. How could one describe the anticipated *proportional* population growth trends among the various ethnic groups?

   a. The populations of Asian Americans, Hispanics, and whites will rapidly increase. African Americans will experience a slight decline in growth.
   b. Whites and African Americans will experience steady growth, Asian Americans will experience rapid growth, and Hispanics will experience a decline in growth.
   c. Asian Americans, Hispanics, and African Americans will make significant gains in growth; whites will experience a decline in growth.
   d. African Americans and Hispanics will make large gains in their populations; whites and Asian Americans will experience rapid declines in their growth.

5. The United States is undergoing some significant population changes. As of the year 2000, minority students will make up what percent of the school-age population of the nation?

   a. 49 percent.
   b. 13 percent.
   c. 25 percent.
   d. 37 percent.

6. In a public school that embraced multiculturalism, which of the following would be evidenced?

   a. Posters of American Revolutionary heroes would be displayed throughout the school.
   b. Class discussions would debate the worth of the value systems of other cultures.
   c. In December, no decorations denoting any celebration would be allowed.
   d. Selections for literature classes would represent a broad collection of authors.

7. What is the purpose of multiculturalism in schools?

   a. To help assimilate students' cultures into the American "melting pot"
   b. To reduce prejudice, foster tolerance, and improve the academic achievement of minority students
   c. To support students in the maintenance and preservation of their own cultures
   d. To assimilate students into the "melting pot" of the United States as well as to foster students' respect for the existence of various cultures

8. Critics of multiculturalism contend that if multicultural education were accepted uncritically, it could

   a. result in the failure to transmit the essential information about shared culture.
   b. blur the contributions of each separate culture.
   c. cause children to forget their individual cultural heritage.
   d. offset the effect of the "melting pot" approach.

9. Which of the following is the most commonly used criterion for identifying gifted students?

   a. Academic record
   b. Individual intelligence test scores
   c. Group intelligence test scores
   d. Standardized achievement test scores

10. Which student group is probably underrepresented because of current gifted identification practices?

   a. Girls
   b. Asian students
   c. White males
   d. Economically disadvantaged minority students

11. Which of the following would fit into the newer definition of giftedness?

   a. A ten-year-old who can add a series of three-digit numbers in her head
   b. A twelve-year-old who can hit a three-point throw in basketball 95 percent of the time
   c. An eight-year-old who can read at a tenth-grade level
   d. All of these would be considered gifted.

12. Why have gifted and talented programs met with resistance from many Americans?

   a. Having a gifted and talented program, to some, implies a superiority or an elitism that does not favorably impress many Americans.
   b. Too many children have been identified as "gifted" or "talented," so the phrase has lost its currency.
   c. The programs have not had any discernible effect on the students.
   d. Because of the structure of the gifted and talented programs, they disrupt the running of the school.

13. According to William Glasser's choice theory, why would a person feel discontented or be unsatisfied with his or her life?

   a. He or she lacks the power to control people and events in his or her life.
   b. He or she has unmet basic needs.

c.   He or she does not yet know how to attain personal empowerment.

d.   He or she has unmet basic needs and does not have the capacity to attain personal empowerment.

14.   Ms. O'Neill, a sixth-grade teacher, knows that Song feels proud of herself when she can construct something. Therefore, Ms. O'Neill provides Song with many opportunities to make models, draw pictures, and create objects. After Song has completed one of her creations, Ms. O'Neill can tell that she has fulfilled her needs for power, or self-esteem, and fun. Ms. O'Neill's classroom practices are clearly influenced by

   a.   Maslow's hierarchy of needs.

   b.   Gardner's theory of multiple intelligence.

   c.   Glasser's choice theory.

   d.   the Comer model.

15.   Lynn Kaiser is an outstanding sales broker in real estate. She can immediately strike up a conversation with anyone, and half of her clients are repeat clients. She frequently remembers small details about her clients, such as their favorite color or their birthday, which makes them feel special. According to Howard Gardner's theory, what strong intellectual capacity does Lynn possess?

   a.   Intrapersonal

   b.   Interpersonal

   c.   Linguistic

   d.   Kinesthetic

16.   If Howard Gardner's theory of multiple intelligence took hold in public schools, what would be a close approximation of the educational practices he would advocate?

   a.   Students would be tested to determine the breadth and range of their multiple intelligences; then they would follow an individually determined course of study.

   b.   Students would enroll in courses that would maximize their strongest type of intelligence. Gradually, they would focus almost entirely on their strongest abilities.

   c.   Students would be exposed to activities and content that involved many of the areas of intelligence.

   d.   Traditional academic courses would be eliminated, and schools would design each new course so that it targeted a particular intelligence.

17.   Learning style models concern themselves with the process of learning. Which of the following process descriptions is matched with the correct learning style?

   a.   The understanding style looks for images implied in learning and uses feelings and emotions to construct new ideas.

   b.   The self-expressive style prefers to learn socially and judges learning in terms of its potential to help others.

   c.   The interpersonal style focuses more on ideas and abstractions through questioning, reasoning, or the use of logic.

   d.   The mastery style processes information sequentially and judges it in terms of its clarity and practicality.

18.   Regular teachers who are effective in teaching children with disabilities

   a.   have students with disabilities work together in pairs.

   b.   find one teaching strategy that is most effective and stick with it.

   c.   are open to the idea of including students with disabilities.

   d.   stand back and let the special education teacher manage the disabled student's program.

19.   What does IDEA establish?

   a.   The right of non-English-speaking children to instruction in their native language

   b.   The right of children with disabilities to a free, appropriate public education

   c.   The right of children to a public education based on the wealth of the state, not the wealth of the community

   d.   The right of families and students to examine the administrative records kept on the student

20. IDEA mandates special services for students who

     a.   dislike school.
     b.   have any kind of disability.
     c.   have a low socioeconomic status.
     d.   cannot speak English.

21. The Americans with Disabilities Act (ADA) protects the rights of individuals with disabilities in society. Because of this act,

     a.   handicap facilities must be provided in all public places.
     b.   people with disabilities qualify for free medical care.
     c.   people with disabilities qualify for free dental care.
     d.   handicap facilities are not necessary in churches.

22. Congress passed the Bilingual Education Act in 1968 in order to

     a.   develop fluency in another language by all Americans.
     b.   encourage foreigners to visit the United States.
     c.   cope with the large number of students who did not speak English.
     d.   promote linguistic awareness in all students.

23. Which of the following supplies the best description of the goals for bilingual education?

     a.   Non-native non-English-speaking children could learn content in their native language while gradually developing English fluency, and eventually joining English-only classes.
     b.   Non-native non-English-speaking children would learn content in their native tongue and would develop pride in their ethnic heritage.
     c.   Non-native non-English-speaking children would be taught a culturally appropriate curriculum and would not be required to join English-speaking students.
     d.   Non-native non-English-speaking children would attend some classes in English and some in their native tongue, hastening their assimilation into Anglo-American culture.

24. One result of the *Lau* v. *Nichols* decision might be seen in which of the following cases?

     a.   A Vietnamese child is taught entirely in English with English textbooks in order to speed the process of assimilation.
     b.   A Spanish-speaking child is sent to a school where only Spanish is spoken so that she can learn basic skills.
     c.   A German-speaking child is given textbooks and basic skill instruction in German and English until he or she is fluent enough in English.
     d.   The experiences of the Vietnamese child, the Spanish-speaking child, and the German-speaking child all demonstrate the influence of the decision.

25. How did the *Lau* remedies affect public education?

     a.   They concluded that non-English-speaking children would best learn from submersion in English-speaking classrooms; therefore, schools felt little impact.
     b.   They required that non-English-speaking students be taught academic subjects in their native language until their command of English allowed them to benefit from English instruction.
     c.   They required schools to limit the amount of time any student could spend in a bilingual education program.
     d.   They provided for intensive language education programs for children in the elementary grades. They made little provision for students in secondary schools.

26. Juan is a non-English-speaking student who has recently enrolled in a public school in the United States. He has been placed in a classroom with some native English speakers and some non-English-speaking students. Although he is encouraged to practice English, when he gets stuck he can speak Spanish to his teacher, because she is fluent in Spanish. However, she will only answer him using English. The model for this type of instruction is

     a.   immersion.

     b.   submersion.

     c.   transition.

     d.   maintenance.

27.   Amber, a three-year-old, was born with mild cerebral palsy, which reduced her motor coordination on her left side and delayed her speech development. Her parents want her to receive special therapy, but have been told by the school system in their town that nothing is available for her. Based on the Education of the Handicapped Act Amendments (PL99--457), what should Amber's parents do?

     a.   Seek a private school that could provide services for Amber and cover the costs themselves

     b.   Remind the school system that it is required to provide Amber with free appropriate education from age three on

     c.   Ask for federal government assistance to cover Amber's education in a private school

     d.   Keep Amber at home until she is five and eligible to be enrolled in a public kindergarten

28.   Mr. and Mrs. Wells are meeting with their daughter's teacher to discuss her individualized education plan (IEP) for the next school year. Their daughter, Donna, has a learning disability that affects her reading skills. When Mr. and Mrs. Wells review Donna's IEP, they should expect to find

     a.   information on how Donna compares to the rest of the students in the class.

     b.   a complete list of curricular materials that will be used with Donna.

     c.   the services that will be provided by the school for Donna during the upcoming year and an assessment plan.

     d.   the maximum potential level that Donna will achieve as an adult.

29.   An individualized education plan (IEP) is a document required for special education students. Which of the following elements must be included in it?

     a.   Criteria for evaluating student progress

     b.   The student's personality profile

     c.   The student's learning style inventory

     d.   The mean score of same-age students on the school-authorized standardized test (such as the CAT or Iowa tests)

     e.   A plan for the student's education for the next two years

30.   *Inclusion* of students with disabilities refers to

     a.   including those students in schoolwide activities.

     b.   including the study of a wide range of subject areas in the special education curriculum.

     c.   educating those students to the maximum extent possible in the regular classroom.

     d.   pairing those students up with regular education students.

31.   Many school systems have been urged to understand the "least restrictive environment" clause of the IDEA to mean mainstreaming or inclusion of students with disabilities into the regular education classroom. This policy is supported by many special educators who feel that

     a.   segregated education for special needs students is inherently unequal.

     b.   segregated education for special needs students is ineffective.

     c.   special needs students don't really need a lot of specialized services.

     d.   special needs students will suffer from being labeled in a separate program.

32.   The "Comer Model" of schooling emphasizes the social context of teaching and learning because of the belief that

     a.   learning can only take place in a positive environment where teachers, students, administrators, and parents work together.

     b.   students are primarily interested in socializing with their friends, not learning.

     c.   the causes of problems within a school need to be identified and the situation or the personnel employed need to be changed.

     d.   social differences create problems in schools.

33. If the vast majority of teachers are white, middle-class females, how can they avoid misunderstandings with their students, who may reflect wide diversity in background?

    a. They can pursue increased pedagogical training to help them develop their range of teaching skills and knowledge of how people learn.

    b. They can consciously focus their attention on becoming more aware of the differences between white, middle-class culture and other cultures represented in their schools.

    c. They can announce at the beginning of the year that they are always available if any student wants to talk to them after school.

    d. They can take courses concerning the major cultures of the world.

34. What function does belonging to a group serve in the life of the adolescent?

    a. Belonging to a group helps the student be more successful in school.

    b. Groups are a channel through which the teen's values are clarified and defined.

    c. Membership in a group facilitates communication between the student and his or her school, family, and community.

    d. Membership in a group satisfies adolescent needs for belonging, power, and fun.

35. What is the most likely conclusion to explain why jocks adapt and succeed in school more often than burnouts?

    a. Jocks are more conscientious workers and are generally better-prepared students than burnouts.

    b. Jocks have a cooperative, hence positive relationship with the school, while burnouts have an adversarial, hence negative relationship with the school.

    c. The jocks learn at a young age how to use egalitarian social networks of friends to get help studying, locating a job, or meeting other needs. Their interpersonal skills enable them to succeed in school. The burnouts do not have the same drive to succeed or the same system of working with people.

    d. The jocks succeed in school because they are conscientious, strongly motivated to succeed in the real world, and very comfortable in the school's world.

36. Studies of peer relationships among adolescents show that

    a. high school has become a social system with its own set of values and activities.

    b. adolescent relationships with adults are more important than with other adolescents.

    c. more and more adolescents have the self-confidence to act independently from their peer group.

    d. the values of adolescents are the same as those of their parents.

SHORT-ANSWER QUESTIONS

Respond to each of the following questions briefly, but specifically, in complete sentences.

1. Explain what the term *least restrictive environment* means. Give an example.

2. Which types of intelligence have traditionally been rewarded in schools? Explain how Gardner's theory of multiple intelligences would affect public schools.

ESSAY QUESTIONS

Read each of the following questions, and respond by composing an organized essay that includes an introduction, fully developed paragraph(s), and a conclusion.

1. Analyze the concept of multiculturalism by examining the major arguments in support of multiculturalism, then by examining the major arguments opposing it. What perspective do you think best serves public education? Support your position.

2. The debate over full inclusion of special needs students continues to rage. Discuss the issue by presenting the major arguments from both sides of the debate.

3. The debate over how to best assist students with a Limited Proficiency in English has recently become more heated. Cite the laws that are relevant, contrast the bilingual programs (both traditional and in the new policies), and give brief pro and con statements about the proposed changes.

ANSWERS TO MULTIPLE CHOICE QUESTIONS

1. b
2. a
3. d
4. c
5. d
6. d
7. b
8. a
9. b
10. d
11. d
12. a
13. d
14. c
15. b
16. c
17. d
18. c
19. b
20. b
21. a
22. c
23. a
24. c
25. b
26. a
27. b
28. c
29. a
30. c
31. a
32. a
33. b
34. d
35. b
36. a

ANSWERS TO SHORT-ANSWER QUESTIONS

1. *(suggested answer)*

    The term *least restrictive environment* means that a child with a disability should participate in regular education classes to the greatest extent possible consistent with what is best for his or her learning. Examples will vary.

2. *(suggested answer)*

    Traditionally, linguistic and logico-mathematic abilities have been the most emphasized in schools. If Gardner's theory took hold in public schools, teachers and administrators would design activities with greater attention to how they draw out one intelligence or another. Because the definition of intelligence would be broadened, it would give greater numbers of students the opportunity to develop the intelligences they have.

ANSWERS TO ESSAY QUESTIONS

1. *(suggested answer)*

    Multicultural education is in many ways "a reaction against assimilation and the melting pot myth." The most prominent argument for multiculturalism is that all ethnic groups and minorities have contributed to the United States. To only focus on the white, male, European perspective results in an incomplete vision. Multiculturalism seeks to value all groups and their unique perspectives, lifestyles, traditions, and contributions. It also seeks to include more ethnic and minority groups into the mainstream and to critically assess the tradition of the male, European dominance in America. Therefore, multiculturalism, some would say, offers a radical perspective of how to view history and culture.

    The arguments against multiculturalism take two basic positions. One is that an appreciation of various cultures is to be hoped for, yet schools cannot realistically teach the important elements of every culture. Furthermore, many argue that students should focus on the ideas and the forces that have worked to create the United States. They argue that some people, events, and ideas do have greater importance than others. If we focus on multiculturalism to its extreme, some fear, we will lose our commonalities as Americans. The other major argument against multiculturalism is based on the perceived relativism of multiculturalism. Some argue against multiculturalism on a moral basis, claiming that the values of a particular group do not necessarily make something moral.

2. *(suggested answer)*

    Students should identify and explain the arguments in favor of full inclusion such as greater social interaction and learning to function in a "real world" environment, as well as the arguments against inclusion, which revolve around adequate services for special needs students.

3. *(suggested answer)*

    Both *Lau* v. *Nichols* and California Proposition 227 should be reviewed on this issue.

    Of the old immersion, submersion, transitional, and maintenance models, the new proposal of one-year intense instruction is most comparable to submersion (also known as English as a Second Language, ESL).

    Pros for the new policy include that it is fast; students acquire English faster and it does not result in long term "tracking" caused by placement in bilingual (transitional or maintenance) programs for years. Advocates would point to improved standardized test scores in California. This new policy also reduces the number of bilingual teachers needed, which is beneficial since there is a shortage.

    The cons include a possible affect of slowing down the curriculum for all the students in a class where students with less developed language abilities are included, with subsequently less learning for all.

CHAPTER 3

What Social Problems and Tension Points Affect Today's Students?

MULTIPLE CHOICE QUESTIONS

(An additional ten multiple-choice items and two short answer items are available in the sample quiz for this chapter.)

Read each item carefully. Select the letter of the choice that represents the best answer.

1. Perry is a student in your class, and you know he is homeless. What potential problems might Perry face in light of his living situation?

    a.   His parent(s) may not participate at school.
    b.   He may not be allowed to attend school without a permanent address.
    c.   His teacher may not know how to meet his particular needs.
    d.   He may have trouble making friends because of poor personal hygiene, and may frequently miss school because of transportation difficulties.

2. Jenna is seventeen years old, the mother of an infant, and a full-time employee at a small manufacturing company. What else is likely true about Jenna's life?

    a.   She is making progress advancing in her company.
    b.   She lives below the poverty line.
    c.   She is enrolled part-time in college.
    d.   She and her child are physically healthy.

3. Darla LeMan suspects that her student Sheila is being abused at home. After she reports her suspicion to the principal, how can Darla best serve Sheila's needs?

    a.   Offer Sheila extra attention by spending time with her after school
    b.   Informally stop by Sheila's home to visit with Sheila and her family
    c.   Provide a stable class environment to foster student learning
    d.   Uphold very high standards for Sheila and her work so that Sheila knows that Darla believes in her

4. Which of the following is uppermost among a teacher's responsibilities toward a child who is disadvantaged, neglected, or abused?

    a.   Giving the child lots of attention and affection
    b.   Offering the haven of a well-run, orderly classroom
    c.   Maintaining a cool but fair approach to help the child learn independence and feel a sense of accomplishment when he or she completes work
    d.   Showing the child that you care, perhaps by buying the child a toy or an ice-cream cone

5. It is the third week of September, and you are just beginning to know your first-grade students. One child, Marcus, stands out in your mind. He has not made friends with any playmates so far, and he rarely talks to the other children. Yesterday, during playtime, after playing with a cardboard puzzle for several minutes, he stomped on it. Later, he told you he got mad at it because "it wasn't all fitting in." During the past several days, he has had several such outbursts, usually when things get busy in the class, such as lining up for lunch or recess, or marching to music. Given his behavior, you think he may

    a.   have dyslexia.
    b.   have a low IQ.

c.   be suffering from abuse.
d.   be homeless.

6.   Singleton is a divorced mother of two children who works at a local shipping company. If she is representative of most divorced mothers, what is the most significant problem she is facing?

a.   Deep feelings of depression after her marriage ended
b.   The relocation of her family, including finding a new home and a new school for her children
c.   The financial strain of supporting her family on limited income
d.   Harassment from her ex-husband

7.   Over 60 percent of all children live in homes where the only parent or both parents work. What significance does this have for teachers?

a.   Teachers need to assume the parent role.
b.   Teachers should not try to involve parents in the school as much as they used to.
c.   Parents are now generally expecting teachers to monitor children much more closely than the parents will.
d.   Parents' work schedule(s) may make participation in the school more difficult and teachers may have difficulty contacting them.

8.   A teacher notices that Victor, a student in her class, has been acting differently. He has quit the hockey team and stopped spending time with his friends. When she asks Victor about it, he withdraws. The teacher feels that she has seen a happy, popular, attractive boy become a disheveled-looking loner. She raises the issue with a guidance counselor, who thinks Victor may have a drug or alcohol problem. Given Victor's behavior, the guidance counselor and teacher should also consider that he

a.   may be contemplating suicide.
b.   has abused a child.
c.   may just be going through a stage of adolescent development.
d.   has joined a gang.

9.   A teacher has serious concerns, based on a student's behavior, that the student is contemplating suicide, and one day the student admits that the possibility has occurred to him. The teacher should

a.   have a long talk with the student, telling him why he should want to live.
b.   tell the student that he or she will always be available if the student needs to talk.
c.   call the student's parents.
d.   contact the school psychologist or guidance counselor and explain the situation.

10. Relief from a high incidence of school violence and vandalism seems to come directly from programs that

a.   strictly enforce rules and punish offenders.
b.   establish a firm, fair, and consistent system.
c.   generously and publicly reward compliant student behavior.
d.   do all of these.

11. Mrs. Wasserberg is the principal of Kenmont High School, located in an urban area. She has managed to develop ways for all staff members to have positive and productive interactions with students, while maintaining order. Such an atmosphere in a school, according to research, helps reduce which of the following problems?

a.   Teenage pregnancy
b.   Child abuse
c.   Violence and vandalism in schools
d.   Teenage suicide

12. The national dropout rate during the 1990s has

a.   remained steady.
b.   sharply increased.
c.   gradually decreased.
d.   gradually increased.

13. Youth join gangs

    a.   to belong to and identify with a group.
    b.   for protection.
    c.   because they feel ignored.
    d.   for all of the reasons above.

14. To minimize the influence of gangs, educators can

    a.   hire more security personnel.
    b.   ignore minor activity.
    c.   establish programs that stress positive youth involvement.
    d.   investigate the use of metal detectors and dogs.

15. Besides poverty, what is the reason most cited by students for dropping out of school?

    a.   Pregnancy
    b.   Poor grades
    c.   Dislike of school
    d.   Employment opportunities

16. Equality of educational opportunity was defined as equal allocation of resources *until* the U.S. Supreme Court ruled on which of the following cases?

    a.   *Swan* v. *Charlotte-Mecklenburg*
    b.   *Brown* v. *Board of Education*
    c.   *Wolman* v. *Walter*
    d.   *Lau* v. *Nichols*

17. After the *Brown* v. *Board of Education* decision, what new component was added to considerations of whether educational opportunities offered to all children were equal?

    a.   The amount spent on teachers' salaries
    b.   Amount of resources
    c.   The quality of the textbooks provided
    d.   The measurable achievement

18. The educator who advocated using structured environments with supplies and equipment that give children the learning opportunities they needed while they engaged in "free play" was

    a.   Herbert Kohl.
    b.   Maria Montessori.
    c.   Jonathon Kozol.
    d.   Johann Pestalozzi.

19. What might be found in a classroom designed according to Montessori's methods?

    a.   Dozens of storybooks and puzzles
    b.   Colorful workbooks with carefully sequenced lessons in math and reading
    c.   A child-sized kitchen and dining area with appropriate supplies and equipment
    d.   Small desks with old-fashioned inkwells and little drawers for children's toys

20. Magnet schools were initially designed to do which of the following?

    a.   Contribute to the desegregation of schools in urban areas
    b.   Provide musically and artistically talented students with a school tailored to their talents
    c.   Provide a rich academic environment for children at risk
    d.   Fill the need for public schools that demand rigorous academic work from their students and have high expectations for their academic success

21. Mrs. Li's son shows a strong interest for and aptitude in science. He is enrolled at P.S. 101 in Manhattan, where he is doing superior work; however, Mrs. Li is not satisfied with the science facilities at her son's school, and she doesn't have enough money to send him to a private school. What other options would she have?

    a. She can arrange for her son to go to a magnet school.
    b. Her only option is to enroll him in a private school.
    c. She can ask the school district to provide a science tutor for her son.
    d. She can move out of the city to a rural school.

22. Charter schools are public schools with a large amount of autonomy in decision making. A charter school is judged and allowed to continue to operate based on which of the following criteria?

    a. How well they meet student achievement goals stated in their charter and manage their fiscal responsibilities
    b. How much demand is generated by enrollment applications
    c. The strength of their students' achievement test scores on state or national exams
    d. Philosophical and political changes on the board of education as new members are selected

23. Opponents of vouchers cite which of the following as a reason vouchers should not be implemented?

    a. Parents are not well enough informed to choose a school for their student.
    b. They would increase the size of the budget needed for education.
    c. They would increase the school's drive to serve the public good and not the need to earn profits.
    d. The public schools would lose money and have the major burden for special needs students.

24. Ms. Bradley, a high school math teacher, teaches a trigonometry class with thirteen boys and eight girls. One day, she was in the middle of a lesson reviewing answers to a test when her overhead projector malfunctioned. Looking up, she asked, "Do any of you boys know how to fix this machine?" One boy, Ed, came up and quickly fixed the projector. Which of the following indicates sexist behavior on Ms. Bradley's part?

    a. She teaches a class dominated by males.
    b. She asked only if one of the boys could fix the machine.
    c. She is unable to fix the machine herself.
    d. She uses an overhead projector in her class.

25. Features that indicate gender bias in a history textbook include

    a. descriptions of common occupations held only by men.
    b. women mentioned infrequently, usually with reference to their husbands or fathers.
    c. generic use of masculine pronouns.
    d. all of these.

26. How have different social expectations affected behaviors of boys and girls?

    a. Boys are ruder whereas girls are more polite and courteous.
    b. Girls tend to be more aggressive now than they were twenty years ago.
    c. Boys are expected to be aggressive and independent, whereas girls are expected to be passive conformists.
    d. Boys aren't as noisy as they were ten years ago.

27. A recent report by the American Association of University Women contends that schools are not meeting girls' needs because

    a. boys are always making trouble in class and girls are not.
    b. boys get more attention from teachers and have higher expectations placed on them.
    c. girls always have to clean up in the classroom and boys do not.
    d. girls are not allowed to use the computers in the classroom.

28. Melissa, a seventh-grader at East Highwater Middle School, is afraid to go to her locker because every time she does, a group of boys is standing around making lewd comments to her. Melissa's grades are beginning to suffer. Melissa's case is an example of

    a. sexual harassment.
    b. gender bias.
    c. sexual preferential treatment.
    d. gang intimidation.

29. Interpretation of the implications of Title IX means that

    a. females must be offered equal educational opportunities in institutions that receive any federal dollars.
    b. females must be offered equal opportunities for participation in a program that is funded by federal dollars.
    c. females must be permitted to play on any team that is fielded at federal expense.
    d. educational achievement awards of students must be equally distributed between males and females.

30. Which of the following statements about gay and lesbian students is true?

    a. They have a higher rate of attempted suicide than other groups of students.
    b. They have been recognized as an at-risk group for several decades.
    c. They face less hostility in the high school environment than they do in society at large.
    d. Teachers are as vigilant about not tolerating homosexual name calling as they are regarding racial slurs.

31. Sex education is a very controversial topic. However, most people would agree on which of the following?

    a. School is the most appropriate institution to offer sex education.
    b. Young people need information about sex.
    c. Students should receive only factual information about sex.
    d. Young people can learn enough about sex from television.

32. It is unlikely that the debate over sex education will be resolved soon because sex education is

    a. too costly for most school systems.
    b. too complex for most students to understand.
    c. linked to people's religious and moral beliefs, which represent a wide range of views.
    d. tied to people's socioeconomic standing.

33. The Tyler school system would like to implement a sex education course in the seventh and eighth grades, but administrators have met with considerable resistance from the community. What information should the administration present to the community to convince them of the need for the course?

    a. Programs that teach abstinence only are the most effective.
    b. Effective sex education courses have been shown to delay the onset of sexual activity.
    c. Short sex education programs are the most effective.
    d. The incidence of sexually transmitted diseases is decreasing.

34. Proponents of school choice argue that if parents can choose their children's school, then

    a. some teachers will have to work sixteen hours a day.
    b. parents will be able to move from one community to another more easily.
    c. free-market principles of competition will help to improve the quality of education.
    d. some schools will be able to make a lot of money.

35. Charter schools, one option of school choice, have certain advantages over public schools because they

    a. have considerable autonomy to operate as they wish.
    b. have more money to operate than the other public schools.
    c. are usually larger and more economical than other public schools.
    d. have a clearly delineated hierarchical structure.

36.   A second school choice option is the voucher plan in which parents would

    a.   vouch for their children when they enroll them in the school of their choice.

    b.   receive a voucher for their children's books and school materials.

    c.   receive a voucher worth a specified amount and use it to enroll their children in whatever school they choose.

    d.   vouch for the quality of the instruction the children would be receiving.

SHORT-ANSWER QUESTIONS

Respond to each of the following questions briefly, but specifically, in complete sentences.

1.   Compare and contrast school choice and voucher plan programs.

2.   Describe the components of a charter school.

3.   Education has been proposed as a solution to poverty, yet despite numerous programs and great expense, the vicious cycle of poverty remains. Discuss the reasons why schooling does not seem to be an effective solution to poverty.

ESSAY QUESTIONS

Read each of the following questions, and respond by composing an organized essay that includes an introduction, fully developed paragraph(s), and a conclusion.

1.   Pick one of the issues regarding sexuality discussed in the text. Describe the issue and the teacher's role in response.

2.   Consider the following quote by Neil Postman: "If you heap upon the school all of the problems that the family, the church, the political system, and the economy cannot solve, the school becomes a kind of well-financed garbage dump, from which very little can be expected except the unsweet odor of failure." To what degree does this statement represent public schools? What do you see as the role of the public school in solving or ameliorating social problems?

ANSWERS TO MULTIPLE CHOICE QUESTIONS

1.   d

2.   b

3.   c

4.   b

5.   c

6.   c

7.   d

8.   a

9.   d

10.   b

11.   c

12.   a

13.   d

14.   c

15.   b

16.   b

17. d
18. b
19. c
20. a
21. a
22. a
23. d
24. b
25. d
26. c
27. b
28. a
29. b
30. a
31. b
32. c
33. b
34. c
35. a
36. c

ANSWERS TO SHORT-ANSWER QUESTIONS

1. *(suggested answer)*

    School choice is any of a variety of programs that allow parents to choose public schools within their own or neighboring districts including magnet, charter, and alternative schools. Vouchers would change the flow of money to those public as well as private schools based on the parent's choices.

2. *(suggested answer)*

    It is a public school, which by its charter, is allowed more independent decision making and is allowed to continue to operate based on its success in achieving the goals set forth in the charter and its management of fiscal and operational responsibilities.

3. *(suggested answer)*

    Students should recognize that schools are a middle-class concept with middle-class values that are in conflict with the circumstances of the poor. Consequently, economically disadvantaged youth often feel alienated in schools and do not succeed academically.

ANSWERS TO ESSAY QUESTIONS

1. *(suggested answer)*

    Students should choose one of these issues: Title IV, gender differences between male and female students, sexual harassment, sexual orientation, or sex education. Answers will vary for teacher roles and responsibilities.

2. (Answers will vary.)

CHAPTER 4

What Is Taught?

MULTIPLE CHOICE QUESTIONS

(An additional ten multiple-choice items and two short answer items are available in the sample quiz for this chapter.)

Read each item carefully. Select the letter of the choice that represents the best answer.

1. A school's curriculum could best be defined as

    a. all of the organized and planned experiences of students for which the school assumes responsibility.
    b. a scope and sequence plan for the subjects to be learned by students from grades K–12.
    c. the written document in which the school outlines its goals for the school district for the next decade.
    d. an explanation of the minimum skills in each of the required subject areas for students in grades K–12.

2. Which of the following has had the most influence over the content of the curriculum in the past decade?

    a. Back to basics movement
    b. Standards-based movement
    c. Decreases in financial support
    d. Technology revolution in education

3. Critics of the standards-based movement cite all of the following reasons for their objections *except*

    a. attention and money should be focused on preexisting urgent needs.
    b. too much focus on testing.
    c. high stakes of accountability based test scores.
    d. lack of support from parents and taxpayers.

4. How has the content of textbooks been affected by the standards-based movement?

    a. The content standards in a few large states determine the content in the books.
    b. Fewer textbooks are being used in most states.
    c. Publishers prepare individual texts to meet each state's standards.
    d. Teachers have been creating their own curriculum rather than using textbooks.

5. A student listens to an editorial response on the TV news in which the speaker charges that a city politician is acting like Macbeth. The student immediately knows by the reference to Macbeth that the city politician is trying to usurp power, according to the speaker. The student is able to make that connection because

    a. of her critical thinking skills.
    b. of her powers of memorization.
    c. she is culturally literate.
    d. she has had courses in British history.

6. Why did the back-to-basics group push for the return to a "basic" curriculum?

    a. They believed that schools did not have the financial resources to support a wide range of programs.
    b. They believed that schools should prepare students to work hard and persevere at difficult tasks.
    c. They believed that students were being exposed to topics and concepts that only a small percentage would actually need.
    d. They vehemently opposed any inclusion of multiculturalism in the curriculum.

7. In general, educational writers comment that textbooks

    a.   provide sufficient depth of coverage.
    b.   are written in a lively, varied style.
    c.   typically pique students' interest and stimulate student learning.
    d.   match none of the descriptions given here.

8. Current trends in math instruction are likely to lead to graduates who are able to

    a.   add long columns of numbers accurately in their heads.
    b.   explain math theories and concepts with insight and ease.
    c.   use mathematical reasoning to solve real problems that confront them.
    d.   find exact answers speedily by referring to texts and tables.

9. In addition to using technology and emphasizing problem solving, mathematics instruction is moving toward

    a.   back-to-basics arithmetic.
    b.   blending of the traditional subject-matter areas—algebra, geometry, etc.
    c.   compartmentalization of subject areas.
    d.   more skill drills.

10. Foreign language departments have sought to attract more students by

    a.   making more use of language labs.
    b.   expanding their course offerings and integrating the study of language with the study of culture.
    c.   using the audiolingual approach.
    d.   decreasing the course requirements for most language classes.

11. According to the recent trends in foreign language instruction, which of the following would one expect to see in foreign language classes?

    a.   More programs starting early in elementary schools
    b.   More integration of international and multicultural education content
    c.   Use of the Internet to access current materials from other countries
    d.   All of these.

12. In the past, school programs in the arts have focused on the creation of art forms, but recently they have attended more to

    a.   individual performance.
    b.   drama, music, and dance.
    c.   aesthetic education as a means of perception.
    d.   art history.

13. Which of the following are guiding the development of physical education curricula?

    a.   Focus on individual rather than team sports skills
    b.   Coordination, endurance, and strength goals
    c.   Information on nutrition, mental health, and sexuality
    d.   Development of aerobic capacity and appropriate levels of body fat

14. In contemporary health education, a unit on AIDS directed toward adolescents would focus on

    a.   changing attitudes to get students to take fewer risks.
    b.   how to identify symptoms of AIDS.
    c.   how to resist peer pressure and information on avoiding risk of infection.
    d.   lectures on the dangers of sexual activity and how to resist peer pressure.

15. Current trends in English instruction include

    a.   selecting literature that is relevant to student interests and representative of accepted literary tradition.
    b.   writing across the curriculum with increased focus on grammar.
    c.   isolated instruction in reading and writing.

    d.   specialists teaching the skills while subject area teachers teach content.

16.   In the controversy over methods of teaching reading, recent research seems to support the use of

    a.   basal reader series.
    b.   a balance of explicit phonics instruction and whole language approaches.
    c.   whole language methods as superior to phonics.
    d.   phonics methods only.

17.   The U.S. Department of Labor's SCANS report argues that in order for all high school graduates to be prepared for the world of work, they need to

    a.   go to a vocationally oriented high school.
    b.   do extensive part-time work as an apprentice in a school-sponsored program.
    c.   develop higher sets of competencies and a foundation of skills.
    d.   receive on-the-job training.

18.   Leslie Taylor is a twelve-year teaching veteran. She has taught seventh grade and has recently moved to fifth grade. She is concerned about the lack of active involvement the students have in their science lessons and the simplistic memorization that the science materials seem to emphasize. Leslie's desire to make changes would be supported by

    a.   the work of E. D. Hirsch.
    b.   Project 2061 and the work of Jerome Bruner.
    c.   the work of Mortimer Adler.
    d.   the advocate of the core curriculum.

19.   If Project 2061, sponsored by the American Association for the Advancement of Science, came to fruition, which of the following would occur?

    a.   A core science curriculum would be instituted for all high school students.
    b.   Finer distinctions would be made between the scientific disciplines, and the use of interactive videos would be widespread.
    c.   Elementary science education would actively engage children in the scientific processes of experiments.
    d.   All of these.

20.   According to the text, which is the greatest problem impeding the social studies curriculum?

    a.   The traditional Eurocentric emphasis in the social studies curriculum
    b.   The lack of coherence and the randomness of approaches in the social studies curriculum
    c.   The lack of change in the social studies curriculum over the past few decades
    d.   The emphasis on the memorization of facts rather than on historical analysis of events

21.   A teacher in New England is planning a social studies unit on the Revolutionary War. According to the text, which of the following typically has the largest influence on the teacher's planning?

    a.   Teacher-made materials (notes, worksheets, activities)
    b.   Accessibility to various historical sites (Bunker Hill, Lexington, Concord, and so on)
    c.   A district curriculum guide
    d.   The textbook adopted for use in the school

22.   Among the trends in the social studies curriculum are

    a.   an emphasis on enabling students to develop an analytical perspective of the human condition.
    b.   more emphasis on geography and civics.
    c.   a focus on global issues instead of American issues.
    d.   a unification and emphasis on themes across the Social Studies.

23.   Which of the following statements regarding American students' scores on the Third International Mathematics and Science Study (TIMSS) is true?

    a.   U.S. students start out behind in fourth grade and stay behind.
    b.   U.S. students are behind because they study fewer topics but in greater depth.

    c.   U.S. students perform just below average in both science and math.

    d.   U.S. students start out above average in fourth grade but are below average by the time they graduate.

24.   Which of the following is *not* a contributing factor to U.S. students scoring lower in mathematics than their international counterparts?

    a.   Lower expectations of students

    b.   Students working

    c.   More time spent on nonacademic activities

    d.   Less sophisticated texts and instructional materials

25.   Which of the following is an accurate statement about the 2000 National Assessment of Education Progress (NAEP) scores?

    a.   Students in the U.S. score significantly lower in the fields of history, geography, and civics than in other fields.

    b.   There is a gender gap in scores for males and females on the math and science tests.

    c.   Over the past 20 years, scores on the math and science tests have declined.

    d.   NAEP scores indicate that American students fall far below students in other developed countries.

26.   Successful cooperative learning strategies include the following:

    a.   group goals, even distribution of labor, and equal opportunities for participation.

    b.   equal opportunities for success, heterogeneous grouping, and individual goals.

    c.   homogeneous grouping, individual accountability, and goals.

    d.   group goals, individual accountability, and equal opportunities for success.

27.   In order to avoid the problem of the smart student in a group doing all the work, cooperative learning strategies

    a.   focus on group accountability and group assessment.

    b.   develop a sense of community within the group.

    c.   involve formal group presentations and individual mastery assessment.

    d.   entail specific, clearly articulated steps to complete an activity.

28.   Proponents of interdisciplinary teaching contend that such an approach helps students

    a.   prepare for the real world where disciplines are interrelated.

    b.   memorize facts and figures necessary to pass standards tests.

    c.   become better readers and writers and well acquainted with classical knowledge.

    d.   develop oral communication skills and use them to access information.

29.   If an art teacher's goal were to foster critical thinking in his/her students, which of the following activities would he/she most likely include for their students?

    a.   A listing of the characteristics of impressionism

    b.   A project evaluating various works by Andrew Wyeth

    c.   A unit in acrylic painting in which the students would paint a still life

    d.   An essay requiring students to describe the art of the Romantic age

30.   Socratic questioning, problem solving, identifying biases or assumptions, weighing evidence, and studying philosophy are among the many activities recommended to develop a curriculum in

    a.   critical thinking.

    b.   discovery learning.

    c.   basic skills.

    d.   mastery learning.

31.   Block scheduling is a more efficient use of time because it reduces

    a.   the number of courses students take during high school.

    b.   time spent passing between classes.

    c.   the hours in the school day.

    d.   homework and study hall time.

32.   The primary purpose of using writing across the curriculum is to

    a.   focus on new, creative ways for students to express themselves.
    b.   develop writing as a tool for learning.
    c.   demonstrate the student's mastery of key concepts in the discipline.
    d.   strengthen the student's communication skills by emphasizing grammar, syntax, and usage.

33.   Evidence suggests that the use of writing activities in other curriculum areas

    a.   enhances writing skills but adds nothing to the mastery of the other areas.
    b.   enhances achievement in the other areas without changing skills in writing.
    c.   enhances writing skills as well as achievement in other areas.
    d.   does not change achievement in either writing or the other areas but adds interest to both.

34.   Differentiated instruction is a teaching philosophy that encourages teachers to meet the needs of academically diverse students by adapting which three elements of instruction?

    a.   Tests, lectures, and demonstrations
    b.   Content standards, assessment, and communication
    c.   Content, process, and products
    d.   Reading readiness, learning preferences, and interests

35.   The term *looping* refers to:

    a.   repeating the same topic at even more complex levels on the K–12 curriculum spiral.
    b.   reinforcing the same content and skills several times during the same grade level.
    c.   a particular format of lesson plan, which introduces a topic, provides instruction, and then reviews within the same class period.
    d.   the practice of promoting the teacher along with the students so that they have the same teacher for several grade levels.

36.   Which of the following school-level actions represents a type of problem highlighted by the parable "The Saber-Tooth Curriculum"?

    a.   Dropping a French course to make room for a course in modern Japanese
    b.   Adding a Latin course while dropping two computer courses
    c.   Adding a course in Japanese by dropping a Latin class
    d.   Adding courses in ancient Egyptian art and dropping Russian

SHORT-ANSWER QUESTIONS

Respond to each of the following questions briefly, but specifically, in complete sentences.

1.   Since 1987, when E. D. Hirsch published his work on cultural literacy, the concept has generated much attention. Briefly define the term and explain Hirsch's major argument for cultural literacy (now known as core knowledge).

2.   Choose one of the innovative instructional approaches and explain how it seeks to improve student learning.

ESSAY QUESTIONS

Read each of the following questions, and respond by composing an organized essay that includes an introduction, fully developed paragraph(s), and a conclusion.

1.   Identify and describe the impact of at least three events, philosophies, or movements that have influenced changes in the curriculum over the last 50 years. Give specific examples of the changes in the curriculum.

2.   Pick one of the current curriculum controversies. Present both sides of the controversy and state and justify your own personal choice of action.

ANSWERS TO MULTIPLE CHOICE QUESTIONS

1.   a

2. b
3. d
4. a
5. c
6. b
7. d
8. c
9. b
10. b
11. d
12. a
13. d
14. a
15. a
16. b
17. c
18. b
19. c
20. b
21. d
22. b
23. d
24. d
25. b
26. b
27. c
28. a
29. b
30. a
31. b
32. b
33. c
34. c
35. d
36. c

ANSWERS TO SHORT-ANSWER QUESTIONS

1. *(suggested answer)*

Hirsch argues that cultural literacy is the ability to recognize and understand the central ideas, stories, characters, events, and scientific knowledge of a culture. It is necessary for a person to understand references to these ideas that authors assume readers know because without knowing those allusions, the person will not understand fully the society in which he or she lives, and as a result may have limited participation in it. Hirsch also argues that schools should teach cultural literacy to develop a shared national framework and unity.

2.   Answers will vary, but should include elements of the following:

Interdisciplinary teaching: Students become aware of the interrelatedness of disciplines and see learning and school as a coherent unit rather than fragmented pieces. Student learning is enhanced because students are hearing the same message in different subjects; in this way their knowledge is reinforced.

Cooperative learning: Students see learning as a social process and appreciate the abilities of their peers. Students take charge of their own learning and have greater motivation to do well. Individual accountability ensures that all members of the group participate.

Critical learning and problem solving: Students learn to evaluate the worth of ideas before making a decision. The focus on critically evaluating ideas helps make students better thinkers. Students appreciate their own learning strategies.

Writing across the curriculum: Students come to see writing as a tool for learning, not as a skill to be mastered. Through writing, students can learn more in the disciplines, focusing on expanding their knowledge.

Differentiated instruction: Because of the broad diversity among students more than one instructional approach should be used to address their diverse learning styles and needs.

Block scheduling: Students save time through a smaller number of passing periods and teacher attendance taking, etc. This structure also allows for more flexibility in instructional methods and activities.

ANSWERS TO ESSAY QUESTIONS

1.   (Answers will vary.)

Possible events, philosophies, or movements include:

Interdisciplinary curricula	Whole language/phonics
Cooperative learning	Tracking/detracking
Core knowledge/cultural literacy	NAEP and TIMSS scores
Goals 2000	Critical thinking/problem solving
Writing across the curriculum	Textbooks
State standards	Block scheduling
Multicultural curriculum	Back-to -basics

2.   (Answers will vary.)

Controversies include:

Influence of the textbooks

Tracking

Core curriculum (cultural literacy) vs. multicultural

Phonics vs. whole language

Cultural literacy

CHAPTER 5

What Makes a Teacher Effective?

MULTIPLE CHOICE QUESTIONS

(An additional ten multiple-choice items and two short answer items are available in the sample quiz for this chapter.)

Read each item carefully. Select the letter of the choice that represents the best answer.

1. Before starting a new unit, Sally White reviews her notes on students, refers to written goals for them, and collects materials that she will need for her class. During this process, what kind of decisions is Sally making?

    a. Planning
    b. Evaluating
    c. Instructing
    d. Managing

2. After giving her class several algebra problems to work on individually, Melina observed that half the students were stuck. She called the class's attention and asked them to work on their algebra problems in pairs so they could help each other. What kind of decision did Melina make?

    a. Adopting
    b. Evaluating
    c. Planning
    d. Implementing

3. When teachers choose questions to ask, reflect on the student understanding that the answers demonstrate, and then decide how to adjust their instruction to improve the results, they are making what kinds of decisions?

    a. Planning.
    b. Managing.
    c. Implementing.
    d. Evaluating.

4. Which of the following is the best description of reflective teaching?

    a. Teaching that mirrors the culture in which the teacher is working
    b. Teaching that incorporates a teacher's self-examination and self-evaluation
    c. Teaching that puts current theoretical research into classroom practice
    d. Teaching that responds to the interests and needs of the students

5. Which of the following teachers best exemplifies the behavior of a reflective teacher?

    a. Keshia reviews her lessons each day after teaching and keeps a teaching journal.
    b. Anselm talks frequently to veteran teachers to see how they teach particular topics.
    c. Darnell uses commercially prepared instructional materials when he begins a unit.
    d. Tina prepares detailed thematic units demonstrating the most recent research on different learning styles.

6. A teacher's attitude toward students plays an obvious role in influencing teacher behavior. Which other attitude also plays an important role?

    a. A teacher's attitude toward his or her teacher education program

    b.   A teacher's attitude toward his or her colleagues

    c.   A teacher's attitude toward professional associations

    d.   A teacher's attitude toward his or her own parents

7.   Teaching is significantly affected by the teacher's attitude toward

    a.   work, toward learning, and toward the practice of habits.

    b.   being a professional and toward being a good staff member.

    c.   other teachers and parents and toward the subject.

    d.   training, students, and toward oneself.

8.   An essential part of understanding and dealing with the feelings of students is

    a.   watching students' behavior out of class.

    b.   taking courses in adolescent psychology.

    c.   studying students' records and talking to their previous teachers.

    d.   knowing and understanding one's own feelings.

9.   How does recognizing one's own feelings of anxiety help a teacher?

    a.   She cannot rid herself of unhealthy emotions if she doesn't accept them.

    b.   It can help her understand how a student's anxiety can affect his or her learning.

    c.   It enables her to control the feelings of her students.

    d.   She can draw on them for energy and inspiration in her work with students.

10.   Which of the following is an example of "self-fulfilling prophecy"?

    a.   If a teacher believes in herself, she will be effective.

    b.   Students will achieve to match the teacher's expectation of them.

    c.   If the students believe in the teacher, he will be effective.

    d.   Students can only be successful when they believe in themselves.

11.   According to David Berliner, which of the following is a characteristic behavior of effective teachers?

    a.   They ask lots of questions requiring students to recall and comprehend knowledge.

    b.   They have strict classroom management skills and silent classrooms.

    c.   They aim instruction at average achievement.

    d.   They pace instruction rapidly.

12.   Brian, frustrated by his math worksheet, tears the paper in half. Which of the teacher's following responses would best characterize what psychologist Carl Rogers calls "empathic understanding"?

    a.   "Joanna, why don't you sit with Brian and help him with his math worksheet? He needs your help."

    b.   "Brian, tearing your math worksheet is not a constructive way to solve your problems."

    c.   "You were working on those problems for some time without getting many done. Why don't you show me where you got stuck?"

    d.   "Math was always my worst subject, too. Finally, I just realized I was better at other things."

13.   Effective teachers demonstrate certain traits in their dealings with peers, administrators, and parents. What are those traits?

    a.   Intellectual rigor, fair-mindedness, and competitiveness

    b.   Vision, cooperation, and innovativeness in problem solving

    c.   Creativity, competence, and control of students

    d.   Cooperation, collaboration, and acceptance of others

14.   During an Open House night, Tyrone Green met with parents of his Algebra I students. He briefly mentioned some of the fundamental concepts in Algebra I and spent most of his time explaining his techniques for teaching Algebra I to ninth-graders. What kind of knowledge did Tyrone use to explain how he taught algebra?

    a.   Discipline content knowledge

    b.   Pedagogical content knowledge

    c.   Curriculum content knowledge

    d.   Theory-in-use knowledge

15. David Kornfeld, a college senior majoring in history, was concerned that his knowledge of history would be insufficient to teach high school. He was considering enrolling in more American history courses to prepare himself for the classroom. According to research about teacher effectiveness, what is most likely a better use of David's time as he prepares to teach?

    a.   Developing tests in American history for his use with students
    b.   Studying history from an interdisciplinary perspective so he could draw upon those other areas in his teaching
    c.   Learning alternative strategies for facilitating a group process in the classroom
    d.   Developing an understanding of the content of the school curriculum that students will be expected to know

16. A theory-in-use is best described as

    a.   a hypothesis designed to bring facts and concepts into systematic connection.
    b.   an explanation used to justify action.
    c.   a common-sense idea proven throughout repeated experiences.
    d.   a practical solution to a theoretical problem.

17. A panel of educators is asked to review a new "fifth-year" teacher training program that focuses almost exclusively on presentation and evaluation methods, or "practical" skills. One shortcoming the panel might expect to find in the program is that its graduates

    a.   will lack adequate content knowledge (for example, in history or math).
    b.   will be unable to use some of the more innovative methodologies they learn in their school settings.
    c.   will resist using some of the methodologies to which they have been exposed.
    d.   will lack the theoretical knowledge that would help them interpret the complexities of the classroom.

18. Gigi Underwood's class has been doing a hands-on unit on World War I. First, the students were enthusiastically responding. Yesterday, Gigi noticed that the class's interest seemed to be flagging. Which of the following would be most helpful to help Gigi interpret the situation?

    a.   Theoretical knowledge
    b.   Discipline knowledge
    c.   Her own common sense
    d.   Curriculum content knowledge

19. Vygotsky's theory of the "zone of proximal development" refers to

    a.   tasks students can accomplish only with the assistance of someone with more skills.
    b.   tasks students can do successfully and independently.
    c.   tasks students have not developed enough skills to do.
    d.   tasks students can only do in cooperative groups.

20. Which of the following would be most consistent with recent cognitive research on teaching and learning?

    a.   Ask students to talk about how they complete a task and structure cooperative learning experiences for them.
    b.   Establish high expectations for all students and structure frequent competitive activities for all them.
    c.   Arrange for students to have cognitive apprenticeships and teach students mnemonic devices to help improve their memory.
    d.   Observe students as they work through problems and prevent students from attempting problems that are beyond their ability.

21. Lois and Charlotte are considered successful teachers. Charlotte revises her units each year, working to improve them, whereas Lois rarely teaches the same unit twice. Lois is able to cover much material with her class by adhering to lesson plans, whereas Charlotte will alter her lesson plan if she thinks it is necessary. Which teacher demonstrates the behavior of an effective teacher?

    a.   Charlotte, because she will modify her lessons if she thinks it's necessary.
    b.   Lois, because she is able to teach her students a large amount of material by adhering to her plans.

    c.   Lois, because she never teaches the same unit twice.
    d.   Both teachers are equally likely to be effective.

22. A teacher smoothly makes transitions from one activity to another so that no time is wasted. She clearly explains what she wants her students to do during activities, and she sets up a system by which they can quickly and quietly have their work checked by her before moving on to the next activity. These tasks of the teacher all fall under the description of

    a.   teaching methodology.
    b.   academic engaged time.
    c.   classroom management.
    d.   pre-active decision making.

23. Raoul Fernandes is able to create a purposeful learning environment in his class through behaviors that focus on instruction and help him run the classroom smoothly. This skill can best be described as

    a.   pre-active decisions.
    b.   classroom management.
    c.   momentum.
    d.   engaged time.

24. Which of the following best describes the concept of "academic engagement"?

    a.   Students work quietly on tasks without any break in their involvement, mastering skills.
    b.   Students work sequentially through more varied and complex material.
    c.   Students show a high degree of interest and demonstrate independence in pursuing new tasks.
    d.   Students work on activities relevant to the instructional goals and work with a high degree of success.

25. A student was overheard saying to his friend, "There's no way I would act up in her class. She acts like she knows what's going to happen before it happens. Ted tried to fool her, but she got him right away. You can't pull anything on her." According to Kounin, this teacher has

    a.   "with-it-ness."
    b.   smoothness.
    c.   "realness."
    d.   pedagogical content knowledge.

26. In Liz's class, some students worked quickly through tasks and sat with nothing to do. Liz often had to stop other students in the middle of their work to clarify the assignment. As a result, the class usually took much longer than Liz planned to complete their work. What elements of classroom management does Liz lack, according to Jacob Kounin's ideas?

    a.   With-it-ness and realness
    b.   Smoothness and momentum
    c.   Clarity and appropriateness
    d.   Planning and consistency

27. Ms. Salama frequently scans her classroom to see how students are working, varies the type and difficulty of questions she asks students, and reinforces the expectations she has for them. All of her behaviors best match which of the following terms?

    a.   Reflective teaching
    b.   Interactive decision making
    c.   Theory-in-use
    d.   Classroom management

28. Mike Hsu, a sixth-grade teacher, is having difficulty with Benny, one of his students. Benny finishes his tasks quickly and then distracts other students. According to Jim and Kevin's suggestions for classroom management, what should Mike do?

    a.   Use assertive discipline to control Benny's behavior.
    b.   Review his teaching to see if it is appropriate for Benny.
    c.   Pair Benny with a student who needs assistance.

d.   Design activities to boost Benny's self-esteem.

29.   Which of the following is consistent with the tone of "Kevin and Jim's Suggestions for Classroom Discipline"?

a.   Be discreet about your problems. Don't tell anyone until you have tried everything.
b.   Make polite but firm corrections to individuals publicly so everyone gets the benefit of the instructions.
c.   Confront student misbehavior immediately. Don't let things slide.
d.   Make unilateral decisions about the kinds of disciplinary action a student needs. The administration should support you as a professional.

30.   Although Noam's math students are bright and interested, their responses to his questions are minimal. Which is the best suggestion for Noam to improve the length and quality of his students' responses?

a.   Have them practice giving oral reports.
b.   Have them write their own questions to ask and answer.
c.   Wait longer between asking a question and calling for a response.
d.   Tell them that their final grade will also include "contribution to class."

31.   When asking questions, the authors of the text would recommend:

a.   asking long questions.
b.   asking questions of volunteers and non-volunteers equally.
c.   asking yes/no questions.
d.   limiting feedback about students' responses.

32.   To use questions effectively, teachers should

a.   ask abstract questions.
b.   ask long questions.
c.   call a student's name before asking the question.
d.   probe students' responses.

33.   According to research, what typically happens when teachers increase their wait-time when questioning students?

a.   The momentum of the class lesson slows down, and advanced students lose their concentration.
b.   The teachers' questions change from being primarily recall questions to questions that require higher-order thinking.
c.   The students provide lengthier responses without being asked.
d.   The students' attitude about the subject improves, and they are more willing to follow the teachers' lead.

34.   Colbie will soon be entering second grade. Which of the following will most likely *not* affect the academic expectations her teachers will have for her?

a.   How much money her parents earn
b.   Scores from the standardized tests she took in first grade
c.   Her race and ethnicity
d.   Whether her parents think she is gifted

35.   How do teachers' expectations influence students' achievement?

a.   Students somehow perceive how the teacher feels and achieve consistent with the expectation.
b.   In subtle, often unconscious, ways, teachers "teach" good students differently than they teach "bad" students.
c.   Teachers consciously work harder with the slower students.
d.   When teachers indicate, in subtle and clear ways, that they don't think the students will succeed, the students try especially hard to succeed to prove them wrong.

SHORT-ANSWER QUESTIONS

Respond to each of the following questions briefly, but specifically, in complete sentences.

1. Identify and explain the attitudes that can foster and those that can impede effective teachers.

2. Teachers used to be noted for having good "disciplinary skills." Now researchers talk about teachers' "classroom management styles." Describe the skills that are encompassed in the meaning of the term *classroom management*.

3. Drawing from your experiences as a student or from the classroom, give an example of a theory-in-use. If the person in the example had had better or different theoretical knowledge, how would the theory-in-use fare?

4. According to Jacob Kounin, teachers who are effective classroom managers emphasize the prevention of disruptions. Describe and give an example of each of the three skills he identified from studying effective teachers.

ESSAY QUESTIONS

Reach each of the following questions, and respond by composing an organized essay that includes an introduction, fully developed paragraph(s), and a conclusion.

1. List and describe the four areas of competence that need to be developed to become an effective teacher and give an example of each.

2. List five of Kevin and Jim's rules of management. Explain each.

ANSWERS TO MULTIPLE CHOICE QUESTIONS

1. a
2. d
3. d
4. b
5. a
6. b
7. c
8. d
9. b
10. b
11. d
12. c
13. d
14. b
15. d
16. b
17. d
18. a
19. a
20. a

21. a
22. c
23. b
24. d
25. a
26. b
27. d
28. b
29. c
30. c
31. b
32. d
33. c
34. d
35. a

ANSWERS TO SHORT-ANSWER QUESTIONS

1. *(suggested answer)*

    Effective teachers demonstrate collaborative, cooperative, accepting attitudes toward others. Resentment toward authority, competition for recognition, and prejudicial or superior attitudes impede a teacher's effectiveness.

2. *(suggested answer)*

    Classroom management includes maintaining an appropriate and orderly environment for student learning, but it also includes developing teacher-student rapport, and housekeeping duties like record keeping and managing time and resources.

3. (Answers will vary.)

4. *(suggested answer)*

    Effective teachers are skilled in *"with-it-ness"* (they pick up the first sign of misbehavior and deal with it quickly), *"smoothness"* (they minimize teacher behaviors that interfere with the flow of instruction); and *"momentum"* (they eliminate teacher behaviors such as *overdwelling* and *fragmentation* that slow down the pace of lesson.) Examples will vary.

ANSWERS TO ESSAY QUESTIONS

1. *(suggested answer)*

    The four areas of competence are attitudes (toward self, students, peers and parents, and subject matter), knowledge of the subject matter, theoretical knowledge about learning, and skills that are necessary to promote learning.

2. *(suggested answer)*

    Kevin and Jim's rules for classroom management are when students misbehave, check teaching; make sure everyone knows the rules; monitor the class regularly; squelch flagrant misbehavior quickly; correct in private; don't make empty threats; don't put hands on a child in anger; think through problems; get help; have a backup; and make sure your rules are consistent with the school's. Examples will vary.

CHAPTER 6

What Should Teachers Know About Technology and Its Impact on Schools?

MULTIPLE CHOICE QUESTIONS

(An additional ten multiple-choice items and two short answer items are available in the sample quiz for this chapter.)

Read each item carefully. Select the letter of the choice that represents the best answer.

1.   When a new technology is first introduced in the classroom, it is often proclaimed that

   a.   the materials will be too expensive.
   b.   students won't have to work in order to learn.
   c.   it will be the end of instruction as we now know it.
   d.   teachers will automatically know how to use it.

2.   Which one of these is *not* one of the stages of technology maturity?

   Technology

   a.   is applied to tasks we already do.
   b.   makes the tasks unnecessary.
   c.   is used to improve the tasks we do.
   d.   is used to do tasks that were not possible before.

3.   When elementary school classes from all over the world go online to add ozone measurements from their community to an online database and then analyze the data and draw conclusions, this is an example of

   a.   distance education.
   b.   a digital archive.
   c.   a newsgroup.
   d.   telecollaboration

4.   When Mrs. Sanchez creates a multimedia project to individualize for her gifted and talented students, she is using her computer as a

   a.   cognitive tool.
   b.   facilitator of instruction.
   c.   communication tool.
   d.   poor substitute for her personal attention.

5.   Students who use word processors to write are more likely to

   a.   finish the assignment more quickly.
   b.   make more substantial revisions.
   c.   include more errors.
   d.   learn less about proofreading and editing.

6.   Which of the following is allowing the social studies teacher to do something innovative with technology?

   a.   Online activities
   b.   Virtual field trips
   c.   GIS software
   d.   Encyclopedia or CD-ROM

7.   Which one of the following is one way to restrict students from inappropriate Web sites?

    a.   An acceptable use policy agreed to by teachers, students, and administrators
    b.   A broadcast system where all the Internet connections flow through one base station
    c.   Require students to obtain teacher permission for every site they visit
    d.   Allow students to use the Internet only from computer stations in the library

8.   Which one of the following is an argument against the use of Web filtering software?

    a.   The software is too expensive
    b.   The filters are imperfect and lead to false confidence
    c.   The software is too difficult to use
    d.   Student's parents don't like the filtering software

9.   The Berkeley public school district has just invested a considerable sum of money on computers for classroom use. If the administration and the faculty want to encourage widespread, habitual use of computers by the students, they should ensure

    a.   a one-to-one ratio of computer to student.
    b.   that students are rewarded with "computer time."
    c.   that the students have adequate access to computers during and after class.
    d.   that each student has a computer at home.

10.   Teachers will be able to use computers effectively only if

    a.   they receive proper training in their use.
    b.   they have on-site support.
    c.   each teacher has adequate access to appropriate hardware and software.
    d.   all of these.

11.   Equity concerns regarding the integration of technology revolve around

    a.   the rapidity with which technology advances, making most hardware obsolete within three years.
    b.   the potential for increased resource disparities between rich and poor schools and students' home access.
    c.   the lack of space in many schools for technology hardware.
    d.   the difficulty of finding qualified maintenance personnel.

12.   The use of new technology in the classroom, which includes the computer, CD-ROMs, and multimedia, can enhance the curriculum by

    a.   accessing data banks from diverse sources.
    b.   creating simulations to solve real-life problems.
    c.   linking students in different states or countries to one another.
    d.   doing all of these.

13.   Carr High School, located in a remote region of New Hampshire, has several students who are ready to enroll in calculus and others who wish to take Latin, but there aren't any teachers who can teach either course. Based upon the most recent advances in education, which proposal would be the best solution for Carr High School's problem?

    a.   An individualized correspondence course for each student
    b.   Tell students that they should postpone taking such courses until they enroll in college
    c.   Institute a distance education program whereby the students can enroll in calculus and Latin
    d.   Bus the students to other schools that do offer such courses

14.   What is the most significant benefit for instituting distance education within a school district?

    a.   Establishing and maintaining a program is less expensive than paying a teacher.
    b.   It provides a way to provide educational equity between rural and poorer students and those who come from larger, more affluent districts.
    c.   At-risk students who are enrolled in distance education programs demonstrate greater academic achievement than those who are not participants.

      d.   Distance education programs have proved to stimulate student productivity and time on task.

15.   Simulation software's advantages include all of the following *except*

      a.   management of information.
      b.   reaction to student input.
      c.   immediate feedback for the students.
      d.   substitution for the teacher as instructional mentor.

16.   One of the main problems with using the Internet in schools is that

      a.   it's too expensive.
      b.   it contains unverified information.
      c.   it's too hard for students to learn to use.
      d.   it's not readily available.

17.   Distance education provides for all of the following *except*

      a.   overcoming problems of budget, size, and location.
      b.   using two-way audio and video interaction.
      c.   offering upper division or advanced placement courses.
      d.   flexibility of time.

18.   Which of the following is *not* a common type of computer arrangement in schools?

      a.   A computer for each student
      b.   Computer labs
      c.   Single-computer classrooms
      d.   Classroom computer clusters

19.   The provision of assistive technology in the classroom for students with special needs is mandated by

      a.   ADA—Aid for Disabled Americans.
      b.   IDEA —Individuals with Disabilities Act.
      c.   the Bill of Rights.
      d.   Goals 2000.

20.   One problem with using computers in instruction is that

      a.   many teachers focus their activities on learning about computers rather than using computers to learn.
      b.   teachers must move from whole-class instruction toward smaller group projects.
      c.   teachers must view themselves as coaches or facilitators.
      d.   classrooms evolve into cooperative rather than competitive social structures.

21.   Which of the following is a major obstacle in implementing more technology in the curriculum?

      a.   There are no technology applications in some subject areas.
      b.   Students resist using technology.
      c.   Teachers need more training.
      d.   Technology has not kept up with the needs of the field of education.

22.   A disadvantage to organizing the computers in a school into a computer lab is that

      a.   labs do not lend themselves to cooperative learning activities.
      b.   labs do not provide open table space.
      c.   labs foster instruction about technology.
      d.   all of these are true.

23.   Mrs. Brown teaches in an inner-city school district. Each of the classrooms in her school has one computer for student use. The equal opportunity issue in this school may be related to

      a.   inadequate funding.
      b.   inadequate electrical systems and network wiring.
      c.   inadequate access to the Internet.

<ol start="24">
<li>all of these.</li>
</ol>

24. In regard to gender differences in the use of computer technology, which of the following statements is true?

    a.   Girls are *more* likely to participate in out-of-school computer programs.
    b.   Families of boys are *less* likely to have computers at home.
    c.   Girls are *more* likely to use technology for solving authentic problems.
    d.   Boys are *less* likely to choose computer electives.

25. Which of the following is evidence of the disparity in the quality of educational technology between affluent and disadvantaged students?

    a.   Affluent students are more likely to have a computer at home.
    b.   Disadvantaged students are more likely to be using computers for drill and practice.
    c.   White students are more likely than minority students to have a computer at home.
    d.   All of these.

26. In a technology-assisted classroom, the role of the teacher

    a.   is expanded and involves more higher-level evaluation of performance and more coaching of student learning.
    b.   changes minimally. The teacher will still be the dispenser of information, directing the students' learning.
    c.   becomes obsolete. The students can learn better on their own with the technology available.
    d.   is reduced to technology maintenance. The teacher ensures that the hardware is functional.

27. Joey was born with a birth defect that left him unable to use his vocal cords and consequently to speak. Yet Joey has successfully completed his high school studies and looks forward to a challenging college career. How has assistive technology helped Joey communicate in class?

    a.   He has a full-time interpreter who speaks for him.
    b.   He makes use of a voice output device that produces synthesized sound.
    c.   He uses a voice input device to translate spoken words to written text.
    d.   He uses an adaptive word processing program to write his papers.

SHORT-ANSWER QUESTIONS

Respond to each of the following questions briefly, but specifically, in complete sentences.

1. Briefly identify and explain a benefit of, as well as, an obstacle to installing educational technology within classrooms.

2. Choose one of the four ways that computers can be distributed in a school. Describe the advantages and disadvantages of this arrangement and tell why you prefer it.

ESSAY QUESTIONS

Read each of the following questions, and respond by composing an organized essay that includes an introduction, fully developed paragraph(s), and a conclusion.

1. Clearly describe a specific topic or subject area which you will be teaching and then indicate *all* of the ways you could use educational technology with your students to support and enhance effective instruction and learning.

2. Pick one of the controversial issues surrounding the use of technology in education. Clearly state *all* points of view on the issue and then give your own opinion and support it.

3. The equity issues surrounding educational technology regarding gender and socioeconomic status create many problems for educators. Clearly describe one of these issues (gender, or economic advantage) and your solution for the problem.

4.   Discuss the pros and cons of using a web filtering system or software. Also include information relating to the issue of censorship versus free access to the Internet.

ANSWERS TO MULTIPLE CHOICE QUESTIONS

1.   c
2.   b
3.   d
4.   b
5.   b
6.   d
7.   a
8.   b
9.   c
10.   d
11.   b
12.   d
13.   c
14.   b
15.   d
16.   b
17.   d
18.   a
19.   b
20.   a
21.   c
22.   a
23.   d
24.   c
25.   d
26.   a
27.   b

ANSWERS TO SHORT-ANSWER QUESTIONS

1.   *(suggested answer)*

The benefits that can be gained by using educational technology are many, including the benefits of distance education, interactive video software, individualized instruction, and greater access to educational information. The biggest obstacle for bringing educational technology into the classroom is the sometimes prohibitive cost of starting up programs with technology: the costs of computers, software, printers, CD-ROMs, and the like.

2.   *(suggested answer)*

Computer labs are one way. Advantages are that all students can use computers simultaneously, labs are best for teaching about the computer, and they facilitate demonstration. However, they are not useful for cooperative or interdisciplinary learning because of the lack of table space. Access is sometimes limited.

Single-computer classrooms are another way. They are good for record keeping and can be used to facilitate cooperative groups. However, there is limited opportunity for each student.

Classroom clusters are a third way. They encourage education *with* technology. This is the most flexible use of computers. However, they are costly, they require more printers, and they are not very useful for training *how* to use technology.

Laptops and handheld computers are becoming more common for individual use. In the future they may be as common as calculators.

ANSWERS TO ESSAY QUESTIONS

1. *(suggested answer)*

    Answers will vary. Look for the widest variety of applications suggested in the text.

2. *(suggested answer)*

    Answers will vary depending on the issue selected – infrastructure and budgeting, education of teachers, parents, equity or integration into the curriculum.

3. (Answers will vary.)

4. *(suggested answer)*

    The pros include protecting students from pornography, late literature, or dangerous information like instructions on how to make a bomb as well as some quality control and liability protection for the school.

    The cons include over reliance on the filtering system making the school more vulnerable if it fails, which could also lead to students not learning to evaluate the authority of Web sources and the First Amendment issues of censorship.

CHAPTER 7

What Are the Ethical and Legal Issues Facing Teachers?

MULTIPLE CHOICE QUESTIONS

(An additional ten multiple-choice items and two short answer items are available in the sample quiz for this chapter.)

Read each item carefully. Select the letter of the choice that represents the best answer.

1. When a community develops expectations about the conduct that people ought to exhibit, they are discussing which of the following?

    a. Law
    b. Due process
    c. Ethics
    d. Psychology

2. A system of rules that members of a community, state, or nation formally develop is called

    a. ethics.
    b. due process.
    c. the law.
    d. a cultural code.

3. Which of the following is the best distinction between ethics and law?

    a. Ethics is based upon religion, whereas the law is not.
    b. Law is primarily concerned with what people are required to do, whereas ethics is concerned with what people ought to do.
    c. Ethics is a system of rules articulated to guide human conduct, whereas the law suggests what people should do.
    d. Law deals with human rights, whereas ethics rarely does.

4. Gene Kruczek listens attentively to his students and understands when they feel upset or anxious. Gene exemplifies which of the following characteristics of ethical teaching identified by Kenneth Howe?

    a. Moral deliberation
    b. Knowledge
    c. Empathy
    d. Moral insight

5. Howe's six dimensions of professional codes of morality include

    a. appreciation for moral deliberation and sincerity in purpose.
    b. knowledge and courage.
    c. subject-matter knowledge and sympathy.
    d. reasoning and integrity.

6. Mayumi Ikebe responds to students' papers with suggestions and encouragement. She carefully plans each lesson, even though sometimes she could take shortcuts. In this aspect, she demonstrates

    a. minimum teaching competency.
    b. adherence to the NEA code of ethics.

c. the everyday ethics of teaching.

d. the legal obligations of a teacher.

7. Duane teaches in an industrial city where residents are concerned about groundwater contamination. Duane is elected president of a citizens' environmental group that some residents consider controversial. Near the end of the school year, Duane's principal quietly tells him that he will not be offered a third-year teacher's contract because of his reputation as a "radical environmentalist." Which of this teacher's rights has been violated?

a. The everyday ethics of teaching

b. The right to substantive due process

c. The right to a teaching contract

d. The right to procedural due process

8. A veteran teacher is suspected of drinking on the job. The principal tells this to the teacher and apprises him of the process that will be followed concerning his hearing, retaining an attorney, and other facts. The teacher asks if he will be given the name of his accusers. According to the laws concerning procedural due process, how will the principal answer?

a. To prevent any possibility of retaliation, their identities will remain hidden.

b. The accusers' names will be provided if a preliminary investigation rules that there are reasonable grounds to suspect the teacher of drinking on the job.

c. The accusers' names will be provided to the teacher's attorney only after he has filed for them.

d. The accusers' names will be provided to him.

9. In June, a nontenured teacher has not been informed of her employment status for the following year. On August 16, she is informed that she will not be rehired by the school district because of her "ineffective classroom management." How has this situation violated the Supreme Court decision of *Goldberg* v. *Kelly*?

a. The teacher was not given timely notice of her dismissal.

b. The teacher was not given a clear reason for her dismissal.

c. The teacher was not given a chance to improve her deficiencies in teaching.

d. The teacher was not given the chance to demonstrate her teaching abilities to the school board.

10. Shoshona and Patti are both tenured foreign language teachers. In the Latin courses, which Shoshona teaches, there has been a 30 percent decrease in student enrollment. Patti has assigned numerous papers to students without ever grading them, has shown films in class week after week, or many times has given the students a study hall. According to tenure law, what can their administrators do regarding both teachers' future teaching assignments?

a. Because of tenure, Shoshona cannot be laid off even if there is a reduction in force. However, despite tenure, Patti may lose her job if the administrators demonstrate that she is incompetent.

b. Shoshona can be laid off; however, Patti has a contractual right to teach and cannot be fired because of classroom performance.

c. Tenure protects and ensures the teaching jobs of both Shoshona and Patti.

d. Tenure does not protect the jobs of teachers who are proven to be incompetent or when schools have a reduction in force.

11. In which of the following instances is the teacher most likely to be held liable?

a. Two students begin to speak to each other hostilely. The teacher tells them to stay away from each other. Even though they appear to have calmed down during the class, they begin fighting as soon as they leave class.

b. While a teacher is circulating through the classroom assisting students with their work, a student unexpectedly jumps out of her seat to show a friend a dance move. In doing the move, she dislocates her shoulder.

c. A teacher ignores two students who begin to wrestle playfully, and one of them breaks a wrist.

d. A student enters the teacher's class very angry about a fight he has just had with his father. In his emotional state, he puts his fist through a window, cutting his hand.

12.   In considering whether a teacher should be held liable for a student injury, which of the following facts will a judge consider most important?

    a.   The pupil-to-teacher ratio in the classroom
    b.   Whether the teacher had established rules for the students
    c.   The age of the students in the teacher's classroom
    d.   Whether the teacher had determined the extent and severity of the student injury

13.   As a social studies teacher strolls through the halls during lunch, he finds a group of students clustered around two boys who are fighting. When he intervenes to stop the fighting, the teacher must also be aware of

    a.   the right to due process.
    b.   the *in loco parentis* position.
    c.   his liability insurance.
    d.   the use of reasonable force.

14.   Willful attack resulting in harm to a person is called

    a.   battery.
    b.   liability.
    c.   injury.
    d.   assault.

15.   Which of the following instances would be protected by the *Pickering* decision?

    a.   A teacher would be able to select the movie *The Crucible* for a history unit on the Salem witchcraft trials.
    b.   A teacher would be able to report suspected child abuse without fear of recrimination by the parents.
    c.   A teacher would be assured that she would have a chance to defend herself before being dismissed from a teaching position.
    d.   A teacher would know that she could march in a parade calling for increased federal spending on AIDS research without recrimination from the school administration.

16.   A small group of angry parents threatens to sue a school board for their support of an English teacher and her choice of texts for her class, including the work of J. D. Salinger and Judy Blume. The parents claim that Salinger's *Catcher in the Rye* and Blume's *Forever* are inappropriate to teach in school because of their subject matter. If this case reached the courts, what would a judge consider in deciding the case?

    a.   A review of the personal lives of both Salinger and Blume
    b.   The relevance of the two books to the formal course objectives
    c.   The literature selections of other teachers in the department
    d.   The merit and quality of each literature selections, as viewed by literary critics and scholars

17.   A group of angry parents comes to a PTO meeting, demanding that Ms. Montero never teach *Romeo and Juliet* in school again, because it glorifies teen suicide. This demonstrates

    a.   justified censorship.
    b.   an infringement of the teacher's academic freedom.
    c.   an infringement of procedural due process.
    d.   a violation of Ms. Montero's teaching contract.

18.   Although challenges to censorship have appeared to be on the upswing in recent history, members of particular educational organizations are staunchly opposed to removing a book from a school or library because

    a.   it implies that suppressing an idea is an acceptable way of dealing with controversy.
    b.   they believe that teachers and school librarians should have complete academic freedom from any parental or community input.
    c.   many of the books that come under censorship challenges are the very books that are of high interest to students, prompting them to read.
    d.   they do not want to include parents in education or curricular discussions.

19. According to recent court rulings, which of the following situations is *not* protected as a teacher's right?

    a. To choose any lifestyle, as long as it is not advocated for students
    b. To express any sexual orientation, as long as it is not advocated for students
    c. To wear any hairstyle or dress in any fashion, as long as it is not advocated for students
    d. To belong to any political party, as long as the party is not advocated for students

20. Under copyright law, which of the following is allowed?

    a. Making a class anthology of poems from different poets if you use the anthology for only one class, not to be repeated during the following or subsequent years.
    b. Making enough copies of a newspaper article for your whole class.
    c. Making copies of workbook pages for extra practice by students if the school district has bought at least a classroom set of the workbooks.
    d. Making additional copies of sheet music when the school already owns two dozen copies.

21. A school librarian is allowed to do which of the following under copyright law?

    a. Videotape a television program on the request of a teacher for a one-time use.
    b. Videotape television programs of her own accord that would be of general interest to the faculty and students for their one-time use.
    c. Videotape programs of interest so that she can build up their video library.
    d. Videotape reruns of educational programs to keep for future use.

22. Copyright laws regarding the use of software

    a. are the same as laws for the use of text and video clips.
    b. are the same rules for material taken off the Internet.
    c. are the same rules for printed materials.
    d. specify that software should not be passed around and copied.

23. Lanlan Sheng wants to show her science class a television documentary on tidal pools she has taped. In order to do that in compliance with the copyright laws, what must she do?

    a. Erase the taped program after forty-five days
    b. Write to the producers of the television program for permission
    c. Ask the school librarian for permission to tape the program
    d. Tape over the program at the end of the school year

24. Rose Huang, a second-grade teacher, notices that Donnie, one of her pupils, frequently arrives at school with bruises and cuts. Rose suspects physical abuse by the parents, yet she can't be entirely certain. According to the law, what must Rose do?

    a. Report her suspicions
    b. Call the parents for a conference
    c. Offer the child emotional guidance and counseling
    d. Interview the child and look for additional evidence

25. Hildi Chinigo suspects that one of her students is the victim of child abuse. However, the parents are politically and socially prominent in town, and Hildi worries about any repercussions of reporting her suspicions. What protects her from the possible negative consequences of reporting suspicions to the principal?

    a. The law forbids the parents to take action against the teacher.
    b. The principal is not obliged to report the incident to the parents.
    c. The law requires that the source of the report be kept confidential.
    d. There must be more than two teachers reporting suspected child abuse before further investigation will be made.

26. Several students would like to begin an after-school Bible study to meet in a classroom. According to the recent court cases cited in the text, what is the most likely response from the principal?

    a. Yes, because forbidding the club is a violation of the First Amendment.

b. No, because starting a Bible reading group within the school suggests the promotion of religion.
c. Yes, as long as the club is held after school hours and is student initiated without teacher participation.
d. Only if the Bible reading group reflects the religious affiliation or orientation of the majority of the students in the school.

27. What impact did the *Scopes* trial ruling have upon public schooling?

a. Public schools had to reflect the religious orientation of the majority of the school's students.
b. Public schools were permitted to teach evolution because it is a scientific theory as opposed to a religious belief.
c. Evolution could not be taught in a public school because it was anti-religious.
d. Public schools had to spend an equal amount of time teaching both evolution and creationism.

28. The legal policy that educators should consider when dealing with disciplinary actions, such as suspension or expulsion, of students is

a. due process.
b. probable cause.
c. academic freedom.
d. reasonable prudence.

29. To what extent is corporal punishment permitted?

a. It is forbidden in all states.
b. It is permitted without restrictions in most school districts.
c. It is permitted in most districts for middle and high school students but prohibited for elementary students.
d. It is permitted in many states, but only with restrictions in many school districts.

30. Under what conditions may a school official search a student's locker?

a. When the official is searching for evidence so he or she can expel the student from school
b. When the official has a suspicion that a student is hiding illegal substances or weapons in her locker
c. When the official wants to reduce drug trafficking in school by having frequent surprise locker searches
d. When the official knows that the student is friends with others who have broken the law earlier

31. Which of the following best represents the recent court decisions regarding the extent of students' freedom of speech?

a. A student's First Amendment rights should be in no way abrogated merely because he or she is within the walls of a school.
b. A minor's right to free speech is not as extensive and far-reaching as an adult's.
c. An individual student's writing or speech is covered by the First Amendment, but symbolic speech is not.
d. Public schools have the right to restrict students' free speech so that it is consistent with the goals of the school.

32. Under the terms of the Buckley Amendment (the Family Educational Rights and Privacy Act), what might happen to a school that refused parents access to the school files on their own children?

a. The school is denied federal funds.
b. The school is closed.
c. The school loses accreditation.
d. The school officials are arrested.

33. Kristi Mandelbaum keeps extensive personal notes on the progress of her students. A parent of one student finds out about her notes and demands to see the notes Kristi has kept on her son. Which of Kristi's responses is most reflective of the Family Educational Rights and Privacy Act (i.e., the Buckley Amendment)?

a. "Certainly, here are all my notebooks."

b. "I will let you see what I have written about your son, but I cannot show you what I have written about the other students."

c. "Your request must be approved by the school board before I can share any of my notes with you."

d. "I'm sorry, but these are my personal notes, so I am not required to share them with you."

34. According to the text, with recent supreme court rulings regarding the responsibility of schools to address charges of sexual harassment which of the following is *not* one of the perceived dangers?

a. Courts will be flooded with cases.

b. Sexual harassment will be easier to prove.

c. School districts' budgets will be drained by the costs of litigation.

d. More cases against teachers will be filed.

SHORT-ANSWER QUESTIONS

Respond to each of the following questions briefly, but specifically, in complete sentences.

1. According to Kenneth Howe, a teacher who strives to be ethical must have "an appreciation for moral deliberation." What does that phrase mean? Give an example to illustrate.

2. To what extent is academic freedom available to public school teachers?

3. How has the Buckley Amendment proved somewhat problematic for teachers?

ESSAY QUESTIONS

Read each of the following questions, and respond by composing an organized essay that includes an introduction, fully developed paragraph(s), and a conclusion.

First subsection

1. In practicing their profession, teachers frequently face issues that have ethical or legal dimensions. Listed here are five situations that require ethical or legal decisions. For each, tell whether the decision involves professional ethics or law and explain what the ethical or legal consideration is. For each, describe one solution that represents sound legal or ethical thinking.

a. One of your students appears to be abused at home.

b. You think you see a student cheating on a test. The evidence is fairly convincing, but there is room for doubt.

c. You write a letter to the editor of the local paper expressing your view that sexual preference is a private matter and should not be used as a basis for employment. Your letter elicits a response, and you would like to continue the dialogue in another letter. Your principal reports this civic activity to the superintendent.

d. You have used only one or two of your sick leave days this year, and today is the first warm, lovely day of spring. You would like to take what you privately call a "mental health day."

e. After months of good-faith negotiation, your professional association has determined that only a strike can persuade the school board of the teachers' seriousness about getting improved working conditions. The board continues to put off making any decisions and has said that working conditions are good as they are. You agree that the current board offers are not fair. The strike is supported by a clear majority of members. You feel very uneasy about joining it because you are by nature very reserved and quiet in public.

Second subsection

2. Explain current court interpretations of issues involving religion in schools. Mention specifically teaching prayer in school, religious clubs, and discussion of religious practices.

3.   How does the right to due process affect a school administrator's dismissal of a teacher? What is the difference between substantive and procedural due process?

ANSWERS TO MULTIPLE CHOICE QUESTIONS

1.   c
2.   c
3.   b
4.   c
5.   b
6.   c
7.   b
8.   d
9.   a
10. d
11. c
12. b
13. d
14. a
15. d
16. b
17. b
18. a
19. c
20. b
21. a
22. d
23. a
24. a
25. c
26. c
27. b
28. a
29. d
30. b
31. d
32. a
33. d
34. b

ANSWERS TO SHORT-ANSWER QUESTIONS

1.   *(suggested answer)*

The text states that "appreciation for moral deliberation" means that the teacher must be able to see a situation as containing conflicting and competing moral interests. The teacher must be able to see the complexities of moral problems and take care that the rights of all parties are protected. Examples to demonstrate that definition will vary, but all examples should illustrate the teacher's ability to see moral problems as containing competing moral claims.

2.   *(suggested answer)*

Academic freedom is available to some degree to public school teachers, although they certainly have less freedom in their choice of teaching materials than teachers in private schools, colleges, or universities. Academic freedom in a public school is moderated by particular questions regarding the relevance of the material to the stated course goals, the appropriateness of the material for the students involved, the quality of the material, and the purpose of the teacher in using the material.

3.   *(suggested answer)*

Because students now have the right to see everything in their student files, teachers are more careful about what they write there. In many cases, that is a positive change. However, teachers are also cautious about what they write for fear of potential lawsuits. As a result, to protect themselves teachers may concentrate on writing vague or extremely general comments about students. The Buckley Amendment may have inhibited many teachers from writing fully and honestly about students for fear that something in their descriptions would in some way offend a student or parent.

ANSWERS TO ESSAY QUESTIONS

1.   a.   Law. Teachers are required to report suspected abuse. Tell the principal.

   b.   Ethics. Teachers are supposed to help students achieve their best and also to behave honestly. Several different responses might be ethical.

   c.   Law. Teachers are permitted public expression of conviction, just as are all citizens. You may write your second letter and may decide to remind the principal that you never use the classroom as an arena to advocate your beliefs.

   d.   Ethics. You have agreed to serve in good faith, and only you can judge when you are capable of working and when you are not. However, you are clearly bound to teach when you can. In real life, people have various responses to this common problem. Any answer supported by an ethical interpretation is correct.

   e.   Ethics. By becoming a member, you have agreed to work collectively. The call for a strike is warranted by the board's inaction. As this case is described, joining the strike is probably the ethical response.

2.   *(suggested answer)*

Current interpretations require teachers to steer away from any behavior that advocates a particular set of beliefs or practices. No form of prayer is permitted at a formal event because it puts social pressure on all students to participate. Students may as individuals pray silently whenever they desire. Bible reading as a form of prayer is forbidden. Religious clubs can meet in the school before or after school hours as long as they are student initiated and no teachers participate. The Bible may be studied as literature. Religious practices may be discussed as features of a pluralistic society but not conducted as forms of observance.

3.   *(suggested answer)*

The right to due process means that an individual's rights should not be violated and that the individual should be treated fairly. Due process affects the way in which a school board may dismiss a teacher, because the teacher must know why he or she is being fired, must have timely and adequate notice of his or her dismissal, must have the opportunity to defend himself or herself and to cross-examine witnesses, must also be allowed the counsel of an attorney, and must have an impartial decision maker. Substantive due process concerns the fairness of the issue itself. For example, it would violate substantive due process for the school board to dismiss a teacher because she became a Muslim. Procedural due process has to do with the fairness of the procedure followed. A school board can inform a teacher that it wants to dismiss her. But it would violate procedural due process for the school board to inform the teacher that her hearing at which she could defend herself was scheduled for the next day, because that would not give her adequate time to prepare her own defense.

CHAPTER 8

What Are the Philosophical Foundations of American Education?

MULTIPLE CHOICE QUESTIONS

(An additional ten multiple-choice items and two short answer items are available in the sample quiz for this chapter.)

Read each item carefully. Select the letter of the choice that represents the best answer.

1. What is a philosopher's primary mode of inquiry?

   a. Through reason and argument
   b. Through the analysis of historical patterns
   c. Through intuition
   d. Through experimentation and data gathering

2. A veteran teacher considers his thirty-year career and asks himself, "Has my career had a core purpose?" What kind of philosophical question is this?

   a. Aesthetic
   b. Epistemological
   c. Metaphysical
   d. Ethical

3. A young child asks his teacher, "How can love be real if you don't ever see it?" Which branch of philosophy has that child's question tapped into?

   a. Axiology
   b. Epistemology
   c. Logic
   d. Metaphysics

4. The study of axiology provides one with an understanding of

   a. the way knowledge is comprehended.
   b. the values people hold concerning beauty and conduct.
   c. the nature of humankind.
   d. the elements of reasoning.

5. An art teacher is prompting his Sculpture I students to identify the elements of beauty that exist in Michelangelo's *David*. This activity is focusing on developing students' comprehension of

   a. aesthetics.
   b. ethics.
   c. logic.
   d. metaphysics.

6. Two kindergartners are fighting over a Power Ranger toy. Ms. Hernandez tells the children gently, "Brian, you promised Ali you would share that toy with her. It's not fair to Ali if you go back on your promise." Ms. Hernandez is giving the children a simple lesson in which of the following?

   a. Axiology
   b. Ethics

    c. Logic
    d. Aesthetics

7. A teacher education class is discussing the duties of a teacher and the principles that should guide a teacher's conduct with students. This class's discussion concerns which of the following?

    a. Metaphysics
    b. Epistemology
    c. Ethics
    d. Axiology

8. Two historians debate the merits of a recent historical analysis. One claims it is the definitive account of that period; the other argues that the historical period could be legitimately analyzed through several other perspectives equally as well. What kind of philosophical discussion are these historians having?

    a. Axiological
    b. Logical
    c. Epistemological
    d. Metaphysical

9. Mr. Nguyen, an algebra teacher, emphasizes the epistemological aspects of mathematics to his students. Which of the following kinds of questions is he most likely to ask students?

    a. "When are you likely to use algebra?"
    b. "What is the purpose of the quadratic equation?"
    c. "If I know $b = c$, then what is the value of a?"
    d. "Explain how you know that $x = 12$."

10. When a long-term heavy smoker was sixty-five, she was fitted for dentures. Months later, she was diagnosed with throat cancer. Her neighbor explained, "I don't want to have my denture fitting now. Getting dentures gave my neighbor throat cancer!" A background in one area of philosophy would have helped the neighbor come to a stronger conclusion. Which one would be of most help?

    a. Logic
    b. Ethics
    c. Aesthetics
    d. Metaphysics

11. A student completing a project on bird identification knows that insect-eating birds have narrow, pointed bills. One day, her mother and she look out the window and see a bird they don't recognize with a narrow bill. The mother exclaims, "What an unusual bird. I've never seen a bird like that all through this snowy winter." The daughter replies, "You wouldn't. That bird must migrate to warmer climates during the winter." Which of the following is the girl using?

    a. Metaphorical thinking
    b. Inductive reasoning
    c. Correctional thinking
    d. Deductive reasoning

12. At Bowker High School, students take many required courses, including Latin, history, humanities, mathematics, and science. The students study those disciplines as a way of developing their intellect and discovering the universal truths of humankind. Bowker High's philosophy of education is derived from

    a. asceticism
    b. essentialism
    c. romanticism
    d. perennialism

13. A frustrated faculty member stated at a department meeting, "We have one female author in the curriculum! Shakespeare, Sophocles, Dickens, Homer! When are we going to acknowledge that other people have contributed to the universe of knowledge? When are we going to provide a broader framework for our students?" This teacher would be *least supportive* of which of the following educational philosophies?

    a. Essentialism
    b. Romanticism
    c. Perennialism
    d. Progressivism

14. Mrs. Svensen, the school principal, explained to parents that because human nature does not change, students can discover rich truths through studying biographies of significant people from history. What educational philosophy is Mrs. Svensen supporting?

    a. Perennialism
    b. Humanism
    c. Romanticism
    d. Progressivism

15. Which of the following best depicts a classroom of a progressive teacher?

    a. Students are sitting quietly reading the *Odyssey*, while the teacher writes key passages on the chalkboard for the students to memorize .
    b. A list of computer assignments for math and writing is on the board for the students to complete; students are clustered around computer terminals, and the teacher is explaining the commands for several of the most common functions of the computer.
    c. A group of students is working cooperatively on a student-initiated project to discover how gears operate; the teacher acts as a facilitator for their experimentation.
    d. The teacher and a student meet individually to decide which topics could best help a student discover the meaning within of his life.

16. Which of the following would most closely represent a progressive's philosophy of education?

    a. Human nature is static, and knowledge is absolute; therefore, people will learn by imitating the practice of our wise ancestors.
    b. Human nature is constant, but new knowledge is constantly being discovered; therefore, people must learn from the past and present.
    c. Human nature is ever changing; therefore, people must continually rediscover and redefine knowledge and its application.
    d. Human nature is an illusion; there is no reality outside the individual; therefore, the individual must make meaning for himself or herself.

17. The social studies department at a high school noted that the students' achievement, by and large, was mediocre. One teacher told the others: "The students' achievement will probably always be mediocre if we continue to teach them without using interactive groups and activities. We need to examine our curriculum for possible revision." How would this teacher describe herself?

    a. As a conceptual empiricist
    b. As a progressivist
    c. As an essentialist
    d. As a perennialist

18. During a one-on-one conversation, a student asks a trusted teacher what kind of knowledge is the most important for him to know. The teacher, a progressivist, would reply:

    a. "All of the traditional academic disciplines, like mathematics, science, literature, history, and foreign languages."
    b. "Whatever enables you to explore anything you chose to learn."
    c. "The knowledge that will give you an edge in the competitive world in which we live. Subjects like computer programming and science are important."

d.   "There is no 'most important' knowledge. It is up to you to make meaning out of your life; don't look for others to do it for you."

19.   The Oak Valley school board is conducting a very heated board meeting in which board members and residents are debating the educational goals of the school district. One parent, an essentialist, stands up and asserts that

a.   the school district should shy away from all the group emphasis on teaching methods, for that does not allow the individual student to truly learn the meaning of his or her existence.
b.   the school needs to focus on stimulating the students' natural curiosity and eagerness to learn, which it is stifling by emphasizing the study of traditional disciplines.
c.   the school's current emphasis on "relevance" for students is completely misguided; students will benefit most from the self-discipline and the intellectual growth that studying the classics fosters.
d.   the school board will best serve the needs of the students and of the community if it emphasizes the subject areas that will most help the students become functioning, productive members of society.

20.   Alma is meeting with her guidance counselor to select courses. She tells her counselor, "I know that course would be interesting, but will it help me get a job or help prepare me for college?" Alma is probably supportive of which of the following philosophies?

a.   Eclecticism
b.   Essentialism
c.   Romanticism
d.   Progressivism

21.   In the recent past, U.S. policymakers, elected officials, and educational experts have warned that the United States is losing its competitive edge in the global economy. They have also warned the public that U.S. students lack skill in mathematics, science, and technology. These policymakers, officials, and educational experts are probably most aligned with

a.   essentialism
b.   romanticism
c.   perennialism
d.   progressivism

22.   Which of the following best depicts a romanticist teacher's classroom?

a.   Some students work together on a scale model of the Globe Theater, and others work on sewing costumes for a play they will perform.
b.   Students in a French class chorally read a passage from their textbook, and the teacher corrects the pronunciation of several students.
c.   Students work individually on worksheets or exercises to help reinforce their skills in computation.
d.   A student, after checking in the school and local library, draws up a reading list and meets with the teacher to inform her of his course of study for the semester.

23.   Mrs. Boxleitner tells her students at the beginning of the year: "You need to find out who you are and what you are interested in. Each of you needs to discover these areas for yourselves. Don't look to me to provide you with answers." Mrs. Boxleitner represents which of the following philosophies?

a.   Perennialism
b.   Essentialism
c.   Romanticism
d.   Progressivism

24.   Which of the following statements best reflects romanticism?

a.   Students naturally drift toward others in order to learn.
b.   Students must follow their own interests.
c.   Students learn best by adapting wisdom from the past to their own lives.
d.   Students can only thrive by learning what is necessary to prosper in their society.

25. Which of the following might be found in a school following the romanticist philosophy?

    a. Character education
    b. Individualized instruction
    c. Instruction in citizenship
    d. Cooperative learning

26. Which two of the four educational philosophies were developed first in the American education system?

    a. Progressivist/perennialist
    b. Essentialist/progressivist
    c. Essentialist/romanticist
    d. Romanticist/progressivist

27. Which two of the four educational philosophies are more teacher centered?

    a. Essentialist/perennialist
    b. Essentialist/progressivist
    c. Essentialist/romanticist
    d. Romanticist/progressivist

28. Mr. Sharif thinks that there is a core body of knowledge that most students can master, that this core knowledge is important for students to become productive members of society, and that students can best learn this knowledge through a problem-solving approach to learning, motivated by their own curiosity. His philosophy of education is that of a(n)

    a. eclectic.
    b. essentialist.
    c. romanticist.
    d. perennialist.

29. Rebecca Landis is a teacher who ascribes to several different philosophies of education. She believes that children are naturally good and curious and learn best by discovery. She also believes that as a teacher she has the responsibility and authority to pass on to the next generation the wisdom of our ancestors. As a result of her eclecticism, what is likely to happen?

    a. The students will naturally choose to learn about the past.
    b. Rebecca will experience conflict as the result of choosing disparate elements of educational philosophies.
    c. Rebecca will alternate between requiring students to memorize passages and to choose their own projects.
    d. Rebecca's teaching will progress unimpeded, facilitated by her coherent educational philosophy.

30. John Dewey thought that ideas

    a. were divinely inspired, allowing us to transcend the confines of our temporal existence.
    b. should be passed on from one generation to the other so the younger generation could learn the wisdom from the past.
    c. were important in and of themselves, without any link to action.
    d. were instruments that enabled people to work together to solve problems.

31. John Dewey, an educator of the twentieth century, was most noted for his contributions to

    a. essentialism.
    b. romanticism.
    c. perennialism.
    d. progressivism.

32. Which hypothetical teaching situation would John Dewey be most likely to support?

    a. Teaching geometry by studying the lives of Greek mathematicians
    b. Teaching geometry by making up songs and stories the students enjoy
    c. Teaching geometry by giving many examples of its uses

d.   Teaching geometry by explaining principles when the need arises as the students build a tree house

33.   In the twentieth century, psychological theory has influenced educational practices. Which of the following would be typical in a classroom where the teacher's practices were based on behaviorism?

a.   A lot of student decision making
b.   Focus on the process rather than the answer
c.   Hands-on activities
d.   Close monitoring and direct feedback

34.   The theories in cognitive psychology developed in the twentieth century have influenced educational practices. Which of the following would be emphasized in a classroom where the teacher based his/her practices on constructivist theory?

a.   A focus on the process of thinking
b.   Teacher telling the students information
c.   Passive students
d.   Rewards for correct answers

35.   Which of the following technologies is a constructivist teacher *least* likely to use?

a.   Have students sort things and look for clues
b.   Have students use reference resources to find the answer
c.   Have students connect new ideas to what they already know
d.   Have students look for patterns

SHORT-ANSWER QUESTIONS

Respond to each of the following questions briefly, but specifically, in complete sentences.

1.   You are a romanticist teacher, and in your high school curriculum you are expected to teach ethics to your high school students. How would you respond to this element of the curriculum?

2.   An elementary school committee is designing an updated curriculum for the mathematics program. Explain how epistemology will affect the work the members do in designing the curriculum. Provide an example of a question they may have regarding math instruction that would reveal the epistemological influence.

3.   Compare the perennialist's and the essentialist's conception of metaphysics.

4.   Why is it important for teachers to have an understanding of philosophy?

ESSAY QUESTIONS

Read each of the following questions, and respond by composing an organized essay that includes an introduction, fully developed paragraph(s), and a conclusion.

1.   Explain the differences among the four schools of philosophy with regard to the role of the teacher and the role of the student. Answer these two questions for each philosophy (perennialism, progressivism, essentialism, romanticism): What is the role of the teacher? What is the role of the student?

2.   Two of the philosophies discussed were somewhat distorted in popular practice. Dewey's progressivism was sometimes twisted in ways that reduced its real value. Romanticism, on the other hand, was trimmed of some of its ideas regarding isolation from society and made into a greater force for personal growth. Briefly explain the important elements of Dewey's educational philosophy, and note some of the abuses eventually perpetrated in its name. Also explain the educational effects of the romantic emphasis on self-determination and self-definition.

3.   Consider the school in which you now observe. If you are not currently observing in a school, consider your high school. What is the dominant educational philosophy of the school? To answer that question, describe the role of the teacher, the choice of curriculum, and the goals set for the students.

ANSWERS TO MULTIPLE CHOICE QUESTIONS

1. a
2. c
3. d
4. b
5. a
6. b
7. c
8. c
9. d
10. a
11. b
12. d
13. c
14. a
15. c
16. c
17. b
18. b
19. d
20. b
21. a
22. d
23. c
24. b
25. b
26. b
27. a
28. a
29. b
30. d
31. d
32. d
33. d
34. a
35. b

ANSWERS TO SHORT-ANSWER QUESTIONS

1.   *(suggested answer)*

Since romanticists believe that students need to learn individually through experience with their environment, I would ask my students to focus on developing a code of ethics for students in their own high school or, another environment of their choice (their family, church, community, etc.) supported by examples of incidents in their own experience and their own description of their value system.

2.   *(suggested answer)*

Epistemology is the study of knowledge and knowing. It also concerns itself with how we know. Therefore, the curriculum committee will be influenced by epistemology at any time when it wants an explanation or evidence of how children know mathematical concepts. Some selected questions that could occur in the curriculum could include "What constitutes fourth-grade competency in mathematics?" or "How will the students learn subtraction?"

3.   *(suggested answer)*

For the perennialist, reality is found in the collective wisdom of Western culture. Our association with that enables us to discover and confirm the reality and the meaning of our existence. The essentialist, on the other hand, has respect for but not complete adherence to the wisdom of the past. The essentialist is very much influenced by pragmatism. Whatever is relevant and helps an individual survive and prosper is what has meaning. Whatever helps humans improve the condition of humanity is real and meaningful.

4.   *(suggested answer)*

Because teachers are fundamentally associated with education, they should be familiar with different conceptions of knowledge and meaning. Having a clear understanding of philosophy and having their own philosophy of education enable them to work under a coherent system of principles that guides both their goals and their methodology. A clear understanding of philosophy transforms a teacher from being a mere skilled technician to being a professional.

ANSWER TO ESSAY QUESTIONS

1.   *(suggested answer)*

Answers are summarized in Table 8 of the textbook.

2.   *(suggested answer)*

Dewey said that school should be instructive participation in life, not preparation for life, and that school should be a microcosm of democratic society in which students learn the skills of citizenship. Dewey's curriculum was built around the activities and occupations of adult life. Corruptions of Dewey's philosophy hold that content is virtually unimportant, that only process counts. To the romantics in the absence of preexisting relationships with the world, people are independent. Ultimately, educators seized on the romantic focus on self-determination and self-definition. Activities deriving from the human potential movement, such as self-determination and individualized learning are examples of methods that build on the notion of self-creation.

3.   *(suggested answer)*

Answers will vary; however, the answer should match its description of teacher's role, curriculum, and student expectations with one of the educational philosophies presented in the chapter.

CHAPTER 9

What Is the History of American Education?

MULTIPLE CHOICE QUESTIONS

(An additional ten multiple-choice items and two short answer items are available in the sample quiz for this chapter.)

Read each item carefully. Select the letter of the choice that represents the best answer.

1. Since colonial times in this country, formal education of some kind has almost always been available to

    a. middle-class and upperclass white males.
    b. immigrants from various countries.
    c. immigrants from England.
    d. white males and females of any class.

2. How were dame schools organized?

    a. An unmarried woman would travel from village to village conducting lessons in reading, writing, and religion.
    b. A housewife would teach children basic literacy and household skills in her home.
    c. Several women joined to form a cooperative school that taught reading, writing, and arithmetic.
    d. Female teachers taught young women in a boarding school domestic arts, French, music, and art to prepare them for marriage.

3. During the colonial period, which type of formal education was most typical in New England?

    a. Secular public schools attended in large part by one ethnic type
    b. Individual tutors hired to work with one or two families in a home
    c. Private religious schools supported by tuition
    d. Public schools with a religious orientation

4. Why did Massachusetts's colonists pass the Old Deluder Satan Act?

    a. They wanted to eradicate all signs of satanic influence from the colony.
    b. They wanted to ensure that religion would be taught in all schools so that children would not be tempted into doing the devil's work.
    c. They wanted to guarantee the religious education of non-Christians so they would convert to Puritanism.
    d. They wanted to ensure that all children would learn how to read and be able to understand the teachings of the Bible.

5. Which of the following were the predominant forms of elementary schooling in New England during the colonial period?

    a. Private venture schools, dame schools, and religious schools
    b. Private academies, individual tutors, and Quaker schools
    c. Latin schools, dame schools, and individual tutors
    d. Town schools, moving schools, and district schools

6. A child has been born to a Southern plantation family during colonial times. . How would he most likely be educated?

    a. At home with traveling scholars or local ministers
    b. Through a tax-supported community school
    c. Through a small local school run by the Anglican church
    d. In a boarding school in a large Southern town

7. What is the best description of private venture schools?

   a. Schools formed so different ethnic groups could be instilled with American democratic values and learn reading, writing, and arithmetic

   b. Schools designed to provide an elementary education for children within the tenets of their faith

   c. Schools that prepared young men to enter commerce and trade

   d. Small, community-run and financed schools designed to teach reading, writing, vocational skills, and religion

8. What change did the Northwest Ordinances of 1785 and 1787 effect?

   a. The federal government required townships to hire a teacher for the children.

   b. The federal government taxed households to support and sustain public high schools within their district.

   c. The federal government required each township to set aside land for the maintenance of public schools.

   d. The federal government instituted public elementary/secondary schools and agricultural colleges on parcels of tax-supported public land.

9. Which of the following ideas was the basis for the establishment of common schools?

   a. Equal educational access for upperclass men and women

   b. The need for a literate citizenry to maintain a democracy

   c. The need for strong instruction in religion and morals for U.S. youth

   d. The importance of vocational training for those who could not afford further schooling

10. One obstacle for establishing common schools was economic. Which of the following best exemplifies the economic argument against common schools?

    a. The number of teachers needed for the establishment of common schools would cost too much for residents to support.

    b. There appeared to be no feasible, economically viable way to build and maintain the necessary school buildings.

    c. People should be held responsible for paying only for their own children's education, not for the children of others.

    d. Paying for instructional materials and teachers' salaries would unduly burden taxpayers.

11. For parents who enrolled their child in a private venture school, what is the most likely reason they would be opposed to common schools?

    a. The numbers of students would prevent individual attention for their child.

    b. Their child would be required to follow the common academic curriculum given to all students.

    c. Common schools would not provide their child with the necessary background to succeed in a trade.

    d. Their child would not be instructed in the tenets of his or her faith or about his or her own ethnic heritage.

12. For what educational innovation is Friedrich Froebel, a German educator, best known?

    a. Developing the kindergarten

    b. Designing a system by which to teach blind children

    c. Instituting grade levels for students

    d. Writing the curriculum that became the standard high school curriculum

13. Why did many of Johann Pestalozzi's contemporaries scoff at his educational philosophy?

    a. He believed that the teacher should demonstrate respect and affection for each student.

    b. He believed most children learned best through memorization and drill.

    c. He thought the only subjects that should be included in elementary school were art and music.

    d. He contended that the only real learning that occurred happened when students focused on abstract learning.

14. Today, many of Horace Mann's ideas about education are commonly accepted. Which of the following ideas of Mann were considered radical during his day?

    a. That teachers should not hit students; that religious education did not belong in the schools

b.   That religious education belonged in public schools; that teachers should be highly educated

c.   That formal education should focus on practical as well as academic skills; that cooperative learning was highly effective

d.   That schools should admit both sexes; that a core curriculum should be provided for all students

15.   Which of the following best describes Horace Mann's advocacy of common schools?

a.   He thought common schools were the only way to forge national unity.

b.   He thought that common schools would be easier to control and regulate, ensuring some consistency in students' education.

c.   He believed that common schools would provide an education for all, and that was the best means for social mobility.

d.   He thought that common schools would turn out a literate work force, especially important for worker productivity and worker loyalty.

16.   A new school in the early part of the twentieth century builds its curriculum on its students' natural development and natural interests. Teachers act as guides for student discovery, rather than as presenters of information. This school is carrying out the principles of which of the following groups?

a.   National Education Association

b.   Progressive Education Association

c.   Committee of Ten

d.   Association of Middle Schools

17.   Which of the following would be a likely occurrence in a school following the principles of the Progressive Education Association?

a.   Students individually reciting their lessons at the teacher's desk

b.   Students progressing through a highly sequential mathematics curriculum

c.   Students working in ability level groups

d.   Students working in groups to design and produce projects

18.   During the 1700s, if a boy wanted to prepare for college, the best choice of preparation would have been

a.   an English grammar school.

b.   an academy.

c.   a common school.

d.   a Latin grammar school.

19.   It is 1763, and Thomas Smith is attending an English grammar school. What is the primary purpose of Thomas's schooling?

a.   To prepare him for college

b.   To prepare him for the ministry

c.   To teach him the humanities

d.   To prepare him for commerce and trade

20.   A young woman living in the Middle Colonies during the 1700s is attending a secondary school. Given the types of secondary schooling available at that time for women, which of the following schools would she attend?

a.   A Latin grammar school

b.   A private venture school

c.   A public high school

d.   A female academy

21.   During the 1800s, which type of secondary school had a curriculum that included both classical and commercial subjects?

a.   Latin schools

b.   English schools

c.   Academies

d.   Private venture schools

22.   What was the significance of Emma Willard, Mary Lyon, and Catharine Beecher in the history of American education?

    a.   They were the first women to graduate from an academy.
    b.   They started a grassroots movement protesting the exclusion of women from Latin schools.
    c.   They each started a female academy.
    d.   They were the first graduates of a normal school.

23.   What would a young woman expect to learn at a female academy?

    a.   How to be an intelligent companion for her husband or how to be a teacher
    b.   The traditional subjects of a Latin school, including reading, Latin, writing, rhetoric, and mathematics
    c.   The fundamentals of commerce and trade
    d.   How to raise children, along with advanced mathematics, science, philosophy, and languages

24.   Which of the following was the underlying argument for the Kalamazoo case ruling in 1874?

    a.   Public high schools were necessary to ensure employment of the middle class.
    b.   Providing a free elementary education but a secondary education to only those who could afford tuition was inherently unequal.
    c.   Establishing public high schools would foster national unity and loyalty in the same way common schools did.
    d.   Instituting public high schools would allow greater economic opportunity for the working class and the middle class, as well as recent immigrants.

25.   What is the distinction between junior high schools and middle schools?

    a.   Middle schools typically place students in teams where they follow a core academic program whereas junior highs typically track their students on the basis of ability.
    b.   Middle schools usually put more emphasis on the adolescents' emotional and cognitive development and the junior highs emphasize subject content.
    c.   Junior highs typically place greater emphasis on academic and less emphasis on athletic competition than middle schools do.
    d.   Junior highs usually offer a greater and wider range of courses suited to adolescents than middle schools do.

26.   Which of the following is characteristic of a middle school?

    a.   Strong emphasis on competition in sports and academics
    b.   Great emphasis on skills proficiency for students and the consistent use of one teacher for all subjects for students
    c.   Interdisciplinary team teaching and a curriculum that focuses on students' personal development
    d.   Multi-age grouping and highly competitive sports teams

27.   To what degree have instructional practices in high school changed during the last century?

    a.   No change at all
    b.   Relatively little change
    c.   Substantial change
    d.   Dramatic, radical change

28.   Approximately what percentage of the school-age population attends private schools?

    a.   5 percent
    b.   10 percent
    c.   15 percent
    d.   20 percent

29.   Historically, private education has met the needs of various groups of people. Which of the following groups have most often been served by private institutions throughout American education history?

    a.   African-American separatists and Baptists
    b.   Women and Protestants
    c.   The wealthy and Roman Catholics
    d.   Bilingual students and new immigrants

30. When an African American was educated before the Civil War, who typically taught him or her?

    a. A business member or a clergy member
    b. A clergy member or an abolitionist
    c. An abolitionist or a plantation owner
    d. A plantation owner or a Puritan

31. Which of the following was a prevalent reason for educating African Americans before the Civil War?

    a. To stir up slave discontent and to encourage rebellion
    b. To teach African Americans how to be diligent, loyal workers
    c. To convert African Americans to Christianity
    d. To help teach African Americans new trades

32. It is the early 1900s, and a young black man dreams of becoming a success. He doesn't want to just have a skilled job, though. He dreams of an education, of becoming an intellectual leader. He sees advanced education as the way for African Americans to make real progress in a white world. This young man's beliefs are most closely associated with the ideas of

    a. Booker T. Washington.
    b. Horace Mann.
    c. Catharine Beecher.
    d. W. E. B. Du Bois.

33. Booker T. Washington, founder of the Tuskegee Institute, believed that

    a. African Americans should learn practical skills and demonstrate they could be productive members of society.
    b. there must be an intellectually rigorous program for the "talented tenth" who would make up the bulk of African-American leaders.
    c. if African Americans learned the classics, they could ease the tensions between blacks and whites.
    d. the only real hope for African-American advancement was repatriation to Africa.

34. After the Morrill Acts of 1862 and 1890, which of the following would apply to a college in order for it to receive federal money?

    a. If sufficient interest is demonstrated by African Americans in attending an agricultural college, the land-grant college is responsible for establishing it. Otherwise, it is under no legal obligation to provide that kind of facility for African Americans.
    b. The college would be prohibited from discriminating against African Americans unless a separate agriculture college for African Americans existed nearby.
    c. The college would be required to admit certain percentages of each ethnic and racial group that applied.
    d. The college would be prohibited from discrimination of any kind.

35. According to the case of *Plessy* v. *Ferguson* (1896),

    a. separate facilities for minorities were inherently unequal.
    b. separate schools for black students were inherently unequal, but other facilities might be separate.
    c. separate but equal facilities for minorities were constitutionally acceptable.
    d. separate facilities were consistently equal, despite claims to the contrary.

36. According to *Brown* v. *Board of Education of Topeka* (1954),

    a. separate facilities for minorities are inherently unequal and therefore constitutionally unacceptable.
    b. the determination of whether separate facilities for minorities are equal is the right of each state.
    c. separate facilities for minorities may be found to be equal.
    d. separate facilities represent a viable choice for those districts that want to maintain cultural heritage and identity.

37. Although the 1954 Supreme Court decision ended de jure school segregation, de facto segregation continued because of

    a. widespread refusal to obey the law.
    b. federal regulations.

    c.   neighborhood housing patterns.
    d.   unequal distribution of magnet schools.

38. Cross-region busing was an attempt to integrate metropolitan regions in response to

    a.   white flight, in which many white families moved out of urban cities into the metropolitan areas.
    b.   magnet schools, which were built primarily in urban areas.
    c.   federal court orders to desegregate public schools.
    d.   recent waves of immigrants settling in metropolitan areas.

39. Which of the following is true concerning recent developments in desegregation?

    a.   An increasing number of students are being bussed to integrate schools.
    b.   Federal desegregation rulings are intended to continue until students are equally mixed.
    c.   Desegregation efforts must continue until differences in student performance are eliminated.
    d.   Schools are becoming resegregated and some leaders feel that efforts should be shifted to improving the quality of single race neighborhood schools.

40. Which of the following best explains the underlying reason that whites initially wanted to teach Native Americans?

    a.   The whites' goal was for greater social harmony and cultural understanding through educating Native Americans.
    b.   The whites believed that Native Americans would coexist more easily with whites if they knew how to read and write.
    c.   The whites wanted to teach Native Americans how to read and write so they would convert to Christianity.
    d.   The whites saw Native Americans as a potential labor force and wanted to teach them basic literacy so they could be employed.

41. Once the federal government assumed control for Native Americans' education, the government had a particular goal. Which of the following best identifies the goal that the federal government had for Native Americans?

    a.   Maintaining their cultural identity and practices
    b.   Improving upon the basic standard of living for Native Americans
    c.   Aiding Native Americans in their assimilation into white American culture
    d.   Fostering the education of a talented minority who would then become the liaisons between the white American government and the Native American nations

42. During the 1970s, the federal government made changes in the Native American schools. Which of the following were included in those changes?

    a.   Curricular changes, emphasizing a college preparatory course of study rather than vocational skills
    b.   Establishing mentoring programs for Native American high school graduates to work with Native American high school students
    c.   Identifying minimum competencies that Native American students would be expected to achieve before graduation
    d.   Establishment of a Native American advisory committee and adding culturally relevant material to the subjects and skills taught

43. Current public education for Native Americans is threatened by a number of problems. Which of the following are the most direct problems affecting the public education of Native Americans today?

    a.   Crime, violence in schools, and a breakdown in the family structure
    b.   Poverty, absenteeism, and a high dropout rate
    c.   Isolation, loneliness, and lack of respect for teachers
    d.   Lack of cultural cohesion, acting out in schools, and friction between students and teachers

44. Historically, a common stereotype existed that Hispanic-American children were intellectually less capable than Anglo-American children. Which of the following best describes how standardized testing compounded that misconception?

    a.   It demonstrated that Hispanic-American children's Spanish grammar was less logical than Anglo-American children's English grammar.

b. Many standardized tests included advanced cognitive skills that many Hispanic-American children could not perform.

c. The time limit on standardized tests was rigid, not allowing Spanish-speaking children sufficient time to complete the tasks, and their scores suffered.

d. Standardized tests like the I.Q. test were written in a language other than their native language and reflected Anglo middle class values; questions that would be common knowledge for Anglo-American children but unfamiliar to Hispanic-American children.

45. Why is the success of Hispanic students in the public school of particular concern to American schools?

a. Their high school completion rate is lower than whites but higher than blacks.
b. They are economically and politically powerful.
c. There will not be enough low skilled jobs.
d. They are the fastest growing segment of the U.S. population and their success has consequences for society.

46. Which of the following is not typically characteristic of Asian American community involvement in education?

a. Industriousness
b. A sense of honor for students' work
c. Attention at home to the academic work of the child
d. The assertive, visible participation of the parents in the child's school

47. What is a disadvantage for Asian Americans in being perceived as the "model minority"?

a. No agencies are willing to assist in housing or education because they believe that Asian Americans can succeed or their own.
b. It minimizes the needs Asian Americans have for English language instruction and multicultural education.
c. It may become more difficult for them to blend in with other groups.
d. They may assimilate too quickly into the mainstream culture, quickly losing their cultural identity.

SHORT-ANSWER QUESTIONS

Respond to each of the following questions briefly, but specifically, in complete sentences.

1. Identify and explain two of the characteristics of middle schools. Why are these particular characteristics considered important in middle school education?

2. Explain the difference between universal education and comprehensive education in the history of American education.

3. What role did the academies play in American education?

4. The 1896 *Plessy* v. *Ferguson* decision was overturned by *Brown* v. *Board of Education* in 1954. The effects of the *Brown* decision were far-reaching, although much work remains to be done in establishing equality of educational opportunity. Explain the basic nature of each decision, and tell how the *Brown* decision affected U.S. education.

ESSAY QUESTIONS

Read each of the following questions, and respond by composing an organized essay that includes an introduction, fully developed paragraph(s), and a conclusion.

1. Education in New England, the Middle Colonies, and the South took three different forms. Each form of education reflected the beliefs and the social organization of the area in which it predominated. Describe the differences among the predominant forms of education in each of these three areas. Explain the features of community life that seemed to influence education to develop as it did in each area.

2. Some would argue that the history of American education has been the history of education for the middle-class to upperclass white male. Identify three significant changes in the history of American education that expanded educational opportunities for others. Explain the impact that each of these changes had upon the education of Americans.

3. In the beginning of the chapter, the authors identified six major forces in American educational history: local control, universal education, public education, comprehensive education, secular education, and the changing ideas of the basics. Many of the contemporary educational problems or issues emanate from these forces. Select two contemporary education issues or problems, and briefly explain them. Then describe how each one is associated with one of the major forces of American education.

ANSWERS TO MULTIPLE CHOICE QUESTIONS

1. a
2. b
3. d
4. d
5. d
6. a
7. b
8. c
9. b
10. c
11. d
12. a
13. a
14. a
15. c
16. b
17. d
18. d
19. d
20. b
21. c
22. c
23. a
24. b
25. b
26. c
27. b
28. b
29. c
30. b
31. c
32. d
33. a
34. b

35. c

36. a

37. c

38. c

39. d

40. c

41. c

42. d

43. b

44. d

45. d

46. d

47. b

ANSWERS TO SHORT-ANSWER QUESTIONS

1. *(suggested answer)*

    Answers will vary. A correct answer will identify two of the following characteristics and explain how each one supports the middle school philosophy of dealing with adolescents' particular emotional and developmental needs. The following are the characteristics of a middle school: 1) interdisciplinary team organization; 2) long-term teacher-student relationships, including advisory homerooms; 3) block scheduling; 4) exploratory activities and courses.

2. *(suggested answer)*

    Universal education is the concept that all people have a right to be educated. Early in American history, only upperclass white males were educated.

    Gradually, during the 1800s, the common school was instituted, in which white children of town residents could obtain a grammar school education. During different stages of American history, universal education became more inclusive of groups of people previously excluded: women, African Americans, Native Americans, and the disabled. A comprehensive education is an education that includes both the traditional curriculum for college preparation and training for trades. The need for comprehensive education was first seen during the nineteenth century, and the comprehensive high school was founded to address the needs of students requiring job training and college preparatory studies.

3. *(suggested answer)*

    Some would call the academies the precursors of the comprehensive high school. Through the 1700s, Latin grammar schools were run to teach young men the classical subjects that they would need to continue their education in college. English grammar schools focused on more practical skills and subjects, preparing their students to work in commerce and trade. Academies sprang up during the second half of the eighteenth century. They combined elements of the Latin and English grammar school. The instruction was conducted in English, not Latin, but classical subjects were also offered in the curriculum. Gradually, as academies grew, they began to emphasize a college preparatory curriculum but held to the ideal of a utilitarian curriculum.

4. *(suggested answer)*

    Plessy v. *Ferguson* said that operating separate facilities for members of different ethnic groups was not inherently unconstitutional as long as the facilities were equal. The Brown decision said that separate facilities could not help being unequal and that operating separate school systems for black students ensured their unequal treatment for a variety of reasons. As a result of Brown, school districts all over the country were obliged to come up with plans to desegregate school populations and to demonstrate equality of treatment. A common strategy was to bus black students to white schools. The problem of ensuring equality of educational opportunity has not yet been solved.

ANSWERS TO ESSAY QUESTIONS

1.   *(suggested answer)*

New England: Settled by Puritans who lived in compact communities and believed that everyone should be able to read and interpret the Bible. The Puritans first had town schools, one in each town of fifty families or more, then moving schools, which went to remote farmlands. District schools were finally established in each township. Schools were funded by the town treasury and included moral instruction according to Puritan ideas because in terms of religion the population was fairly homogeneous. Middle Colonies: Settled by a variety of religious and ethnic groups, each of which valued separate education. Promoted private venture schools licensed by civil government but funded by parents, not by taxes. Religious training was offered, but differed among schools, according to the religion of those sponsoring each school. South: Settled by Anglican Englishmen of the upper class who established large plantations and settlements quite distant from each other. They did not believe in a religious imperative to learn to read. Southerners hired tutors to educate children. Schools might be established by government authority, but run by a corporation that collected tuition and administered the school.

2.   *(suggested answer)*

Answers will vary. However, some of the changes that may be included are the advent of the common schools and the public high schools; the opening of female academies; the Kalamazoo case; the Morrill Acts; *Brown* v. *Board of Education*; the inclusion of Native Americans within public education; the beginning of bilingual education and special education; and the education of the gifted and disadvantaged.

3.   *(suggested answer)*

Answers will vary. The answers should show an identification of an issue and a clear link with one of the educational forces. An example might be the current debate on school choice and its tie to public education and/or secular education. Another example might be technology education and its link to the changing ideas of the basics.

CHAPTER 10

How Are Schools Governed, Influenced, and Financed?

MULTIPLE CHOICE QUESTIONS

(An additional ten multiple-choice items and two short answer items are available in the sample quiz for this chapter.)

Read each item carefully. Select the letter of the choice that represents the best answer.

1. What effect did the Tenth Amendment to the U.S. Constitution have upon public education?

   a. The state department of education was established.
   b. Legal responsibility for school governance was delegated to the states.
   c. Responsibility for the majority of funding for public education was assumed by the federal government.
   d. Equal educational opportunity was guaranteed for all.

2. Which of these bodies makes law and is considered the most influential in setting up educational policy?

   a. State legislature
   b. State department of education
   c. State board of education
   d. Local school board

3. The state of Illinois wants to establish a policy regarding its public education in the twenty-first century. Illinois wants to create a broad-based policy outlining its priorities and establishing its goals for the state's students. Which agency would issue this policy?

   a. The state department of education
   b. The federal Department of Education
   c. The local school boards
   d. The state board of education

4. Overseeing the administration of teacher licensure requirements, organizing programs of study, supervising elementary and secondary education program assessment, and applying school finance laws are all tasks of

   a. the chief state school officer.
   b. the state department of education.
   c. the federal Department of Education.
   d. the school principal.

5. The agency that administers and distributes state and federal funds, certifies or licenses teachers, and accredits professional training programs is the

   a. state department of education.
   b. state board of education.
   c. office of the state superintendent.
   d. local school board.

6. Heidi Pfluger is interviewing for a teaching position in the Florham Park school system. According to school management and organization, which of the following is the formal hiring authority?

   a. Building principal

b.   Assistant superintendent of instruction
c.   Local school board
d.   School superintendent

7.   The typical holder of this position is white, male, college-educated, and has a managerial or professional job unrelated to the position. The position is

a.   state superintendent.
b.   school principal.
c.   local school board member.
d.   state department curriculum specialist.

8.   Which of the following people is most representative of the typical school board member?

a.   Loretta Padovani, a white, 68-year-old retired bookkeeper with grandchildren in the public schools
b.   Carla Wilson, African American, 40 years old, with a master's degree in nursing, is a nurse practitioner at a large hospital
c.   John Baster, white, 51 years old, who has an M.B.A. and is an executive at a computer software company
d.   Joe Eichler, white, 44 years old, a high school graduate who works in a tool and die factory

9.   Brian Bomberger spends part of his work time interviewing and promoting personnel. He ensures that there are adequate funds to run school facilities through his planning and administration of the budget, and he also is responsible for administering curriculum and instruction. What is Brian's occupation?

a.   Chief state school officer
b.   Curriculum coordinator
c.   Chairman of the board of education
d.   District superintendent

10.   Susan Breiner has just completed interviewing two prospective faculty members, has sent in a large teaching supply order, has proofread the new school discipline policy written by a team of teachers, and has reviewed the school budget for the next academic year. Based upon those activities, what is Susan?

a.   Department chairperson
b.   Superintendent of schools
c.   Assistant superintendent of personnel
d.   School principal

11.   During recent presidential elections, hundreds of thousands of educators have been mobilized to support a particular party platform and the candidate endorsed by that party. Which organization has been instrumental in influencing the educators to support a particular candidate?

a.   National Association of School Boards
b.   National Education Association
c.   Association of Teacher Educators
d.   National Parent Teacher Association

12.   Mary Ellen DuPree, a teacher at Belleville High School, also volunteers as the drama coach. The school musical selected this year, *Little Shop of Horrors,* has generated widespread student involvement; however, because of the tight school budget Mary Ellen has not been able to get the necessary costumes or props for the show. Which of the following would be the most likely or most able to provide her with the help she needs for the school play?

a.   District superintendent
b.   Assistant superintendent for curriculum and instruction
c.   Parent-teacher organization
d.   Local school board

13.   Which of the following most typically describes the relationship between a superintendent of schools and the local school board?

a.   Both have educational training and they argue over policy.

b.   The board makes policy without advice from the superintendent.
c.   The superintendent makes policy and the board carries it out.
d.   While the superintendent is the employee of the board, he/she also serves as the professionally trained consultant.

14.   Bill Hickey is an employee of the Middleburg school district, and John Morgan is associated with that district as well. At meetings, Bill frequently has to push to get new school programs approved or to hire particular personnel whereas John frequently derails Bill's proposals, looking to cut costs or to recommend his own candidate for employment. Which of the following most likely describes their positions?

a.   Bill is a teacher, and John is the department chairperson.
b.   Bill is the assistant superintendent of instruction, and John is a building principal.
c.   Bill is the superintendent of schools, and John is the chair of the school board.
d.   Bill is the assistant superintendent of instruction, and John is the assistant superintendent of personnel.

15.   Which of the following most aptly characterizes the historical stance that business has had toward public education?

a.   Business was and still is interested in educational efficiency, standardization, and productivity.
b.   Business was interested in standardization and regulation; now, it is almost exclusively concerned with commercialization of education.
c.   Business was more concerned with efficiency and quantitative evaluation; now, it is much more concerned with authentic evaluation and student satisfaction.
d.   Business used to be exclusively concerned with productivity; now, business is exclusively concerned with educational expenditures, seeking to lower costs.

16.   Corporations have been increasingly involved in local school programs. Which of the following best characterizes the reason for this development?

a.   A corporation needs workers who are competent in basic skills.
b.   A corporation needs the opportunity to practice training programs.
c.   A corporation believes it owes a debt to the community that supports it.
d.   A corporation can collect state school funds for participating in education.

17.   A local business needs more trainees who are highly proficient in math and language skills. In keeping with the current trend, the business addresses this problem by

a.   relocating the business to an area where there are more qualified workers.
b.   eliminating positions that require these advanced skills.
c.   extending its recruitment to a wider area.
d.   working with the local high school to improve the school's basic skills program.

18.   One problem in using statewide standardized tests to measure a school's effectiveness is that

a.   too many students may pass the minimum basic competencies.
b.   the typical standardized test is limited in what it can measure.
c.   such tests are cost prohibitive to administer and grade.
d.   numerous school districts have had problems with widespread cheating and test score alteration.

19.   Which is an accurate statement of the proportion of contribution to a public school district from the federal, state, and local governments?

a.   The federal government provides most of the school district's funds. The state provides the next largest amount, with the local district supplying the least amount of money for the public school district.
b.   The state and local governments generally provide almost equal amounts to run the public schools, with the federal government's support a distant third.
c.   The state government provides the most amount of money, the federal government closely follows with its support, and the local government is a distant third.
d.   The local, state, and federal governments contribute equal amounts to the funds for the public school district.

20. The percentage of a district's education budget that is contributed by federal, state, and local agencies varies from state to state. Which of the following represents a typical distribution of funding sources?

    a.   Federal, 2 percent; state, 61 percent; local, 37 percent
    b.   Federal, 7 percent; state, 46 percent; local, 47 percent.
    c.   Federal, 15 percent; state, 33 percent; local, 52 percent
    d.   Federal, 32 percent; state, 46 percent; local, 22 percent

21. Local districts rely primarily on property taxes to fund schools. Which revenue is most commonly used by the state for support of education?

    a.   "Sin" taxes from cigarettes and alcohol
    b.   Property taxes
    c.   Sales and income taxes
    d.   Vehicle taxes

22. Wichita Falls is a small city containing several retail malls, several corporations, and numerous neighborhoods. Assuming that Wichita Falls is a typical school district, which of the following is its primary source of funds for public education?

    a.   Property taxes
    b.   Sales taxes
    c.   Corporate taxes
    d.   Income taxes

23. In the *Serrano* v. *Priest* and *Serrano II* decisions, the Supreme Court of California determined that according to the laws of the state, the quality of a child's education must reflect the wealth of the

    a.   local school district.
    b.   child's family.
    c.   state, based on the provisions of its constitution.
    d.   nation, because the Constitution guarantees equality.

24. How has federal funding for education changed from the 1980s through the 1990s?

    a.   Funding has increased and has been issued almost exclusively in categorical aid.
    b.   Funding has remained about the same, shifting from categorical aid to block grants.
    c.   Funding has increased, shifting from block grants to categorical aid.
    d.   Funding has decreased and has emphasized categorical aid.

25. The national average per-pupil expenditure from all sources in 2001-2002 was closest to

    a. $5,600.
    b. $6,900.
    c. $7,500.
    d. $8,300.

26. Which of the following statements about year-round schools is accurate?

    a.   Year-round schooling increases achievement.
    b.   The main benefit is enrichment and remedial activities during breaks.
    c.   Year-round schools increase overall spending in the district.
    d.   In districts where it has been tried, students, teachers, and parents now support it.

27. All of the following have been documented as advantages of privatization *except*

    a.   more individualized instruction.
    b.   greater access to computers.
    c.   cleaner buildings.
    d.   academic improvement.

28. Compensatory education was designed to overcome learning deficiencies in students who

    a.   do not speak English as a first language.

b.   are from a disadvantaged socioeconomic background.
c.   have developmentally delayed speech.
d.   are not very smart.

29.   Critics have charged that compensatory education programs are ineffective because students served by the programs

a.   have not shown improved IQ and achievement scores.
b.   are still placed in special education classes with the same frequency as before the program.
c.   take longer than originally planned to move out of their bilingual classrooms and into English-speaking classes.
d.   drop out at the same rate before high school graduation.

30.   Compensatory education is primarily aimed at

a.   all underachieving kindergartners.
b.   economically disadvantaged students.
.c   most academically deficient middle school students and disadvantaged high school students.
d.   female students who have been victims of sexual discrimination.

31.   Which of the following is *not* a requirement of the "No Child Left Behind" Act of 2002?

a.   Annual testing must be done in reading and math.
b.   Each state must raise the level of proficiency leading to 100% proficient.
c.   Beginning in 2002, all teachers hired must be "highly qualified."
d.   Schools must increase per-pupil funding.

SHORT-ANSWER QUESTIONS

Respond to each of the following questions briefly, but specifically, in complete sentences.

1.   Why might one say that the school district superintendent's job is precarious? What are the potential difficulties in the position?

2.   Why are the demographics of a typical school board member important? What are the implications of those demographics to the running of public schools?

3.   Many would argue that a principal is the single most important person for ensuring the success of a particular school. Explain how this could be true.

4.   Oakdell is a town with a sizable portion of its residents living on fixed incomes. Explain why Oakdell potentially could have difficulty passing school budgets from year to year.

ESSAY QUESTIONS

Read each of the following questions, and respond by composing an organized essay that includes an introduction, fully developed paragraph(s), and a conclusion.

1.   Assess the involvement of the corporate world in public education. Is greater business involvement in public education a benefit, a disadvantage, or a mixed benefit to public education? Explain.

2.   Define and explain the relationships among the state legislature, state board of education, the state superintendent, and the state department of education.

3.   Explain the relative contributions of the federal, state, and local communities to schools, and tell how state and local funds are raised. Describe the implications of the *Serrano* decision for equity of educational opportunity.

ANSWERS TO MULTIPLE CHOICE QUESTIONS

1.   b

2.   a

3. d
4. a
5. a
6. c
7. c
8. c
9. d
10. d
11. b
12. c
13. d
14. c
15. a
16. a
17. d
18. b
19. b
20. b
21. c
22. a
23. c
24. b
25. c
26. d
27. d
28. b
29. a
30. b
31. d

ANSWERS TO SHORT-ANSWER QUESTIONS

1. *(suggested answer)*

    Since the superintendent does not have tenure, he or she may lose his or her position at any time that he or she loses the confidence of the school board. In addition to having the knowledge, experience, and expertise required for running a district's schools, the superintendent must have finely polished interpersonal skills. Much of his or her time will be spent either in conflict resolution between groups who have competing claims, or in diplomatically trying to answer demands that may be very difficult or impossible. He or she must also possess strong leadership to direct the schools forward, without getting mired in the politics that frequently engulf school systems.

2. *(suggested answer)*

The typical school board member is a white, middle-aged, college-educated male who is working in a managerial or professional position and who is middle class or upper middle class. The demographics are important because if the overwhelming number of school members fit this profile, then the particular interests associated with this demographic group may be better attended to than other interests. For example, the school boards may pay greater attention to college preparatory education than to vocational education; they may adopt a favorable attitude toward greater business involvement in the public schools; they may emphasize the values of the dominant middle class. Such representation may not be problematic; however, it is important to recognize that if any particular demographic group is overwhelmingly represented on school boards, the concerns of that group usually take precedence over others' concerns.

3.   *(suggested answer)*

Principals are responsible for management, supervision, and inspection of the school and its operation.

4.   *(suggested answer)*

Because public schools are funded in large part from local property taxes, a community with large numbers of residents on fixed incomes may resist any increase in the school budgets from year to year because they feel they are not able to afford increases in their property taxes.

ANSWERS TO ESSAY QUESTIONS

1.   Answers will vary, but they should give logical, well-supported reasons and clear examples.

2.   *(suggested answer)*

The state legislature enacts laws that govern the work and goals of the other entities. The state board of education is the chief educational policy-making agency in the state. Its chief executive officer is the state superintendent, who carries out its directives through the work of the state department of education. The state department oversees operations, assessment, provides technical assistance, and certifies/licenses teachers.

3.   *(suggested answer)*

The federal government provides the least amount, about 7 percent of the total budget on average. On average, the state and local communities each now contribute about half of the remainder. States raise money by income and corporate taxes, excise taxes, and lotteries. Local governments usually raise funds by means of a property tax. *Serrano* resulted in some states' reapportioning funds to various districts to equalize per-pupil expenditures. If a state has an "equal protection" clause in its constitution, the amount spent on each pupil in the state must be roughly the same, reflecting the state's wealth, not the local community's. Not every state is affected by *Serrano* because not every state has an "equal protection" clause that includes education.

CHAPTER 11

How Should Education Be Reformed?

MULTIPLE CHOICE QUESTIONS

(An additional ten multiple-choice items and two short answer items are available in the sample quiz for this chapter.)

Read each item carefully. Select the letter of the choice that represents the best answer.

1. A major reason that it is difficult to implement educational reforms and achieve the desired effects is

    a. they take so much financial support and taxpayers are unwilling to raise budgets.
    b. American education is a giant institution with standard operating procedures that set certain expectations.
    c. teachers are set in their ways, and they refuse to change unless they can make all the decisions.
    d. no one gives the changes enough time to take effect before they start assessing their success or failure.

2. The long-term goals that undergird school reform are threefold:

    a. develop academic excellence, world dominance, and social graces.
    b. nurture self-esteem, confidence, and a positive outlook on life.
    c. develop the good worker, educate the people, and increase productivity.
    d. develop the democratic citizen, the good worker, and the good person.

3. Which of the following was *not* listed as a key element of true school reform as defined by Ryan and Cooper?

    a. Active learning
    b. Lifelong learning
    c. A sense of community
    d. School choice

4. The "call to excellence" movement places high expectations on both students and teachers. The focus of this movement is to

    a. set higher standards for both students and teachers.
    b. set high standards and *earn* self-esteem by achieving them.
    c. help students succeed on standardized tests and in life.
    d. individualize education and build self-esteem.

5. In a constructivist approach to learning, learners

    a. actively make their own meaning from new knowledge.
    b. learn new facts and knowledge without questioning them.
    c. question all new information.
    d. believe that there are no universal truths; all truths are relative.

6. Mildred teaches a fifth-grade class in which she applies a constructivist approach to learning. What would Mildred's classroom probably look like?

    a. Students sit quietly in their seats and work independently on worksheets.
    b. Mildred does a lot of whole-class instruction, presenting lecture-type lessons.
    c. Students make frequent use of library resources to prepare written reports on various topics in social studies and science.
    d. Students work on projects in small groups or independently. There are a lot of "hands-on" activities.

7. Authentic assessment grew out of a concern that

   a.   student performance was declining on standardized tests.
   b.   the emphasis on standardized test scores caused a narrow emphasis of lower-order thinking skills.
   c.   multiple-choice tests were too difficult for the majority of students.
   d.   students were focusing on critical-thinking skills and not performing well on competency tests.

8. Portfolio assessment allows the teacher to determine a student's progress toward certain learning goals or standards. Still, concerns about authentic assessment remain, in particular

   a.   the feasibility of quantifying scores from authentic assessments.
   b.   the reliability and validity of the assessments from site to site and evaluator to evaluator.
   c.   the ability of the students to complete the portfolio on time.
   d.   the interest of teachers in authentic assessment.

9. Smaller schools are a recommended component of school reform because they

   a.   are less expensive to operate.
   b.   require a smaller administrative staff and less cost.
   c.   allow for a greater sense of community within the school.
   d.   make it easier to keep track of books and supplies.

10. Reformers criticize large schools and fault them with being partly responsible for the decline in academic achievement because they

   a.   foster poor discipline and classroom management problems for new teachers.
   b.   are so costly to run that money cannot be spent on updating books and school supplies.
   c.   cause students to be constantly late for class because of the distance between classrooms.
   d.   create an aura of impersonality in which students feel lost, disengaged, and unmotivated.

11. Ryan and Cooper contend that the New Basics, a set of academic learning skills, ought to be a major component of school reform because these skills

   a.   can train students' thinking to make them more efficient learners.
   b.   provide job training to make high school students more marketable.
   c.   keep students from mixing up facts.
   d.   help students do better on standardized tests.

12. Character educators would like to redefine a "good" student as being one who

   a.   has a good sense of right and wrong.
   b.   excels in a particular sport.
   c.   gets good grades in school.
   d.   is considered a "good kid" by his or her teachers.

13. Joshua is a high school history teacher who believes that his role as teacher extends to teaching his ninth-grade students certain core values, such as honesty, justice, kindness, and respect. Which of the following would most likely be found in Joshua's classroom?

   a.   A multiple-choice test on important events in World War II
   b.   A geography unit identifying the locations of all the major battles of World War II
   c.   A fine arts unit in which students develop appreciation for the music and dance of the United States in the 1940s
   d.   A discussion of the responsibilities of the United States toward Europe in the early 1940s

14. Although much debate revolves around whether schools should teach values, and if so which values, character educators maintain that students

   a.   have a moral "Teflon coating" and absorb little teaching of values.
   b.   are constantly and unavoidably learning values from their teachers, so it would be beneficial to formalize this instruction in the curriculum.
   c.   practice good moral behavior already and have little need for character education.
   d.   have such a narrow focus on academics that they block out any other instruction.

15.   A second approach to character education is service learning, in which students participate in a service activity. The goal of service learning is

    a.   to teach students the core values of honesty, respect, and kindness.
    b.   to instill in students a work ethic.
    c.   to give students the opportunity to practice the core values that they have been taught.
    d.   to provide students with work experience in an ethically good environment.

16.   *A Nation at Risk* was published in 1983 and declared that due to the quality of education being offered, the United States was

    a.   in peril of being attacked by hostile nations in the near future.
    b.   in serious peril of losing the state of California.
    c.   losing its economic and military competitiveness in the world market.
    d.   facing serious and significant problems in the major urban areas.

17.   The Education Summit of 1989 was one of the most visible efforts to bring about education reform at a national level. The summit ended with

    a.   a commitment by the governors present to work toward meeting the six established goals by the year 2000.
    b.   a commitment by the governors present to remain in office until the year 2000 in order to bring about change in the educational system of their respective states.
    c.   an ambiguous statement from the governors present, indicating an absence of consensus on educational reform.
    d.   disagreement over what needs to be done to reform the educational system of the United States.

18.   A number of national curriculum reform efforts have come from

    a.   the federal government.
    b.   elementary school teachers.
    c.   national associations representing specific academic areas.
    d.   national curriculums in other countries around the world.

19.   State reform efforts, focusing on the call to excellence, share a number of common elements, which include

    a.   more students to graduate, more time in school, and more money in education budgets.
    b.   better test results for students and teachers, and more graduates.
    c.   more time in school, increased graduation requirements, and higher standards and salaries.
    d.   more homework, career ladders for teachers, and higher standards.

20.   Many state reform efforts have tried to improve the quality of instruction in the schools. A frequently heard proposal calls for a career ladder in teaching that would

    a.   allow the more experienced teachers to teach in the better classrooms.
    b.   extend the salary schedule for teachers to an unlimited number of steps.
    c.   make it easier for teachers to assume administrative positions in the same schools.
    d.   recognize expert teachers with rewards, while allowing them to remain in the classroom.

21.   One residual of the state reform efforts has been

    a.   a loss of local authority and autonomy as more and more funding for reform comes from the state.
    b.   an increase in the number of teachers teaching at the elementary level.
    c.   more teachers leaving the teaching profession.
    d.   greater recognition of the strengths and weaknesses of teacher education programs.

22.   The limited involvement of teachers in state reform efforts would indicate that most of the reforms have been

    a.   unsupported by the rank and file.
    b.   ineffective.
    c.   top-down.
    d.   bottom-up.

23. The Kentucky Education Reform Act is notable because it

    a. has state-mandated testing in grades 4, 8, and 12, which determines school funding.
    b. was one of the first states to shift the power controlling what is taught from the local to the state level.
    c. was declared unconstitutional by the U.S. Supreme Court.
    d. was initiated by the state legislature without economic funding to support the changes.

24. Any successful reform of education will require

    a. the approval of Congress.
    b. funding from the federal government.
    c. the active participation of the teachers involved.
    d. the creation of a new body to oversee the changes.

25. What is a possible explanation for the disappointing findings of the relationship between smaller class sizes and level of achievement?

    a. When class sizes are smaller, teachers and students relax more and don't accomplish as much.
    b. The class size and increased achievement theory was invented by the teacher associations to make the job easier.
    c. Students need to learn from each other and reducing this opportunity by having fewer students in a class affects their achievement.
    d. When class sizes are reduced on any large scale, it creates a shortage of teachers and more less experienced, emergency, and first-time teachers are hired.

26. According to the text, one of the keys to accomplishing educational reform is

    a. longer school years.
    b. staff development.
    c. significantly increased educational budgets.
    d. smaller class sizes.

27. One of the reasons why current staff development is not as effective as it could be is

    a. the activities teachers choose to participate in are so broad and not focused on specific goals.
    b. there is no financial incentive for the teachers to participate.
    c. teachers have not been required to participate in continuing education.
    d. teachers were not required to obtain advanced degrees.

28. According to Michael Fullam, which of the following is *not* a characteristic attitude of teachers who are seeking to improve?

    a. They accept that it is possible to improve.
    b. They are ready to be self-critical.
    c. They are motivated by extrinsic rewards for their learning.
    d. They are willing to learn what has to be learned.

29. In California's effort to reform public education all of the following are being tried *except*

    a. reducing the use of social promotion.
    b. merit pay for teachers with the highest performing classes.
    c. smaller class sizes.
    d. special staff help and money for poorly performing schools.

SHORT-ANSWER QUESTIONS

Respond to each of the following questions briefly, but specifically, in complete sentences.

1. Explain why the New Basics are seen as a way of improving the schools.

2. Describe the "three people" representing the goals for reform that should be kept in mind as a focus when educational reforms are being planned and implemented. Include examples of the motivations each of these three provide for reform.

3.   Explain what is meant by a constructivist approach to learning and why this approach is seen as part of educational reform.

ESSAY QUESTIONS

Read each of the following questions, and respond by composing an organized essay that includes an introduction, fully developed paragraph(s), and a conclusion.

1.   Which one of the seven key elements of reform described in the text do you think is the most important and will lead to the greatest improvement?

2.   One of the most frequently debated components of educational reform is character education. The debate revolves around two important questions. Identify these two questions and present the opposing positions on each question.

ANSWERS TO MULTIPLE CHOICE QUESTIONS

1.   b
2.   d
3.   d
4.   b
5.   a
6.   d
7.   b
8.   b
9.   c
10.   d
11.   a
12.   a
13.   d
14.   b
15.   c
16.   c
17.   a
18.   c
19.   c
20.   d
21.   a
22.   c
23.   b
24.   c
25.   d
26.   b
27.   a

28. c

29. b

ANSWERS TO SHORT-ANSWER QUESTIONS

1.   *(suggested answer)*

The New Basics are a variety of skills that can make the brain a more efficient tool by improving memory strategies. These skills include note taking, study reading, test preparation, researching, systematic problem solving, creating thinking, and goal setting. Proponents of the New Basics believe that these skills can help learners access more knowledge more easily, an essential ability in most, if not all, work situations.

2.   *(suggested answer)*

Democratic Citizen

      differences in education of the poor and the rich need to be eliminated

      students need to know how democracy works

      need for understanding of global role

Good Worker

      need to maintain economic leadership

      rapidly changing work skills

Good Person

      children need to develop a moral compass

      students need to accept their responsibility for education

3.   *(suggested answer)*

A constructivist approach to learning recognizes that humans are meaning makers. Constructivists maintain that learners do not simply take in new knowledge and information, but that they actively construct it, using their prior knowledge and experiences to make sense of the new knowledge. In this way, learners take responsibility for their own learning since they are making meaning for themselves. A constructivist classroom encourages experiential learning. This is seen as part of reform because this active method of learning has not been used much in our traditional approach to teaching and learning.

ANSWERS TO ESSAY QUESTIONS

1.   *(suggested answer)*

The elements are high standards, active learning (constructivism), accountability, sense of community, lifelong learning, character education, and professional development. Answers will vary significantly but students must provide their rationale for their choice.

2.   *(suggested answer)*

The first question deals with whether or not the school as an institution is an appropriate venue for character education. Opponents argue that character education is primarily the responsibility of the family and of religious institutions, not the school. Supporters insist that, historically, the schools always had a moral component that was lost sometime in the 1960s. They agree that the family should be the primary moral educator but too frequently is abandoning that role, leaving many children in a moral and ethical vacuum. Therefore, the schools must reclaim their moral responsibility to educate the whole child.

The second question revolves around what values to teach if values are indeed taught in school. Opponents maintain that values are culturally and religiously based, and teaching values in school would necessarily mean teaching values particular to a certain religion to the detriment of others. Supporters argue that there is a core of civic values, such as honesty, respect, tolerance, kindness, and justice that are common to all cultures and religions.

CHAPTER 12

What Are Your Job Options in Education?

MULTIPLE CHOICE QUESTIONS

(An additional ten multiple-choice items and two short answer items are available in the sample quiz for this chapter.)

Read each item carefully. Select the letter of the choice that represents the best answer.

1. A recent college graduate targets a particular district for his job search because he knows a number of teachers are retiring and the student enrollment is increasing. What other information should he look at that could impact on his being hired?

    a.   The number of alternative-route certificate teaching candidates in the area
    b.   The pupil-teacher ratio in the schools
    c.   The educational level attained by most teachers in the district
    d.   The strength of the local school budget and the local economy

2. The increase in teaching positions expected over the next ten years is due in part to

    a.   decreasing student enrollments.
    b.   increasing student enrollments.
    c.   decreasing teacher retirements.
    d.   increasing federal funding.

3. Chantal has just started college and is interested in pursuing a career in teaching. Her advisor tells her that she shouldn't have any trouble getting a job when she graduates. Why does her advisor think this?

    a.   Municipal funding for education is expected to increase 15 percent in the next ten years.
    b.   There is a shortage of teachers in every area and community.
    c.   Half of the nation's teachers are expected to retire in this decade.
    d.   The student-teacher ratio will decrease to 15 to 1.

4. Minority teachers serve as positive role models for both minority and white students because

    a.   minority students develop self-esteem and white students break stereotyping and racism.
    b.   white students develop self-confidence and minority students achieve better results.
    c.   both minority and white students perform better academically.
    d.   minority students break stereotyping and teach white students minority culture.

5. The shortage of minority teachers is problematic because

    a.   there are many minorities in urban areas.
    b.   many minority students have no positive minority role models.
    c.   too many white students do not have positive white role models.
    d.   minority teachers represent a disproportionately large percentage of the teaching population.

6. Which of the following has contributed to the decline in the number of minority teachers?

    a.   Wider recruitment of minorities in other professions and the increased use of competency testing for teachers
    b.   The decline of minority students enrolled in education because of the anticipated teaching surplus in the 1990s
    c.   The lack of respect and worth given to teachers and the increased use of alternative licensure in hiring teachers

d.   The refusal of many school systems to recognize alternative licenses of teachers

7.   Which of the following is *not* a suggested strategy for brining more minorities into teaching?

a.   Creating minority magnet schools
b.   Higher teaching salaries
c.   More valued status for teachers
d.   Assistance programs for competency tests

8.   LaMar, an African American, is majoring in English at a state college. He took an education course and really enjoyed the experience and so is thinking about a teaching career after college. What are LaMar's chances of getting a teaching job when he graduates?

a.   Good. The call for excellence recommends smaller class sizes, so more teachers will probably be hired.
b.   Mediocre. The teaching job market does not look very promising over the next ten years.
c.   Weak. There is a surplus of English teachers in most parts of the country.
d.   Excellent. Minority teachers are needed in every subject area and geographical location.

9.   After ten years of working in journalism, Ellen decided to pursue a teaching career. She received her teaching license through the alternative licensing program and is currently seeking a teaching position. She has a degree in English and would like to teach middle school English in a rural school district. Which of the following will work most in her favor as she searches for a job?

a.   Her willingness to teach in a rural community
b.   Her status as an alternative-route teaching candidate
c.   Her experience working in journalism
d.   Her interest in teaching in a middle school

10.   It is helpful to verify published reports on teacher supply and demand with your own research on local conditions because

a.   projections are based on information that changes unpredictably.
b.   published reports are inherently unreliable.
c.   local communities sometimes exaggerate the facts in publications to make their community appear more desirable.
d.   many communities are ignored in the broadly based statistical surveys.

11.   Nancy White and David Tepper were both hired as recent college graduates by the same school district in 1992. After ten years of teaching, Nancy's salary is considerably more than David's. Which of the following most likely explains this salary difference?

a.   Nancy has advised the AFS club and debate team over the course of her tenure.
b.   Nancy has been awarded merit pay increases for her outstanding teaching.
c.   Nancy has earned a master's degree in her field.
d.   Nancy teaches high school whereas David teaches elementary.

12.   Most public school teachers' salaries are still based on level of education and

a.   grade level or academic subject taught.
b.   additional coaching or advising activities.
c.   recommendations and evaluations of administrators.
d.   years of teaching experience.

13.   One of the common errors in searching for a teaching position is

a.   portfolios that are overwhelming.
b.   individualized cover letters.
c.   a passive attitude and lack of follow through.
d.   applying for too many positions.

14.   Ryan and Cooper suggest that an effective way of preparing for a job interview is to

a.   do stress-relieving exercises for a week before the interview.

b.   role-play the interview with a friend to practice your skill in answering questions.
c.   buy a new pair of shoes.
d.   talk to your college professor about job openings.

15.   All of the following may be components of traditional teacher licensure *except*

a.   a bachelor's degree.
b.   special examinations.
c.   demonstration of competence through student test scores.
d.   completion of an approved licensure program.

16.   According to the text, alternative licensure programs vary widely from state to state and are designed to meet the various conditions under which traditional teacher education will not or cannot suffice. Which of the following is the *least* likely to be a rationale for a state's alternative teaching route?

a.   The provision of licensed teachers when the state suffers a teacher shortage
b.   The need for teaching licenses by adults making a career change
c.   An alternative license program is the most appropriate route for secondary school teachers
d.   The enhancement of a college-approved teacher education program

17.   Alternate teaching licensure programs indicate a belief by some legislators that

a.   adults with training in other fields are better qualified to teach than teachers.
b.   teacher preparation is too long and arduous for most people.
c.   traditional teacher education courses are ineffective in preparing people to teach.
d.   subject-matter knowledge is sufficient to teach.

18.   Mark is a sophomore in college and has decided to become a biology teacher. What could he do *now* to enhance his marketability for a teaching position in two years?

a.   Take additional chemistry courses so that he can become licensed in both biology and chemistry
b.   Research the anticipated teaching shortages in various states
c.   Prepare a credential file including a résumé and letters of recommendation from current professors
d.   Transfer to a school in a state that is expecting a teacher shortage

19.   As the new century begins, the *national* average salary *for beginning* teachers is about.

a. $22,000
b. $25,000
c. $28,000
d. $31,000

20.   Experienced teachers who want to change occupations will find that their skills transfer well into such settings as

a.   federal agencies.
b.   philanthropic organizations.
c.   businesses.
d.   all of these.

21.   Consuela is a senior in college and is interested in a career in school administration. What should she be advised to do in order to achieve her goal?

a.   Send out résumés and actively seek an administrative position
b.   Work in the private sector for a few years, then apply for administrative positions
c.   Pursue a teaching career for a couple of years and then move into administration
d.   Apply to a master's program to earn an advanced degree in school administration

22.   Which of the following accurately describes the characteristics of many teachers who seek alternative licensure?

a.   Lower academic qualifications, older, more likely to teach in the inner city
b.   Younger, more males, likely to teach in the suburbs
c.   More work experience, fewer minorities, more likely to stay in teaching

d.   Less likely to stay in teaching, higher academic qualifications, with more previous work experience

23.   Many nonteaching jobs in education, such as staff developer, curriculum coordinator, or guidance counselor, usually require

a.   a cut in salary.
b.   teaching experience and an advanced degree.
c.   a terminal degree in the field of practice.
d.   key contacts in the right places.

24.   Portfolios are being used more often to inform potential employers of a candidate's skills and preparation. Some candidates are using electronic portfolios. Which of the following is *not* an advantage of an electronic portfolio?

a.   It's permanent.
b.   It's easily accessed.
c.   It can be used simultaneously be several hiring committees.
d.   It's easily updated.

SHORT-ANSWER QUESTIONS

Respond to each of the following questions briefly, but specifically, in complete sentences.

1.   Imagine that an education professor at a state college has just received a statistical report projecting demand for teachers for the next ten years. In the report, the professor sees that there is expected to be a considerable shortage of elementary teachers in the college's geographical region. The next day, a student comes to the professor, wishing to declare her major in elementary education. What information should the professor encourage the student to seek to determine the availability of a position after graduation?

2.   Briefly describe the role of alternative licensure. What is its purpose? How effective has it been to date in preparing teachers?

3.   Let's say that although you have performed well as a teacher, at the end of your second year of teaching, you decide to pursue another career. Given the training you have had as a teacher, identify another field or occupation in which you could be successfully employed and explain why.

ESSAY QUESTIONS

Read each of the following questions, and respond by composing an organized essay that includes an introduction, fully developed paragraph(s), and a conclusion.

1.   The text includes sobering data on the number of minority teachers in America. According to the text, 91 percent of all teachers are white, and the percentage of minority teachers continues to shrink. How do minority teachers fulfill a vital role in education for students of all races, and what would be your suggestions for recruiting more minority teachers into the field?

2.   Ryan and Cooper speak of employment trends in teaching in the United States. What are the factors that affect the supply and demand of teachers?

ANSWERS TO MULTIPLE CHOICE QUESTIONS

1.   d

2.   b

3.   c

4.   a

5.   b

6.   a

7.   a

8. d

9. a

10. a

11. c

12. d

13. c

14. b

15. c

16. b

17. d

18. a

19. c

20. d

21. c

22. a

23. b

24. a

ANSWERS TO SHORT-ANSWER QUESTIONS

1. *(suggested answer)*

   Although statistical reports can be helpful in determining trends, at times, statistical data changes rapidly. Therefore, it is unwise to base a career decision solely on a review of *projected* teacher supply and demand. The professor should encourage the student to seek information regarding the type of shortage: minority teachers, certain subjects, certain grade levels, and the contributing factors of retirement rate, growth in student population, budget changes, etc. Finally, as the text mentions, there is never a surplus of good teachers.

2. *(suggested answer)*

   One of the major purposes of alternative licensure is supplying teachers when states experience shortages. Because of many of the commission reports during the early to mid-1980s, which sharply criticized the quality of education majors and the quality of teaching in public schools, alternative licensure received attention as a way of luring liberal arts graduates and people with extensive backgrounds in math and science into teaching. The alternative license programs vary widely from state to state, and at this point there are few data demonstrating their effectiveness in preparing teachers.

3. *(suggested answer)*

   Answers will vary, but students should mention the skills they have learned in teacher training, including managing people, planning, organizing and implementing those plans, researching, speaking in public, and communicating in general.

ANSWERS TO ESSAY QUESTIONS

1. *(suggested answer)*

   Students should discuss the function minority teachers serve as role models for both minority and white children. The need for positive role models is particularly strong in troubled school districts where children sometimes have few positive influences in their lives. In addition, minority teachers also reflect the diversity of the U.S. population.

Answers will vary on recruiting more minority teachers into the field.

2.   *(suggested answer)*

Answers will vary, but students should speak about the social and economic factors that influence supply and demand including growth of the student population, changes in pupil/teacher ratio, varying needs by geographical region, and specific subject areas. Students should recognize the dependence of public school funding on the economic well-being of the community and country. When there is an economic downturn, public school budgets suffer and teaching positions are lost. Students should also mention the current demographics of the teaching population, which will potentially lead to a large number of retirements in the near future. However, the economy will continue to play a dominant role in the availability of teaching positions.

CHAPTER 13

What Can the New Teacher Expect?

MULTIPLE CHOICE QUESTIONS

(An additional ten multiple-choice items and two short answer items are available in the sample quiz for this chapter.)

Read each item carefully. Select the letter of the choice that represents the best answer.

1. During Patty Miller's first week of teaching, she finds it odd to walk past the cafeteria and into the faculty lunchroom. Even more peculiar is having students call her "Ms. Miller." What is Patty likely experiencing?

    a.   Extreme insecurity about her ability as a teacher
    b.   Culture shock
    c.   Overexcitement from her first week of teaching
    d.   Feelings of regret that she entered teaching

2. In one day, principal Toni Radano explained the statewide curricular changes to a group of teachers, fielded an angry phone call from a parent about a teacher, and publicly recognized two teachers for their outstanding work directing the school play. Which of the following best describes her roles on this particular day?

    a.   Coach, crisis manager, evaluator
    b.   Educator, facilitator, judge
    c.   Initiator, buffer, reward dispenser
    d.   Helper, sacrificial lamb, evaluator

3. Mr. Gulick usually represents the school to the local press. He also orders instructional supplies for the school, facilitates student-teacher disagreements, observes and evaluates teachers, and meets directly with parents at times. Based upon that description, what is Mr. Gulick?

    a.   Master teacher
    b.   Curriculum coordinator
    c.   Principal
    d.   Superintendent

4. In what way does the principal act as a liaison between the larger school organization and the faculty? He or she

    a.   guides teachers toward achieving districtwide goals.
    b.   is chosen to be the "sacrificial lamb" if the public isn't satisfied with the school.
    c.   frequently visits teachers to make classroom observations.
    d.   keeps up-to-date on current research and reform initiatives.

5. Because of the complexity of the principal's role, a teacher may lack the principal's support in certain instances. Which of the following describes the most likely instance in which a teacher would lack administrative support?

    a.   A student with a serious behavior problem fails to live up to the terms of a learning contract.
    b.   The teacher does not want to complete the routine paperwork demanded by the office because it takes time away from instruction.
    c.   A custodian regularly fails to perform routine tasks clearly defined in the posted description.
    d.   An irate parent charges into the teacher's classroom, disrupting the class.

6. Seeing that Marc was having difficulty making classroom transitions between activities, Claire, his supervisor, provided him with several practical suggestions. What else falls under the typical ways a supervisor helps a new teacher?

    a. Observing and providing constructive feedback
    b. Sitting in with the new teacher during parent-teacher conferences and contributing additional information to the parents
    c. Loaning lesson plans and unit tests
    d. Arranging the students' assignments so that the more difficult students are assigned to more experienced teachers

7. Which of the following are typical ways a supervisor can help a beginning teacher?

    a. Help the new teacher respond to the principal's written observation; review the new teacher's lessons
    b. Advise the new teacher which faculty members are burnt out; provide suggestions for follow-up activities for a unit
    c. Conduct a minilesson to demonstrate a new teaching strategy; point out ways to minimize class distractions
    d. Coach him or her on how to conduct parent conferences; provide assistance in evaluating students' work

8. According to the text, what is the most useful attitude for beginning teachers to have toward their colleagues?

    a. Be ever skeptical. A great many experienced teachers have developed bad habits.
    b. Be cautiously optimistic. Although poor teachers exist, dedicated teachers abound.
    c. Be unworried. With rare exceptions, other teachers will be generous, helpful, and supportive.
    d. Be persistently friendly. Other teachers, if they like you, will always be able to help lighten your workload by giving you materials.

9. Darla Desiderio is somewhat apprehensive about surviving her first year of teaching, and she would appreciate having a mentor. According to the text, which approach would be the wisest for Darla?

    a. Announce in the teacher's lounge that you would like to work with a mentor and choose whoever volunteers.
    b. Observe teachers in their day-to-day work to see who would be the most receptive to being a mentor and who would have the most to offer you.
    c. Let a relationship emerge naturally. The teacher who becomes her best friend will be the best mentor for Darla.
    d. Wait for a teacher to approach her with the offer. She should not appear too eager or too unsure of her abilities in front of other teachers.

10. It is your first year of teaching. A few days before classes start, a very friendly teacher stops by to welcome you to the school. By the end of the second week of school, she stops by your room regularly, frequently giving you information about other faculty and the administration. What would be the best approach for dealing with this teacher?

    a. Try to avoid her in the future. You don't want to get involved with any teacher who is too friendly this early in the year.
    b. Encourage her friendship. She's friendly and has taken an interest in you.
    c. Be polite but reserve your friendship until you know her and the school system better.
    d. Find out more by asking other teachers for their opinion of her.

11. What is the best measure of a teacher's success?

    a. The amount of respect shown by colleagues
    b. Ratings earned on formal evaluations
    c. The degree of student's progress as learners
    d. The size of the raise in salary for the second year

12. During a year-end meeting, the principal asked Mark Steinberg how he would assess his performance as a teacher over the past year. What would be the strongest answer from Mark?

    a. "My students like my class. In fact, they tell me they enjoyed my class better than any other."
    b. "My department chairman told me that I have a fine future ahead of me based upon this year of teaching."
    c. "Other members of the department frequently ask if I'll share my lesson plans and unit evaluations with them."
    d. "I've just finished reviewing my students' cumulative folders. Generally, their problem-solving abilities have increased."

13. Many beginning teachers are concerned that they will lack subject-matter knowledge. In reality, though, most beginning teachers have the most difficulty with which of the following?

    a. Learning how to work in a bureaucracy
    b. Designing adequate lesson plans
    c. Maintaining classroom discipline
    d. Evaluating student work

14. Consider the following summary of beginning teacher Rocco Mandala's class. While his class was working on projects, one student asked a question that puzzled Rocco. Two students quietly doodled. Then one activity ran long, so Rocco had to change his lesson plan in the middle of the period. As a beginning teacher, what should Rocco do?

    a. Review his subject matter so he does not get stumped by a student's question
    b. Confront students who are not on task and reinforce for them his expectations
    c. Review his lesson plans more thoroughly to make sure he has timed activities correctly
    d. Adhere to his original lesson plan, even if he has some momentary digressions

15. According to research, which of the following comments typifies the attitude of a beginning teacher?

    a. "This is just what I expected teaching would be like! The students are basically enthusiastic and eager."
    b. "When I student-taught, the students I worked with were horrible. I began to doubt if I even wanted to teach, but these students are wonderful!"
    c. "I am surprised at how demanding and difficult these students are. They're more difficult than the students I had in student teaching."
    d. "I began to wonder about my feelings for children when I student-taught because I didn't like them. My feelings haven't changed."

16. What is the typical attitude of teacher education students toward children?

    a. They think of them as "blank slates" needing to be filled with information and knowledge.
    b. They think of them as essentially good students filled with curiosity and willingness to learn.
    c. They see students ambivalently. Although they know students will be good students, they are fearful of many.
    d. They see them as needing the civilizing influence of education and discipline.

17. Becky Osuchowski is a first-year math teacher at Bernards High. One Monday morning, a student drapes his arm around her should as class starts and asks, "So, Ms. Osuchowski, go to any clubs this weekend like you said you wanted to?" The student's comment indicates Becky is having difficulty with which of the following areas?

    a. Setting up appropriate pre-lesson activities for students
    b. Preparing solid instructional lessons for her classes
    c. Maintaining consistent classroom discipline procedures
    d. Establishing social distance from her students

18. Why is establishing an appropriate social distance from students difficult for so many new teachers?

    a. Many are guided by other teachers' advice rather than following their instincts.
    b. Many want to be liked by students, so they become overly friendly.

c.   Many suffer from poor self-esteem and seek to build their own esteem by becoming close to students.

d.   Many lack interpersonal skills necessary for teaching.

19.   Heidi Pfluger, a first-year history teacher, is quite popular with students. One day after school, Julien, a student, asked her to come to his party as his special guest. What is the best way for her to handle this situation?

    a.   She must decline and report the incident to the principal in case he finds out from someone else.

    b.   She must decline and let Julien know in a firm way that his question was completely inappropriate.

    c.   She must decline, yet do so in a way that will not hurt Julien's feelings.

    d.   She must decline and resolve to speak to him as little as possible in the future.

20.   Bob Federbusch is a beginning teacher. He's aware that he may feel attracted to one of his students, yet he thinks he will be able to handle that situation. Which of the following previous experiences will be most helpful to him as he establishes an appropriate relationship with his students?

    a.   Working as an assistant coach for the YWCA swim team

    b.   Completing an internship at a local newspaper

    c.   Being an active member of the school soccer team

    d.   Observing various teachers during his pre-practicum

21.   During Kaye's first day of teaching, she assigned locker numbers and all books, she passed out "mystery bags" and asked students to write a story based upon the objects inside, she collected phone numbers of her students' parents, and she assigned homework. According to Jim and Kevin's suggestions for the first day of school, what made Kaye's day successful?

    a.   She dealt with administrative details and taught an interesting lesson.

    b.   She taught an interesting lesson and collected parents' phone numbers.

    c.   She collected parents' phone numbers and assigned homework.

    d.   She taught an interesting lesson and assigned homework.

22.   Which of the following is usually at the heart of problems parents have in communicating with teachers?

    a.   The parent lacks the time to see the teacher after school or during conferences.

    b.   The parent believes that the teacher is a low-status person who chose teaching as a safe job.

    c.   The parent thinks the child has significantly more or less talent than the teacher recognizes.

    d.   The parent is philosophically opposed to the curriculum implemented by the child's teacher.

23.   According to the authors, which one of the following teachers is most closely following the author's practical teaching tips for surviving the first year of teaching?

    a.   Randy has phoned each of his students' parents to introduce himself, and he exercises regularly.

    b.   Donna has enrolled in several teaching workshops offered by an educational association, and she keeps a diary of her daily thoughts and feelings.

    c.   Ed has established strict disciplinary rules and has planned his lessons far in advance of when he will teach them.

    d.   Kellie reads over all her evaluations, taking notes on how to improve, and she has agreed to serve as the advisor of several co-curricular activities.

24.   According to the authors, which is the best description of a teaching journal's use?

    a.   It would serve to remind the teacher of how much he or she has progressed in his or her field throughout the year.

    b.   It could be used as a sourcebook for teaching ideas, particularly when one is searching for a new way to approach a topic.

    c.   It is a daily notebook in which the teacher records every class he or she taught and how it proceeded.

    d.   It is a place where the teacher writes all his or her feelings about what teaching has meant. By examining those feelings, a teacher will be inspired in the future.

SHORT-ANSWER QUESTIONS

Respond to each of the following questions briefly, but specifically, in complete sentences.

1. What does the term *social distance* mean? Why is maintaining social distance between yourself, as a teacher, and students particularly important?

2. What is some practical advice for beginning teachers regarding their relationships with teaching colleagues?

3. What is the most reliable indicator of a new teacher's success? What are other factors that teachers may think measure success? To what degree may those other factors be accurate?

4. Why are teacher education students' attitudes toward children typically much more positive than those of first-year teachers?

ESSAY QUESTIONS

Read each of the following questions, and respond by composing an organized essay that includes an introduction, fully developed paragraph(s), and a conclusion.

1. Explain the kinds of problems that a first-year teacher might face in three of the following six areas: shock of the familiar, instruction, and dealing with students, administrators, teaching peers, and parents. Include a definition of *culture shock*.

2. Parents and teachers often have communication problems that stem from one of three areas. Tell what the areas are, and given an example of a problem in each area.

3. To what degree are the principal's and teacher's roles in a school system complementary? To what degree can each help the other do the best possible job?

ANSWERS TO MULTIPLE CHOICE QUESTIONS

1. b
2. a
3. c
4. a
5. b
6. a
7. c
8. b
9. b
10. c
11. c
12. d
13. c
14. b
15. c
16. b
17. d
18. b
19. c
20. a
21. b

22. c

23. a

24. a

ANSWERS TO SHORT-ANSWER QUESTIONS

1. *(suggested answer)*

    Social distance between teacher and student is the appropriate level and tone of interactions that characterize their relationship. A teacher should be friendly and warm toward students, but not so friendly that the student-teacher relationship becomes more personal than professional. It is particularly important that a beginning teacher know how to strike the balance between friendliness and professionalism because when a teacher does not maintain an appropriate social distance, he or she will have trouble being an effective teacher.

2. *(suggested answer)*

    Beginning teachers should know that although many teachers have goodwill and are valuable associates, not all teachers are. As in any organization, people fulfill different roles: the role of the gossip, the busybody, the ally seeker. A teacher needs to see who is genuine and who has ulterior motives for the beginning teacher's confidences. It behooves a beginning teacher to be friendly to all as she or he begins school, but to observe the school climate and the people in the school before aligning oneself too closely to any one teacher or group of teachers.

3. *(suggested answer)*

    The best indication of how well a teacher has performed is the growth and advancement of the students' learning. Ultimately, that is the single most important reason teachers teach: to help students learn. Other factors may provide some helpful information, but they are not always accurate measures of how much the students have learned. Such other factors include the teacher's reputation among colleagues, the teacher's written evaluations, the popularity of the teacher with students, and the relationship of the teacher with students' parents.

4. *(suggested answer)*

    The answer lies in two potential areas: philosophy and experience. Many times prospective teachers' underlying philosophy emanates from Romanticism. They conceive of children as essentially good, thwarted by the stifling influence of education, curious and willing to learn if supported and nurtured in the proper environment. Although that is a tenable philosophy for many and has had a long history in education, most prospective teachers have not had the opportunity to test out their philosophy, to match it against real situations. For that reason, they may feel shocked when their best attempts to nurture students are rebuffed.

    Furthermore, most prospective teachers have not had extended experience as authority figures with children and adolescents. They may experience some awkwardness moving from student to teacher and the change in authority that requires. For that reason, the authors suggest any experience, such as coaching, tutoring, and camp counseling, can help prospective teachers make that transition.

ANSWERS TO ESSAY QUESTIONS

1. (Answers will vary.)

2. *(suggested answer)*

    Different perspectives, differing evaluations of the student's work, different socioeconomic status. Examples will vary.

3. *(suggested answer)*

    Whereas both principals and teachers are educators, their function in the school organization is different. Teachers work individually with particular students, instructing them and designing activities to help their individual class or classes advance. They are the primary instructor in a school organization, and, as a result, they will know details about their students' learning that others will now know. They are typically most concerned with how the curriculum impacts their classroom or their department. Principals are, in large degree, the managers of the school building. They oversee the general processes of education, trying to keep the entire school heading toward district and state curricular goals. They are responsible for evaluating the teachers' performance as well as being the official spokesperson to the community of that school.

Teachers and principals are most helpful to each other when they recognize what the other one brings to education. Principals can look to teachers to provide feedback and input on the implementation of the curriculum. Teachers can discuss, with more authority than other school personnel, how students are learning under particular conditions and what students are undergoing at any particular time. Principals can provide the general leadership a school needs by articulating general goals, fostering a sense of purpose, making connections between individual teachers and departments, and otherwise working to create a unified school.

CHAPTER 14

What Does It Mean to Be a Professional?

MULTIPLE CHOICE QUESTIONS

(An additional ten multiple-choice items and two short answer items are available in the sample quiz for this chapter).

Read each item carefully. Select the letter of the choice that represents the best answer.

1. Which of the following must be included for an occupation to be considered a profession?

    a. High status of those in the field
    b. The potential for great financial reward
    c. Strict control of the numbers of people allowed into the field
    d. Extensive special training required, using one's intellectual ability

2. If someone wanted to *discount* the claim that teaching is a profession, which of the following statements could he or she use?

    a. The teacher's work emphasizes service, not rewards.
    b. The teacher's power is limited.
    c. The teacher earns an impressive salary.
    d. The teacher's job is not essential to the community.

3. Some of public teachers' harshest critics state that teachers do not fool the public even if they fool themselves; teaching is not a profession, and it will not be until teachers

    a. recognize the fallibility of man.
    b. build better relations with the parent community.
    c. develop more compassion for the students with whom they work.
    d. can govern their own, including weeding out incompetent teachers.

4. The recommendations made in the text for ensuring the place of teaching among the professions are

    a. higher pay, more strikes, and better negotiations.
    b. fewer workdays, higher pay, and better training.
    c. more self-governance, better training, and better policing of teachers.
    d. higher pay, fewer workdays, and better negotiations.

5. By saying that teaching is *in the process of becoming a profession*, Ryan and Cooper want to emphasize

    a. the legislation that Congress is working on to make teaching a profession.
    b. the continuous education of teachers, which makes them more and more effective.
    c. a case before the Supreme Court that will soon decide if teaching is a profession.
    d. the significant changes that teaching has experienced over the years.

6. One drawback to teaching at the imitative maintenance level of professionalism is

    a. it takes too much time to be creative and innovative.
    b. it is complicated and confusing for the student.
    c. the teacher has too many areas to maintain at one time.
    d. it doesn't promote individualized responses to the unique needs and special circumstances of students.

7. The teacher at the meditative level of professionalism

    a. has a broad perspective of many education systems and classrooms.

    b.   is reflective about his/her own teaching practice within his/her own classroom.

    c.   is only able to imitate teaching practices he/she has seen other teachers use.

    d.   doesn't deviate from prescribed instructional guidelines.

8.   The classrooms of teachers at the generative creative level of professionalism are characterized by

    a.   a variety of instructional practices and problem centers.

    b.   instruction focused on teaching to the test.

    c.   teacher proof materials and adherence to prescribed guidelines.

    d.   lots of art projects, drama, and music integrations.

9.   The National Board for Professional Teaching Standards (NBPTS) is developing board certification assessments for teachers in order to

    a.   relieve the states of the responsibility of certifying teachers.

    b.   create a career ladder for more qualified and talented teachers.

    c.   identify the knowledge base of teaching.

    d.   raise the standards in teaching and recognize teachers who meet them.

10.   The (NBPTS) designation will be earned by a teacher after

    a.   passing a national norm referenced test such as PRAXIS.

    b.   undergoing an extensive assessment procedure, including observations, interviews, and submitting a portfolio.

    c.   earning a master's degree and undergoing a rigorous examination of his or her teaching abilities.

    d.   undergoing an extensive assessment and being nominated by fellow teachers.

11.   Melanie is applying for board certification from the NBPTS. What will she probably have to do?

    a.   She will have to take a written exam to evaluate her knowledge of her subject area.

    b.   She will have to have an oral interview with a group of school board members from her town.

    c.   She will have to send in videotapes of her teaching in her classroom.

    d.   She will probably have to do all of these.

12.   Critics of the (NBPTS) argue that

    a.   teaching has no recognized common knowledge base on which to ground assessments.

    b.   teaching has no need for any kind of standards.

    c.   historically, teaching has been dominated by women.

    d.   these standards seek to make teaching even more elitist than it already is.

13.   Which of these are possible effects of NBPTS certification?

    a.   Salary increases for certificate holders

    b.   Easier portability of state certification from one state to another

    c.   Research on characteristics of superior teaching

    d.   All of these

14.   A teacher who is selected to serve as a mentor may receive any of the following *except*

    a.   automatic recertification in their state.

    b.   specialized training.

    c.   reduction in teaching responsibilities.

    d.   monetary compensation.

15.   The need for continuous education for teachers seems to be even greater for teachers in today's schools due to

    a.   the number of poorly trained people being hired to teach.

    b.   the high cost of a college education.

    c.   the growth of new knowledge and the demand for new skills.

    d.   the growing class size, especially in rural areas.

16. Which of the following would *not* be considered a way for an elementary school teacher to continue to grow professionally?

   a. Attend a summer workshop in cooperative learning
   b. Take many trips to other countries
   c. Serve as a cooperating teacher for a student teacher
   d. Enroll in a master's program at a local college

17. The NEA initially resisted

   a. collective bargaining for teachers' salary negotiations.
   b. efforts to improve preservice teacher education.
   c. the establishment of the National Board for Professional Teaching.
   d. multicultural education.

18. The AFT is known as more aggressive than the NEA because it

   a. instituted QUEST (Quality Education Standards in Teaching).
   b. instituted collective bargaining for teachers' salaries.
   c. has supported greater decision making by teachers.
   d. works against parents having choices in public schools.

SHORT-ANSWER QUESTIONS

Respond to each of the following questions briefly, but specifically, in complete sentences.

1. Describe the five distinguishing characteristics of the National Board for Professional Teaching Standards.

2. Describe the benefits NEA and ACT provide to their teacher members.

ESSAY QUESTIONS

Read each of the following questions, and respond by composing an organized essay that includes an introduction, fully developed paragraph(s), and a conclusion.

1. List four of the elements that characterize a profession. For each one, summarize the arguments both for and against calling teaching a profession.

2. The NEA and the AFT both represent large numbers of teachers. Each ranks its priorities in slightly different ways, emphasizing slightly different factors. Describe the similarities and differences between the organizations with respect to size, age, representation, history of issues, positions on educational reform, and collective bargaining.

ANSWERS TO MULTIPLE CHOICE QUESTIONS

1. d
2. b
3. d
4. c
5. d
6. d
7. b
8. a
9. d
10. b
11. c

12. a

13. d

14. a

15. c

16. b

17. a

18. b

ANSWERS TO SHORT-ANSWER QUESTIONS

1. *(suggested answer)*

    It is for experienced teachers and is voluntary. It involves submitting to a set of exams and assessments in specific subject areas. The assessments involve videotapes and a portfolio rather than relying only on traditional paper and pencil testing. The control of NBPTS is in the hands of practicing teachers.

2. *(suggested answer)*

    Responses should include references to publications, collective bargaining, travel, insurance and other support services, legal representation, and a political voice.

ANSWERS TO ESSAY QUESTIONS

1. *(suggested answer)*

    A profession provides a definite, unique, essential service; relies on intellectual skills; requires special training; permits autonomy for members; assumes personal responsibility for consequences; emphasizes services rather than rewards; is self-governing; and has a code of ethics. Evidence in support of calling teaching a profession includes the fact that teachers are specialists who pass on key skills, they teach thinking skills, they train continuously, they exercise a great deal of personal control, they are accountable for effectiveness, and they attempt to influence law and licensure and to maintain standards. Evidence arguing against calling teaching a profession includes that everyone and everything is a teacher, many people have education equal to that of teachers, relatively little training is required, teachers' power is greater only than that of students, teachers' influence on professional governance is limited, there are no repercussions for ineptitude, there is limited interest in excellence, and teachers have low status and low pay.

2. *(suggested answer)*

    The NEA represents nearly two-thirds of elementary and secondary teachers in the United States. It seems more conservative about educational reform than the AFT. The NEA was founded in the mid-1800s. It resisted collective bargaining at first. The AFT, representing about 25 percent of all teachers, is a strong advocate of educational reform. It was begun in the mid-1900s. The AFT is a member of the AFL-CIO and brought collective bargaining into teachers' salary negotiations. The AFT is noted for hard bargaining over bread-and-butter issues and is a defender of academic freedom and of greater participation by teachers in decision making.

CHAPTER 15

Why Teach?

MULTIPLE CHOICE QUESTIONS

(An additional ten multiple-choice items and two short answer items are available in the sample quiz for this chapter.)

Read each item carefully. Select the letter of the choice that represents the best answer.

1. Denise, a medical sales representative, is considering a career switch to teaching. She is bright, outgoing, and likes the high pay she has earned in sales. Yet she has felt drawn to teaching because of the positive contribution she could make to students' lives. If she makes the career switch, which reward is Denise *least* likely to experience in teaching

    a. a lively intellectual atmosphere with colleagues and students.
    b. a work schedule offering generous personal time.
    c. the satisfaction of contributing positively to others' lives.
    d. a salary that rivals other professional salaries.

2. Telly, the president of the senior class at State U., thinks he would enjoy teaching history and civics, because he has always taken a prominent role in student government and finds politics fascinating. If Telly decides to become a teacher, which of the following of Telly's interests would *least* likely be satisfied in a teaching career?

    a. His pleasure in working with other people
    b. The opportunity to learn more about history and civics
    c. His attraction to status
    d. The opportunity to help create change in people's lives

3. Juan, a talented young artist, has already had some of his watercolors displayed at showings. In addition to painting, he also enjoys teaching painting to young children. He feels strongly that art should be part of every child's education. If Juan decides to become an art teacher, which of the following extrinsic rewards will he most certainly experience?

    a. The status and recognition of being an accomplished teacher
    b. A generous work schedule, providing him time to paint
    c. A secure and high salary
    d. The sense of power that he will be able to change curriculum

4. Tai is a college sophomore with numerous interests. Public service has always appealed to her, yet she is not sure if teaching will be the most satisfying career. Which of the following would be the best indicators that Tai would find satisfaction in teaching?

    a. She feels a strong desire to contribute to society and wants a secure salary.
    b. She wants recognition for her work, and she enjoys working with people.
    c. She enjoys intellectual stimulation and wants to perform a service to society.
    d. She wants to work with others and wants a work schedule with ample personal time.

5. Of the following extrinsic rewards, which is most closely associated with teaching?

    a. A competitive salary
    b. High status and prestige
    c. Power over one's subordinates and working associates
    d. A work schedule allowing generous time for oneself

6. What is the best indicator that you will be satisfied teaching?

    a. Listening to your parents, friends, and others who know you well who think that teaching would be a good career for you
    b. Being attracted to performing an important social service
    c. Knowing that children usually like you very much
    d. Enjoying the power and influence you can have upon others

7. Intrinsic rewards in teaching include

    a. the close work with young people, the actual teaching, and the power in the career.
    b. performing a significant social service and the flexible work schedule.
    c. the salary, the actual teaching, and the status.
    d. the actual teaching and satisfaction from the performance of an important social service.

8. During Noam's twelve years of teaching, he has coached an award-winning chemistry team, successfully taught advanced placement chemistry, chaperoned numerous overnight camping trips, coached the girls' volleyball team, and worked as a class advisor. In his career, Noam is probably most rewarded by

    a. his actual work with adolescents.
    b. the prestige of being a chemistry teacher.
    c. the power he has over the lives of so many.
    d. his salary and stipends earned as a coach and advisor.

9. A direct way to find out if you will enjoy the realities of teaching is to

    a. get frequent, long-term baby-sitting jobs.
    b. seek the counsel of a career placement counselor and let him or her direct you.
    c. volunteer several hours a week at a school or supervise extracurricular activities.
    d. study the teachers' benefits and salaries where you would like to teach.

10. After reading several novels about teaching, Jameel has become fascinated with teaching as a career. According to the authors, what else would be a fruitful way to help him decide if teaching is the right career for him?

    a. To work in a variety of part-time jobs to see if teaching is still appealing
    b. To get advice from his former teachers about the realities of teaching
    c. To take a career preference test
    d. To read some more novels and watch movies about teaching

11. Tina suffered a vicious assault when she was a college senior and still feels the aftereffects. Now, several years later, she actively organizes rape awareness seminars for her high school students. During a recent class discussion about date rape, one student raised the possibility that people can be, at times, wrongfully accused. Tina barely contained her anger and dismissed the student's comment immediately. What does this scenario suggest?

    a. Tina's effectiveness as a teacher may be diminished because of her unresolved personal problems.
    b. Tina must continue to work to raise students' awareness levels.
    c. Tina must include more material in her curriculum about violence in contemporary society.
    d. Tina needs to improve her classroom management skills.

12. One of the most effective ways teachers can aid in the renewal of society is to

    a. pick a service project for their classes and require that all students participate.
    b. work on political campaigns with fellow teachers.
    c. enthusiastically teach their favorite subjects.
    d. teach students to become involved and informed citizens.

13. Cleo, an earth science teacher, spends considerable time working with her students on environmental projects that demand their critical-thinking and problem-solving skills. Most recently, they have been working on a project exploring groundwater contamination and its effects on the environment. Cleo most likely sees the purpose of her teaching as a means of

    a.   aiding in the renewal of society.
    b.   preparing her students for the expectations of college.
    c.   gaining recognition for her innovative teaching methods.
    d.   helping students memorize important facts in science.

14. According to the authors of this text, the question "Why teach?" is important because our answer is a good indicator of

    a.   what kind of institution is best for our training.
    b.   what subjects we will teach.
    c.   what we will accomplish as teachers.
    d.   whether we will be effective teachers.

15. Based on the study of teachers in the first five years of their career, which of the following is a *true* statement of the conclusions of that study?

    a.   The majority report that their more experienced colleagues share their enthusiasm for teaching.
    b.   The new teachers are described by their administrators as intelligent and skilled.
    c.   Few of them claim that teaching is their lifelong career choice.
    d.   The vast majority have extremely altruistic/attitudes about contributing to society.

SHORT-ANSWER QUESTIONS

Respond to each of the following questions briefly, but specifically, in complete sentences.

1.   In most respects, teaching ranks rather low in all extrinsic rewards except for one. Which extrinsic reward is it, and how can teachers use it best?

2.   One way of deciding if a teaching career is for you is through vicarious experience. Although very helpful, vicarious experience also has its limitations in helping you decide if teaching is for you. Name and explain the strengths and limitations of using vicarious experience in your decision to become a teacher.

3.   In one of the short narratives in the text, Julia recognized that her deep interest in science was both an advantage and a disadvantage. Describe the advantages and disadvantages of a teacher's deep commitment to their subject area as well as how Julia could change her instruction to solve her problems.

4.   In the text, Fred repeatedly asks for "low-achieving" classes in history because he has a strong commitment to helping those students become involved, reflective citizens. He strongly believes that preparing those students to become participating citizens is vital for the renewal of society. In the teaching field you are considering, what could you do in your classes to enhance students' abilities in active citizenship? How does that relate to the renewal of society?

ESSAY QUESTIONS

Read each of the following questions, and respond by composing an organized essay that includes an introduction, fully developed paragraph(s), and a conclusion.

1.   Many would argue that the rewards of a task are what propel people to become actively engaged in their work. Rewards, both intrinsic and extrinsic, reside in all occupations to some degree or another. What are the extrinsic rewards of an occupation, and to what degree would you claim that teaching supplies those extrinsic rewards? What are the intrinsic rewards associated with teaching? Identify and explain them.

2.   One teacher recalled that he decided to go into teaching because of a daydream he had. He imagined teaching biology to students and having them really interested in him and what he was teaching them. He also imagined himself acting as a counselor and mentor to his students. Other than that pleasant daydream, he had little opportunity to test out his attraction to teaching. For someone attracted to teaching, what are

some useful sources of experience to help in the career choice? Analyze three types of useful experience, explaining the benefits of each.

ANSWERS TO MULTIPLE CHOICE QUESTIONS

1. d
2. c
3. b
4. c
5. d
6. b
7. d
8. a
9. c
10. b
11. a
12. d
13. a
14. c
15. d

ANSWERS TO SHORT-ANSWER QUESTIONS

1. *(suggested answer)*

    The one extrinsic reward most noted in teaching is the work schedule. Because of the frequent vacations throughout the school year and during the summer, teaching offers a work schedule that allows the teacher more time at his or her disposal than most other professions. Professional development and planning ahead for the next school year are two constructive ways to use the time.

2. *(suggested answer)*

    Vicarious experience can help by providing you with experience you may not have had. Therefore, reading a book or watching a movie about teachers may show you intriguing aspects of the profession. However, one must also remember that the vicarious experience you gain from reading a book or watching a movie may not always be completely realistic. In literature, movies, and other art forms, particular facets are emphasized to create interest, so the actual book or movie may not be factually correct in every detail.

3. (Answers will vary.)

4. *(suggested answer)*

    Answers will vary, but ideas should clearly demonstrate how a teaching strategy or activity helps enhance students' critical thinking. Also, educating students to become active, reflective citizens aids in the renewal of society because participating citizens are fundamental for the maintenance of a democracy. Active citizens can successfully work toward the improvements of society.

ANSWERS TO ESSAY QUESTIONS

1. *(suggested answer)*

    The extrinsic rewards are salary, status, power, and work schedule. Teaching does not typically reward teachers with high salaries; however, some could argue that teachers' salaries are improving in certain geographical areas, based on the attention to education and the increased expectations for teachers. In the

United States, teaching has never been considered a high-status job, perhaps partly because of the lack of power a teacher has in comparison to other professions. A teacher's work schedule, with its frequent vacations, is the strongest extrinsic reward.

The intrinsic rewards in teaching are teaching itself, working with students, working in a collegial atmosphere, and performing a vital social service.

2.   *(suggested answer)*

The authors contend that actual work with children and adolescents is a very useful way of determining if one would be happy as a teacher. Several possibilities exist for prospective teachers to test out their interest in the profession. They are baby-sitting, working as a camp counselor, working at the Y or other club as an instructor, serving as an assistant coach for Little League or other athletic team, either assisting or working as a religious teacher at a church or temple, serving as a Big Brother or Big Sister, working at a preschool, day care center, or the like, and tutoring a younger student. With each possibility selected, the answer should demonstrate how that particular experience adds to one's useful knowledge of teaching. For example, tutoring or baby-sitting usually involves only one or two children, whereas coaching a Little League team requires work with many children. Another distinction is that tutoring, coaching, or instructing involves actual teaching whereas baby-sitting or serving as a Big Brother or Sister may not involve direct teaching.

APPENDIX I

Media Distributor Contact Information

Annenberg CPB Videos
P.O. Box 2345
S. Burlington, VT 05407-2345
1-800-532-7637
Fax: (802) 846-1850
http://www.learner.org

Association for Supervision and Curriculum Development1703 N. Beauregard St.
Alexandria, Virginia 22311
1-800-933-2723 press #2
Fax: (703) 575-5400
http://www.ascd.org

Films for the Humanities & Sciences
P.O. Box 2053
Princeton, New Jersey 08543
1-800-257-5126
Fax: (609) 275-3767
http://www.films.com

Insight Media
2162 Broadway
New York, New York 10024
1-800-233-9910
Fax: (212) 799-5309
http://www.insight-media.com

Public Broadcasting System (PBS)
PBS Home Video
P.O. Box 751089
Charlotte, North Carolina 28275
1-800-645-4727

Pyramid Media
P.O. Box 1048
Santa Monica, California 90409
1-800-421-2304
Fax: (310) 453-9083
http://www.pyramidmedia.com

Other videotapes listed as resources in this manual are available through a variety of distributors. Please contact a media reference librarian at your institution's library for current distribution information.

APPENDIX II

Teaching with Case Studies

The case study approach has been gaining popularity in teacher education programs. Long a common approach in law, medicine, counseling, and psychology, it is now being used more frequently in teacher preparation and even in teacher in-service programs. By reading a case study, prospective teachers can appreciate the complexities of teaching and can learn more about the contingencies involved in teaching. As they discuss the issues and propose viable solutions, prospective teachers can apply their theoretical knowledge of teaching in realistic contexts and can explore alternate courses of action, thereby expanding their thinking about teaching.

The case studies we have included deal with topical themes that confront teachers: pedagogical issues such as educational philosophy, teaching styles, grading practices, classroom management, and ability grouping, and practical or professional issues such as disagreements with the principal and decisions to strike.

When using a case study with your students, we suggest that the first part of the discussion focus on identifying the issues at hand and the key players involved as well as other factors that affect the issues. The second part can explore the issues themselves, discussing the different positions on the issues and the rationale (if there is one) for these positions. Finally, possible solutions can be evoked with the subsequent consequences of these solutions.

FOR USE WITH CHAPTERS 2 OR 7

From *Case Studies for Teacher Problem Solving* by Rita Silverman, William M. Welty, and Sally Lyon. Copyright © 1992. Reproduced with permission of The McGraw-Hill Companies.

Leigh Scott

A high school social studies teacher gives a higher-than-earned report card grade to a mainstreamed student on the basis of the boy's effort, and is confronted by another student with identical test grades who received a lower report card grade.

Leigh Scott felt the flush slowly leave her face as she watched Aaron Washington leave the classroom, slamming the door behind him. It was the end of the second grading cycle; students had received their report cards the day before. Leigh had just taken off her coat and was on her way to the teachers' room to get a cup of coffee before the bell rang when Aaron came into the room.

He began, "We got to talk about my American government grade." It was clear that he was angry.

Leigh moved to her desk and responded, "Hi, Aaron, What's up? You're upset about your grade?"

"You gave me a D."

"You did D work."

"So did Dale, and he got a C." Aaron was leaning over the desk toward Leigh.

"Aaron, this is not a good time to talk about this. The bell is going to ring in a few minutes. Why don't you see me after school this afternoon."

Aaron shook his head at her suggestion. "I have practice after school. We have to talk now."

Now it was Leigh's turn to shake her head. "This is not a good time; I have to get ready for homeroom. Besides, there's not really anything to talk about."

Aaron straightened up, took a couple of steps back from the desk, and said, "You gave a white kid who got the same grades I did a C, and you gave me a D. I even did more homework than Dale. I say we do have something to talk about."

Leigh capitulated. "Come in tomorrow morning at 7:30, and we'll talk before homeroom period."

Aaron nodded, strode out of the room without another word, and let the door slam as he left.

Leigh had been teaching social studies at Littleton High School for eleven years, and this was the first time a student accused her of racial bias. Students sometimes complained about their grades, and Leigh was always willing to reconsider a grade. But she never had a student suggest she was biased. Leigh had spent her entire teaching career at Littleton, so she had been teaching classes that were mixed racially and ethnically for a long time. She considered herself color blind when it came to assigning grades.

At Littleton High School, students were placed into one of four academic tracks: honors, above average, average, and remedial. Teachers were responsible for five classes a day, with the honors classes typically assigned to senior faculty. Newer faculty taught mostly average and remedial sections. Leigh taught a senior-level honors American history course, two freshman above-average sections of world history, and two sophomore average-level sections of American government.

Leigh graded her two sophomore American government sections on the following requirements each cycle:

- Tests (usually three or four, depending on the material)
- Homework (collected three times a week)
- A project
- Participation in class discussions based on the textbook readings

The textbook was written on an eighth-grade reading level. Leigh's tests were a combination of vocabulary, multiple-choice, and short-answer items. Leigh didn't require that students in the average sections answer essay questions. Students selected projects from among several choices: writing papers, constructing something appropriate to the topic, making a presentation to the class, or writing book reports on pertinent readings.

During homeroom period, Leigh consulted her grade book and confirmed that Aaron's information was accurate. Neither he nor Dale had done particularly well this grading cycle. Both had received mostly D grades with an occasional C. Neither participated in class discussions unless called on. However, she knew that she had given Dale the higher grade because of his effort, not because of his color. Dale was a learning disabled student mainstreamed into Leigh's class.

Typically a mainstreamed student would be placed in a remedial section, but Dale's case was an exception. He was in an average-level class because his resource room teacher, Meg Dament, requested the placement, feeling that Dale needed a more academic environment and a higher-achieving peer group than he would have had in a remedial section. Meg and Leigh had known each other since Leigh came to Littleton. Leigh admired Meg's dedication and her tenacity on behalf of her students. It was clear that Meg cared deeply about the students she served and wanted them to have whatever educational normality she could engineer for them. Meg was able to mainstream her "best" students into average-level, not remedial, classes. She actively sought teachers who would be responsive to her students' needs and to their efforts. It was not easy to convince high school teachers to work with classified students, but of the four resource room teachers in the high school, it was Meg who made the most regular class placements.

When Meg requested Leigh as Dale's teacher, Leigh understood that Dale was not a very good reader and that he would not volunteer in class. Leigh and Meg spoke regularly about Dale's progress, as well as the classroom requirements. Meg helped Dale prepare for Leigh's class, and he was showing real improvement since the first cycle, when his grade had been a low D.

Additionally, Dale's attitude in class was positive. He had learned to exhibit "teacher-pleasing behaviors": He looked attentive, he tried to take notes, he almost always carried his textbook and notebook and a pencil, and he never disrupted the class. Aaron had a different style: He would put his head on his desk during class discussions, he seldom brought materials to class, and he often talked to friends while Leigh was lecturing.

Nevertheless, their grades during the cycle were nearly identical, and Aaron was demanding an explanation. Leigh drove home that day wondering what she would tell Aaron during their appointment the following morning. Aaron's anger, coupled with his charge of racism, exacerbated her anxiety about their meeting. She also knew that she would have to figure out what she might do to prevent this from happening in the future, since she anticipated that she would continue to have mainstreamed students in her classes and she believed they should be rewarded for effort and improvement.

Discussion Questions

Two issues dominate this case: grading practices and mainstreaming, both of which are complicated by the charge of racism that Aaron has leveled at Leigh.

Grading

What is Aaron's complaint with his grade? Does he have a legitimate complaint? Is Leigh Scott's grading system fair? What is her grading system? Is it clearly articulated to the students? On what does Leigh base her grades? What is she rewarding in students, outcomes only, or progress toward a specified outcome? Is she consistent in her grading practices? What are the strengths and weaknesses of her system?

Mainstreaming

Should mainstreamed students be evaluated on different criteria or the same ones as the regular education students? Who should decide the criteria? How should they be decided? What role does the mainstreamed student's individualized education plan (IEP) play in grading? What is more important for mainstreamed students: feelings of social well-being or academic achievement?

Teacher-Student Interactions

How should Leigh respond to Aaron? Should she respond to his demands for an explanation of her grading? Should Aaron be encouraged (allowed) to challenge Leigh's grading? How should Leigh respond to Aaron's charges of racism?

How should Leigh prepare for the meeting with Aaron? Where should it be? Who should be present? Should she be willing to change Aaron's grade?

FOR USE WITH CHAPTER 2

From *Case Studies for Teacher Problem Solving* by Rita Silverman, William M. Welty, and Sally Lyon. Copyright © 1992. Reproduced with permission of The McGraw-Hill Companies.

Marsha Warren

An experienced third-grade teacher is overwhelmed by the problems created by her heterogeneous class, which includes seven students who have unique home and personal situations that are affecting their schooling.

José glared at Tyrone. "Quit looking at me, you jerk!"

"I wasn't lookin' at nothin', creepy," replied Tyrone vehemently.

Marsha Warren looked up sharply at the two boys and made a cutting gesture through the air. "That's enough from both of you. You should both be looking at your books, not each other."

"I was lookin' at my book!" protested Tyrone.

"Just stop!" repeated Marsha. "Please continue reading, Angela."

Angela rolled her eyes at no one in particular and resumed reading aloud in a bored, expressionless tone. Her progress was slow and halting.

Marsha Warren was a third-grade teacher at the Roosevelt Elementary School in Littleton. She was trying to conduct a reading group with the eight slowest readers in her class of twenty-two while the other children worked in workbooks at their seats. But each time an argument erupted among the children in the reading group, most of the children at their desks snapped to attention to watch the sparks fly.

"You can stop there, Angela," interrupted Marsha as Angela came to the end of a paragraph. "Bettie Ann, will you read next?" As she spoke, Marsha also put a hand out to touch another child, Katie, on the shoulder in an attempt to stop her from bouncing in her chair.

Bettie Ann didn't respond. She was gazing out the window at the leafless November landscape, sucking her thumb and twirling her hair with her other hand. "Bettie Ann, I'm talking to you," repeated Marsha.

"Your turn," yelled José, as he poked Bettie Ann's shoulder.

"Shut up, José," interjected Sarah. Sarah often tried to mediate between the members of the group, but her argumentative streak pulled her into the fray as often as not.

"Quiet!" insisted Marsha in a hushed, but emphatic tone. As she spoke, she turned her head to glance over her shoulder at the rest of the class. The hum of conversation was growing in the room. Tension crept into her voice as she addressed the reading group. "We're distracting the other children. Do we need to discuss rule 3 again? Everyone pull out the class rules from your notebook, now."

The chemistry in the reading group—and in the class in general—had been so explosive since September that Marsha had gone beyond her normal first-of-the-year review of rules and procedures. All the children in the class had copied four class rules into their notebooks, and she had led long discussions of what they meant. Rule 3 was "Be considerate of other people."

Loud groans from the reading group greeted Marsha's mention of rules. Simultaneously, a long BANG sounded in the back of the room. Marsha turned and saw a student reaching to the floor for a book as his neighbor snickered. She also noticed three girls in the far-left row leaning into a conversation over a drawing, and she saw most of the students quickly turn back to their work, as if they were not enjoying the entertainment of the reading group once again.

"That's it!" Marsha exclaimed. She slammed her hand down on the reading-circle table and stood to face the entire class. "Put your head on your desks and don't say another word—everyone!" By the time she finished her sentence, Marsha realized she had been shouting, but she didn't care. Her class glazed at her in stunned disbelief. Mrs. Warren had always been so gentle! "Now!"

Marsha quickly turned and walked from the room, not bothering to look back to see if her command had been obeyed. She closed the door to her classroom, managing not to slam it, and tried to control her temper and collect her thoughts. "What in God's name am I going to do with this class?" she asked herself. "I've got to calm down. Here I am in the hallway with twenty-two kids inside who have driven me out—they've absolutely won." Marsha suddenly felt paralyzed.

Marsha tried to remember if there was ever a time in her eleven years of teaching when discipline and control were such a challenge. "It's not as though I were a rookie. I ought to know what to do!" she agonized. But Marsha had tried everything she had ever learned or done before to interest and control this group, and the class as a whole, yet there she was, standing in the hall.

Marsha's third-grade class was indeed a difficult group of children. There were a few students who liked school and really tried to learn, but overall it was a class full of children who were just not focused on learning. It was impossible to relax with them. If Marsha let down her guard and tried to engage them on a more friendly or casual level, the class would disintegrate. Marsha's natural inclination in teaching was to maintain a friendly, relaxed manner; she usually enjoyed her students and her enjoyment showed. But with this class she constantly had to be firm and vigilant ("witchlike," she thought) in order to keep the students under control.

Academically the class was fairly average, but Marsha did have two instructional challenges: There were three really bright students, whom Marsha tried to encourage with extra instruction and higher expectations, and there were three students (besides the Hispanic children in her slow-reading group) who spoke little or no English. The most remarkable characteristic of the students, though, was their overall immaturity. Each child seemed to feed off the antics of the others, and every issue was taken to its extreme. For example, whenever one child laughed, the entire class would begin to giggle uncontrollably. The students' behavior was simply inappropriate for their age and grade.

The core of Marsha's problem was the lowest-level reading group. This group provided the spark that set off fireworks in the entire class, day after day. The slow readers were rude and disruptive as a group, and they were instigators on their own.

When Marsha thought of each child in the lowest reading group individually, she was usually able to summon some sympathy and understanding. Each of the eight had an emotional or academic problem that probably accounted, at least in part, for his or her behavior.

José, for instance, topped her list of troublemakers. He was a loud, egocentric child. His mother, Marsha thought, probably had surrendered long ago, and his father did not live with them. José had little respect for or recognition of authority; he was boisterous and argumentative; and he was unable to take turns under any condition. When something didn't go his way, he would explode. This low flash point, Marsha felt, was just one of many signs of his immaturity, even though José was repeating the third grade and was actually older than his classmates.

José had a slight learning disability in the area of organizational skills, but Marsha didn't think this justified his behavior. His mother spoke only Spanish, and—although José was fluent in both Spanish and English—when Marsha sent notes home, she would first have to find someone to translate for her. Conferring with José's mother on the telephone was out of the question.

Angela was also repeating the third grade, and Marsha thought the child's anger over this contributed to her terrible attitude in class. The child just refused to learn. She could be a low-average achiever if she would apply herself, but it was clear that Angela's agenda was not school. She was concerned with her hair, her looks, her clothes—preoccupations that Marsha found inappropriate for a third-grader. Angela came from a middle-class black family, and her parents were also angry that she had been held back; consultations with them were not usually fruitful. Angela seemed truly upset if Marsha asked her to do any work, and Marsha was sure her frustration with the child was occasionally apparent.

Tyrone, on the other hand, was a very low average learner, but he, at least, worked to his capabilities. He even tried to mediate arguments among the members of the group. But Tyrone had a very stubborn streak, which was typical, Marsha thought, of slow learners. If he was on the wrong track, he just would not get off of it. She frequently asked him to redo work and helped him with his errors, but when he presented it to her the next day as though it were different, it would contain the same mistakes.

Sarah, too, knew right from wrong and generally wanted to do her work, but she was easily pulled into the fray. Sarah had appointed herself protector of Bettie Ann, an overweight, emotionally insecure child who had difficulty focusing on the topic at hand. Bettie Ann was the baby of her family, with several near-adult siblings at home. Marsha wondered if Bettie Ann's position in the family was the reason she assumed no responsibility for her own actions and no control over her own fate. Bettie Ann seemed hungry for Marsha's attention, but she exhibited no independence or initiative at all.

Katie was one of the brighter students in the reading group, but her hyperactivity caused her to be easily distracted and argumentative. She could neither sit still physically nor pay attention mentally. Katie had a rich home background, full of books and middle-class aspirations, but Marsha thought she also encountered pressure at home to perform, perhaps to levels beyond her capability.

Rhea, another child with at least average intelligence, was one of the more heart-rending cases. Her mother was an alcoholic who neglected her, and Rhea had to do the housework and care for her older brother, who was in a special education class. She had no time for homework, and there were no books or even conversation at home. Rhea had been held back in the second grade, and while she tried to do her work, the language deficit at home was so severe that she kept falling further behind.

Finally, there was Maria, a petite immature native of El Salvador. She had average intelligence and a cooperative spirit, but Spanish was spoken in her home and her limited English vocabulary severely limited her progress.

Marsha tried to analyze what it was among these children that fostered such animosity. Not a day passed that they didn't argue, fight, or insult one another. The reading group was not the only arena for these combatants; they fought in the playground, in line, on the bus, and in the cafeteria. They were troublemakers in previous grades, and some of the teachers at Roosevelt called them "Infidels."

They tended to be at their worst as a group, and so Marsha had tried separating them, but with little improvement. Three weeks before, in early October, she rearranged and reorganized all three reading groups, distributing the students in the lowest section among three new groups. But she found that the inappropriate behavior did not stop; it only spread. Now all three of her reading groups, rather than one, were disrupted, and mixing her slow and average readers dramatically reduced the pace of both groups. Finding this arrangement unfair to her other students, she reorganized back to her original group assignments last week.

Marsha also tried other remedies. She introduced popular reading material for the reading groups and tried innovations such as having the children act out the stories they read. She wrote a contingency contract with the groups when she reconstituted them last week, promising that they could use the school's audiovisual equipment to make filmstrips illustrating their current book if they behaved, but so far that wasn't working either.

Marsha did not think she was generally too lax. She had procedures for incomplete work (the students had to come to her room during lunch hour or after school to finish); she had rules for appropriate behavior in school; and she never hesitated to involve parents. She praised the children for completing work, and she sent positive notes home when they did so. She also sent home disciplinary cards (much more frequently, unfortunately), which parents were supposed to sign, and she telephoned parents when she thought it would help.

Marsha also tried punishment. She sent individual troublemakers to the office, and she held detention during lunch. She isolated children for misbehavior by separating their desks from the rest of the class, and she used denial of privileges (the children really liked using the class computer, so she withdrew that privilege frequently). Marsha even tried talking honestly with the children, giving them pep talks about the value of education and their need to read and write and think in order to participate in life. But nothing was fundamentally altering the course of the class's behavior.

Besides having the desire to teach the "Infidels," Marsha knew that the progress of the rest of the class was being slowed because of the time she was forced to spend on policing. Her patience, her ideas, and her fortitude were fast evaporating, and she knew she had to solve the problem even though she felt like giving up.

Marsha stood on tiptoe to look through the window of the classroom door. The children were sitting in their places looking at each other uneasily and at the door, clearly wondering what would happen next. With a sigh, Marsha turned the knob.

Discussion Questions

The first task with this case is to decide what is happening in Marsha's classroom—that is, what are the different problems that Marsha has to manage? Once the problems have been identified, the discussion can turn to possible solutions. A suggested outline for discussion contains the following:

Problem Identification

What are the problems in the class, from Marsha's perspective? What is known about the students in the class? How can the behavior of the "Infidels" be explained?

How has Marsha contributed to these problems? What has she already tried to solve the problems? Why weren't her efforts successful? How does Marsha explain her lack of progress?

Solutions

Short-term: Marsha has to return to the classroom. What should she do when she walks back into the room?

Long-term: What can Marsha do to improve the environment of her classroom? What areas should she focus on first? Classroom management? Ability grouping? Motivation? What specific plans could she try?

FOR USE WITH CHAPTERS 2 OR 7

From *Case Studies for Teacher Problem Solving* by Rita Silverman, William M. Welty, and Sally Lyon.
Copyright © 1992. Reproduced with permission of The McGraw-Hill Companies.

Erica Kaiser

Erica Kaiser was busy teaching her fifth-period Spanish class at Centerville Middle School. It was a seventh-grade class and the students were engrossed in some language puzzles that Erica had made up for them. She was pleased to see them working so hard at the puzzles because she had spent a lot of time developing them. As Erica wandered around the classroom, checking on the groups' progress, she thought about her work. She was in her second year of teaching and had already received notes from parents praising her work, and very positive feedback from her department coordinator. She enjoyed teaching at the middle school level and working with her colleagues, many of whom had become Erica's good friends. She was delighted with the professional development opportunities, which the Centerville school district offered and regularly took part in these activities. Erica thought she had found her niche.

As she was circulating around the class, Dr. Fraelich, the principal, came in. Erica started toward the door, but he waved her away. She knew what that meant: he was just on one of his spot visits. He didn't stay long, but then he rarely did. He circled around the class, chatted with a few students, checked their work, and then he was off to another class. As he strolled out the door, he stopped near Erica and murmured, "Well, Miss Kaiser, looks like you've got the troops under control today. But then again, they're not doing much, are they? I'll come back another day when you're doing some real teaching! After all, it's Friday, and I'm sure you have other things on your mind besides verb conjugations!" He winked playfully at her and left the room.

Erica gaped at the open door. She had worked on these vocabulary puzzles for two weeks; they were hardly spur-of-the moment "busy work" for the students. Besides, her social life after school hours was none of his business. The bell rang and brought Erica back to the classroom as the students filed out. Erica tried to forget Dr. Fraelich's remark, yet, as the afternoon wore on, Erica found her irritation growing as she thought about the incident and other similar comments Dr. Fraelich had made in the past. She tried to excuse him to herself, since he was an older man and basically nice. Maybe he just didn't realize that he sounded patronizing.

As the weeks went by, Dr. Fraelich's comments seemed to become more frequent and more irritating. Erica tried to remain pleasant, but she found herself cutting her conversations with him short out of fear of saying something that she might regret. The situation came to a head in May when Erica received her yearly evaluation from Dr. Fraelich. Because she was an untenured teacher, Erica received a "full" evaluation every year, which consisted of a checklist and a narrative evaluation. She scanned down the checklist and was pleased to note that she had received "outstanding" for every item there. She turned to the next page to read Dr. Fraelich's written comments about her teaching. She read:

> Miss Kaiser is a fine, courteous young woman. She comes to school promptly every day, and she hands in her plan book on the date assigned. She has eagerly volunteered for after-school events and has the knack of adding a special touch to every activity, whether it's bringing in some homemade baked goods or staying behind to help with the clean-up crew. Finally, Miss Kaiser's professional appearance is to be commended. Her dress is neat, modest, and attractive. I recommend her without hesitation for a contract for the 1994–95 school year.

Erica's stomach churned. She stared at her evaluation in disbelief. She knew that Dr. Fraelich could be patronizing at times, but she couldn't believe what he had written. This report was part of her permanent record and he was talking about her culinary talents! He made no reference at all to her teaching, her professional development activities, or her participation on the school committees. She shoved the report in her briefcase and headed out the door.

On her way home, Erica tried to remember what he had written in her evaluation last year, but she couldn't. She could only remember being so nervous about the two classroom observations he did that when she saw that he had recommended her to be rehired, she only gave a cursory glance at the rest of the report. She was overjoyed to have survived her first year and to be coming back for a second year.

That evening, she showed her evaluation to Mike and Laurie, two close college friends.

"I don't believe he wrote this!" exclaimed Laurie. "I thought it was bad in med. school, but this is ridiculous! Where has this guy been? Doesn't he know about sexual harassment? Can't you file some sort of complaint? What's he going to write next year? A recommendation that you make coffee and sew curtains?"

Mike stared at Erica and shook his head. "Yeah, that's really too bad because except for him, you're happy at Centerville, aren't you? And your position seems secure, unlike mine. I'm pretty sure I'm getting pink-slipped next week. I have the least seniority in the science department and every department has to cut one teacher. Modern languages has to cut two."

Laurie interrupted Mike. "So, what are you saying, Mike? That she should just ignore this? This is part of her permanent record. What happens when she applies for another job and they call here for a reference and find out she bakes good cookies and dresses nicely? I certainly wouldn't be impressed by that!"

"No, no, no. The guy's definitely chauvinistic and patronizing and everything else. I'm just saying that before Erica does anything, she should find out more about what's going on. I mean, the bottom line is that he did recommend that her contract be renewed, so would it hold up as sexual discrimination or harassment? I'm not sure. Besides," he added as he picked up the report to look at it more carefully, "don't you have to sign the report and give it back to him? Why don't you write on the report that you're not happy with it because it doesn't evaluate your teaching? Or maybe you could just talk to the principal about it and ask him to redo it or something. That's what we do at my school if we have a problem with our annual reports."

"Mike is right," Erica sighed. "First I need to find out what procedures are in place to deal with this. I can check with Bill, who's our teachers' association rep. But I really wonder what other teachers' evaluation reports are like. Is he this way just with me or with everyone?"

Over the next few days, Erica learned a lot. She found out from Bill the district policy regarding teacher evaluations (which was in her teacher handbook, but she had never paid much attention to it). He told her that teachers had to sign and return their reports within ten working days. If a teacher was unhappy with the report, he or she could draft a rebuttal, sign that, and not the evaluation report, and submit the two of them. The next step, he explained, was up to the principal, who could rewrite the report and, assuming the teacher was satisfied with the revised report, submit that one to the superintendent. However, if the principal felt that the evaluation was an accurate representation of the teacher's performance, then the two reports, the principal's original and the teacher's rebuttal, would be submitted. At that point, it was up to the superintendent to resolve the issue by either meeting with the two people concerned or having a third party observe the teacher in question and write up an evaluation.

"But, just a friendly reminder before you do anything, Erica. Dr. Marston, our superintendent, and Dr. Fraelich came to Centerville at the same time and have both been here for a long time. They are frequent golf partners, if that makes any difference to you. But, whatever you decide, keep me informed in case you need the support of the teachers' association."

"I will, Bill, and thanks for the information—and the advice."

At lunch, she asked some of her closer friends about their evaluation reports and found that hers was not unique, nor was her reaction.

"Yeah, that fries me, too," remarked Tracy. "He always says that I 'dress sensibly.' That's so demeaning. But, you know, Erica, other than those stupid remarks, he doesn't bother me. I can teach and be left to do what I like just about all of the time. Besides, he would always recommend that my contract be renewed. Of course now that I'm tenured, that is less of a concern for me."

"But what about those of us who aren't tenured?" asked Maggie. "Why should we have to put up with those kinds of comments when we all know that they're inappropriate? It's not fair that someone like that is the one deciding whether or not we will have jobs in the fall."

Erica looked over to Drew. "Well, what do you think, Drew? Are you comfortable with what he says?"

Drew looked at her sheepishly. "I don't know what to say. My evaluation reports have been fine. He always gives a full evaluation of my teaching and lists all the extracurricular and professional activities I participate in. I hate to say it, but I have no complaints about my evaluations. I really don't."

"Boy, that makes it sound even worse, doesn't it?" Erica commented. "Now what do we do? What do *I* do?"

"I don't know, but I do know that you should really think this through before you do anything," Drew advised, "and I don't say that to sound patronizing. You know about Dr. Fraelich and Dr. Marston, don't you?"

"Yeah, more or less," Erica responded.

"But do you know about Lucy? She got fed up with Bob, too, and called him a chauvinist. Actually, she did more than that. She filed a grievance against him. Not much really came of it, though, except that Lucy got transferred to the high school the following year when she hadn't even requested it."

"And then there was Charlotte," Tracy added. "Remember her?"

Mary Jane continued, "First, she also complained about her evaluations and about Dr. Fraelich's comments. Then she was assigned to all the lousy duties and Bob started being very subtly vigilant about making sure she was at the bus stop, at detention, you know, the whole deal. Then, the next year, we had a classroom shortage, and Bob reassigned Charlotte to this closet space instead of a classroom, saying that she had the smallest number of students, so she didn't need her own classroom. Ever since, her 'space' has been down in the corner of the book closet.

"And Charlotte applied to be language arts coordinator four years ago. Even though she was the most qualified, they hired someone else, saying they wanted someone from the outside."

Drew added, "We're not exactly sure that Bob had anything to do with that, but it does seem awfully coincidental."

Erica looked at them squarely. "So you're telling me he's not a man to make enemies with, that he has friends in high places, is that right? So what do I do?"

"Well, if you'll forgive my sports analogy," Drew said, "the ball is in your court. What do you want to do? You have been recommended to be rehired."

Discussion Questions

Problem Identification

What is Erica's problem? Why is it a problem? Is this really a case of gender bias or sexual harassment? What are important factors that Erica needs to keep in mind?

Problem Solution

What should Erica do? Her options are clear: either let it go or write a rebuttal. Or is there another option? What are some potential consequences if she does nothing? If she writes a rebuttal? If she talks to Dr. Fraelich?

FOR USE WITH CHAPTER 7

From *Case Studies on Teaching* by Theodore J. Kowalski, Roy A. Weaver, and Kenneth T. Henson. Copyright © 1992 by Longman, a division of Addison-Wesley Publishing Co., Inc. Used by permission of the author.

Karen Washington

Karen's first year of teaching starts off very well, but the threat of a strike forces Karen to examine her priorities and to make some hard decisions fast.

Karen Washington faces what she believes is the greatest decision of her life. She must decide if she will participate in a teachers' strike. The predicament angers Karen. She sits alone in her newly acquired apartment mulling over her options and trying to determine how she got herself into this situation.

Just four months ago, Karen graduated from North State College after completing her student teaching. Everything seemed magnificent. She had received an outstanding evaluation for student teaching; she was going to graduate summa cum laude; she had four solid job opportunities; and most important, she was convinced that she had made an excellent career choice. Karen was in love with teaching!

The youngest of four children, Karen had been reared in the industrial area of Pittsburgh. Her father was an ardent union loyalist who, after thirty-one years of employment in the steel mills, was forced to take an early retirement. Her mother, who managed to complete her high school education after she got married, works as a clerk in a meat packing company—a job she has held for twenty-two years. In the Washington household, education is a high priority. Karen's siblings all attended college. One of her brothers left after his freshman year to join the army, and after twelve years, has decided to make the military his career. Karen's sister is a nursing supervisor in a suburban hospital and her other brother is finishing his Ph.D. in sociology at the University of Texas.

Karen has a very close relationship with her mother. She would preach to Karen, "Getting your degree is your ticket to job security. Look at what happened to your father. Thirty-one years and they just tell him he has to retire."

As Karen sits in her room pondering the issue before her, memories of home and college are comforting. But she also thinks about the major decision she made just two months ago—accepting a teaching position in the Glennville schools. Karen had applied for four positions. Each school district had pursued her vigorously. In a way, she had been surprised because the districts were located in quite different environments. One of the school systems was large and urban; one was an affluent suburban district; one was a "blue collar" suburb; and Glennville was a quiet, sleepy little community of 5,000 nestled in the mountains of central Pennsylvania. Perhaps it had been her mother's urgings to seek job security that had prompted Karen to select Glennville. After all, it offered the lowest salary of the four.

The first month of teaching had been superb. Karen had a second-grade class with nineteen healthy and happy students. She had become very good friends with the other second-grade teacher, Martha McKewan, a veteran of twenty-seven years in the classroom. To the unending pleasure of her mother, Karen had also become a member of the choir at the local church in Glennville and had begun dating the assistant pastor, David Simms.

As a matter of routine, Karen had joined the Glennville Teachers' Association (GTA) the first day she reported to work. She hadn't asked any questions—it seemed like the thing to do. About the second week of school, Karen began receiving an association newsletter entitled, "Negotiations Update." The publication had made it clear that the GTA was most unhappy with the progress of its salary negotiations with the school board. Discussions in the lunchroom and teachers' lounge centered almost entirely around the contents of the newsletter. It was obvious that tensions were mounting.

During a routine visit with the principal, Mrs. Armand, Karen had raised the issue of negotiations. "I just don't understand it," Mrs. Armand said. "I've been in this community longer than I care to admit and nothing like this has ever happened before. I really think we're headed for a showdown. The school board has decided to get tough."

Karen asked, "What do you mean by getting tough?"

Mrs. Armand thought a moment and responded. "We never had negotiations here until five years ago. The board reluctantly participates in the process. Each year they get a little more bitter. This is not a union town. Even though our salaries are not very high, and even though the board knows that, they find if difficult to accept collective bargaining. Maybe they feel they have to teach the GTA a lesson."

Karen was surprised that the situation was so severe. She asked further, "If there is a strike, Mrs. Armand, what do you recommend that I do?"

"Karen, you know, I have to be on the board's side in this matter," she responded. "I don't believe in strikes. You have to decide what is best for you. As a first-year teacher, you'd better be careful."

Two days after her conference with the principal, the officers of the GTA held a strike vote. Karen did not vote because she was torn by mixed emotions. The teachers voted overwhelmingly to strike. A majority of the teachers believed that the board would not make salary concessions without a strike. The strike would begin in the morning.

Sitting in her room alone now, Karen also recalls other pleas she had made for advice.

Mrs. McKewan, a professional role model for Karen, had told her, "I'm going out on strike. I never thought I would. But this has become a matter of honor and professional integrity." Karen's recently acquired friend, Reverend Simms, had responded by saying that a strike would not go over very well in the community. "As a first-year teacher, Karen, you could be very vulnerable," he advised.

Karen had reluctantly called home and discussed the matter with her parents. Even they disagreed on what she should do. Her father told her to honor the strike; her mother told her to protect her job.

Ralph Hopson, president of the GTA, had said, "Karen, your best friends are in the GTA. Stand with us and we'll stand behind you. Don't make the mistake of turning your back on your professional colleagues."

All of this would not be so bad if Karen didn't really like her job, the community, and most important, the children in her classroom. Karen had received two letters from parents urging her not to go on strike. One father had pleaded, "Only the children suffer in a strike. Why should they be made the innocent victims of a political fight?"

Just two weeks ago, everything was so perfect, so rosy. Karen wanted her experiences in Glennville to continue to be positive. Yet she knew she had to make a decision that could change her future in this community.

Discussion Questions

The major issue here has to do with where Karen's professional loyalties should lie. Should she honor the strike and support her colleagues, thereby signaling her adherence to her professional community, or should she honor her professional obligations to teach the students?

Problem Identification

What are the arguments in favor of Karen supporting the strike? Consider professional as well as personal arguments. What are the arguments against Karen supporting the strike? Once again, consider both personal and professional arguments. Who else could Karen consult to help her make her decision?

Solution

What advice would you give Karen? Should she support the strike or not? What do you imagine to be the consequence of her supporting the strike? Of her not supporting the strike?

INSTRUCTOR EVALUATION OF *THOSE WHO CAN, TEACH*, TENTH EDITION, *INSTRUCTOR'S RESOURCE MANUAL*

Please complete the questionnaire and mail it to: Marketing Services, College Division, Houghton Mifflin Company, 222 Berkeley Street, Boston, MA 02116-3764.

1. Indicate how often you use each of these features in this instructor's manual.

2. Do you provide or require your students to use the following student resources in this manual?

3. Which of the following assessment resources do you use?

	Frequently	Occasionally	Never
Chapter Outline			
Supplementary Lecture and Discussion Topics			
Student Activities			
Ready-to-Copy Assignment Sheets			
Additional Resources for Instructors			
Media Resources			
Study Guides			
Sample Chapter Quizzes			
Test Bank Questions on Disk			
Test Bank Questions in Print			
Multiple-Choice Items			
Short-Answer Questions			
Essay Questions			
Reflective Papers			
Journal Writing			

4. Do you use the case studies in the Appendix?

5. Do you use *Kaleidoscope* in conjunction with this course?

6. Please provide the following information about yourself to help us better understand who uses our manual and how we can support you. Please circle or write in your rank and status.

Rank:

Professor   Assistant Professor

Lecturer   Associate Professor

Graduate Assistant   Other: _____

Full Time   Part Time

Tenured: Yes   No

7. How many years have you taught this course? _____

8. How many sections of this course do you teach in one year? _____

9. Do you consider the foundations of education to be your major area of expertise?   Yes   No

10. What else would you like to suggest we add to the *Instructor's Resource Manual* to assist you?

_____

_____

_____

11.   Is there anything we should delete?

_____

_____

12.   We would like to know how you rate our textbook in each of the following areas:

	Excellent	Good	Adequate	Poor
Selection of topics				
Detail of coverage				
Order of topics				
Writing style/readability				
Accuracy of information				
Study aids and test questions				
Illustrations and cartoons				
Student reaction to book				
Examples/applications				
Explanations of concepts				

13.   We invite you to cite specific examples that illustrate any of the above ratings.

_____

_____

14.   Describe the strongest feature(s) of the book.

_____

_____

15.   Describe the weakest feature(s) of the book.

_____

_____

16.   What other topics should be included in this text?

_____

_____

17.   What recommendations can you make for improving this book?

_____